Virginia Principles of Life/Health

Second Edition

Printed in the United States of America.

Published by Cape School

© 2016 by Cape School

Great care is taken to insure that information supplied in this text is accurate and current. However, many of the general principles and conclusions are subject to interpretation and court case revisions. The reader is urged to consult legal counsel regarding points of law. This publication should not be used as a substitute for competent legal counsel.

Table of Contents

HEALTH 113

VA PPL LH-2_16298

Single Line Sections

Life Only

Sections I-V, Section XII, and Life and Health Insurance Glossary of Terms

Health Only

Sections VI-XI, Section XII, and Life and Health Insurance Glossary of Terms

VA PPL LH-2_16298

LIFE

VA PPL LH-2_16298

VA PPL LH-2_16298

Section I: Types of Life Insurance Policies

This section begins our exploration of life insurance. Topics include:

- Traditional whole life products
- Interest- and market-sensitive life products
- Term life products
- Annuities
- Combination life insurance plans

A glossary is at the end of this course and includes the definition and explanation of many important insurance terms. When a word or phrase *looks like this* it can be found in the glossary.

Traditional Whole Life Insurance

Simply put, *insurance* is an agreement between an insurance policyholder and the insurer where the payment of premium by the policyholder requires the insurance company, through an insurance contract, to provide payment for certain losses.

Whole life insurance is a form of permanent life insurance. Permanent life insurance accumulates cash values and is designed to provide coverage during the insured's entire life, not just for a term. Ordinary whole life insurance was one of the first forms of whole life insurance developed.

The *insured,* the person, group or organization whose life is covered by the policy, is the life measured by the life insurance policy. At the insured's death, the insurance policy pays a death benefit.

The various types of whole life policies are generally distinguished by the structure of premium payments. The shorter the premium payment period, the faster cash values grow in whole life policies.

Premiums are money paid to the insurer to pay for the risk the insurer assumes for paying claims and for meeting the life insurance contract's provisions. Premiums must be paid to keep the policy in force.

Continuous Premium (Straight or Ordinary Life)

Straight or *ordinary life insurance* includes the following characteristics:

- *Level Premium* Payments
- Coverage to Age 100
- Cash Values
- Level Face Amount

Level premiums are premiums that normally do not change over the life of a straight life policy and that cannot be arbitrarily changed while the policy is in place.

Cash Values

Because premium payments are level in ordinary life, premiums are higher at policy inception than needed to cover the insurance risk and lower than needed to cover the insurance risk as the insured ages. The additional premium, meaning that above what is needed to pay the mortality and administrative expenses, goes to *cash values*.

Mortality and Administrative Expenses in Life Insurance

Administrative expenses are the portion of premium that goes to pay the insurer for administration of the policy. These expenses may include producing annual statements, processing customer service changes on the contract, providing ongoing customer service through the insurer's home office, and so on. Some administrative expenses may be charged directly to policyholders rather than being paid through the premium. For example, a $25 annual administrative fee may be charged by an insurer to cover the expense of issuing statements and addressing customer service needs.

The insurer bases and collects premium based on statistical data that indicates that a certain percentage of insureds will suffer losses at a certain frequency percentage. In life insurance the loss the insured suffers is death. The frequency that death occurs within a population is called the mortality risk. The portion of premium charged based on mortality risk is known as *mortality expense.*

Cash Values Belong to the Policyholder

The cash values of the policy belong to the policyowner. Under whole life policies, the policyowner may take loans against the cash values, but may not generally make withdrawals of cash values. Should the policy be surrendered, however, the cash values, less surrender charges if any, are paid to the policyholder.

The *policyowner* is the party on a life insurance contract who is normally the premium payer and has the right to change the beneficiary, to withdraw funds, take loans, make premium payments, and in some cases add or change beneficiaries.

A *surrender charge* is a percentage charged against certain withdrawals and surrenders taken from life insurance and annuity contract cash values. It is generally in effect for a specified period of time, such as for 7 years beginning with the issue date of the policy. The period of time that the surrender charge applies is known as the *surrender charge period*.

Cash Value Earnings

Cash values are credited with interest by the insurer and accumulate earnings on a tax-deferred basis. A *minimum guaranteed rate* for cash values is included within the contract.

Death Benefit

The death benefit under whole life policies is guaranteed. The *death benefit* is the amount specified in the life insurance contract that is to be paid out at the death of the insured.

Generally, the *face amount* and the death benefit are the same in life insurance policies, but strictly speaking, the face amount is the amount of the death benefit of a life insurance policy on the effective date of the policy. It is listed on the front page, or face page, of an insurance policy. Depending on the life insurance policy type, the face amount may differ from the actual death benefit payable over the life of the policy, due to withdrawals or features in the policy that cause the death benefit to increase or decrease.

The *effective date* of an insurance policy is the date on which an insurance policy goes into effect and provides protection. This date is also known as the issue date and the policy inception date.

Limited Pay Whole Life Insurance

Limited pay whole life insurance requires payments for a certain, or limited, period. *Single premium life* is actually a form of limited pay life with a period extending for one premium payment. Limited pay life policies can have premium periods of any length, such as twenty years, or up to age 65.

Premiums are generally higher under a limited pay life policy than under an ordinary whole life policy (assuming the two policies are issued at the same time to the same insured) since the premium payment period is shorter. The higher premiums may be accepted by a policyholder who wants to have his or her policy paid off by the time of retirement, or plans to borrow against cash values for a child's college education and wants cash values to grow as quickly as possible. Another use of limited pay life insurance is as a gift. *For example, parents may purchase a limited pay policy on the life of a newborn and gift the paid-up policy to the child once the child reaches age 21.*

If a limited pay policy requires premiums for seven years or less, it may be classified as a modified endowment contract.

Single Premium Whole Life Policies

Single premium whole life policies are issued requiring only one, single premium. Because they are purchased with a single premium, they create a relatively high amount of cash value immediately. These cash values grow tax-deferred. Up until legislation taking effect after June 20, 1988, these cash values could be accessed through policy loans which were not taxable. This changed, however, with legislation that created the insurance product classification modified endowment contract (MEC). Single premium life policies are MECs.

Any life insurance product that does not pass the *seven-pay test* is treated for tax purposes as a modified endowment contract. The seven-pay test is a complicated computation, but generally, if the calculated net level premium (which is calculated based on assumptions laid out in the IRS Code) during the first seven years of the contract is less

VA PPL LH-2_16298

than the amount paid in the first seven years of the contract, the contract is considered a MEC.

MEC policies are taxed as though interest is received first in distributions. For tax purposes, both withdrawals and loans are considered distributions under a MEC policy, so single premium life policies do not provide tax-free loans, as non-MEC life insurance policies can provide.

Graded Premium Whole Life Policy

The premium for a *graded premium* whole life policy gradually increases, generally for a period consisting of the first five years of the policy. A graded premium policy has the advantage of lower premium payments at the beginning of the policy, like the modified whole life policy. One of the major differences between this policy and the modified policy is that the graded premium policy always provides permanent whole life insurance coverage and does not use term insurance coverage. The cost of the premium is structured to level off at the end of the graded period (i.e. five years) and then remain level. The policy builds some cash value in the early years of the policy.

Modified Whole Life Policy

A modified whole life policy combines both term insurance and whole life insurance. Coverage begins with term insurance and automatically converts into whole life insurance coverage after a short period of time (usually 3-5 years). One of the major advantages of the modified policy is the lower initial premium needed for the term insurance. A major disadvantage is that there is no cash buildup in the early policy years while the term insurance is in effect. This type of policy is meant for persons who need affordable, term insurance premiums at policy issue, but expect that increased earnings will allow larger premiums to be paid in the future.

Indeterminate Premium

Indeterminate premium whole life is a product that sets two premium rates – one is a guaranteed maximum premium rate and the other is the premium amount payable. The premium amount payable is reset after a specified period of a few years or annually, and then annually thereafter. The premium rate payable is based on the experience of the insurer. The premium rate payable may increase or decrease, based on the insurer's experience. The premium amount payable will never exceed the guaranteed maximum.

Adjustable Life Insurance

Adjustable life insurance was developed for those persons who want to change their insurance coverage, either up or down, while reacting to their changing life situations such as marriage, buying a home, having children, etc. The insured can increase or decrease the death benefit. The amount or frequency of premium payments can be changed. The death benefit may be increased but the insurance company may require evidence of *insurability*. These policy changes are normally allowed at the policy anniversary date. Also, the policy can be converted from whole life to term life and back to whole life again.

Term life insurance is a life insurance policy that does not accumulate cash values, but pays a death benefit only. The policy is in force for a certain period of time, or term, and generally may be renewed for additional terms.

Insurability is the overall acceptability of an individual as an insurance risk. Factors used to determine insurability include health, financial situation, occupation, life expectancy, exposure to risks and other factors determined by the insurance company.

Interest- and Market Sensitive Life Products

Universal Life Insurance

Universal life insurance was developed to be a flexible form of insurance that can be used to meet almost any need. Premium amounts can be changed, premium payments may be skipped or suspended for a time, and the death benefit can be changed, all during the life of the policy.

A universal life policy's components – the cost of insurance, the policy expenses, and the rate paid by the insurance company – are separated or *unbundled*. Basically, under a universal life policy, when premium is paid, it is placed in the reserve fund. From it, the cost of insurance and policy expenses are subtracted, and the rate of return is applied to the amount remaining in the reserve account. The minimum rate paid on cash values is guaranteed, and universal life policies may pay a higher current interest rate.

Universal life policies allow the policyholder to skip premium payments. In such a case, the premium will be paid from the reserve account. If funds within the reserve account are not sufficient to pay the premium, however, the policy will lapse and coverage will terminate. *Lapse* is a cessation of coverage due to the failure to pay premiums as required.

Universal life is a form of *flexible premium* insurance policy. Flexible premium policies, unlike single premium products:

- allow for premiums to be paid throughout the life of the policy.
- are a more affordable option for many than a single premium product.
- have cash values with the potential to increase due to additional premium amounts.

can be structured as non-MEC policies, so that tax-free loans are available.

Universal Life Death Benefits

Two death benefit options are available under universal life policies. Under Option I, also known as Option A, the death benefit is level. In the later years of the policy, as cash values increase, the death benefit is also increased in order to meet the parameters required in the tax code to ensure that the policy retains the tax treatment of a life insurance policy.

Under Option II, or Option B, the death benefit increases as the cash value in the policy increases.

Access to Cash Values

Universal life policies allow both withdrawals and policy loans as methods of accessing cash values. This is in contrast to ordinary whole life policies, which allow only policy loans as a way to access cash values. However, the policy provisions in universal life contracts generally give the insurer the right to cancel the policy if cash values fall below a certain level. During the first five to ten years of the policy, withdrawals are generally

assessed withdrawal charges, also known as *surrender charges*.

Uses of Universal Life Insurance

As mentioned, universal life insurance was designed to be as the name suggests, universal: to meet just about any insurance need a policyholder may have.

For example, a young couple may open a universal life policy plan, designed initially with low premiums and minimum accumulation of cash values while their children are growing and finances are tight. As income grows, premiums are increased and cash values accumulate more rapidly. When the couple wants to help send their children through college, premium payments are suspended and cash values are withdrawn or borrowed against. After the college years, premiums begin again, perhaps at an increased level now that the child-rearing years are behind the couple. During retirement, the couple may opt to access cash values to supplement retirement income.

Universal life plans may be used in business situations as well. Its flexibility and its potential to earn higher crediting rates than a traditional whole life policy can be attractive to businesses. Universal life may be used in conjunction with buy-sell agreements, for a deferred compensation plan or for key employee insurance.

Business insurance is life or health insurance written to cover business situations such as key employees, owners, sole proprietors, buy-sell agreements, partnerships and corporations.

Key employee insurance is an insurance policy on the life of a key employee, such as an executive, researcher or salesperson, whose death or disability would cause the employer financial loss. The company is the beneficiary, and the payout is intended to replace the financial loss incurred by the company due to the death or disability of the key employee.

Variable Whole Life Insurance

Variable life insurance is a form of whole life insurance that provides the opportunity for growth in cash values through variable account investing. Variable whole life shares the characteristics of a guaranteed minimum death benefit and level

VA PPL LH-2_16298

premiums with ordinary whole life insurance. It differs from ordinary whole life in that cash values are not credited with interest guaranteed by the insurer, but instead are placed in variable subaccounts.

The agents who sell variable insurance products must be licensed by the securities regulators and must comply with the variable licensing requirements of the state in which they do business. An agent is authorized to sell variable life and annuity products if the agent holds a Virginia life and health insurance license and is a registered representative of a FINRA member firm. Along with the federal authority of the SEC and FINRA, the Department of Insurance is charged with authority to enforce the insurance laws and regulations applicable to variable insurance transacted in Virginia and to Virginia citizens.

Investment Accounts

Variable accounts, known as **subaccount**s, are part of an insurer's **separate account**. Separate accounts:

- are not part of the insurer's general assets.
- hold contract amounts which are invested in shares of an investment company.
- are registered under the Investment Company Act of 1940, which places the management of the account and solicitation activities related to variable life products under the authority of the Securities and Exchange Commission (SEC) and the Financial Industry Regulatory Authority (FINRA).
- are made up of subaccounts, that are pools of securities managed with specified objectives that are disclosed and explained in the variable product's prospectus.
- hold cash values that belong to the policyholders and cannot be attached by the insurer's creditors.
- hold cash values that are not guaranteed by state life and health insurance guaranty associations.

State insurance guaranty associations are associations made up of insurance companies doing business in a particular state and/or domiciled within a particular state. Insurance companies that are part of a state guaranty

association are liable for a specified amount of an insurer's contractual obligations if that member is not able to meet them.

Variable accounts, known as **subaccount**s, are part of an insurer's **separate account**.

Many variable life policies also offer a **fixed account** investment option. A fixed account:

- may be an investment account that is part of the **general account** of the insurance company.
- offers a guaranteed rate for a specified time period and a minimum guaranteed rate.
- is a contractual obligation of the issuing insurance company.

Advantages of subaccount investing include:

- diversification through placing amounts in a variety of subaccount investments.
- money management by professionals engaged by the investment company.
- opportunity for growth that may exceed that of guaranteed, less risky alternatives.
- no taxation when moving amounts from one subaccount to another within the variable product, which is unlike mutual funds where a movement of amounts between funds causes a taxable transaction.

Subaccount returns are not guaranteed, so there is also risk that subaccount returns will be lower than the return on a guaranteed rate product.

The Prospectus

The prospectus:

- is a condensed version of the registration statement filed by the insurer with the SEC in order to offer variable subaccounts.
- contains information about the subaccount, managers and insurance company.
- is designed to assist a purchaser to make an informed decision.
- must be updated at least annually.

Variable Life Death Benefit

The variable life death benefit:

- is variable.
- is equal to the policy's face amount plus the cash value, and can vary over time.
- increases with cash value increases and decreases with cash value decreases.

- includes a guaranteed minimum amount payable, generally equal to the face amount of the policy at policy inception.

Access to Cash Values

Variable life policies allow policyholders to access cash values through policy loans. These loans:

- are generally limited to 75% to 90% of the cash value at the time of the loan.
- charge low interest rates.
- while outstanding reduce accumulations within the variable subaccounts by the amount of the loan.
- must be paid back and if not paid back, will reduce distributions by the amount of the loan plus interest at time of death or, if allowed, at the surrender of the policy.

Variable life policies may allow withdrawals. Withdrawals of cash values:

- may cause a reduction in the death benefit.
- may trigger a percentage withdrawal charge each time a withdrawal is made or a surrender charge fee when withdrawals are made for a specified period of time after issue.
- may trigger a nominal administrative fee for processing withdrawals.

Variable Universal Life Insurance

Variable universal life insurance:

- combines features of variable whole life and universal life insurance.
- requires a minimum premium amount, at least initially similar to variable whole life.
- includes cash value subaccount investing.
- allows, premium payments to be skipped or suspended once cash values are sufficient
- allows additional premium payments in order to increase cash values.
- may require evidence of insurability for additional premiums above certain levels.
- includes a guaranteed minimum death benefit.
- contains two death benefit options, where Option I/Option A is a level death benefit and Option II/Option B has a death benefit that varies with cash values
- generally allows withdrawals and allows policy loans, generally up to a maximum of 75% – 90% of cash values.

Interest Sensitive or Current-Assumption Life

Current-assumption whole life is a whole life insurance product that includes some of the features of universal life policies. It is designed to allow the policyholder to more directly participate in the actual experience of the insurer as that experience relates to the policy.

Insurers use certain assumptions to determine the premium charge for and the cash value accumulation of an insurance policy. These assumptions are based upon the statistical likelihood of a certain level of mortality, policy expenses, lapses and surrenders associated with its policies, the current interest rate environment and other variables. A current-assumption whole life policy recalculates cash values and premium expenses at scheduled intervals, based on the actual expenses and returns experienced by the insurer, and updated with the current assumptions the insurer is using. This recalculation is done regularly throughout the life of the policy, for example every five years.

Unbundled Policy Components

In order to be able to recalculate cash values, the insurer has to be able to track the elements involved in recalculating them, and so uses an unbundled approach, similar to that used with universal life products. Basically, each premium payment is placed in an accumulation account. From that account, expenses are withdrawn and the insurer applies a crediting rate to the remaining values. The crediting rate may be linked to a specific index, such as a Treasury Bill index. A minimum crediting rate is guaranteed in the policy.

Features of Current-Assumption Whole Life Policies

- Mortality charges and expense rates may vary and are guaranteed not to exceed a specified maximum, and:
  - if these rates are reduced, the policyholder will benefit from this reduction; and
  - if these rates increase, the policyholder will bear the increase in these charges.
- Premium payments and premium amounts remain level during each recalculation period.
- Death benefit provisions vary, and:

- some policies provide a guaranteed death benefit, like other whole life policies.
- other policies offer two death benefit options, similar to universal life policies.
- Current-assumption whole life policies generally allow both partial withdrawals and policy loans as methods to access cash values.
- Most policies include withdrawal charges for withdrawals made in the first five to ten years from policy inception.
- As a form of permanent insurance, current-assumption whole life can be used in situations that permanent life insurance is used in the family and business markets.

Current-assumption whole life is for the policyholder who wants to make a regular premium payment, desires a guaranteed minimum crediting rate on cash values and the opportunity to participate in potentially higher cash value accumulations than those that may be found in traditional whole life policies.

Equity Indexed Universal Life

Another form of life insurance that allows for flexible premiums is equity indexed universal life. This product allows for the possibility of cash value returns that mirror stock returns and provide minimum death benefit and return guarantees.

The return in the cash values is linked to an index, such as the S&P 500 Composite Index or the Nasdaq-100. The insurer manages the portfolios used for these products by purchasing options on the index as part of the insurer's general account.

Features of Equity Index Universal Life Products

- Premiums first go toward paying for the mortality and administrative expenses and the remainder generates cash values.
- If cash values are sufficient, premium payments may be reduced or skipped and the policy will not lapse and the death benefit will not decrease.
- If cash values are not sufficient, it is possible that a reduced premium payment or skipped payment could cause the death benefit to decrease or the policy to lapse.

- Some policies segment the index return by time periods and premium amounts not used for the cost of insurance and administrative expenses are allocated to a segment based on date of premium payment receipt. *For example, for five years, the cash values reflect the index return of Portfolio-A1. The next five years, the cash values reflect the index return of Portfolio-A2.*
- There is a minimum guaranteed return on cash values.
- The return may fluctuate over time.
- Potential gains could be lost when a withdrawal of cash values is made or the policy is surrendered.
- The return calculation may only be performed at certain intervals of time, such as every 5 or 10 years.
- If a withdrawal or surrender is made prior to the end of the recalculation period, some insurers may not credit the index return to the amounts withdrawn or surrendered at all, because the return calculation is based on the cash value at the end of the period.

Important Terms

- Cap – the limit on a percentage increase from one return period to the next in some equity-indexed contracts. If a contract includes a cap, when the return on the cash values is calculated, the new return cannot increase by more than the cap percentage.
- Term – the contract length and/or the recalculation period length. Terms have a variety of lengths, from one to ten years. For example, an equity-indexed contract may have a six-year term. After the six-year term, it may be renewed for additional one-year periods. During the initial term, surrender charges generally apply to withdrawals or surrenders. Surrender charges may not apply during a renewal term.
- Participation rate – refers to the percentage of change in the index that is used in the return calculation. For example, if the participation rate in a contract is 85% and the index increases by five percent, the rate of return that will be applied to the cash values is 4.25 percent.
- Floor – the minimum index-based rate the insurer will pay on cash values. If the contract

 VA PPL LH-2_16298

has such a provision, the floor is generally 0%. If a contract has a floor of 0%, the insurer will never credit a negative amount of return to a contract.

- Vesting – a contract feature where the entire cash value of the contract is not available for withdrawal until the end of the policy's term and there is no surrender charge percentage applied to the cash values withdrawn or surrendered.
- Averaging – a method of calculating the index-based return in some equity-indexed products. The change in the index is averaged over a specified period, for example, monthly or annually, and the result is used in the index-based return calculation.
- Compounding – a contract feature where the earnings from one rate calculation period are added to cash values before the next earnings rate is applied. Some equity-indexed products do not compound earnings and only premiums contributed to the product are considered when calculating earnings and the calculation does not include any prior earnings in the calculation.

Term Life Insurance

Term life insurance is life insurance that pays a death benefit only, and does not build up cash values. Term life insurance issued to individuals is issued based on the risk of death of the *insured*. *Life expectancy* and health factors are taken into consideration. The insured with a lower risk of death is charged a lower rate of premium per $1000 of coverage than is an insured with a higher risk of death. The premium charged for term insurance does not include an amount that goes toward building cash values in the policy.

The *life expectancy* of an insured with a life or health policy that pays a death benefit is statistically determined based on mortality tables that are approved through state and federal laws.

Term life insurance policies pay a death benefit if the insured dies during the policy period. Unlike permanent insurance, which is generally designed to cover the insured for all of the insured's life, term insurance is designed to cover the insured for a specified period, or *term*. Term insurance policies

generally accrue no cash values and have no non-forfeiture values.

Term Lengths

Term insurance policies are available for various term lengths. The most common terms are one, five, ten and twenty years, but they are also available for longer terms, such as 30 years. Generally, premiums during the term of the policy remain constant and are increased when the policy is renewed for an additional term.

Level Term Policies

A level term policy is a term policy that has a face amount/death benefit that remains constant during the term. At the end of the term, the insured must generally prove insurability in order to renew for an additional term. If the policy is renewed for another term, the premium increases. Level term policies may allow for renewal without proving insurability.

Decreasing Term Policies

A *decreasing term* policy is a term policy that has a face amount that decreases over the policy term. By the end of the term, the face amount decreases to zero.

A decreasing term policy is used in both business and personal situations to protect against the financial risk assumed when a loan is taken. For example, a decreasing term policy may be purchased by an individual to coincide with the term of a mortgage loan. Should the insured die before the mortgage is paid off, the proceeds from the policy may be used to pay- off the loan. This protects the heirs of the mortgagor from having to pay this debt.

In the case of a business, the owners of the business may be required to personally guarantee a business loan. To protect their heirs as well as the business, an owner may take out a decreasing term policy to cover the loan. In some business loan situations, the creditor may require that life insurance is in force on the business owners or key shareholders for the term of the loan. Decreasing term insurance can be used in this situation as well

14

Term – Return of Premium

Term insurance policies are available that include a *return of premium* feature. If the term policy is held for the entire term, for example 10, 20 or 30 years, and the insured is still living, a full refund of the premiums paid is made.

Annual Renewable Term

Annual renewable term is term insurance that is effective for a 12 month period. The premium charged for the coverage increases annually as the insured increases in age. The policy may require the insured to prove insurability at each renewal. Some annual renewable term policies are guaranteed renewable for a specified period without the requirement to show insurability. The premium also increases annually on guaranteed renewable annual term contracts.

Life Expectancy Contract

A term insurance policy may be issued for a term based on the life expectancy of the insured. This may be attractive to an applicant who believes the insurance coverage will be needed over his or her entire lifetime and who does not want to run the risk of losing insurability as the applicant ages.

Term-to-65 Contract

Term policies to age 65 are designed to cover insureds for their working years. These products are designed for those who determine they will not need term insurance coverage once they stop working. *Group* term insurance is often used as an employee benefit in the business markets. (*Group insurance* is insurance that is issued to groups that are approved through state law to offer insurance to group members. Employer sponsored group insurance is the most common form of group insurance.)

Increasing Term Policies

Under an increasing term policy, the face amount increases over the term of the policy. This type of policy is often used in family coverage situations to supplement a permanent insurance policy when the financial situation of the family does not allow them to pay the premium required for sufficient permanent insurance coverage.

Special Features

Term – Renewable

A term policy can generally be renewed for a new term, and at renewal, premiums will normally increase.

For example, a 5 year term policy has a monthly premium of $80. At the end of the five years, the policy automatically renews, and the premium is now $92 per month. As long as the insured pays the new premium, the policy remains in force.

Many term policies are not renewable at later ages, or require proof of insurability at these later ages in order to renew. Term policies that can be renewed at later ages (later than age 70 or 75) may have premiums that make them virtually unaffordable.

Term – Convertible

Term policies may include the option to convert to a permanent policy without requiring evidence of insurability. This feature greatly adds to the utility of term insurance as part of an overall coverage plan.

For example, convertible term insurance can be used to cover children under a family plan of insurance. When the children reach a certain age, such as age 21, the term coverage can be converted to an individual, permanent plan on the now adult child, without the child having to prove insurability.

Convertible term may also be used along with a permanent policy covering the insured to cover a spouse of the insured. When finances allow, the term policy may be converted to permanent coverage on the spouse. Or, convertible term may be used to supplement coverage on the primary earner in a family policy situation and may be converted to permanent insurance when finances allow.

Convertibility is especially important should the insured become uninsurable. Being able to convert to a permanent plan, lock in the premium rate upon conversion, and not have to worry about renewing a term policy at increasing rates can be of great benefit to an insured and beneficiaries.

VA PPL LH-2_16298

Convertibility provisions may suspend the offer of conversion once the insured reaches a certain age, such as after reaching age 65.

Conversion Options

Term policies that are convertible generally offer conversion on an *attained age* basis. Some offer the option of *original age* conversion as well. Under the attained age option, rates for the permanent policy are based on the insured's age at the time of conversion.

Under the original age option, the premium is based on the insured's age when the term policy was originally issued. If the original age conversion option is selected, generally an extra premium amount is due upon conversion. At conversion, an amount equal to the adjustment of premium for the difference between the term insurance premium amount and the permanent policy premium amount since policy inception, increased by a specified annual percentage rate, must be paid to the insurer. This required payment can make the selection of original age conversion unaffordable unless conversion occurs just a few years after policy inception.

Annuities

An annuity is a life insurance contract that pays income for a specified period of time or for life. Annuities are used to pay out life insurance settlements upon death to beneficiaries. For example, the death benefit can be paid as a life annuity. Annuities are also purchased specifically to provide income to the purchaser during the purchaser's lifetime. Insurers pay a return on the money contributed to purchase the contract and pay the income out over the period of time the purchaser requests. When an annuity is purchased to pay income from its inception, it is known as an *immediate annuity*. Annuities can also be purchased that do not pay out income from their inception. This kind of annuity is called a *deferred annuity*.

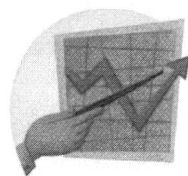

Annuity products are an important tool used to meet many retirement savings and income needs.

Insurers offer them with a number of different features and benefits and risk levels.

Clients looking for	can purchase...
a steady return with guarantees	a fixed deferred annuity with long-term rate guarantees
more opportunity for growth with few guarantees	a variable deferred annuity with subaccount options
market returns with guarantees	an equity index annuity
immediate income	an immediate annuity
income at retirement, but not now	a deferred annuity

Single and Flexible Deferred Annuities

There are two basic types of deferred annuities. One is a flexible premium deferred annuity, which allows for contributions to be made any time prior to converting the policy to an income annuity. The other is a single premium deferred annuity. This contract allows only one contribution to be made to the product.

Immediate and Deferred Annuities

Single Premium Immediate Income Annuities

Immediate annuities begin making a payout "immediately" after making the annuity contribution. "Immediately" doesn't mean the day or week after purchase; there may be a period of delay, such as month or a quarter after purchase before the first payment is made. Under tax laws, a product is considered an immediate annuity if it begins paying out the income stream within 12 months of purchase. These annuities are always single premium products, and are known as single premium immediate annuities (SPIA).

The interest rate credited on SPIA contributions is not published. For this reason, when selecting a SPIA, the insured should compare payout amounts among insurers (along with other factors such as the financial health of the company) when determining which product to buy.

Deferred Annuities

Deferred annuities have an accumulation period where the contributions made to the annuity accumulate earnings. During the accumulation phase, earnings are not taxed as they accumulate

VA PPL LH-2_16298

within the product; the earnings grow tax-deferred, unless withdrawn. The insurer applies surrender charges for withdrawals during the accumulation period, generally with some exceptions. If they are withdrawn prior to age 59 ½, there is a 10% tax penalty, with some exceptions.

Deferred annuities may be purchased as fixed or variable products. *Variable annuities* pay a return based on the variable subaccounts selected by the annuity owner, similar to the return paid on cash values of variable life and variable universal life products. A *fixed annuity* contract is an annuity contract that earns a fixed interest rate, guaranteed by the insurance company.

Annuity Benefit Payment Options

SPIAs offer several different payout options. These same payout options are generally available through deferred annuities upon annuitization.

The *annuitant* is the insured party on an annuity contract. If an annuity contract is annuitized, the annuitant's life is used to determine the amount of the annuity payments. *Annuitization* is the conversion of annuity contract values to an irrevocable stream of income payments.

Life Contingency Options

Life Income

The life income payout option, also known as the straight life option:

- provides payments for the entire life of the insured.
- is advertised as "income you can never outlive."
- pays a specified amount each payment period until the annuitant passes away.
- payment periods may be monthly, quarterly, semi-annually, or annually.
- ends payments at death.
- may provide a total payout that is less than the amount paid to purchase the contract or greater than that amount, depending upon when the annuitant passes away.

For example, if an annuitant with a life expectancy of 18 years dies 2 years after purchasing the life income annuity, the payout will be much less than the amount contributed. However, if the annuity exceeds his life expectancy and lives 25 years, the amount received will be greater than the amount used to purchase the annuity.

There are other life options available from annuities that include a guaranteed minimum payable. These options include life income with period certain and life income with refund.

Life Income with Period Certain

Under a life income with period certain, the payments are guaranteed for a certain period, or for life, whichever is greater. *For example, a life income with 20 year period certain will make payments for at least 20 years. If the annuitant dies during the 20 year period, the payments continue to a beneficiary. If the annuitant lives beyond the 20 year period, the payments continue until the annuitant's death.*

(The *beneficiary* is the party receiving proceeds at the death of an insured on a life insurance policy, including annuities.)

Life Income with Refund

A life income with refund annuity:

- pays out income for the life of the annuitant.
- continues to pay income or pays a lump sum to a beneficiary if the annuitant passes away before an amount equal to the payment(s) made to the annuity is paid out
- pays a beneficiary in installment payments when the annuity is a Life Income with Installment Refund annuity.
- pays a beneficiary in a lump sum when the annuity is a Life Income with Cash Refund annuity.

For example, the policyholder who is also the annuitant contributes $75,000 to a SPIA. He chooses the life income with cash refund payout option. He receives payments of $293 a month from this product. He passes away after seventeen years. He has received $59,772 in payments. His beneficiary will receive $15,228 as a cash refund upon his death.

Temporary Life Income

Under a temporary life income annuity, payments are made for the annuitant's life or a period certain, whichever is shorter. *For example, the annuitant has a life expectancy under the insurance company's tables of 22.7 years. The annuitant chooses to take a temporary life income annuity with a period certain of 20 years. The annuity will make payments for at least 20 years. The reason the annuitant selected this option is that the payout amount was slightly higher than the life income only option, since the term certain is shorter than his life expectancy. Depending on the age of the annuitant, his life expectancy and expense factors and the term period selected, temporary life annuities may pay out more than a life income contract, or may pay out less.*

Multiple Life Annuity Payment Options

Joint and Survivor Life Payouts

There are several annuity income payout options that are based on the lives of two beneficiaries, known as joint and survivor life payouts.

Joint and survivor life	Payments are calculated based on two life expectancies and continue until the death of the last annuitant to die
Joint and survivor specified percentage	Annuity payments after the death of the first annuitant to die are a lower percentage, such as 75% or 50%, of the payment amount made while both annuitants were alive
Joint and survivor period certain income	Payments are made for a specified period or until the death of the second annuitant, whichever is later
Joint and survivor life payouts with refund	After the death of both annuitants, if the amount paid out does not equal the principal paid for the annuity, a beneficiary will receive the remainder in installments, or as a lump sum

Installments for a Fixed Period or Annuities Certain

Installments for a fixed period or annuity certain options, or *period certain* payouts:

- allow the purchaser to specify a fixed period of time that the payments continue.
- generally, have a minimum period of five years, but some annuity companies issue them for as short as three years.
- may have a maximum term- an insurer may not allow any annuity with longer than a forty year period or may not allow a period certain that exceeds the annuitant's life expectancy.

Installments for a Fixed Amount

Annuity payment options may also be selected that allow the purchaser to specify a fixed dollar amount of payments. The payment period varies based on the payment amount selected by the purchaser.

Fixed Annuities

Fixed annuities are products that have a guaranteed rate for fixed periods of time. They include a minimum guaranteed rate, and often allow for withdrawals without penalty prior to the payout period. Upon payout, or *annuitization*, they offer a variety of fixed payout options.

Fixed annuities may either be flexible premium annuities or single premium annuities. A *flexible premium annuity* is one that accepts premiums throughout the life of the annuity, although some states may require that premiums stop once the owner reaches a certain age, such as age 85. A *single premium annuity* is one that accepts only one premium contribution.

Fixed annuity contracts are also referred to as tax-deferred annuities or *deferred annuities:*

- This title emphasizes tax-deferral of earnings, which is a key benefit – earnings on cash accumulations are not taxed until withdrawn.
- This title differentiates a fixed annuity contract from a single premium immediate annuity contract.
- Annuitization may be deferred until a later date, or funds may be held in the annuity until the death of the contract owner, when the beneficiary receives a lump sum or an income stream.

Interest Rate Guarantees

Interest rates on fixed annuities may be guaranteed for a variety of periods. Some guarantee the rate for one year, and then the rate is subject to change. Other's guarantee the rate for several years, known as the period or *term*, and then give the owner the option to renew the contract for another period at the rate being paid at that time.

Interest Rate Crediting

Fixed annuities may earn guaranteed rates, *bonus rates, base rates* and *renewal rates.*

VA PPL LH-2_16298

Guaranteed rate	Earn a stated fixed interest rate for 1 year or longer
Bonus rate	Earn 1% or more higher than the base rate for the first year or more
Base rate	The rate before a bonus rate is applied
Renewal rate	The rate after the first guaranteed rate period is over
Minimum guaranteed rate	The lowest rate, stated in the contract, that the annuity will pay, and which is regulated by state law

The renewal rate is generally lower than the bonus rate, unless the interest rate environment merits the insurer crediting a renewal rate from its general account as high as the initial bonus rate.

Level Benefit Payment Amount

Fixed annuities pay income streams that do not vary from payment to payment. For example, a life annuity will pay the same monthly payment of $500 a month until the annuitant passes away, a period certain annuity will pay $500 a month for a period such as 10 years and a *joint life annuity* will pay $500 until both annuitants pass away unless the purchasers selected a joint life annuity that decreases the payment upon the first to die.

Variable Annuities

Variable annuities are annuity contracts which allow the accumulation of earnings based on subaccounts that are similar to mutual funds as we discussed concerning variable life products:

- Each subaccount has a specified objective
- Securities in subaccount managed by investment manager
- Risk and opportunity for growth varies in subaccounts
- Insurer does not guarantee return on subaccounts, but may offer value guarantees by pegging value of annuity every several years or guaranteeing death benefit

Because these products utilize securities and the risk of return is borne by the policyholder and not the insurer, variable annuities are **securities** products. *Agents* offering them must be licensed for selling securities products by registering with FINRA, as well as being life insurance agents.

Deferred Annuity Surrender and Withdrawal Charges

Deferred annuity contracts generally have back-end charges levied when a contract is surrendered or when withdrawals are made. The surrender charge period is generally from five to seven years, but the period varies. Some contracts have a level surrender charge percentage during that period, but more commonly, the surrender charge percentage decreases each year.

Deferred annuities generally waive normally applicable surrender or withdrawal charges for withdrawals that are within a specified amount. For example, withdrawals of up to ten or fifteen percent of the annuity value may be considered a *free withdrawal*, meaning that no withdrawal charges apply. Another form of free withdrawal found in some contracts is allowing all earnings from the contract to be withdrawn without normally applicable withdrawal charges.

Medical Waivers

Many deferred annuities also waive withdrawal or surrender charges under provisions known as *medical* or *nursing home waivers*. Under such a provision, if the owner, or in some cases, the annuitant or a spouse of the owner or annuitant, undergoes nursing home, hospice or hospital care for a specified number of days, withdrawals can be made without charges applying. The length of the stay that these provisions require vary, and may be anywhere from thirty to ninety days.

For long-term care insurance, life insurance and annuity accelerated death benefit and premium waiver provision purposes, *nursing home* is generally defined as a state licensed residential facility which provides 24-hr skilled nursing care to elderly or disabled persons. Other services consist of room and board, personal and custodial care, medication, therapy, rehabilitation, and communal dining. Rooms may be private or semi-private.

Systematic Withdrawals

Another type of withdrawal provision found in annuity contracts is the systematic withdrawal provision. Under a systematic withdrawal provision:

VA PPL LH-2_16298

- a specified amount or a specified percentage of contract values may be withdrawn periodically, monthly, quarterly, semi-annually or annually
- withdrawals may be stopped and started.
- if the systematic withdrawal amount exceeds penalty free limits, surrender charges generally apply.

Bail Out Provisions

A surrender provision in some annuities includes a waiver of surrender charges if the rate ever falls below a specified percentage or falls more than a specified percentage lower than the initial rate. This percentage is referred to as a bail out rate or as the rate floor. This provision may be effective only the first time the rate falls to the floor rate. If the policy holder does not invoke this right at that time, he or she may not have the right to do so at a later date.

Equity-Indexed Annuities

Equity-indexed annuities are annuities that provide a return based on a stock index. They include some of the guarantees of fixed annuities along with the potential for growth that may exceed that of a fixed annuity product.

In calculating the return on equity-indexed annuities, the most commonly used index is the S&P 500 Composite Price Index. This index represents ninety different industry groups. The major industry groups represented include industrial, utilities, financial and transportation. Another popularly used index is the NASDAQ-100 Index, which also reflects companies across a wide spectrum of major industry groups including computer hardware and software, telecommunications, retail/wholesale trade and biotechnology and excludes financial company securities.

An equity-indexed annuity is different from other fixed annuities because of the way it credits interest to the annuity's value. Equity-indexed annuities credit interest using a calculation method based on changes in the index to which the annuity is linked, just as equity-indexed universal life insurance products do, using the annual reset, point-to-point, or high water mark methods.

Guarantees in equity-indexed annuities include minimum guaranteed rates, minimum index returns and minimum death benefit guarantees. For example, an insurer may guarantee that a minimum rate of 3% will be credited to the amounts contributed during the accumulation phase. Some insurers also guarantee a rate of return during payout. Minimum death benefit guarantees may provide that the proceeds will be the greater of the annuity value or the amount based on a minimum index return or minimum rate.

Combination Plans and Variations
Joint Life Insurance

Joint life insurance, also known as first-to-die insurance, is life insurance that covers two or more insureds and pays a death benefit upon the insured first-to-die. A joint life plan may be structured in various ways, but generally, a permanent life insurance policy is used.

In the family market, joint life is usually utilized in order to save the expense associated with writing two separate individual policies. Joint life policies may also include a provision that allows the survivor to decide whether to continue the coverage after the first death.

Joint Life with a Guaranteed Insurability Rider

A *rider* is an optional insurance policy benefit added to the policy that requires the payment of additional premium.

Joint life insurance is used in a variety of situations. It is a more flexible tool when a **guaranteed insurability** rider is attached. A guaranteed insurability rider gives the policyowner the ability to add to or continue insurance coverage without proving insurability.

For example, a husband and wife may purchase joint life insurance, planning that an important debt, such as the home mortgage, be paid off upon the first-to-die. A guaranteed insurability rider or provision then gives the

VA PPL LH-2_16298

surviving spouse the option to purchase additional insurance without having to prove insurability.

Survivorship Life Insurance

Survivorship life pays a death benefit upon the death of the last to die of two or more insureds. The most common use of survivorship life is to supply insurance coverage to pay for **estate taxes** at the death of a surviving spouse, as well as other expenses that erode the value of an estate. Purchasing survivorship life ensures there is more to pass onto beneficiaries than if estate assets must be sold or used to pay expenses upon death.

Estate taxes are federal taxes due on transfers of property or wealth at the death of the property owner.

At the death of the first spouse, estate taxation is largely avoided due to the unlimited marital deduction. The unlimited marital deduction allows property to pass from a deceased spouse to the surviving spouse without estate taxation. However, at the death of the second spouse, the marital deduction does not apply, and estate taxation can be significant. Having a survivorship life policy in place provides funds needed to pay estate taxes and other estate expenses upon the death of the second spouse.

Another use in the family market is for dual-income spouses. At the death of one spouse, the survivors may not need an insurance benefit, due to the continuing income of the surviving spouse. However, upon the death of the surviving spouse, the death benefit will be needed to provide for beneficiaries.

Some survivorship life policies allow for the splitting of the policy into two policies under certain conditions. For example, such a provision may state that a policy may be split into two separate policies if tax laws change and replace the current unlimited marital deduction rules so that the structure of the survivorship life policy is no longer needed, or if a married couple divorces.

Adding a First-Death Rider

In some cases, a relatively small death benefit may be needed upon the first insured to die. A first-death rider, which is a term insurance rider, may be added to the survivorship life policy so that the needed death benefit may be paid.

Section I Review

1) Ordinary whole life:
   a. allows premium payments to be skipped.
   b. includes an adjustable death benefit.
   c. requires level premium payments.
   d. includes lower premiums the first few years of the policy and higher premiums after that time.

2) The type of whole life insurance that requires payments for a certain, or limited, period is:
   a. limited pay
   b. single premium
   c. permanent
   d. level-pay

3) Universal life insurance policies:
   a. include bundled policy elements.
   b. offer one death benefit option.
   c. allow premium payments to be skipped.
   d. require level premium payments.

4) Of the following, which type of life insurance policy is regulated as a security?
   a. Single premium whole life
   b. Universal life
   c. Variable life
   d. Ordinary whole life

5) The type of life insurance product that combines features of universal life and variable life is called:
  a. subaccount life
  b. uni-var life
  c. combination life
  d. variable universal life

6) Current-assumption whole life insurance policies:
  a. allow premium payments to be skipped.
  b. may offer an adjustable death benefit.
  c. never allow withdrawals.
  d. include bundled policy components.

7) The type of term insurance that is generally used to protect against the risk that an insured will die before an outstanding loan is paid off is:
  a. level term
  b. increasing term
  c. decreasing term
  d. non-renewable term

8) A variable annuity:
  a. pays a fixed, constant rate over the entire life of the annuity.
  b. pays a stated rate of interest, established by the insurance company, and includes a guaranteed minimum rate of return.
  c. pays a variable return, based on subaccount performance.
  d. pays a return based on an index benefit calculation.

9) The measuring life of an annuity policy is generally the:
  a. annuitant.
  b. beneficiary.
  c. policy owner.
  d. insurance company.

10) The type of immediate annuity or annuitization option that pays a specified amount for a specified period is a:
  a. term certain or period certain annuity
  b. straight life annuity
  c. specified period annuity
  d. interest only annuity

11) A fixed annuity where a single, cash payment establishes the contract is a:
  a. single premium annuity
  b. deferred annuity
  c. equity-index annuity
  d. variable annuity

12) When a client takes a withdrawal out of their deferred annuity, the insurance company may charge the client which of the following?
  a. a surrender charge
  b. an annuity fee
  c. a systematic fee
  d. income taxes

13) A deferred annuity has a provision that states that if the rate ever goes below 2%, the annuity can be surrendered without the application of surrender charges. This provision is called a:
  a. Bail-out provision
  b. Systematic withdrawal provision
  c. Surrender charge provision
  d. Early withdrawal provision

14) _____ is the type of insurance that pays a death benefit upon the death of the last to die of two or more insureds.
  a. Key employee insurance
  b. Joint-life insurance
  c. Survivorship life insurance
  d. Benefit life insurance

15) A guaranteed insurability provision or rider:
  a. gives the insured the right to purchase additional insurance without having to provide evidence of insurability.
  b. increases coverage based on an inflationary index.
  c. gives the owner the ability to replace the insured with a current owner or key shareholder.
  d. is also known as a cost of living rider.

Section II: Policy Riders, Provisions, Options and Exclusions

This section looks at the provisions in life insurance contracts, optional provisions, exclusions and policy riders that add benefits. Topics include:

- Policy riders
- Policy provisions and options
- Policy exclusions

Virginia Law and Regulation Cites

Throughout the course, Virginia law or regulation may be cited. The Virginia insurance code is found in Section 38.2 of the Virginia Code. It is cited in the course as *VA Code §38.2*. Virginia insurance regulations are found in Title 14, Agency 5 of the Virginia Administrative Code. These regulations are cited in the course as *14VAC 5*.

Policy Riders

A **rider** is an additional, optional life insurance policy benefit that requires the payment of additional premium.

Life insurance riders provide many benefits such as:

- a way to tailor an insurance policy to meet individual client needs.
- additional insurance coverage for family members.
- policy coverage amounts that increase to keep up with inflation.
- a guaranteed ability to purchase added coverage in the future.
- the ability for a business to change insureds at a later date.
- premium waivers should the owner or insured become disabled.

Waiver of Premium for Disability Rider

A waiver of premium rider provides that the insurer will waive the premium on a life insurance policy should the insured or policyholder become disabled (the policy defines whose disability, the insured or the policyholder, triggers this benefit). The provisions of waiver of premium riders vary regarding the length of time coverage applies, the definition of disability and the length of the waiting period before coverage applies.

Coverage Period

Waiver of premium riders have varying coverage periods.

- Many do not generally continue to age 100 or policy maturity, but end at age 60, 65 or 70.
- Some provide disability coverage up to age 90, but only waive premium up to age 65 or age 70.
- Some provide that if disability occurs before age 60 or 65, premium will be waived for the entire life of the policy.

Definition of Disability

A waiver of premium rider is a form of disability insurance. A key part of disability insurance coverage is the definition of disability. Two categories of disability definitions are generally found in disability coverage: the own occupation definition and the any gainful occupation definition.

Own occupation definition – Unable to perform substantial and material duties of the insured's regular occupation. *Under such a definition, premium would be waived if a teacher can no longer teach, for example.*

Unable to work in any gainful occupation definition – *If a teacher were unable to work as a teacher but was still able to work at a computer, entering data, for example, a policy with an any gainful occupation definition would not waive premium.*

Combination of the own occupation and any gainful occupation definitions – *A policy may waive premium if the insured is unable to perform substantial and material duties of the insured's regular occupation for two years, and would continue to waive premium after that time if the insured was then unable to work in any gainful occupation after the two-year period.*

Premium waivers generally include conditions that are automatically considered to meet its definition of total disability. For example, loss of sight or loss of a limb are both generally considered *presumptive disabilities*, or disabilities that are presumed to cause total disability.

Waiting Period

The waiting period is the length of time from disability inception to when the benefit will apply. Most waiver of premium riders include a waiting period of four to six months.

Waiver of Cost of Insurance for Disability Rider

A waiver of cost of insurance for disability rider:

- provides that the cost of insurance (COI) is waived when the insured or policyholder meets the definition of disability in the rider.
- applies only to universal life (UL) policies because of the unbundling of the premium in these policies of the mortality and administrative expenses (the COI) and the premium amounts that are applied to the cash value.
- in some policies is a waiver of premium for more than COI and waives the amount of premium the insured would have paid had the disability not occurred.

Waiver of Premium with Disability Income Benefit Rider

Waiver of premium with disability income riders include the features of a waiver of premium rider **and** pay disability income to the insured or policyholder. *Disability income insurance* is a form of health insurance that compensates the insured for loss of income due to a disability.

These riders:

- pay a specified percentage of the life insurance policy's face amount on a monthly basis. *For example, the rider may pay 1% of a $75,000 policy's face amount, or $750 per month, to the insured if the insured becomes totally disabled.*
- include a cap on the amount of monthly income payable under the rider, regardless of the face amount of the underlying policy.
- do not pay benefits if an insured is partially disabled but only pay for total disability.
- generally include a waiting period of up to six months.

Guaranteed Insurability Riders

A *guaranteed insurability* rider, also known as an *additional purchase option*, gives the insured the right to purchase additional insurance without having to provide evidence of insurability. The rider allows the option to purchase additional insurance at specified time frames, such as every three years, or at the time of identified life events, such as the birth of a child.

Guaranteed insurability riders:

- may limit the ability to purchase additional insurance without proving insurability to age 40.
- may allow additional insurance to be purchased up to ages as high as 65, and so may be suitable for purchase by older insureds.
- are used in situations:
  - where a younger insured cannot initially afford as much coverage as may be needed later.
  - where the rider allows the surviving insured on joint life insurance to increase coverage upon the death of the first-to-die.

Juvenile Life Waiver of Premium for Disability Rider, Payor Benefits

Juvenile life insurance is life insurance on a minor's life. Generally, juvenile life insurance:

- is term coverage that is converted to permanent coverage upon the insured's majority age or at age 25.
- requires very minimal *underwriting* based on age, sex, height, weight and general health information.
- does not require proof of insurability when converted to permanent insurance.
- may allow purchasing increased amounts of insurance without providing proof of insurability through a guaranteed insurability option.

Juvenile life issued with a waiver of premium for disability rider waives the premium when the payor, which is the person paying the premiums, becomes disabled. For example, *a grandfather purchased a juvenile term life policy on a grandchild's life. The grandfather is paying the premiums for the policy and the policy has a waiver of premium rider. If the grandfather becomes disabled, the premiums are waived.*

VA PPL LH-2_16298

Accidental Death (Double Indemnity) Rider

The accidental death rider:

- pays double (or triple) the policy's face amount if death occurs as a result of an accident.
- has a definition of accident that does not include disease – death must be the direct result of accidental injury.
- specifies that death must occur within a specified number of days from the accident, generally 90 to 120 days.
- generally stops coverage at a specified age, such as 70.

Accidental Death and Dismemberment Rider

Accidental Death and Dismemberment insurance, or AD&D insurance, pays a lump-sum benefit in the case of accidental death or in the event of the loss of body members due to accidental injury. This form of insurance may be added as a rider. The accidental death benefit has the same conditions as that provided under an accidental death benefit rider.

Accidental Dismemberment Rider

The dismemberment benefit under the rider pays a portion or all of the death benefit when accidental dismemberment occurs. The benefit is payable for the loss of one or both limbs or for the loss of sight in one or both eyes. The full death benefit is generally paid if the insured loses two limbs or sight in both eyes. A lesser amount, such as ½ the death benefit is paid if one limb is lost as the result of an accident.

Term Riders

Term insurance riders are used in many ways on life policies.

Term Riders added to a Permanent Policy, on a Spouse	Affordable additional coverage Often used for a non-income earning spouse Used to replace and pay for economic contributions of spouse performing childcare, home management, cooking, etc.

Family Coverage – Term coverage on Spouse and/or Children	Children covered for an amount to cover death expenses Children's coverage can be converted to permanent insurance Spouse's coverage for an amount to replace economic contribution to household
Term Riders on Non-Family Members	Covers other owners of policyowner's residence Covers other persons with close financial ties to policyholder
Joint Life Coverage	Both spouses listed as insureds At first death, term policy pays a benefit to pay off mortgage, pay for college, etc. At last death, permanent policy pays larger benefit for heirs
Additional Insurance	Provides additional coverage at a lower price than permanent coverage Can usually be converted to permanent insurance

Accelerated Death Benefit or Long-Term Care Riders

Life insurance policies may include a form of long-term care coverage through riders or provisions that pay all or a portion of the death benefit during life if the insured meets certain criteria. The idea behind these riders is that the death benefit may be needed during life in order to pay for long-term care expenses. These riders or provisions may be called a *living benefit, long-term care rider* or *convalescent care rider*.

Accelerated death benefit or living benefit riders pay a portion or all of the policy's death benefit if the insured becomes terminally ill, enters an eligible health care facility, such as a skilled nursing facility, or meets other criteria of the rider.

Accelerated death benefit riders:

- may limit the benefits payable to a specified percentage of the death benefit, such as 50% or 75%.
- may allow the full death benefit to be paid out.
- may pay the full death benefit for terminal illness and partial benefits for a serious medical condition.
- may pay a lump sum to the insured.
- may pay a monthly amount while the insured is living and the remaining death benefit to

VA PPL LH-2_16298

the insured's beneficiaries upon the insured's death.

- may pay benefits based on the actual long-term care or terminal illness expenses incurred, and require documentation of the expenses before payment is made.

A *skilled nursing facility* is a facility which provides room and board, 24-hour nursing care and rehabilitation, along with other medical services, and has been certified by Medicare.

Long-term care is a form of health care that is comprised of a variety of services that help people with health or personal needs and activities of daily living over a period of time. Long-term care can be provided at home, in the community, or in various types of facilities, including nursing homes and assisted living facilities. Most long-term care is custodial care. Skilled nursing care is generally the type of long-term care that triggers an accelerated death benefit based on long-term care conditions.

Activities of daily living is a term used in the long-term care field and means normal, necessary, everyday activities which include eating, bathing, dressing, mobility, transferring, toileting, and continence. Inability to perform these activities is considered a trigger for needing long-term care.

Return of Premium Riders

A *return of premium* rider allows the insured to request a refund of premium if no claim is filed against the policy within a specified time frame or if the amount of claims submitted do not exceed a specified percentage of premiums paid. The insurer will refund all or a portion of the premium, as the rider's provisions dictate. Return of premium riders are a relatively expensive option.

Policy Provisions and Options
Entire Contract

All life insurance policies must have a provision that states that the policy constitutes the *entire contract*. If, however, the insurance company includes the *application* as part of the contract (which is common procedure), the copy of the application must be endorsed to or be attached to the policy

when issued. In this case, the policy must contain a provision that the policy and application constitute the entire contract between the parties.

The *application* is a document used by the insurance company to evaluate the risk of a proposed insured and policy owner. It includes information concerning the medical condition, occupation and avocation of the insured.

Insuring Clause

The insuring clause in a life insurance contract generally states that the insurer will pay the death benefit in the contract upon the death of the insured, according to the terms of the contract and upon acceptable proof of death.

Free Look – Virginia Requirement

All life insurance policies have a minimum specified right to review period. If the policyholder returns the policy to the insurer within this time frame, the premium paid to the insurer must be returned in full. This right to review period is also known as the *free look period*.

No individual life insurance policy may be delivered or issued for delivery in Virginia unless it has printed on it a notice that states that during a ten-day period from the date the policy is delivered to the policyowner, the policy is surrendered to the insurer or its *agent* with a written request for cancellation, the policy is void from the beginning and the insurer will refund any premium paid for the policy. An insurer may extend this right to examine period to more than ten days if the period is specified in the policy.
VA Code §38.2-3301.

Individual insurance is insurance issued directly to an individual policyowner by the insurer. Individual insurance may cover more than just one individual. An individual policy may cover a family or several partners in a business.

Consideration

The parties to a life insurance contract must each provide valuable *consideration* in a contractual relationship. The **premium** is the consideration by the insured and the **promise to fulfill policy obligations** is the consideration given by the insurer.

The applicant's premium is based on the statements made in the application. The consideration is not commensurate to the insurer's stake in the policy if the applicant makes material misrepresentations or false statements in the application.

The insurer can void coverage in certain circumstances when material misrepresentation or false statements are made, or, the insurer may reduce coverage when misstatements are discovered so that the premium reflects the actual cost to the insurer in providing coverage.

Owner's Rights

The policyowner (or policyholder) is typically the purchaser and payer of the premium. It is up to the owner to name the insured and beneficiaries of the policy. The owner also has rights related to the policy, including the right to:

- Name and change beneficiaries during the life of the policy (unless an irrevocable beneficiary is named)
- Withdraw cash values
- Take policy loans
- Increase or decrease coverage within contract specifications
- Select dividend payment options, if the policy pays dividends
- Surrender the policy
- Policyowners are also responsible for any taxes related to the receipt of taxable income from the policy during the lifetime of the insured. The policy pays a death benefit upon the death of the insured.

Beneficiaries

Beneficiaries receive the policy proceeds upon the death of the insured. Any person, natural or non-natural, may be named as a beneficiary.

Upon the death of the insured, the policy proceeds belong to the beneficiary. If more than one beneficiary will receive the death benefit, each beneficiary can generally make their own decision how to receive the death benefits. The options a beneficiary has regarding the death benefit are called *settlement options*.

Beneficiary Designations

Beneficiary designations should be clearly stated. If a person is named, the full name of the person should be listed. If a charitable organization or other non-natural person is named, the organization should be clearly identified. Unclear beneficiary designations to avoid include simply stating, "wife" (many people have been divorced or widowed, so the question arises, "Which wife?") or "children" (does this include step-children, adopted children or illegitimate children?) and "estate" (whose estate, the owner's or the insured's?). When unclear designations are used, the insurance company may have to use a lengthy investigative process to make certain that the proper beneficiary or beneficiaries are paid. Unclear designations also open the way for heirs to contest the disposition of the insurance proceeds.

Classes of Beneficiaries

Primary or Class I Beneficiaries

Primary and contingent, or Class I and Class II, beneficiaries can be named on life insurance contracts. Some insurers also allow tertiary beneficiaries to be named. The *primary* or *Class I beneficiary* receives the death proceeds, if living. More than one primary beneficiary may be named to share the death benefit from a life insurance policy.

Contingent or Class II Beneficiaries

Contingent beneficiaries (also known as Class II or Secondary beneficiaries) receive the death benefit only if all the primary beneficiaries are deceased at the time of the death of the insured.

Tertiary Beneficiaries

A tertiary beneficiary is the next beneficiary in line if both the primary and contingent beneficiaries pre-decease the insured.

Estate as Beneficiary

If an estate of the insured or the owner is named as beneficiary, the proceeds do not avoid probate. However, leaving proceeds to the insured's estate may be desirable to provide funds to pay estate expenses and other expenses related to the insured's death. *Probate* is the legal process of ensuring clear title to property in an estate prior to

VA PPL LH-2_16298

transferring this property to heirs upon the death of the property owner.

Trusts as Beneficiaries

Trusts may be named as beneficiary of a life insurance contract. A **trust** is a legal relationship under which one person holds the title to property for the benefit of another or others. The person who holds the title to (controls) property is called the **trustee**. The person adding property to the trust and establishing the trust's purpose is called the **grantor**, and the property is called the **corpus**, or body, of the trust.

The trustee:
- must act with the best interests of the beneficiaries of the trust.
- must strictly follow the provisions and instructions within the trust document.
- has specific powers granted him or her in the trust document, generally including:
  - investing and reinvesting assets within the trust.
  - paying trust expenses.
  - collecting income payable to the trust.
  - paying out income from the trust.

A trust established prior to the insured's death could be named as beneficiary and the life insurance proceeds will be added to the other assets of the trust and managed by the trustee. Or a trust may be established to take effect upon the insured's death and become funded by the insurance proceeds at that time.

Trusts may be used for many purposes, including:
- the education of beneficiaries.
- taking care of an individual who is legally incapable of taking care of himself.
- to take care of someone unable to manage property if it were given to the individual directly.
- to donate to charities and by charities to distribute and administer funds.

Revocable and Irrevocable Beneficiaries (Changing a Beneficiary)

Revocable beneficiary – beneficiary that can be changed by the owner during the life of the insured.

Irrevocable beneficiary – beneficiary that cannot be changed without the written permission of that beneficiary.

Irrevocable beneficiaries may be named through a court order, such as a divorce decree or a monetary judgment award, that requires a specified person be named irrevocably to receive proceeds at death

Common Disaster and Beneficiaries

An insurer may include a deferment or *common disaster* period in beneficiary designations. These clauses will pay benefits to the class II or secondary beneficiary only if the primary beneficiary does not survive the insured for a specified number of days.

For example, assume a wife is named as primary beneficiary on a policy where the husband was named as insured. Assume the common disaster period in the life insurance policy is 30 days. The secondary beneficiary is their only daughter. The husband and wife are both in a serious car accident. The husband dies immediately at the scene of the accident. The wife dies ten days later. The insurer will pay the secondary beneficiary, the daughter, the policy's death benefit. However, if the wife had survived for thirty-one days, and then passed away, the wife's estate would receive the insurance benefits, and the daughter as secondary beneficiary would not.

Common disaster periods provided for in life insurance policies vary from 30 to 90 days.

Naming a Minor as Beneficiary

If a minor is named as beneficiary, the insurance company will generally not pay the proceeds directly to the minor. An individual with minor children should name a property guardian in the individual's will. A property guardian is responsible to care for property left to minor children. A trust is sometimes also set up prior to a parent's death or through a will to receive money left to minor children.

Succession and Life Insurance Beneficiaries

Per Capita

Most insurance companies assume per capita distribution when more than one beneficiary is named in the same beneficiary class. *For example, if "John Randolph, son and Paula Cramer, daughter" are named on a life insurance policy assuming a per capita distribution, John and Paula would share equally in the* death proceeds. *If either beneficiary predeceased the insured, the remaining beneficiary would receive the entire proceeds. If both had predeceased the insured, the contingent beneficiary or beneficiaries would receive the death proceeds.*

Per Stirpes

Under a per stirpes designation, if a beneficiary predeceases the insured, that beneficiary's child or children will receive the death benefit. If the beneficiary's child was also deceased, the child's child or children will receive the death benefit. Per stirpes means by stock; which is an old-fashioned term meaning succession by family lines.

For example, if John Randolph, son and Paula Cramer, daughter were named on a policy with a per stirpes designation, and John Randolph predeceased the insured, Paula would receive one-half of the death benefit and John Randolph's children would share the other half. Because of the potential complications arising from a per stirpes beneficiary designation, some insurance companies will not accept them.

Percentage Distributions

The percentage each beneficiary is to receive may also be included in a beneficiary designation. *The percentage designation is used when the policyowner wants to leave more for the adult child that has the most children, or wants to leave less to a child that has regularly borrowed money from the policyowner during life. Or, a policyowner may want to leave 10% of the policy's proceeds to a charity and the remaining 90% to his or her children.* There can be many reasons a policyowner may want to specify the percentage distributed among beneficiaries.

Premium Payment

The policyowner's payment of insurance premiums is a conditional precedent of the insurer's duty to pay a death claim. Details as to when, where and how the premiums are to be paid are set forth in the payment of premium provisions in a life insurance contract. Policies commonly provide that each premium must be payable in advance, either at the home office or to an agent, upon delivery of a receipt signed by one or more officers of the company.

Modes

Premiums are contributions required to open a policy and to keep the policy in force. Some life insurance policies require only one premium. Others accept monthly, quarterly, semi-annual or annual payments. Level premium payments may be required.

Minimum and Maximum Amounts

Life insurance policies have established minimum and maximum premium amounts that they are able to accept. A single premium policy may have a minimum premium amount of $10,000 or higher, a level premium, ordinary life policy may have a minimum monthly premium of $100 or less.

Maximum premium amounts are based in part on the amount of risk an insurance company is willing to accept. Some policies are designed to provide large death benefits and accept large premium amounts. Other policies are designed for more moderate coverage amounts.

Grace Period – Virginia Law

Each individual life insurance policy must contain a provision that the insured is entitled to a *grace period* of not less than 31 days within which the payment of any premium after the first premium may be made. The provision must also state that during the grace period the policy continues in full force, but if a claim arises under the policy during the grace period before the overdue premium is paid, the amount of any earned overdue premium through the policy month of death with interest may be deducted from policy settlement. The grace period starts on the premium payment due date. *VA Code §38.2-3303*

Automatic Premium Loans

Most cash value life insurance policies offer an *automatic premium loan* provision. An automatic premium loan:

- is a provision that authorizes the insurance company to use the policy loan value to pay any premium not paid by the end of the grace period.
- is charged interest like other policy loans from the policy and will be made as long as the cash value allows for a loan in the amount of the premium.

VA PPL LH-2_16298

- prevents the lapse of the policy when the policyholder is having difficulty paying premiums and the death benefit protection is not lost at a time of financial stress.
- must be paid back, and the death benefit and total surrender value will be reduced by outstanding loans and interest.

Level or Flexible Premiums

Premiums required for a life insurance contract may be level or flexible, as discussed throughout explanations of life insurance and annuity products. Here is a summary or premium payment features by product:

Ordinary Whole Life	Level premium payments until death or policy maturity at age 100
Limited Pay Whole Life	Level premiums for a specified period, such as for 20 years. These have higher premiums than an ordinary whole life policy, assuming equal risk characteristics
Universal Life	Flexible premium payments allowed. Owner may change premiums amount paid and skip premiums without contract lapse, if cash values are sufficient. Premium is paid to cash values, then COI and expenses are subtracted. Cash value amounts earn a rate of return established by the insurer, subject to minimum guarantees
Adjustable life	Premiums can be increased or decreased as the face amount is adjusted over the life of the policy.
Term life	Most term life is level premium, but increasing premium and decreasing premium term is also available. Level term products increase premium with age, at policy renewal at the end of the policy term.

Reinstatement – Virginia Law

A life insurance policy where premiums payments are in default is subject to *reinstatement.* Each individual life insurance policy must have a provision that in the event of default in premium payments, if:

- the value of the policy has been applied automatically to the purchase of other insurance;
- the insurance is in force; and
- the original policy has not been surrendered to the insurer and cancelled,

then, the policy may be reinstated within three years from default, upon:

- evidence of insurability satisfactory to the insurer;
- payment of premiums in arrears with interest at a rate not exceeding 6% per year payable annually; and
- the payment or reinstatement of any other indebtedness to the insurer based on the policy, including interest due.

VA Code §38.2-3311

Reinstatement is a restoration and, according to most courts, a continuation of the original contract. Policy holders may prefer to reinstate lapsed policies rather than purchase new ones because older policies may have lower interest rates on policy loans, suicide and incontestability clauses may no longer apply, and premium payments may be lower than on a new policy, due to the insured's age.

Policy Loans, Withdrawals and Partial Surrenders

Cash Loans

A policy loan is a loan against cash values accumulated in a life insurance policy. Fixed permanent life insurance policies generally allow loans up to the full amount of the cash surrender value. Variable life insurance policies may limit loans to 75% to 90% of the cash value at the time of loan.

When a policyowner borrows money directly from the insurer, what is actually occurring is something other than a "loan" in the strict sense. The difference in insurance loans from other types of loans is that in a true loan the borrower must agree to repay the money within a specified time frame. An insurance policy does not require that the borrower repay the loan within a specified time frame, but requires that if the loan has not been paid when a death benefit is paid out, the amount of the loan and any outstanding interest will be deleted from the death benefit payable to the beneficiary. If a policy is fully surrendered and it includes an outstanding loan balance, the surrender value will be reduced by the amount of the loan and applicable interest.

Policy Loan Interest

Insurers charge an interest rate on outstanding loan amounts. The reason for this is that a life insurance premium rate is in part based on the investment return the insurer expects to make. The insurer invests the portion of premiums paid that does not go toward paying for mortality, administration and similar policy expenses. This portion of the premium creates the cash value. The insurer considers the investment return when determining whether it can fulfill its contractual obligations, including paying the death benefit and paying minimum guaranteed rates. If the insurer makes a policy loan, the insurer is paying out cash, and thereby loses the ability to earn income on it. This loss of investment return could jeopardize the insurer's ability to fulfill its policy obligations unless the insurer increases premium rates. So, instead, the insurer charges a rate of interest on its policy loans. And the insurer does not pay more than a specified minimum rate on cash values equal to the amount of the outstanding loan value. Doing this keeps premium rates lower for all policyholders and eliminates a kind of "penalty" being charged non-borrowers. If an interest rate isn't charged on policy loans, premiums for non-borrowers will go up when the non-borrowers didn't receive a commensurate benefit for this higher cost.

Loans are generally offered on a zero cost or low cost basis. A *zero cost loan* is one where the interest charged on the amount of the loan is equal to the amount credited to the cash value equal to the loan amount. A *low cost loan* is one where the interest rate charged on the amount of the loan is a few percentage points higher than the amount credited to the cash value equal to the loan amount. Under some contracts, a loan from a policy may be treated as a zero cost loan if the loan amount meets certain criteria and as a low cost loan if it does not meet the criteria.

Policy Withdrawals or Partial Surrenders

Not all life insurance policies allow withdrawals or partial surrenders of cash values, but some policies do. Depending upon the type of contract, withdrawals may reduce the death benefit payable from the policy. During the first several years of a policy that allows withdrawals, a percentage charge may be applied to the amount withdrawn or may be applied to the cash value and reduce it.

Life Insurance Nonforfeiture Provisions

Nonforfeiture value provisions allow the insured to receive all or a portion of the benefits or a partial refund on the premiums paid if the insured misses premium payments causing the policy to lapse. Generally, there are three nonforfeiture options offered to a policyowner. The life insurance policy includes a nonforfeiture table that discloses the amounts of coverage or periods of time of coverage payable through the nonforfeiture options.

Cash Surrender Value

The first nonforfeiture option is the *cash surrender value* nonforfeiture option. Under a cash value nonforfeiture provision, the policyowner is given the cash value of the policy. If any surrender charges apply or loans are outstanding, the policyowner is given the cash value less the surrender charges, loan amount and any loan interest payable. The insurer has up to six months to pay this amount. The six month period was established under the law to prevent the harm a "run" on insurers could cause, similar to the harm caused by a "run" on a bank, when many people request their cash values all at the same time.

Extended Term

The second nonforfeiture provision found in cash value life insurance policies is the *extended term* option. Under an extended term nonforfeiture option, the policyholder is given a term insurance policy. The term of the insurance is equal to the length of time the cash values will purchase.

Reduced Paid-up Insurance

The third nonforfeiture provision is the *reduced paid-up insurance* option. Under this option, the cash values of the policy are used as a single premium to purchase a permanent life insurance policy on the insured. The amount of the insurance is based on the age of the insured at the time the nonforfeiture option is exercised, and the cash value amount available in the policy.

         VA PPL LH-2_16298

Automatic Option Required

The life insurance policy must specify that the insurer will provide a nonforfeiture option specified in the policy if the person entitled to make the nonforfeiture option election (generally, the policyholder) does not make an alternative election within a specified time frame after the due date of the premium in default. The standard nonforfeiture law states that the alternative election must be made within sixty days after the due date of the premium in default.

Dividends and Dividend Options

Owners of *participating* life insurance policies may be entitled to dividends if the insurer has sufficient earned surplus. The term participating means that the policyowner may participate in such surplus. *Surplus* is the difference between the assets and liabilities of an insurer.

When a policy is *nonparticipating*, it means that the policyholders do not participate in the surplus of the insurer through the receipt of dividends. A *dividend* is the payment of surplus to policyholders due to favorable experience related to return, mortality rates, and/or expense charges. Many policies provide for the policyholder to be paid dividends and to participate in any allocation of the company's surplus. The surplus is derived from excess premiums paid by policyholders with participating policies and apportioned by the board of directors. The owner is given options for using the dividends. These options generally include:

- the option to use dividends to reduce premium payments;
- the option to buy paid-up additional insurance on a single premium basis at the insured's attained age. Evidence of insurance is not required unless the policyholder chooses this option after policy inception;
- the option to buy additional 1-year term insurance at the insured's attained age. Evidence of insurance is not required unless the policyholder chooses this option after policy inception;
- the option to increase cash values;
- the option to apply the dividend to an outstanding loan amount;

- the option to have dividends held by or placed on deposit with the insurance company and accumulate interest; and
- the option to use them to make a policy a paid-up contract when the value of the basic contract plus dividends on deposit or additional paid-up insurance equal the net single premium for the paid-up policy at the insured's attained age. No further premiums are then payable on the policy.

If the company calls for apportionment of dividends the first year and annually thereafter, it may require payment of the next year's premium as a condition of payment of the dividend at the end of the first policy year.

Dividends are not guaranteed, but are based on the experience of the insurance company. If the insurance company has actual premium expenses that are lower than the premium charged, dividends are payable. If not, dividends are not payable.

Incontestability

Life insurance policies include a clause that gives the maximum amount of time the insurer has to contest the validity of the policy. The reason for this is that the policyholder should be able to rely on the coverage for which he or she is paying premium. The allowable contestability period gives the insurer time in which to verify the application representations and supporting information supplied by the insured and policyholder.

Virginia Life Insurance Policy Incontestability Period

A life insurance policy must provide that it is incontestable after it has been if force, during the lifetime of the insured, two years from its date of issue, except for nonpayment of premiums. The insurer can exclude from this incontestability provision benefits related to disability and additional insurance due to death by accident or accidental means (i.e., these may remain contestable).

VA Code §38.2-3305

Assignments

Life insurance contracts can be transferred to another person or entity through assignment. There are two basic ways to assign the contract. The first is *absolute assignment*. An absolute assignment transfers all the policyowner's rights irrevocably. The second type of assignment is a *collateral assignment*. Under a collateral assignment, a portion of the death benefit is assigned as long as necessary to secure a lender's rights. No more of the proceeds can be assigned to the lender than the amount of the debt owed however, because the extent of a lender's insurable interest in a life insurance policy does not exceed the amount of the debt.

Before either an absolute assignment or a collateral assignment can be effective, the insurer must be notified by the policyowner in writing and must approve the assignment. If the insurer is not given notice, the insurer is protected from any transaction initiated by a former owner.

Suicide

Life insurance policies include a provision stating that only a return of premiums will be paid if the insured commits suicide within a specified period of time (usually two years) after the policy's issue date.

Misstatement of Age and Gender

If the age of the insured or a beneficiary is misstated, the amount payable under a life insurance policy is the amount the premium would have purchased at the insured's or beneficiary's correct age. The provision in life policies that includes this or a similar statement is known as the misstatement of age adjustment clause. This provision prevents a company from voiding a contract solely because of an error in the age of the insured at the time of issue, or an error in the age of a beneficiary at the time of a settlement payment. If the gender is misstated, the policy amount payable will also be adjusted based on the premium would have purchased at the insured's or beneficiary's correct age.

Settlement Options

Settlement options on a life insurance policy are normally the same options available as options available as immediate and deferred annuity payouts.

Lump Sum or Cash Payment

Life insurance death benefits may be paid to the beneficiaries in a variety of ways. Each beneficiary who receives a share of the death benefit may select the payment method or *settlement option* for that beneficiary's share. Many select receipt of the proceeds as a lump sum. However, the payments may also be made in installments. The available options to receive the death benefit settlements are found in the life insurance policy.

Interest Only

A beneficiary may elect to leave the death proceeds on deposit with the insurance company and receive interest only payments. A low interest rate is guaranteed to be paid by the insurer. The beneficiary can take a lump sum of the balance at a later date, choose an installment option to begin receiving it in payments at a later date, or leave it with the insurer until the beneficiary's death. At the beneficiary's death, if proceeds are left with the insurer, the proceeds will be paid to the person that had been named as beneficiary by the original beneficiary/payee.

In annuity and life insurance contracts, the *payee* is the person who receives annuitization payments, immediate annuity payments and life settlement payments. In some cases, a person other than the insured or named beneficiary may be a payee. Most commonly, however, the insured or named beneficiary is also the payee.

Fixed – Period Installments

Under fixed period installment settlements, a specified period is selected by the beneficiary. Generally, the minimum period is five years, but some companies allow for a period as short as three years. The maximum term may be limited.

Fixed – Amount Installments

A beneficiary may also opt to be the payee on an installment settlement of a fixed amount. The beneficiary selects the amount and the insurer will make the installments for that amount for as long as the proceeds support paying this amount. The insurer may restrict the payment amount based on the life expectancy of the beneficiary. If the payee dies while installment payments are being made, the remaining amounts are paid to a named beneficiary.

Other Income Settlements

Each of the following are available as income settlements, and are structured just like payments from an annuity. The major difference is that death benefits are received income tax free from life insurance policies, whereas earnings in annuity payments received during life are taxable. Life insurance beneficiaries can name beneficiaries on their life income settlements when a payout is a period certain or life with refund option.

- Life Income, also known as Single Life Income
- Life Income with Period Certain
- Life Income with Installment or Cash Refund
- Joint and Survivor Life Income
- Joint and Survivor Specified Percentage Life Income
- Joint and Survivor Life with Period Certain
- Joint and Survivor Life with Installment or Cash Refund

Accelerated Death Benefits

Accelerated death benefits allow the taking of the living death benefit based on the policyowner/insured meeting specified conditions in the provision. These conditions trigger the payment of benefits, and so are called *triggering conditions*. The requirements for payments of benefits under these provisions are that the insured:

- becomes terminally ill;
- becomes chronically ill;
- suffers a catastrophic illness, such as one that requires an organ transplant in order to save the insured's life; or
- enters a nursing home or a similar long-term facility, or has been diagnosed with some other specified condition.

Chronically or Terminally Ill and Activities of Daily Living

Certain amounts paid as accelerated death benefits under a life insurance contact before the insured's death are excluded from income if the insured is terminally ill or chronically ill. This gives these accelerated death benefits the same tax treatment as a life insurance death benefit, which is generally not taxable to the beneficiary who receives the death benefit.

If the insured meets the definition of chronically ill, the accelerated death benefits paid on the basis of costs incurred for *qualified long-term care services* are fully excludable from income for tax purposes. If the accelerated death benefit is paid on a per day basis, such as $125 per day as long as the insured meets the payment trigger requirements in the contract, the amounts are excludable up to a limit.

Definitions of Terminally Ill and Chronically Ill

The definitions of terminally ill and chronically ill as found in IRS Publication 554, Tax Guide for Seniors, are as follows:

Terminally or chronically ill defined – A terminally ill person is one who has been certified by a physician as having an illness or physical condition that reasonably can be expected to result in death within 24 months from the date of certification. A chronically ill person is one who is not terminally ill but has been certified (within the previous 12 months) by a licensed health care practitioner as meeting either of the following conditions:

- The person is unable to perform (without substantial help) at least two *activities of daily living* (eating, toileting, transferring, bathing, dressing and continence) for a period of 90 days or more because of a loss of functional capacity.
- The person requires substantial supervision to protect themselves from threats to health and safety due to severe *cognitive impairment*.

Cognitive impairment is deterioration or loss of mental capacity which results in the loss of short or long-term memory; difficulty orienting as to person, place, or time; and deductive or abstract reasoning. Ability to perform ADLs may also be affected.

Policy Exclusions

Exclusions are conditions listed in the insurance contract which are not covered and for which no benefits are payable. These conditions must be specifically listed in the policy, addendum or rider. Some exclusions are temporary, and are removed after the policy has been in effect after a specified period.

Life insurance policies generally exclude payment of the death benefit due to death arising out of war or any act of war. They also may include an exclusion related to death due to riding on non-commercial aircraft.

There are policies that cover those in the military and which are designed to cover the risks such as death arising out of war and flying or being transported in non-commercial aircraft. These policies offered to those in active military service and those who are veterans through the Servicemember's Group Life Insurance and Veterans Group Life Insurance programs.

VA PPL LH-2_16298

Section II Review

1) A provision which allows the premium payments to stop after the payor of premium on a policy insuring the life of a juvenile becomes disabled is called _____.
   a. restoration of benefits provision for juvenile life policies
   b. elimination period provision for juvenile life policies
   c. waiver of premium provision for juvenile life policies
   d. guaranteed renewable provision for juvenile life policies

2) Waiver of premium disability riders generally are effective:
   a. to the age of 100.
   b. through the ages of 60 to 65.
   c. only to the age of 40.
   d. to the age of 35.

3) The party on a whole life insurance policy with the right to take withdrawals is the:
   a. owner.
   b. primary beneficiary.
   c. insured.
   d. secondary beneficiary.

4) The party on a life insurance contract with the right to increase or decrease coverage within contract specifications is the:
   a. owner.
   b. insured.
   c. beneficiary.
   d. insurance company.

5) Which of the following constitutes valuable consideration in an insurance contract?
   a. Warranties
   b. Statements
   c. Representations
   d. Premiums

6) The party that receives policy benefits upon the death of the insured is the:
   a. beneficiary
   b. owner
   c. insured
   d. insurance company

7) If an irrevocable beneficiary is named on a life insurance policy, the beneficiary designation may only be changed with the permission of:
   a. the insurance company.
   b. the owner.
   c. the irrevocable beneficiary.
   d. the insured.

8) The type of clause that provides that life insurance death benefit will be paid to the class II or secondary beneficiary only if the primary beneficiary does not survive the insured for a specified number of days is known as a(n):
   a. interest only clause
   b. spendthrift clause
   c. common disaster clause
   d. succession clause

9) Reinstatement occurs when:
   a. a policy has lapsed and is put back into force, once evidence of insurability has been determined and payment of premium in arrears, plus interest has been paid.
   b. the grace period of thirty days has passed.
   c. one policy is exchanged for another.
   d. a late payment is made.

10) Nonforfeiture provisions apply when:
   a. cash value policy holders stop paying premiums and the policy lapses.
   b. premium payments are increased.
   c. policy holders pay premiums regularly and on schedule.
   d. policy holders exchange policies.

11) A clause that gives the maximum amount of time the insurer has to contest the validity of the policy is a(n):
   a. reinstatement clause.
   b. beneficiary clause.
   c. nonforfeiture clause.
   d. incontestability clause.

12) The "entire contract," "incontestability," and "misstatement of age" clauses are found in:
   a. fire policies
   b. property policies
   c. crime policies
   d. life policies

13) A life with cash refund settlement option:
    a. always ends at the death of the payee.
    b. does not continue payments at the death of the payee.
    c. pays a lump sum equal to the remaining principal to a beneficiary at the payee's death.
    d. is not available as a variable income option.

14) Under Virginia law, the minimum number of days an insurer must provide an individual whole life policy owner in which to examine a policy that is not a replacement policy and return it for a full refund is:
    a. five
    b. ten
    c. twenty
    d. forty-five

15) Individual life insurance policies issued or delivered in Virginia must provide a grace period of at least _____ days in which a premium payment may be made after its due date in which the policy will remain in full force.
    a. 10
    b. 31
    c. 45
    d. 60

16) An individual health insurance policy requires quarterly premium payments. The first payment was made at policy delivery and the next payment is due on August 31. If the policy owner does not make the payment by August 31,
    a. the policy lapses
    b. the policy owner has until September 7 to make the payment, or the policy lapses
    c. the policy owner has until September 10 to make the payment, or the policy lapses
    d. the policy owner has until October 1 to make the payment

17) Under Virginia law, an individual life insurance policy may be reinstated within ___ years of default, if the insured provides evidence of insurability, payment of premiums in arrears with interest at no more than 6% per year, and the payment or reinstatement of any other indebtedness to the insurer based on the policy, including interest due.
    a. seven
    b. five
    c. two
    d. three

18) An insurer that issued a life insurance policy to a resident of Virginia discovered three years after policy issue that the insured misstated her age by six months at policy application. The insurer:
    a. must cancel the policy due to this misstatement.
    b. may cancel the policy due to this misstatement.
    c. may not cancel the policy due to this misstatement.
    d. will require the insured to reapply for a policy with the insurer and meet all underwriting requirements as of the date that the misstatement is discovered in order to retain coverage with the insurer.

VA PPL LH-2_16298

Section III: Completing the Application, Underwriting and Delivering the Policy

This section explains the agent's responsibilities in taking life insurance applications, obtaining and submitting documents to underwriting and delivering policies. Topics include:

- Completing the application
- Underwriting
- Delivering the policy

Completing the Application

The agent takes the life insurance application information as a part of the process of finding out about the needs of the client, or subsequent to doing the needs analysis. The agent has the important role of not submitting improper risk to the insurer through the application and supporting documents, if the agent knows the risk will not meet the insurer's standards. The agent also may not turn a blind eye to facts an applicant may try to conceal or misstate on an application if the agent knows the applicant is doing so.

Insurance Applications

The insurance application is a critical underwriting resource. From it, the underwriter finds most of the basic information needed to determine whether to issue a policy, and if so, at what premium and terms.

When an application is received in the insurer's underwriting department, the underwriting process which began with the agent taking an application continues.

Underwriting is the process of evaluating an insurance risk to determine whether an insurance policy should be issued, and if so, at what premium rate and with what conditions or exclusions, if any besides those within the policy's normal terms.

In underwriting:

1. The application is reviewed for completeness, and to determine whether the application as submitted meets underwriting standards, including insurable interest. Insurable interest must exist in order for the application to continue through the underwriting process.
2. It is determined whether or not additional documentation is required beyond that which the agent submitted.
3. If additional documentation is required, the underwriter will request documentation directly from the applicant or will notify the agent or agency that these items are needed.
4. Underwriting and policy issue is governed by state regulations and company standards, so requests for documentation include a date in which compliance must occur.
5. If the information is not received within the specified time, the application file is generally closed, and any premium received is returned.

Life Insurance Applications

Each life application generally requires the following type of information:

- Applicant and insured name, address and other general information
- Medical information
- Producer's report (Agent's statement)
- Selection of riders or optional features
- Signatures

General Information

The general information section of life insurance applications generally asks for the name, address, birth date, social security number and gender of the insured and owner. The relationship of the owner to the insured is also needed. The name or names of beneficiaries is also requested, along with the percentage for each beneficiary or other beneficiary designation, and the relationship of each beneficiary to the owner. Some applications also require the beneficiary's social security number. This is to aid the insurer in identifying the proper beneficiary, if necessary.

Medical Information

Medical questions include direct, simple questions asking whether tobacco or nicotine products have been used, and if the insured had been diagnosed, treated or hospitalized for:

- cancer;
- heart attack;
- stroke;
- diabetes;
- kidney disorders;
- Alzheimer's disease;
- liver disorder;
- organ transplant;
- alcohol or drug use treatments;
- AIDS or HIV;
- irregular heart beat;
- high blood pressure;
- fainting spells;
- emphysema or other chronic lung or respiratory disorder;
- inability to work for more than a week in the past six months or year; and
- other similar questions.

If there is a "yes" response to the medical questions asked, the application will generally ask for more details. Once the application reaches the home office, medical reports or an attending physician statement may also be requested. Or, the insurer may have issued underwriting guidelines to the agent, who requests such reports through his or her agency office.

Producer Report or Agent Statement

The agent has a responsibility to the insurer to report to the insurer on the application to provide information the insurer requests, such as how long the agent has known the applicant, whether the agent has knowledge that the proposed insurance is being purchased to replace existing insurance and to supply basic information of which the agent has knowledge regarding the applicant's health, financial situation and general character. The application includes a section where the agent states this information and signs.

Selection of Features and Options

Depending on the type of policy applied for, the applicant will make several choices regarding the insurance coverage, including:

- Premium payment mode, including monthly, quarterly, semi-annual or annual payments.

- Premium payment method, by submission of a check or by direct withdrawal from the bank by the insurer.
- Additional coverage through riders
- Death benefit options
- Variable subaccount options and amounts allocated to each subaccount selected
- Setting up a Personal Identification Number (PIN) or other method that allows transactions over the phone or internet

Occupation/Hobbies

If the applicant is involved in certain occupations or hobbies, or is surrounded by certain sets of circumstances, a completion of a questionnaire designed for that occupation, hobby or circumstance may be required by the insurance company. Examples of items that may require the completion of a questionnaire include involvement in aviation, skydiving, military service, or having foreign residency. Certain occupations also include a higher likelihood of moral hazards in the submission of fraudulent applications, such as those where the application indicates that the applicant works in a finance company or conducts transactions with a finance company that provides decreasing term life insurance or credit insurance. Some occupations include a higher physical hazard of kidnapping or extortion, especially those where the applicant is a high-profile executive or involved in high-finance. These circumstances can also require the submission of a questionnaire.

Dividend Options

If a life insurance policy is a *participating policy*, the application will include a section regarding the owner's dividend options.

Receipt

Once the applicant has completed and signed the application, in some cases, the applicant gives the first premium check, made out to the insurance company, to the agent. The agent then gives a receipt to the applicant. In other cases, the first premium is not collected until policy delivery.

Required Signatures

Applications become part of the policy, and the signing process is part of execution of the valid insurance policy. Agents have several responsibilities in this process:

- Agents should ensure that the applicant understands the questions in the application and ask the prospective insured to read it to confirm that everything is answered correctly and completely. Only then should the application be signed.
- Under no circumstances should applicants sign blank forms.
- The applicant must read and sign the application statement disclosing that errors or intentional misinformation can void a policy.
- The agent must complete and sign the agent's report as the insurer requires.

Changes in the Application

An agent has no authority to change answers on an application without the knowledge, consent and written approval of the applicant or insured. Likewise, an agent may not alter or waive any term or condition of an application without prior consent.

No contract exists between an applicant for insurance and an insurance company until the application for insurance is accepted. An application for insurance is a proposal which does not become an enforceable contract until it is accepted by the insurer on the terms in which the proposal was made. If the insurer alters any terms of the proposal, then the applicant must accept the alterations before the contract is effective.

Consequences of Incomplete Applications

Concealment by the applicant or insured can cause the denial or loss of insurance coverage. Concealment is the intentional nondisclosure of a material fact to the insurer. Nondisclosure or concealment has the same legal effect as a material misrepresentation. Coverage may be denied based on concealment only if the insured knew the fact to be material and only if the insured intended to defraud the insurer for most forms of insurance.

Warranties and Representations

Representations are made prior to or at the same time as the formation of a contract of insurance. Representations are written or oral statements made by the applicant for insurance. These statements are inducements to the insurer to enter into the contract and issue a policy.

For example, a life policy application asks for health-related information. The answer to these questions affect the risk level the insurer takes on if a policy is issued. If the applicant falsely answers such questions, the applicant has made a misrepresentation.

Misrepresentation may be material or immaterial in nature. If an applicant for a life policy states that he has no heart condition and actually had open heart surgery, the misrepresentation is material and will cause the insurer to deny coverage. If an applicant states that the cosmetic surgery on her nose was in 2001 and it was actually in 2002, this is most likely an immaterial misrepresentation and will have no effect on the enforceability of her life insurance coverage.

A *material fact* is one that, if known to the insurer at time of application, would have caused the insurer to deny coverage or issue coverage under substantially different conditions.

The courts weigh several factors when determining whether coverage should be denied due to a material misrepresentation. Courts may provide that the insurer continue coverage even if a material misrepresentation exists. Or, a court may determine that only the contractual provisions directly affected by the material misrepresentation be considered void and apply other provisions to the insured risk. In other cases, the entire contract is void.

Warranties

Warranties are statements or promises made by an applicant for insurance that are serious or material enough in nature that they must be true or the insurer's liability is ended under the policy. Warranties may be made by agreeing to conditions for coverage under policies.

Virginia Individual Life Policies and Representations

In Virginia, all individual life insurance policies must contain an entire contract provision that states the policy, or the policy and the application for the policy if a copy of the application is endorsed upon or attached to the policy when issued or delivered, constitutes the entire contract between the parties. This provision must also state that:

- All statements made by the insured will, in the absence of fraud, be deemed representations and not warranties; and
- No statement may be used in defense of a claim under the policy unless it is contained in a written application that is endorsed upon or attached to the policy when issued or delivered.

VA Code §38.2-3304

In addition, Virginia law provides that all statements, declarations and descriptions in any application for an insurance policy or for the reinstatement of an insurance policy are deemed representations and not warranties. No statement in an application or in any affidavit made before or after loss under the policy may bar a recovery upon a policy of insurance unless it is clearly proven that the answer or statement was material to the risk when assumed and was untrue.

VA Code §38.2-309

Collecting Initial Premium and Issuing the Receipt

Often, the first premium is collected at time of application. The premium check should be made out to the insurer and a receipt provided to the applicant. If additional premium is required at policy delivery, the agent should follow the same procedure. And, if the policyholder pays premium directly to the agent on a periodic ongoing basis, the agent should also ensure the check is made out to the insurer, and must remit funds to the insurer as required by the insurer's funds handling requirements, and provide a receipt.

When an agent handles a client's money, such as by collecting premium, the agent acts in a *fiduciary* capacity. The agent may not commingle the client's money with his or her own. Typically, the agent uses a trust account at a bank or savings institution that is FDIC-insured. The agent is subject to state law and insurance company requirements pertaining to the length of time after receipt by the agent in which a client's money must be deposited into the trust account and remitted to the insurer.

Conditional Receipt

When premium is provided and accepted at the time of application, a conditional binding receipt or binding receipt may be issued. A *conditional receipt* provides that the coverage will be effective from the date of application, or medical exam, whichever is later, unless the coverage is declined or *rated*, meaning that the insured's risk class is not standard, or issued with riders that exclude coverage.

Replacement

Each application also asks whether this proposed insurance will replace or change any existing or pending insurance. If the applicant answers "yes" to this question or if the applicant has existing life insurance, the agent must follow state regulations to complete state replacement notices and forms with the applicant. State replacement forms include comparative information for the applicant to read regarding the proposed insurance and the policy to be replaced. They also include disclosure statements for the applicant to sign indicating that the applicant understands that there may be surrender charges involved in canceling the existing policy, that the new policy generally includes commission loads and that a new surrender charge period may apply to the new policy.

Commission is a fee paid to an insurance producer by the insurance company for the sale of the insurer's policy. A *commission load* is premium cost of a policy allocated to the payment of commissions.

Disclosures at Point of Sale

Use and Disclosure of Insurance Information

An important piece of federal legislation insurance companies must comply with is the Gramm-Leach-Bliley Act. It regulates the disclosure of nonpublic personal information by financial institutions about their customers to nonaffiliated third parties. Financial institutions governed by this Act include bank holding companies that may include the business of insuring. Many banks, for example, own subsidiaries that offer insurance products to their customers and consumers in their marketplace. Life and health insurers are under the authority of state laws, which the Act charges to adopt privacy policies. The Act requires financial institutions to provide customers with their privacy policies and practices regarding nonpublic personal information.

Provisions in the Act Applicable to Insurers

Title V, Subtitle A, Section 501 of the Act gives the policy of Congress regarding the privacy protection responsibilities of financial institutions, which includes certain insurers:

(a) Privacy Obligation Policy. – It is the policy of the Congress that each financial institution has an affirmative and continuing obligation to respect the privacy of its customers and to protect the security and confidentiality of those customers' nonpublic personal information.

Subsection (b) of Section 501 goes on to give specific requirements to establish safeguards on behalf of customer's records:

(b) Financial Institutions Safeguards – In furtherance of the policy in subsection (a), each agency or authority described in Section 505(a) shall establish appropriate standards for the financial institutions subject to their jurisdiction relating to administrative, technical, and physical safeguards –

   (1) to insure the security and confidentiality of customer records and information;

   (2) to protect against any anticipated threats or hazards to the security or integrity of such records; and

   (3) to protect against unauthorized access to a use of such records or information which could result in substantial harm or inconvenience to any customer.

Enforcement of Gramm-Leach-Bliley

Section 505 states the government entity that is responsible for creating the safeguard procedures and to enforce the Act's provisions for various types of financial institutions. Generally, the states have the responsibility to enforce the provisions of the Gramm-Leach-Bliley Act. The National Association of Insurance Commissioners (NAIC) created the "Standards for Safeguarding Customer Information Model Regulation" to implement the requirements of Gramm-Leach-Bliley into a state's laws. If a state does not enforce Gramm-Leach-Bliley provisions, the Act provides that the provisions of the FDIC Act regarding enforcement apply. This means a federal banking agency will have enforcement powers instead of the state.

NAIC's Privacy of Consumer Financial and Health Information Regulation and HIPAA

A second NAIC Model Regulation addresses the privacy requirements of both the *Health Insurance Portability and Accountability Act* (HIPAA) and Gramm-Leach-Bliley. This regulation is the Privacy of Consumer Financial and Health Information Model Regulation. The states may adopt this regulation for governance of information under HIPAA and of nonpublic personal information or financial information as the regulation refers to it, under Gramm-Leach-Bliley.

Virginia's Privacy of Information Laws

Virginia's Privacy laws implementing the Gramm-Leach-Bliley Act are found in VA Code §38.2-600 through §38.2-620.

Primary Gramm-Leach-Bliley Provisions

The primary Gramm-Leach-Bliley provisions addressed in the Model regulation deals with disclosure of nonpublic personal information to nonaffiliated third parties, and how and why this may or may not be done, as well as the requirement of the financial institution to provide a disclosure of the institution's disclosure process. These regulations are based on Sections 502, 503 and 521 of Title V of the Act.

Obligations with Respect to Disclosures of Personal Information

Section 502 of the Act requires that a notice be given to consumers prior to the disclosure by a financial institution to a nonaffiliated party of a consumer's nonpublic personal information.

Opt-Out

In addition, the consumer must be given the ability to opt-out of the disclosure. The opt-out provisions of the Act are as follows:

502(b)(1) In general – A financial institution may not disclose nonpublic personal information to a nonaffiliated third party unless –

   (1) to insure the security and confidentiality of customer records and information;

   (2) to protect against any anticipated threats or hazards to the security or integrity of such records; and

   (3) to protect against unauthorized access to a use of such records or information which could

result in substantial harm or inconvenience to any customer.

HIV Consent – Virginia Law

Insurers may underwrite for acquired immunodeficiency syndrome (AIDS) or HIV infection provided the underwriting procedures, including the questions used on the application for life or accident and sickness insurance coverage, are consistent and not unfairly discriminatory.

Accident and sickness insurance is a form of health insurance that covers loss by bodily injury and sickness.

All of the following are underwriting requirements related to AIDS or HIV under the Virginia insurance law and administrative code:

- Questions relating to the applicant having or having been diagnosed as having AIDS or HIV infection are permissible if they are factual and designed to establish the existence of the condition.
- An adverse underwriting decision is permissible if, during the underwriting process, it is revealed that the applicant has had positive HIV-related test results following testing protocol, or has been diagnosed as having AIDS or HIV infection.
- An adverse underwriting decision is not permissible if it is based solely on the presence of symptoms, as disclosed in an application for life or accident and sickness insurance coverage. An adverse underwriting decision is permissible, however, if the symptoms disclosed in the application for coverage are confirmed as being HIV-related through the use of medical records or HIV-related tests.
- No inquiry in an application for life or accident and sickness insurance coverage, or in an investigation conducted by an insurer or an insurance support organization on its behalf may be directed toward determining the applicant's sexual orientation.
- No question that is designed to establish the sexual orientation of the applicant may be used on an application for life or accident and sickness insurance coverage.
- Neither the marital status, the living arrangements, the occupation, the gender, the medical history, the beneficiary designation, nor the zip code or other territorial classification of an applicant may be used to establish, or aid in establishing, the sexual orientation of the applicant.
- If information about an applicant's sexual orientation becomes known through other means, no adverse underwriting decision may be made based solely on such information.
- Questions relating to medical and other factual matters intending to reveal the possible existence of a medical condition are permissible if they are not used as a proxy to establish the sexual orientation of the applicant.
- The applicant must be given an opportunity to provide an explanation of any answers given in the application for life or accident and sickness insurance coverage that may result in an adverse underwriting decision.
- Questions relating to an applicant having, or having been diagnosed as having, or having been advised to seek treatment for, a sexually transmitted disease are permissible.
- No adverse underwriting decision may be made solely because medical records or a report from an insurance support organization shows that an applicant has demonstrated AIDS-related concerns by seeking preventative educational counseling or advice from health care professionals. This prohibition does not apply to an applicant diagnosed as having been infected with the HIV or seeking treatment for AIDS.

Testing Requirement

- Insurers may require applicants for life or accident and sickness insurance coverage to be tested for the presence of HIV infection, provided the procedures are consistent, accurate, and not unfairly discriminatory.
- If an HIV-related test is not required for all applicants, insurers may test a specific class of applicants based on type of insurance, face amount, or age and face amount of coverage being requested or late entrance under a

group insurance policy or subscription contract. In all other cases, the insurer must have a medical basis for requiring individual applicants to take an HIV-related test.

Written Consent

Whenever an applicant is requested to take an HIV-related test in connection with an application for life or accident and sickness insurance coverage, the use of the test must be revealed to the applicant and his or her written consent must be obtained. The consent form does not need to be filed with the Commission but must provide an explanation of the meaning of the HIV-related test and must disclose:

- The types of individuals or organizations that will receive a copy of the test results;
- The types of individuals or organizations that will have access to the applicant's insurance file;
- The types of individuals or organizations that will keep the test information in a data bank or other file;
- That if the applicant requests the names of these specific individuals or organizations, the information will be provided to the applicant;
- The name and address of the person to be notified of the HIV test results. The applicant may choose to receive the test results directly or designate another person such as a physician; and
- That if the person being tested does not designate a person or physician, personal face-to-face counseling is available through the Virginia Department of Health. To obtain information regarding counseling, a person should contact their local health department. Additional information concerning AIDS or HIV infection can be obtained by calling the Virginia Health Department HIV/STD/Viral Hepatitis Hotline at 1-800-533-4148.

Test Results and Consent

- Insurers must notify applicants or their designees of positive or indeterminate test results. Insurers must:
  - Notify all applicants or their designees of negative test results; or
  - Permit each applicant to indicate on the consent form whether or not negative test

results are to be mailed to the applicant or his designee.

- Insurers are prohibited from sending HIV test results to the applicant if another person is named on the consent form. If a person other than the applicant is named on the consent form, insurers must, no earlier than seven days after sending the test results to the person designated by the applicant, send the applicant notice of an adverse underwriting decision.
- Insurers must maintain strict confidentiality regarding HIV-related test results or the diagnosis of a specific sickness or medical condition derived from such tests.
  - Information regarding specific HIV-related test results must not be disclosed outside the insurance company or its employees, insurance affiliates, agents or reinsurers, third party contractors, insurance regulators, public health regulators or insurance industry data banks, except to the applicant being tested or persons designated in the consent form by the applicant.
  - Specific HIV-related test results may not be furnished to an insurance industry data bank if a review of the information would identify the individual and the specific test results.
  - The use of an insurance industry data bank code for a general blood disorder which is not specific to the HIV infection is permissible.

Adverse Underwriting Decisions

- No adverse underwriting decision may be made on the basis of positive HIV-related test results unless based on, as a minimum, the following test protocol:
  - two positive enzyme-linked immunosorbent assay (ELISA) tests; then
  - one Western Blot. If the results of the Western Blot are indeterminate and the insurer makes a decision to delay issuing the insurance coverage, an adverse underwriting decision notice must be issued.
- New and more effective HIV-related tests are anticipated to be developed in the future. If, in

the opinion of the Commission, the medical community and public health officials establish that future tests are superior to the existing protocol, they may be used instead of the above.

- An insurer may include questions on the application for life or accident and sickness insurance coverage as to whether the applicant has tested positive for the presence of HIV infection.
  - No adverse underwriting decision must be made concerning an applicant who has tested positive for the presence of HIV infection unless the insurer determines that the applicable test protocol was followed.
  - An insurer may require an applicant to be re-tested if the insurer is unable to make a determination that the proper test protocol was followed.
- An adverse underwriting decision is permissible if the applicant refuses to take an HIV-related test requested by the insurer.
- If an insurer requires an applicant to be tested for the presence of HIV infection as a condition of underwriting, the cost of testing must be borne by the insurer in the same way as for any other tests required in the underwriting process.

VA Code §38.2-613.01 and 14VAC 5-180-50

USA Patriot Act

In response to the 9/11 terrorist attacks, President Bush signed into law the USA Patriot Act on October 26, 2001. This act required:

- government institution information sharing and voluntary information sharing among financial institutions;
- verification of customer identity programs;
- enhanced due diligence programs; and
- anti-money laundering programs across the financial services industry.

Money laundering is the process of engaging in acts with the purpose of concealing the origin of the criminally derived proceeds so that they appear to have been obtained legitimately.

The USA Patriot Act amended the Bank Secrecy Act which was the first instance of anti-money laundering legislation in the United States. The Bank Secrecy Act requires banks to report cash transactions over $10,000 to the government.

The U.S. Treasury department created the Financial Crimes Enforcement Network (FinCEN) to counter insufficient intelligence analysis and resources to support financial investigations. In 2005, FinCEN composed two Final Rules under the USA Patriot Act, which created new responsibilities for the insurance industry. These rules required:

- establishing an anti-money laundering program no later than May 2, 2006; and
- filing Suspicious Activity Reports (SARS) on specified transactions occurring after May 2, 2006.

Insurance Companies

It is important to note that not all insurance companies in the United States are subject to these Rules. They apply only to insurance companies offering covered products, which are those insurance products that have been determined by FinCEN to present a high degree of risk for money laundering.

FinCEN defines the term covered product as:

- A permanent life insurance policy, other than a group life insurance policy
- An annuity contract, other than a group annuity contract
- Any other insurance product with cash value or investment features

Some insurance products, because they pose a lower risk for money laundering, are not covered products. Examples of these products are:

- Group insurance products
- Products offered by charitable organizations
- Term (including credit) life, property, casualty, health, or title insurance
- Reinsurance and retrocession contracts

Insurance Producers

The Rules do not require insurance agents and brokers to report suspicious transactions to the regulatory authorities themselves. And, producers are not required to have separate anti-money laundering programs from that of the insurance company by which they are employed. However,

VA PPL LH-2_16298

since insurance producers are an integral part of the insurance industry because of their direct contact with customers, they have an important role to play in assisting the insurance company in preventing money laundering. Because of their role, insurance agents and brokers must be implemented into an insurance company's anti-money laundering program and must be monitored for compliance.

The Rules require an insurance company's anti-money laundering program to include procedures for obtaining relevant customer-related information necessary for an effective program, either from its producers or otherwise, and using that information to assess the money laundering risks presented by its business.

Anti-Money Laundering Programs

An insurance company is required to develop an anti-money laundering program designed to prevent the company from being used to facilitate money laundering or the financing of terrorist activities. Information on insurance company requirements may be found at FinCEN's website: http://www.fincen.gov/financial_institutions/insurance/.

To begin with, a company's anti-money laundering program must be in writing and must be approved by the insurance company's senior management. The written program must be made available to the Department of Treasury, FinCEN, or their designee upon request.

Insurance companies have four minimum requirements for their program:

1. A compliance officer who is responsible for insuring that the program is implemented effectively
2. Written policies, procedures, and internal controls reasonably designed to control the risk of money laundering, terrorist financing, and other financial crime associated with its business
3. Ongoing training of appropriate persons concerning their responsibilities under the program
4. Independent testing to monitor and maintain an adequate program

Because producers facilitate payment and take customer information, the producers are used for obtaining pertinent customer-related information, and for using that information to assess the money laundering risks presented by its business. It should also be noted that policies, procedures, and internal controls of the insurer's money laundering program must be reasonably designed to ensure compliance with applicable Bank Secrecy Act requirements. The Bank Secrecy Act includes the regulatory requirement applicable to insurance companies to report the receipt of cash or certain non-cash instruments totaling more than $10,000 in one transaction or two or more related transactions.

Ongoing Training of Appropriate Persons

Insurance companies must provide training for their producers concerning their responsibilities under the company's anti-money laundering program. An insurance company may satisfy this requirement by either directly training its producers or by verifying that they have received the required training by another insurance agency or competent third party with respect to covered products offered by the company.

An insurance company should provide for independent testing of their anti-money laundering program on a periodic basis to ensure that it complies with the requirements of the final rule and that it functions as designed.

Penalties for Noncompliance

The negative impacts of failing to maintain an effective anti-money laundering program are as follows:

- Financial penalties (some cases in the banking and brokerage industry have resulted in fines as high as $100 million)
- Injurious impact on share-holder value of a financial institution
- Damage to a company's reputation and integrity (which are fundamental to a company's continuance)

The Importance of Suspicious Activity Reporting

In 1992, Congress authorized the Secretary of the Treasury to require financial institutions to report suspicious transactions. The Bank Secrecy Act, as amended by the USA Patriot Act, subsection (g)(1), states generally that the Secretary may require any financial institution, and any director, officer, employee, or agent of any financial institution, to report any suspicious transaction relevant to a possible violation of law or regulation. The Final Rules require insurance companies offering covered products to detect and report suspicious activity just as other financial institutions have been required to do in the past.

Red Flags

Whether or not a SAR should be filed is based on all the facts and circumstances relating to the transaction and particular customer involved. There are also any number of red flags with regard to insurance products that can alert to suspicious activity. Following is a list of some of the most common red flags, as found in the *Federal Register Vol. 70, No. 212, Thursday, November 3, 2005, Rules and Regulations*:

- The purchase of an insurance product that appears to be inconsistent with a customer's needs
- Any unusual method of payment, particularly by cash or cash equivalents (when such method is, in fact, unusual)
- The purchase of an insurance product with monetary instruments in structured amounts
- The early termination of an insurance product, especially at a cost to the customer, or where cash was tendered and/or the refund check is directed to an apparently unrelated third party
- The transfer of the benefit of an insurance product to an apparently unrelated third party
- Little or no concern by a customer for the investment performance of an insurance product, but much concern about the early termination features of the product
- The reluctance by a customer to provide identifying information when purchasing an insurance product, or the provision of minimal or seemingly fictitious information
- The borrowing of the maximum amount available soon after purchasing the product

SARs Filing Requirements

The requirement to identify and report suspicious transactions applies only to insurance companies offering covered products, and does not apply to their producers. Insurance companies must obtain customer information from all relevant sources (including its producers) and report suspicious activity based on that information.

A transaction must be reported if it is conducted or attempted by, at, or through an insurance company and involves or aggregates at least $5,000 in funds or other assets, and the insurance company knows, suspects, or has reason to suspect that the transaction:

- Involves funds garnered from illegal activity or is intended to hide or disguise funds or assets derived from illegal activity as part of a plan to violate or evade any federal law or regulation or to avoid any transaction reporting requirement under federal law or regulation
- Is designed to evade any requirements of regulations promulgated under the Bank Secrecy Act
- Has no business or apparent lawful purpose or is not the sort in which the particular customer would normally be expected to engage, and the insurance company knows of no reasonable explanation for the transaction after examining available facts
- Involves the use of the insurance company to facilitate criminal activity

The $5,000 threshold amount is not limited to insurance policies whose premiums meet or exceed it; rather it includes a policy in which the premium or potential payout meets the threshold. Insurance companies are also encouraged to voluntarily file SARs, regardless of the threshold amount, if appropriate.

Underwriting
Insurable Interest

Insurance contracts must have a legal purpose to be enforceable. The basic requirement of insurance contracts is that they be made based on *insurable interests.* For example, a business generally owns or leases the property it insures, and has a financial interest in whether the property is lost or damaged.

A husband has a financial stake in the loss of the life of his wife and so may be the policyholder and beneficiary on a life insurance policy insuring the wife. A business has a financial stake in the life of its CEO, so may also be the policyholder and beneficiary on a policy insuring the CEO's life.

Insurable Interest – Virginia Law

The Virginia Code in Section 38.2-301 defines insurable interest for life, accident and sickness policies. This code section states that:

- any individual of lawful age may take out an insurance contract upon himself for the benefit of any person.
- no person is allowed to knowingly procure or cause to be procured any insurance contract upon another individual unless the benefits under the contract are payable to:
  - the insured or his personal representative; or
  - a person having an insurable interest in the insured at the time when the contract was made.

Under Virginia law, insurable interest means:

- in the case of individuals related closely by blood or by law, a substantial interest engendered by love and affection;
- in the case of other persons, a *lawful and substantial economic interest* in the life, health, and bodily safety of the insured. Insurable interest does not include an interest which arises only or is enhanced by the death, disability or injury of the insured;
- in the case of employees of corporations, with respect to whom the corporate employer, a trust established by the corporate employer, or an employee benefit trust is the beneficiary under an insurance contract, the *lawful and substantial economic interest* is deemed to exist in:
  - key employees; and
  - other employees who have been employed by the corporation for 12 consecutive months, provided that the amount of insurance coverage on such other employees is limited to an amount which is commensurate with employer-provided benefits to non-key employees as a group;

- in the case of a party to a contract or option for the purchase or sale of an interest in a business proprietorship, partnership or firm or of shares of stock of a corporation or of an interest in such shares, the *lawful and substantial economic interest* is deemed to exist in each individual party to the contract or option for the purpose of the contract or option only, in addition to any insurable interest that may otherwise exist as to the life of such individual;
- in the case of a trustee, other than the trustee of a domestic business trust or foreign business trust, the *lawful and substantial economic interest* is deemed to exist when the life insurance policy is owned by a trustee, in:
  - the individual insured who established the trust;
  - each individual in whose life the owner of the trust for federal income tax purposes has an insurable interest; and
  - each individual in whose life a beneficiary of the trust has an insurable interest; and
- in the case of a non-profit organization described in §501(c) of the IRC, the *lawful and substantial economic interest* is deemed to exist where:
  - the insured or proposed insured has either:
    - » assigned all or part of his ownership rights in a policy or contract to the organization; or
    - » executed a written consent to the issuance of a policy or contract to the organization; and
  - the organization is named in the policy or contract as owner or as beneficiary.

VA Code §38.2-301

Virginia insurance law provides that:

- A wife or husband may effect an insurance contract upon each other;
- Any person having an insurable interest in the life of a minor, or any person upon whom a minor is dependent for support and maintenance, may effect an insurance contract upon the life of or pertaining to the minor; or
- A corporate employer or an employee benefit trust having insurable interest may effect an insurance contract upon the lives of employees, as long as the employer or trust

VA PPL LH-2_16298

provides the employee with written notice stating:

- insurance has been purchased;
- the amount of coverage; and
- to whom benefits are payable in the event of the employee's death.

VA Code §38.2-302

Medical Information and Consumer Reports

Medical Reports

Besides the application, the underwriters have other resources they may utilize during the underwriting process. For life and health insurance, the medical history of the insured must be examined. The application for the policy includes questions pertaining to basic medical information, including age, height, weight and health history of the applicant and the applicant's family.

Besides the application, if the coverage amount requested is above an insurance company's *non-medical* limit, additional medical information may be requested through a medical report. Generally, a *medical report* may be completed by a paramedic or a registered nurse. If there is information in the application or medical report that requires further explanation, an attending physician's statement, or APS, may be required. An APS must be completed by a physician who treated the medical condition under question.

Attending Physician Statement (APS)

An APS is a questionnaire sent to the applicant's doctor. The doctor must complete the questionnaire in order for the underwriters to complete the underwriting process. The proposed insured must give his or her permission on the application for the attending physician to provide this information.

An attending physician statement is a relatively simple document. It generally includes:

- Patient's (insured's) name
- Patient's address
- If related to an insured's employment, a statement for the physician to designate

whether the patient is able to return to work, and if unable, when it is anticipated the patient will be able to return to work
- An area for the physician to indicate the physician's diagnosis and prognosis
- An area for additional remarks for the physician
- The physician's name, license number, address, phone number and signature

Inspection, Consumer and Credit Reports

If an applicant applies for amounts of insurance above certain levels, the insurer may conduct inspection reports and/or acquire credit reports on the applicant.

Inspection reports:

- are created from interviews with an applicant's neighbors, associates and employees, and sometimes with the applicant.
- are created by national investigative organizations hired by the insurer.
- are requested by insurers to better understand an applicant's overall character, lifestyle, financial situation and risks to which an applicant may be exposed.

Consumer Reports

Credit reports provide information about the financial condition of an applicant. This is important to an insurer because insurance involves a financial commitment from the policyholder. If an insurer accepts policies from people with poor credit, or credit below a certain standard, policy lapses are likely to go up. Lapses cause an increase in expenses to the insurer who has incurred policy issue expenses associated with the policy. In addition, financial problems establish the presence of moral hazard – the applicant may be more likely to submit unfounded claims due to the need for money.

Credit and consumer reports, including investigative consumer reports, are regulated by the federal *Fair Credit Reporting Act (FCRA)*.

Permissible Purposes of Consumer Reports

Under the FCRA, consumer reports may only be furnished for certain purposes by consumer reporting agencies (CRAs). One of these permissible purposes is furnishing a report to a person who intends to use the report in connection with the underwriting of insurance. The CRA must have a reasonable belief this is the intent of the requestor.

Furnishing Consumer Reports

Under the FCRA, a CRA may only issue a consumer report that is not initiated by a consumer request if the consumer authorizes the agency to provide the report or the transaction for which the consumer report is used is considered a firm offer of insurance. If a consumer report is issued because the transaction is a firm offer of insurance and is not authorized by the consumer, the report may only furnish the name and address of the consumer, an identifier used solely to verify the identity of the consumer and other information pertaining to the consumer that does not provide the relationship of experience of the consumer with a particular creditor or other entity.

Disclosing Investigative Consumer Reports

An *investigative consumer report* is a more in-depth form of consumer report that may be obtained by the insurer for underwriting purposes. As defined in the FCRA this report is, "a consumer report or portion thereof in which information on a consumer's character, general reputation, personal characteristics, or mode of living is obtained through personal interviews with neighbors, friends, or associates of the consumer reported on or with others with whom he is acquainted or who may have knowledge concerning any such items of information. However, such information shall not include specific factual information on a consumer's credit record obtained directly from a creditor of the consumer or from a consumer reporting agency when such information was obtained directly from a creditor of the consumer or from the consumer."

In order to have an investigative report prepared, it must be clearly and accurately disclosed to the consumer that an investigative consumer report, that includes information about the consumer's character, general reputation, personal characteristics, and mode of living, may be made. The disclosure to the consumer must:

- be in writing;

- be mailed or delivered to the consumer not more than three days after the date the report was requested; and
- include a statement that the consumer has the right to request information about the nature and scope of the investigation.

The underwriter uses the investigative report to evaluate the risk characteristics of the applicant.

The Medical Information Bureau (MIB)

Besides medical reports and APS reports, insurers have access to medical information through the Medical Information Bureau, Inc., or MIB. The MIB is an association of most life and health insurers in the United States. The MIB contains information about the medical condition of applicants and insureds.

Applicants must authorize the release of information to the MIB. The information may only be used for underwriting and claims purposes, and medical information is released only to the applicant's physician, or directly to the applicant if the applicant requests.

The MIB is considered to be an important tool of the insurance industry because of its role in reducing fraud. By keeping track of important pieces of information used in the application and underwriting of life, health, disability and long-term care insurance, it is more difficult for applicants to falsify applications and claims. Reducing false applications and claims means that premiums do not have to be raised for everyone who purchases such insurance because of expenses related to fraudulent claims. More information about the MIB can be found on its website at www.mib.com.

Fair Credit Reporting Act

(15 USC 1681–1681D)

Consumer Reports

Under the FCRA, a credit report is considered a **consumer report**. Consumer reports can be generated for the following reasons:

- Because of a court order
- Because the consumer has given written authorization to do so

Reasons for Consumer Reports

Credit reports contain private information and can only be generated and used according to specific legal standards. Reports may be generated by a CRA to a person that intends to use the information in connection with a credit transaction involving the consumer for the extension of credit or reviewing their accounts or for collection purposes. They may also be used:

- For employment purposes
- For underwriting insurance
- To determine the eligibility for a government issued license, or other government benefit where financial responsibility or status must be reviewed

Reports are also used by investors or insurers to evaluate the credit risk of a consumer.

Credit Bureaus

The three major credit bureaus (consumer reporting agencies) that issue credit reports are:

- *Equifax® Credit Information Services, Inc.* (800) 525-6285/ TDD 1-800-255-0056; Auto Disclosure Line 1-800-685-1111. P.O. Box 740241, Atlanta, GA 30374-0241 www.equifax.com
- *Experian® Information Solutions, Inc.* (888) 397-3742/ TDD (800) 972-0322 P.O. Box 9532, Allen, TX 75013 www.experian.com
- *TransUnion®* (800) 680-7289/ TDD (877) 553-7803 Fraud Victim Assistance Division P.O. Box 6790, Fullerton, CA 92834-6790; www.transunion.com

Contents of Consumer Reports

Consumer reports include the consumer's credit information, employment information, their current and past addresses, and the source of the information.

They also include information on other persons who have requested a consumer report on the individual, and list the requestor's name or trade name and reason for the request.

Disclosure to Customers

If an **adverse action**, such as denying credit or insurance, occurs due to the information on the consumer report, the user of the report may disclose the contents of the report to the consumer.

The contents of the report are also disclosed to the consumer if the consumer requests this disclosure.

The FACT Act

On December 5, 2003, the federal Fair and Accurate Credit Transactions Act (the FACT Act) was signed into law. It expands some of the consumer protections found in the FCRA. It was passed with the intent to help decrease errors in credit reports and other reporting problems associated with identity theft. Under this Act:

- Consumers are able to view their credit reports for free, once each year
- Consumers are to be given a notice of their Rights to Obtain and Dispute Information in Consumer Reports and to Obtain Credit Scores, from the reporting agency when consumer reports are generated

Consumer Rights Under the FCRA and the FACT Act

Consumers have several rights under the FCRA and the FACT Act. The Federal Trade Commission has created a summary of these rights.

A Summary of Your Rights under the Fair Credit Reporting Act

You must be told if information in your file has been used against you. Anyone who uses a credit report or another type of consumer report to deny your application for credit, insurance, or employment – or to take another adverse action against you – must tell you, and must give you the name, address, and phone number of the agency that provided the information.

You have the right to know what is in your file. You may request and obtain all the information about you in the files of a consumer reporting agency (your "file disclosure"). You will be required to provide proper identification, which may include your Social Security number. In many cases, the disclosure will be free. You are entitled to a free file disclosure if:

- A person has taken adverse action against you because of information in your credit report;

VA PPL LH-2_16298

- You are the victim of identity theft and place a fraud alert in your file;
- Your file contains inaccurate information as a result of fraud;
- You are on public assistance;
- You are unemployed, but expect to apply for employment within 60 days.

Visit www.consumer.ftc.gov for more information.

Other Rights under the Fair Credit Reporting Act
- You have the right to ask for a credit score.
- All consumers are entitled to one free disclosure every 12 months upon request from each nationwide credit bureau and from nationwide specialty consumer reporting agencies. See annualcreditreport.com to get your free credit report.
- You have the right to dispute incomplete or inaccurate information.
- Consumer reporting agencies must correct or delete inaccurate, incomplete, or unverifiable information.
- Consumer reporting agencies may not report outdated negative information.
- Access to your file is limited. A consumer reporting agency may provide information about you only to people with a valid need – usually to consider an application with a creditor, insurer, employer, landlord, or other business. The FCRA specifies those with a valid need for access.
- You must give your consent for reports to be provided to employers.
- You may limit "prescreened" offers of credit and insurance you get based on information in your credit report.
- You may seek damages from violators.

Risk Classification

When evaluating applicants, underwriters determine whether insurance on the applicant will be:
- rejected;
- issued on a substandard basis;
- issued on a standard basis; or
- issued on a preferred basis.

Rejecting Applicants

Insurers reject applications for insurance when they find that the applicant represents a risk that falls outside of the underwriting standards established by the insurance company. These underwriting standards take into consideration many items, such as regulations that require the insurer to establish adequate rates, laws that mandate that certain factors cannot be used to reject an application, insurance principles such as insurability and indemnity, the marketplace in which the insurer sells its products and the profit the insurer hopes to make on its business.

Under the insurance principle of *indemnity*, an insured is to be brought back to the financial position the insured was in prior to the loss or damage the insurance covers. The insured is not to make a profit from the insurance benefits.

Issuing Policies on a Substandard Basis

The decision to issue a policy on a *substandard issue* basis occurs when a risk is not deemed to be outside underwriting standards, but is considered to be of high risk within those standards. The insurer generally has three basic options when it offers a substandard policy issue to an applicant. It may:

1. issue the policy with a higher premium than would be required for a standard policy
2. issue the policy with limited benefits
3. issue the policy with certain exclusions

Higher Premium

The insurer may charge a higher premium to applicants deemed to be of higher risk than those who would be considered a standard risk as long as those higher rates fall within certain parameters. The insurer must charge every insured with the same characteristics the same rate. State and federal laws define which insurance risk elements are considered unfairly discriminatory and higher premium may not be charged based on these elements. The insurer must comply with such laws in determining whether to charge higher premium rates.

Limit Policy Benefits

Insurers may also respond to substandard applicants by offering a policy with limited policy benefits. Again, whether the insurer may limit benefits is regulated by state law. For example, under long-term care policies, some states require that policies offer a minimum home health care benefit limit as a certain ratio of the nursing home benefit limit. Therefore, an insurer offering long-term care benefits could not limit the home health benefit on a policy in a manner that would not comply with such a law. Assuming state regulations are followed, an insurer could offer lower policy limits on certain coverages to a substandard applicant, or could offer lower policy limits for all coverages to such an applicant. Dealing with substandard applicants by limiting policy benefits is most common in commercial coverages.

Excluding Certain Provisions from Coverage

Another option an insurer may have is to offer a substandard applicant a policy that excludes coverage for certain conditions. The exclusion may be permanent or may be in effect for a specified period of time, e.g. for the first six months of coverage. As with the other options discussed, such exclusions must be allowable under state and federal regulations.

Issuing Policies on a Standard Basis

Underwriters base their determination that a policy should be issued on a *standard issue* basis on an analysis of the characteristics of the risk represented by the applicant. Applicants who are issued policies with standard rates fall within the normal boundaries of underwriting standards for that type of policy.

Issuing Policies on a Preferred Basis

If an application falls within the lowest risk boundaries of the underwriting standards, the policy is issued on a *preferred issue* basis. Preferred rates represent the lowest rates offered by an insurer for its coverage. Rates offered on a preferred basis must adhere to the insurance regulations applicable to them, just as rates offered on a substandard and standard basis must.

Stranger-Originated Life Insurance

One of the primary reasons for the requirement of insurable interest is to reduce the moral hazards associated with the possibility of receiving large amounts for a small investment. A person with insurable interest is one who is not in a position to gain or profit from a loss pertaining to the insured.

Rather, because they have a financial interest in the insured, they will be made whole financially by receiving a death benefit amount from the insurer upon the insured's death. Without an insurable interest, there is the hazard that the beneficiary of the insurance will attempt to cause the loss in some way. An uninterested third party who buys a life insurance policy is in the position of profiting from the insured's death.

Stranger-originated life insurance, or STOLI, transactions are generally illegal because they violate insurable interest principles underlying the appropriate issue of insurance products. In STOLI transactions, an unrelated owner purchases a life insurance product on an insured. Or, an entity without insurable interest encourages the purchase of life insurance on an insured by a person with insurable interest with the intent to have the policy transferred or assigned to the entity. The insured on a STOLI product often has no legitimate reason to be an insured on a life insurance policy, such as protecting a spouse, family, business, etc. that will suffer financially from the insured's death. Instead, the insured's life will be used to provide profit to a stranger. The insured is often paid a lump sum for agreeing to be the insured on the STOLI policy or to transfer ownership of an existing policy to the stranger.

Investor Originated Life Insurance

Similar to STOLI transactions, much controversy has existed in recent years regarding investor originated life insurance, or IOLI, transactions. These transactions combine premium financing loans with terms of 2 to 3 years, a substantial amount of life insurance, and life settlements.

A typical IOLI transaction occurs where the life insurance policy is taken out by a senior with excess insurance capacity who does not need to purchase any additional life insurance on his or her own life but has the ability (i.e., has good health) to qualify for the coverage. The original owner and the beneficiary of an IOLI policy is normally an Irrevocable Life Insurance Trust (ILIT), with the insured as *grantor* and an individual with insurable interest in the insured as the beneficiary of the ILIT. The grantor is the person who establishes a trust.

Once the policy is issued, the insured puts the policy in force by paying premiums. Afterwards, the insured gets an offer of a certain percentage of the face amount of the policy (anywhere from 2% to 30%) from an investor with institutional capital sufficient to purchase the beneficial interest in the ILIT. The beneficiary and trustee then sign over their interest or ownership in the ILIT to the funder. The trust remains the owner of the policy. The funder continues to pay the policy premiums through the life of the policy and then collects the full death benefit when the insured dies. In this situation, the policy is opened with legitimate insurable interest in place, and an investor without insurable interest gains interest in the death benefit after the policy's issue.

There has been much debate regarding the legality of such a sale or transfer of insurance policy and death benefit rights. The funders of IOLIs argue that an insured has the ability to transfer any active policy to a third party no matter when the policy was created. Some insurance companies, however, argue that IOLIs break insurable interest laws because the funders do not have a financial interest in the continued life of the insured they purchase the life insurance policy from.

State Regulation

IOLI and STOLI transactions have resulted in many states enacting life settlement or viatical settlement laws that set out when, who and how a life insurance policy may be transferred to a funding company, and when and how an insured may be paid for transferring the policy. A *viatical settlement* is a contract which allows a policy owner to sell his or her life insurance policy to a viatical settlements company or an individual. The owner receives a lump sum equal to the face value of the policy. The buyer then assumes responsibility to pay all premiums, and will receive the death benefit upon the original owner's death.

Life and viatical settlements are regulated by state insurance departments, although not all states have enacted statutes that specifically address the sale and transfer of life insurance policies to those without a traditional insurable interest. Of the regulating states, most require that the viatical or life settlement broker and the provider be licensed.

The National Association of Insurance Commissioners (NAIC) has also created a Model act that has the purpose of providing state legislatures with recommendations for life settlement regulation.

Delivering the Policy
Policy Delivery

After completion of the application and any required additional forms, the agent submits the documents and any premium received to the insurer. The underwriting department of the insurer must complete the underwriting process in a reasonable time frame. Then, the issued policy is generally sent to the agent who delivers it to the policyowner. The agent has the opportunity during delivery to answer any questions the policyowner may have, and explain important provisions within the policy to the policyowner.

Delivery Receipt Requirement

At the time of delivery, a receipt is generally signed by the owner to identify the beginning of the **free look** period or right to return period where the applicant may return the contract and receive any premium paid without penalty.

Many producers see the delivery appointment as an opportunity to solidify their relationship with the policyowner. It is a time when any final questions about the contract may be answered and the policyowner's reasons for purchasing the contract may be reaffirmed. Also, the agent will want to go over all provisions, riders, exclusions and rating determined in underwriting. The sale is not complete until the delivery is made and the free look period has passed.

Review Policy Provisions

When the policy is delivered, its provisions should be reviewed with the policyholder. The policy includes a face page, a copy of the application, and the policy contract.

VA PPL LH-2_16298

The face page summarizes key information about the policy:

- The policyholder's name
- The insured's name
- The insured's age at issue
- The premium amount
- The issue date of the policy
- The policy number

Premium Collected at Policy Delivery – Policy Effective

When premium is not collected at time of application, it must be collected at policy delivery. The policy becomes effective when the premium is collected and a statement of good health is signed.

Policy Inception

It is illegal in most states to backdate a life insurance policy more than six months, and the backdating may only be done if doing so results in a lower premium rate as a result of the insured's age being lowered.

Statement of Good Health

A *statement of good health* is generally required by insurers issuing life polices to be signed at time of policy delivery. If the insured's health has deteriorated between the times the application was taken and the policy was delivered, the agent is required to inform the insurer. If no premium had been collected and the insured's health has deteriorated at the time of policy delivery, the agent should not collect any premium at delivery. The agent must inform the insurer and the insurer will instruct the agent regarding whether the policy can still be delivered and made effective.

Virginia Delivery Period Requirements

Under Virginia law, for purposes of determining the commencement of the free look period during which the owner of an individual life insurance policy may exercise the right to examine, surrender, or return the policy for cancellation, the date of delivery of the policy is:

1. The date of the signed receipt of delivery if the life insurance policy is:
   a. delivered by United States mail or other postal delivery system; or
   b. physically delivered to the owner by a representative of the insurer; or
2. The date of electronic transmission of the policy, provided the electronic transmission has been effected in accordance with applicable laws governing the electronic transmission of documents and information. The insurer must retain evidence of electronic transmittal for the entire period of the life insurance policy.

If an insurer does not deliver a policy by these methods, the burden of proof is on the insurer to establish that the policy was delivered, in the event of a dispute with the owner of the policy.

A policy is deemed to have been received by the owner of the policy as of the date of its issuance if six months have passed since its issue and the owner of the policy has paid the premiums for those six months.

VA Code §38.2-3301.1

Section III Review

1) Taking an accurate and complete application helps to avoid:
   a. the agent from practicing twisting
   b. the insurer and agent from committing unfair claims settlement practices
   c. the insurer from accepting insureds that represent risks that are higher than the insurer is able to accept
   d. the practice of keeping false records

2) An insurance policy may be void if an insured has done any of the following, EXCEPT:
   a. intentionally concealed or misrepresented any material fact or circumstance
   b. made false statements relating to the insurance
   c. engaged in fraudulent conduct
   d. included information about claims history with an application for health insurance

3) The federal Act that regulates the ability of financial institutions to disclose "nonpublic personal information" about consumers to non-affiliated third parties and also requires financial institutions to provide customers with their privacy policies and practices with respect to nonpublic personal information is the:
   a. Gramm-Leach-Bliley Act
   b. Freedom of Information Act
   c. Privacy Act of 1974
   d. Fair Credit Reporting Act

4) When a consumer is provided notice by a financial institution of its policies concerning disclosing nonpublic personal information, the consumer must be given the ability to:
   a. be copied on all disclosures made
   b. be notified of the date(s) any disclosure is made
   c. add comments to the disclosure made
   d. opt-out of the disclosure

5) The three major credit bureaus are:
   a. Equifax, Experian, and the FTC.
   b. Experian, TransUnion, and the FTC.
   c. Equifax, Experian, and TransUnion.
   d. TransUnion, the FTC, and Equifax.

6) Each of the following purposes are legitimate reasons for generating consumer reports EXCEPT:
   a. for employment purposes
   b. for underwriting insurance
   c. to determine the eligibility for a government issued license
   d. for political purposes

7) Which of the following would a consumer report not include?
   a. The consumer's religion
   b. The consumer's employment information
   c. The consumer's past addresses
   d. Information on other persons who requested a consumer report on the original individual

8) A person is denied credit based on information in a consumer report. This is a(n):
   a. Adverse action
   b. Reversal
   c. Denial
   d. Alternative action

9) The federal Act that expands the rights of identity theft victims and their right to receive a free consumer report is the:
   a. Fair Credit Reporting Act
   b. Fair Credit Billing Act
   c. FACT Act
   d. Electronic Fund Transfer Act

10) What is NOT a concern of insurance companies if investor-owned life insurance transactions are allowed?
   a. Death frequency may increase due to the moral hazard that an investor group will directly or indirectly cause harm to insureds in order to obtain the death benefit.
   b. Insurance companies will not be able to keep mortality statistics in order to set premium rates.
   c. Premiums will rise on all life insurance because persistency will increase.
   d. The requirement of insurable interest will be eroded and insurance will be allowed to become a form of speculative investing.

11) John applied for a life insurance policy on August 9. The life insurer had a policy of backdating the policies to the applicant's prior birthday. John's birthdate is June 2. Which statement is true of the policy's effective issue date?
   a. John's policy may not be backdated to June 2
   b. John's policy may be backdated to June 2
   c. John's policy may be backdated only to July 9
   d. John's policy may be backdated only to August 1

12) The threshold amount at which an insurance company must report a suspicious transaction according to SARs filing requirements is:
   a. $10,000
   b. $ 20,000
   c. $ 50,000
   d. $ 5,000

13) Once an agent has been trained in the insurance company's money laundering program:
   a. he or she must be retrained every six months
   b. he or she must be retrained when necessary to understand the most current program requirements
   c. he or she must never be retrained
   d. he or she must be retrained every 12 months

14) If an insurance company fails to implement an anti-money laundering program as required:
   a. it will be ordered to cease operations
   b. it is subject to fines and penalties
   c. the Treasury Department will investigate
   d. the insurance company will be examined by the Treasury Department every three months until a pattern of compliance has been established

15) The act that required banks to report cash transactions over $10,000 to the government is called the:
   a. Money Laundering Control Act
   b. Bank Secrecy Act
   c. USA Patriot Act
   d. Money Laundering Suppression Act

16) According to Virginia law, if an answer to a question in a life insurance application is later found to be have been untrue at the time the policy was issued:
   a. The untrue statement is automatically considered to be fraudulent
   b. The untrue statement will never be considered a misrepresentation
   c. The untrue statement, if fraudulent and material to a claim filed, may cause the insurer to legally deny the claim
   d. The untrue statement is automatically considered to be a warranty

17) When may an adverse underwriting decision be made based on HIV by a life insurance company issuing policies to Virginia residents?
   a. If it is based solely on the presence of symptoms, as disclosed in an application for life or accident and sickness insurance coverage.
   b. if the symptoms disclosed in the application for coverage are not confirmed as being HIV-related through the use of medical records.
   c. If, during the underwriting process, it is revealed that the applicant has had positive HIV-related test results following testing protocol, or has been diagnosed as having AIDS or HIV infection.
   d. If the symptoms disclosed in the application for coverage are not confirmed as being HIV-related through the use of HIV-related tests

18) Virginia law prohibits anyone from knowingly procuring or causing to be procured any life or accident and sickness policy UNLESS the benefits under the contract are payable to the insured or his personal representative, or to:
   a. a person who is an immediate family member of the insured.
   b. a person having an insurable interest in the insured at the time when the contract was made.
   c. a person who is the spouse of the insured.
   d. a person who is an employee of the insured.

VA PPL LH-2_16298

19) A husband purchases a life insurance policy on his wife and names himself beneficiary. This act:
   a. violates Virginia's insurable interest laws.
   b. is in accordance with Virginia insurable interest laws.
   c. violates Virginia's discrimination laws.
   d. violates Virginia's gambling laws

20) Armand delivered a life insurance policy to a client at the client's office and the client signed the delivery receipt on April 1. Armand retained a copy of the delivery receipt and placed it in the client file. While he was driving back to the agency, he had his car windows rolled down and the receipt blew out the window without Armand's knowledge. A little over nine months later, the client called and said he wanted to cancel the policy and receive a full refund of all premiums paid. Armand went to the client file to see the delivery date of the policy and discovered there was no delivery receipt. He also saw that the insured client had paid the premium on time for nine months, since the policy's inception. The insurer:
   a. Must give the client a full refund of premium from the policy inception date because there is no proof that the policy was delivered.
   b. Does not have to provide a full refund of premium from the policy inception because if a policy's premium is paid for six months, the law views it as having been received by the owner of the policy as of the date of issuance.
   c. Must take the premium refund dispute to arbitration to be resolved.
   d. Must give the client a refund of premium above the cost of insurance from the policy inception date because there is no proof that the policy was delivered.

Section IV: Taxes, Retirement, and Other Insurance Concepts

This section explores several concepts underlying insurance transactions and reasons for life insurance purchases. Topics include:

- Third-party ownership
- Group life insurance
- Retirement plans
- Life insurance needs analysis and suitability
- Social Security benefits and taxes
- Tax treatment of insurance premiums, proceeds and dividends

Third-Party Ownership

Life insurance may be owned by a third-party, meaning a person who is not the insured. For example, a husband may own and be the beneficiary on a policy where the wife is the insured. Or, a non-natural person, such as a trust or a corporation, may own life insurance policies on the lives of employees, owners, debtors, individuals donating their life insurance proceeds to charity, etc. The insured, however, must always be a natural person.

The taxation of life insurance can vary based on the type of third-party that owns the policy.

Life Insurance Values Included in the Estate

A basic rule in estate tax rules is that property that is owned by the deceased is generally includable in the estate of the owner. Life insurance is no exception; it is generally always includable in the estate of a policyowner. However, this fact about life insurance is not generally known because many people avoid estate taxation because their estates are not large enough to be taxed. In addition, in many cases, the beneficiary of a policy is the spouse of the policyowner and insured, and the unlimited marital deduction is used against the life insurance proceeds upon the death of the first spouse, resulting in no taxation on the amounts transferred to the spouse at death.

For example, assume a husband is owner and insured on a life insurance policy and his wife is the beneficiary. At the husband's death, the life insurance death benefit is paid to the wife. Since the transfer at death is between spouses, for estate tax purposes, the husband's estate can use the unlimited marital deduction credit against the amount of the insurance proceeds the wife receives from the deceased spouse, which reduces the value of the taxable estate and excludes the life insurance benefit from estate taxation.

When the second spouse dies, or if a policyowner/insured does not have a spouse or does not name a spouse as beneficiary, the unlimited marital deduction will not apply. In such a case, other estate tax reduction measures are often used. The most common method is using an insurance trust. If money is gifted to an irrevocable life insurance trust, and the trust purchases life insurance on the insured, the value of the life insurance will not be included in the insured's estate, since the insured is not the policyowner.

Estate Inclusion

Transfers within 3 Years of Death

Estate planning professionals recommend that money be gifted to an irrevocable life insurance trust and the trust purchase life insurance on the life of the insured because when an existing cash value life insurance policy is transferred to a trust, it can be includable in the estate of the person who transferred ownership if that individual dies within three years of the transfer.

Irrevocable vs. Revocable Trusts

Irrevocable trusts are used rather than revocable trusts to keep the policy value out of the owner's estate in order that the grantor of the trust (the person who places property into the trust) does not retain any ownership or interest in the property within the trust. If property in a trust includes a *retained interest*, as generally occurs in a revocable trust situation, that property can be included in the estate of the person with the retained interest. A retained interest is any interest or authority over the funds in the trust that is retained by the grantor.

 VA PPL LH-2_16298

Policyowner Predeceases Insured

Another circumstance that causes life insurance values to be includable in an estate is if a person other than the policyowner is named as insured and the policyowner dies before the insured. In this circumstance, the value of the policy at the time of death is the amount includable in the deceased policyowner's estate.

For example, Judy Smith is the owner on a life insurance policy. Her father, Tom Smith is the insured. Judy is the beneficiary. If Judy dies before Tom, the value of the life insurance policy as of the date of Judy's death is included in Judy's estate value.

Sole Proprietorships

For tax purposes, life insurance purchased by a sole proprietorship is treated as though owned by the sole proprietor. This means that premiums for insurance are not a tax-deductible expense for the business. Death benefits from the policy are income tax free to beneficiaries. If the sole proprietor or sole proprietorship is the owner of the policy at his or her death, the value of the policy is includable in the proprietor's estate.

Partnership

If a partnership owns life insurance, each partner is considered to have ownership in the policy in the same relationship as the owner has ownership in the business. *For example, if a partnership is owned equally by two partners, life insurance purchased by the partnership would be owned 50% by Owner A and 50% by Owner B.* Premiums paid by the partnership for the policy are not deductible expenses for tax purposes. Death benefits from the policy are income tax-free to beneficiaries.

C Corporations

Premiums for a life insurance policy owned by a C corporation are not a tax-deductible expense for the corporation. Generally, the death benefit proceeds may be received free from income tax, although larger corporations may be subject to alternative minimum tax.

S Corporations

As with a partnership, a life insurance policy purchased by an S Corporation is considered to be owned by the shareholders in proportion to their ownership in the corporation. Premiums are not a tax-deductible expense to the corporation, and the death benefit is received income tax free.

Limited Liability Companies

Life insurance owned by limited liability companies is treated for tax purposes like life insurance purchased by a partnership.

Corporate-Owned and Individually-Owned Annuities

When a non-natural person owns an annuity, the annuity loses its tax-deferral status. Non-natural persons include businesses, such as a corporation, and irrevocable trusts. However, certain trusts are taxed like a natural person, such as living grantor trusts, also known as revocable living trusts. If a business is taxed like a person, as is a sole-proprietorship, the sole proprietor could own an annuity and it would retain tax-deferral status.

Since the annuity has no tax-deferred status when owned by a non-natural person such as a corporation, earnings are taxable in the year they are earned. There is no premature withdrawal penalty because there is no age 59 ½ that applies to a non-natural person. Annuity payments would only be taxable to the extent the amounts had not already been taxed during accumulation; in other words, only the earnings applied at annuitization would be taxable.

Group Life Insurance
Characteristics

Group life insurance has several characteristics that distinguish it from individual life insurance. These include:

- number of lives covered
- coverage terms
- when coverage terminates
- cost and benefits
- sponsor of the plans
- underwriting requirements

Group life insurance is available through a variety of channels, including employers, trade associations, labor unions and lenders.

Number of Lives

With an individual life policy, one or two lives (or a family, if riders are included) are usually covered.

VA PPL LH-2_16298

A group policy covers several lives. Insurers may have underwriting standards that specify the minimum number of lives that must be covered for a particular group insurance product.

Written Coverage Terms

A group policy contract is issued to the policyholder. This policy is called the Master Contract. The insureds within the group are issued certificates that provide their terms of coverage.

The policyholder of the master contract has the contractual rights of the policy. The policyholder assigns the right to name beneficiaries (the persons to whom the death benefit will be paid) to the certificateholders.

(Note: When a sole proprietor is issued a group master contract, and only one or two lives are covered and issued certificates, it is because the sole proprietor qualifies as a group under that insurer's underwriting standards and under state law and is being rated based on this category.)

When Coverage Terminates

A group life insurance policy continues for as long as the group is insured. When an individual insured under the group plan dies, a death benefit is paid to that certificateholder's beneficiaries and the coverage on the rest of the group continues. Only when the master contract is non-renewed or cancelled does the master policy coverage terminate on the group. Group life insurance is often issued as annually renewable term insurance, but the renewal period may be longer.

Contributory and Non-Contributory Premium Payment

Often, the policyholder of a group life contract is an employer. When an employer sponsors a group life plan, the plans may be *non-contributory* or *contributory*.

Characteristics	Contributory Plans	Non-Contributory Plans
Sponsor	Employer	Employer
Premium payer(s)	Employees 100% or Employee/employer share	Employer 100%
Method of payment	Payroll deduction	Employer pays insurer

Costs and Benefits Provided

The amount of death benefit provided under a group life plan may depend upon, among other things, the group sponsor. If the group sponsor is an employer, the group benefit may be based on salary or be flat amounts available regardless of salary.

Some plans may include riders with special benefits, such as waiver of premium or accelerated death benefits. Others may be more "bare-boned" and not include special benefits.

Conversion to Individual Policies

Group life plans, which are normally term policies, generally allow the insureds to convert to an individual policy when the insured leaves the group, and/or prior to a certain age, without having to demonstrate insurability. The premiums for the individual policy are offered based on attained age at time of conversion. For example, if the insured were 45 when leaving the group, the premium rates for the individual policy would be based on the insured's age 45. The option to convert may only be available up to a specified age.

Retirement Plans

Tax-Qualified Plans

A tax qualified plan is a plan that meets Federal law and regulation requirements, and in some cases, state law and regulation requirements, and is therefore treated for Federal tax purposes with certain tax benefits. By meeting legal requirements, the plans qualify for these tax benefits.

Traditional IRAs

Traditional IRAs were created by legislation effective in 1974. Accumulations in Traditional IRAs are tax deductible to the IRA holder, and deductible contributions and all earnings are taxed upon withdrawal from the IRA.

Eligibility and Contribution Limit

Persons under 70½ with compensation may contribute to a Traditional IRA. The maximum contribution that may be made to a Traditional IRA is currently the greater of $5,500 or 100% of compensation (2017).

VA PPL LH-2_16298

Catch-up contributions may also be made to Traditional IRAs by individuals age 50 and over. An additional $1,000 can be contributed for a tax year, so these individuals may make a maximum IRA contribution of up to $6,500.

Spousal IRAs

Traditional IRA rules allow for non-earner spouses, or spouses that earn less than the $5,500 maximum contribution amount to make contributions of up to the maximum contribution amount based on the total compensation earned by both spouses if the couple files a joint tax return.

Distributions and Age 70½ Rules

Distributions must be made from Traditional IRAs no later than April 1st of the year following the year the IRA holder turned 70 ½.

Deductibility of Traditional IRA Contributions

Certain contributions to Traditional IRAs are fully deductible to the IRA holder. If the IRA holder, and spouse if applicable, is not covered by an employer retirement plan, all contributions made up to the maximum contribution amount are deductible to the IRA holder.

Premature Distributions

Withdrawals from IRAs, other than withdrawals of nondeductible contributions, are taxable as regular income to the owner, and are subject to additional taxation prior to the IRA owner's age 59 ½. Withdrawals prior to 59 ½ are subject to an additional 10% tax unless the withdrawal is:

- due to disability;
- due to death;
- part of a series of substantially equal payments made over the owner's lifetime;
- used for certain unreimbursed medical expenses;
- made to unemployed individuals for health insurance premiums;
- used for certain higher education expenses;
- due to an IRS levy of a qualified plan;
- a qualified reservist distribution (for persons called into active military service); or
- used for certain first-time homebuyer expenses.

Roth IRA
Contributions

Contributions may be made to Roth IRAs by individuals with compensation below certain modified adjusted gross income levels (MAGI). For individuals who file their taxes as married, filing jointly, the ability to contribute to a Roth is not available once MAGI is $194,000 or more for 2017.

The current maximum annual Roth contribution is the greater of 100% of compensation or $5,500. Those who are 50 or older may contribute $6,500 (2017).

Qualified Distributions

Distributions from Roth IRAs that are considered *qualified distributions* are not taxable upon receipt. Contributions to Roth IRAs are made with after-tax dollars, so the money has already been taxed. In addition, under the special tax rules that apply to Roth IRAs, earnings accumulate without taxation as long as qualified distributions are made when they are withdrawn.

In order to be a qualified distribution, the distributions must be made after the fifth-tax-year period beginning with the first tax year for which a contribution is made to a Roth IRA and meet one of the following conditions:

- the IRA holder has reached age 59 ½;
- the IRA holder is disabled;
- the IRA holder has died and the distribution is made to a beneficiary or the holders' estate; or
- the distribution is made to buy, build or rebuild a first home, and the distribution is $10,000 or less. The first time home buyer is one who had no present interest in a main home during the two-year period ending on the date of acquisition of the home with the distribution is being used to buy, build, or rebuild.

If a distribution is not a qualified distribution, generally, the earnings are taxable and a 10% additional tax is applied to the tax on the earnings. The exceptions to the additional 10% tax are the same as those for Traditional IRAs. Roth IRA distributions do not have to begin at age 70 ½ and do not have to meet minimum distribution requirements.

62

IRA and Qualified Plan Rollovers and Transfers

Current taxation of distributions is avoided through lawful rollover and transfer of amounts in IRAs and qualified plans.

From IRA Plans

Rollovers may be made from IRA plans to eligible retirement plans. Eligible retirement plans include other IRA plans and qualified plans such as 401(k) and 403(b) plans. Only one rollover is allowed from an IRA plan each 12-month period.

IRA assets may also be moved to another IRA plan through transfers. Transfers occur when IRA funds are moved directly from one IRA plan to another. There is no limit to the number of IRA transfers that may be made from an IRA plan.

From Qualified Plans

Taxable distributions from a defined contribution plan may be rolled over to an eligible retirement plan and avoid taxation. Eligible retirement plans to which defined contribution plan distributions may be rolled over include another defined contribution plan or an IRA.

A rollover occurs when an eligible distribution is moved from one eligible retirement plan to another eligible retirement plan. If the eligible distribution is moved directly from one eligible plan to another, the process is called a *direct rollover* or *direct transfer*. If the distribution is first made to the employee, who then places it into an eligible retirement plan within sixty days, the process is referred to simply as a *rollover.*

Simplified Employee Pension (SEP) Plans

A Simplified Employee Pension Plan, or SEP plan, was created by Congress to be a less complicated form of employer sponsored retirement plan than defined benefit and defined contribution qualified plans. SEP plans are actually a form of individual retirement account, or IRA. Under a SEP plan, the employer is able to make contributions to individual retirement accounts owned by plan participants.

Eligible Employees

Employees eligible to participate in a SEP plan include those who have:

- Reached age 21;
- Worked for the employer for at least three of the last five years; and
- Received at least $550 in compensation during the plan year.

Excludable Employees

Employees who may be excluded from SEPs include:

- Employees covered by a union agreement whose retirement benefits are the subjects of a good faith agreement between the employer and the union
- Nonresident aliens and employees who do not receive U.S. source wages, salaries or other personal services compensation from the employer

Contribution Rules

Contributions to SEPs must be in cash. The employer is not required to make annual contributions, but must make contributions according to a written allocation formula. The allocation formula must not discriminate in favor of highly compensated employees. Contributions for a tax year must be made by the employer's tax due date, including extensions.

Contribution Limits

Contributions to SEPs are generally tax deductible to the employer. In 2017, the maximum deductible contribution to a SEP is the lesser of 25% of compensation or $54,000. Up to $270,000 in compensation may be taken into consideration for this calculation.

SIMPLE IRA Plans

A SIMPLE IRA plan is a savings incentive match plan for employees under which a SIMPLE IRA is set up for each eligible employee. Employers with 100 or fewer employees who received $5,000 or more in compensation for the preceding year may establish and maintain SIMPLE IRA plans. Generally, the employer may not maintain any other qualified plan other than a qualified plan established for collective bargaining employees, in order to utilize a SIMPLE Plan.

VA PPL LH-2_16298

Eligible Employees

Employees who received at least $5,000 in compensation during any two years preceding the current calendar year and who are reasonably expected to receive at least $5,000 in compensation in the current calendar year are eligible to participate in a SIMPLE IRA plan. An employer may establish less restrictive eligibility requirements.

Contribution Limits

Currently, the maximum salary reduction contribution that may be made to a SIMPLE-IRA is $12,500 (2017).

If an employee is a participant in another employer sponsored retirement plan during a year, the total salary reductions, deferred compensation or elective deferrals under all employer sponsored plans is limited to $18,000 (2017).

Individuals 50 and over may also make catch-up elective deferrals to a SIMPLE plan. The additional amount which such individuals may defer is currently $3,000.

Employer Contributions

Under SIMPLE-IRA rules, the employer may choose to do one of the following:

1. the employer may match employee salary reduction contributions up to 3% of the employee's compensation, or
2. the employer may make nonelective contributions of 2% of compensation for each eligible employee who has at least $5000 in compensation (or a lower compensation amount, if the employer adopts a lower amount in the plan) for the year. Nonelective contributions must be made for all eligible employees, even if they do not make salary reduction contributions.

If matching salary reduction contributions are made, the employer must match at least one percent of compensation and the employer may not match less than 3% of compensation for more than two years during a five-year period. Notice must be given to employees of the reduced contribution in the 60 day period before the employer's calendar year (generally November 2 to December 31 if the calendar year starts on January

1). There are exceptions to the 60 day period; e.g. if the employer sets up the plan in mid-year.

SIMPLE 401(k) Plan

If an employer has a 100 or fewer employees who received $5,000 or more in compensation during the preceding year, the employer may establish a SIMPLE 401(k). The plan is similar to a 401(k) plan, except that it does not have to meet the nondiscrimination and top-heavy rules of qualified plans, if certain conditions are met. These conditions include:

- An employee can choose to have salary reduction contributions made to a trust, made up of a specified percentage of compensation up to $12,500 (2017).
- The employer must either make matching contributions up to 3% of compensation or make nonelective contributions of 2% of compensation on behalf of each eligible employee.
- No other contributions may be made to the trust.
- No other contributions may be made, and no benefits may accrue, for any other qualified plan sponsored by the employer on behalf of any employee eligible to participate in the SIMPLE 401(k) plan.
- The employee must have a nonforfeitable right to any contributions under the plan.

Qualified Defined Benefit or Pension Plans

Another type of qualified retirement plan is a *defined benefit* plan, also known as a pension plan. Defined benefit plans promise to pay a specified benefit upon a plan participant's retirement. The benefit is generally calculated by a formula that includes factors such as salary and length of service. Defined benefit plans were once the most popular type of retirement plan offered by an employer. However, establishing new plans has become less popular over the years because defined benefit plans can represent a significant investment for the employer and are subject to federal laws and regulations that cause them to be less flexible and more expensive to maintain than the other types of qualified retirement plans.

The Pension Benefit Guaranty Corporation (PBGC) was created under Employee Retirement Income

Security Act (ERISA) with the purpose of protecting pension benefits of defined benefit plans. The PBGC provides an insurance program that pays benefits up to an amount specified by law to insured participants whose plan ends without enough money to pay their benefits. The employers that sponsor defined benefit plans pay required premiums to the PBGC, and if the plan ends and cannot pay participant's benefits, the PBGC insurance covers their benefit claims.

Qualified Defined Contribution Plans

Defined contribution plans are currently the most common type of qualified retirement plan being established. Defined contribution plans include 401(k) plans, 403(b) plans, employee stock ownership plans (ESOPs), money purchase plans and profit-sharing plans. Defined contribution plans do not promise to pay a specific benefit upon retirement. Rather, the employer and/or the employee contribute to the plan, plan assets accumulate, and the employee determines how to distribute the plan assets to themselves, within legally required limits and amounts. The contributions are invested based on the specifications of the plan and the choices of the employee, and the amount available at retirement is based on the employee's accumulated assets within the plan.

General Requirements of Defined Benefit and Defined Contribution Plans

The basic requirements of establishing a qualified plan are:
- adopting an IRS approved written plan;
- establishing a structure for the investment of plan assets, whether by the company or by the individual participants;
- meeting the minimum funding requirements of the plan;
- not making any prohibited transactions;
- following all reporting requirements;
- following all distribution requirements; and
- administering the plan throughout the plan's life.

Many of the requirements applicable to qualified retirement plans are found in ERISA.

Defined Benefit Plan Minimum Funding Requirements

A defined benefit plan's funding amount requirements are based on the formula used in the plan to determine benefits. All defined benefit plans must generally make quarterly installment payments of 25% of the required contribution amounts.

The maximum amount for a defined benefit plan's benefit for a participant cannot exceed the lesser of:
- 100% of the participant's average compensation for the participant's highest three consecutive calendar years, or
- $215,000 (2017), subject to adjustment annually for inflation.

Defined Contribution Plan Minimum Funding Requirements

Under a defined contribution plan, contributions to the plan by employers and employees cannot exceed certain limits. Annual contributions to a defined contribution plan cannot exceed the lesser of:
- 100% of the participant's compensation, or
- $54,000 (2017), subject to adjustment annually for inflation.

The amount the employer can deduct for contributions to a defined contribution plan cannot be more than 25% of the compensation paid or accrued during the year to eligible employee participants. The maximum amount of compensation that can be included in this calculation for 2017 is $270,000, and this amount is subject to adjustment annually for inflation.

Other Qualified Plan Requirements
Participation and Eligibility

Generally, an employee is able to participate in a qualified retirement plan after one year of service or age 21, whichever is later.

Vesting

Participating in a plan means that the person is accruing hours of service, and may also mean the employer is contributing to and allocating plan assets on behalf of the person. Later, it can also mean the person is receiving benefits. A person who is participating in the plan is not always the same as a person who is *vested*. A person who is fully vested has nonforfeitable rights to benefits funded by the employer's contributions.

Profit Sharing and 401(k) Plans

Profit Sharing and 401(k) plans are all forms of defined contribution plans.

Profit-Sharing Plans

Profit-sharing plans must include a formula that is used to allocate the employer's plan contribution among plan participants. The plan must also include a formula for distributing the plan accumulations after employees reach a certain age, or after a specified number of years, and after other occurrences specified in the plan. Prototype profit-sharing plans that are approved by the IRS can generally be found through plan providers such as banks, insurance companies, mutual funds and similar entities. If a prototype plan is not used for a qualified plan, the plan must be submitted to the IRS for approval before it may be established. If the plan does not use a predetermined formula for determining the amount of profits to be shared (contribution amounts are discretionary), but there must be recurring and substantial contributions, and contributions must not be made so as to discriminate in favor of highly compensated employees.

Self-Employed Plans (Keogh Plans)

Keogh plans were once popular for high income self employed entrepreneurs, but today, most will use SEP IRAs due to them having less paperwork. The Keogh plan has two options: 1) Defined contribution or 2) Defined benefit. The defined contribution version has a maximum amount that can be contributed, which changes annually based on IRS calculations. The defined benefit option works like a traditional pension plan, though it is funded by the self employed

401(k) Plans

The 401(k) plan is "cash or deferred arrangement that allows contributions of before-tax compensation by employees."

Eligibility

401(k) plans cannot require that employees complete more than one year of service in order to be eligible for the plan. All corporations, partnerships and self-employed individuals may establish 401(k) plans. Employers with 100 or fewer employees who received $5,000 or more in compensation during the preceding year may establish a SIMPLE 401(k) plan.

401(k) Plan Contribution Limits

401(k) plan before-tax salary deferrals, or elective deferrals, are limited to $18,000 (2017).

Employers may make matching contributions on behalf of employees who make elective deferrals to 401(k) plans. The maximum annual addition, including elective deferrals, matching contributions and non-elective contributions, are subject to the limits for defined contribution plans: the lesser of 100% of compensation or $54,000. $270,000 of compensation may be taken into consideration for this limit. Employer deductible contributions are limited to 25 percent of eligible employee compensation.

Individuals 50 and over may make additional catch-up elective deferral amounts to defined contribution plans, including 401(k) plans. Currently the additional catch-up amount is $6,000 per tax year.

Investments

401(k) plans include various investment options for which the participant may choose. Fixed and variable annuities may be an option, as may be equity-index annuities. Mutual funds may also be offered, and some plans include investments that are specifically managed for the plan. Virtually any savings product may be included in a 401(k) plan's menu of investment options. Life insurance may be offered as an incidental benefit in the plan.

Section 403(b) Plans (TSA Plans)

A 403(b) plan, or a tax-sheltered annuity is a qualified plan for use of employees of non-profit organizations determined by Section 501(C)(3) of the Internal Revenue Code.

Eligibility

All of the following types of employees are eligible to participate in a 403(b) plans:

 VA PPL LH-2_16298

- Employees of tax-exempt organizations established under the provisions of Internal Revenue Code Section 501(c)(3).
- Employees of a public school system that are involved in the day-to-day operations of a school.
- Employees of a cooperative.
- Employees of hospital service organizations.
- Civilian faculty and staff of the Uniformed Services University of the Health Sciences (USUHS).
- Employees of public school systems organized by Indian tribal governments.
- Ministers who are employed by section 501(c)(3) organizations.
- Ministers who are self-employed.
- Ministers who are employed by organizations of that are not section 501(c)(3) organizations, who function as ministers in their day-to-day professional responsibilities with their employers and who do not share common religious bonds with their employers (for example, a chaplain in the armed forces).

Contributions

Elective deferrals, non-elective contributions and after-tax contributions are all allowed in 403(b) plans.

The maximum elective deferral amount for 403(b) plans is currently $18,000 and the catch-up contribution amount for those age 50 and over, like that to 401(k) plans, is $6,000.

The limit on total annual additions (the total of elective deferrals, non-elective contributions and after-tax contributions) that may be made in 2017 is the lesser of 100 percent of includible compensation for the most recent year of service, or $54,000. The employee's tax year is used to determine the most recent year of service for the purpose of calculating includable compensation, for most people the period from January through December. Includible compensation includes:

- Wages, salaries and fees earned with the employer who maintains the 403(b) plan
- Elective deferrals to the 403(b) plan
- Amounts contributed or deferred under a Section 125 cafeteria plan

- Income otherwise excluded under the foreign earned income exclusion
- The value of qualified transportation fringe benefits

Includible compensation does not include:

- Employer contributions to the 403(b) (nonelective contributions)
- Employer contributions to a qualified plan that are on behalf of the employee and are excludable from income by the employee
- The cost of incidental life insurance benefits

Distributions from Defined Contribution Plans

Required Beginning Date

Defined contribution plan distributions cannot generally be made from a plan until the employee:

- Reaches age 59 ½
- Separates from service
- Dies
- Becomes disabled
- Qualifies for a hardship withdrawal

Distributions from defined contribution plans and IRAs, other than Roth IRAs, must begin no later than April 1 of the year following the year in which the participant reaches age 70 ½, or if later, the year in which the participant retires. This date is known as the *required beginning date*.

Generally, distributions from a plan must be made by December 31 of a tax year. However, the first distribution may be made up until April 1 of the following tax year. If the first distribution is not made until April 1 of the following tax year, two distributions must be made in that year: one by April 1 and the other by December 31.

For example, Joan Smith, who is retired, turns 70 ½ in 2016. She may withdraw her first distribution (for the tax year 2016) from her 401(k) plan up until April 1, 2017. She must take a second distribution, for the tax year 2017, by December 31, 2017.

Annuity Distribution Rules

Rather than using the IRS life expectancy tables to calculate required minimum distributions, an annuity with a life expectancy contingency (straight life annuity, period certain and life annuity, joint life annuity, etc.) may be purchased

VA PPL LH-2_16298

from a life insurance company with the qualified plan accumulations.

Special Rules for Life Insurance
Taxation of Distributions

Generally, with defined benefit plans, employees do not have to include any of the employer's contributions to the plan in their income. However, if a plan is funded with life insurance, the employees must include in income the current economic benefit provided by life insurance. The insurer provides this amount to the employer so that each employee can be informed of the correct amount to include in income. This amount is known as the Table 2001 cost because this is the IRS table used to determine the amount includible in income.

If a lump sum distribution of plan benefits is taken upon termination or separation of service, all amounts are taxable except any cost basis, such as Table 2001 amounts previously included in income. Alternatively, the distribution may be rolled over into an IRA or another qualified employer plan to avoid current taxation. IRAs cannot accept life insurance, so the life insurance must be surrendered by the plan prior to rolling its value into an IRA.

If the employee dies while an active participant in the plan, and there is life insurance on the participant, the beneficiary receives the death benefit from the life insurance partially tax-free. The difference between the cash value and the death benefit is received income tax free. The cash value, less any taxes paid for the current economic benefit or Table 2001 costs, is taxed as ordinary income.

Distribution of Benefits

Distributions of life insurance benefits in a qualified plan can be taken in a few ways.

Lump Sum

If the cash values are taken as a lump sum, the entire amount, other than any Table 2001 costs included in income, is taxable.

Rollover

Alternatively, the policy may be surrendered while inside the plan and the cash values can then be rolled over to an IRA and the participant will avoid current taxation.

Transfer of Life Policy to the Participant

A third method is to have the qualified proceeds distributed as a stream of payments to the participant, and transfer any life insurance policies to the participant. Transfers of life insurance to a participant are taxable based on the cash value and the value of all rights under the policy.

Non-Qualified Deferred Compensation Plans

Under IRS regulations, a non-qualified deferred compensation plan is a plan established by an employer that provides for the deferral of compensation.

A non-qualified deferred compensation plan is a contractual agreement between the employer and employee that states that the employer will pay the employee a certain amount upon his or her retirement. The plan is not considered a qualified plan, and is therefore not subject to ERISA rules, as long as the employee has no rights to any accumulations in the plan.

Types of Non-Qualified Deferred Compensation Plans

There are two basic types of non-qualified deferred compensation plans: account balance plans and nonaccount balance plans.

Account Balance Plans

An account balance plan is a plan made up of a principal amount that is credited to an individual account, and all earnings on the principal amount are also credited to the account for that individual. Benefits from an account balance plan are strictly based on the value of the individual account. Account balance plans often include a vesting schedule, which may be of any length or design the employer desires.

Nonaccount Balance Plans

Nonaccount balance plans are plans that do not include individual accounts and do not base benefits on the amounts within such an account. Rather, benefits are based upon the terms of the deferred compensation plan.

Life Insurance in Non-Qualified Deferred Compensation Plans

Permanent life insurance is commonly used for non-qualified deferred compensation plans. Permanent life insurance is used because it includes tax-deferred growth of accumulations, cash values that may be accessed to pay retirement benefits, death benefits that may be used to pay the employee's beneficiaries and that can be used by the business to recoup its expenses in providing the plan. The employer pays the premium, owns the policy and is also named as beneficiary. The employee is named as insured. Upon the employee's retirement, the company pays the employee retirement amounts as stated in the non-deferred compensation agreement. Upon the death of the employee, the company receives the life insurance proceeds. If the employee passes away before retirement, the corporation makes payments as stipulated in the deferred compensation agreement to the deceased employee's beneficiaries.

When the business makes payments to the employee from corporate funds, the payments are deductible to the business. The payments are also taxable to the employee when they are paid.

Certain withdrawals may be made from the plan. The conditions for these withdrawals are carefully drawn up in the plan and are only allowed under specified conditions.

Life Insurance Needs Analysis and Suitability

Determining the Amount of Personal Life Insurance

An important question that producers resolve for their customers is how much life insurance the customer should purchase. The objective of life insurance is to protect beneficiaries from financial loss due to the death of the insured. The purchaser of life insurance needs to purchase sufficient amounts to meet this objective, keeping in mind affordability and utility of the life insurance product chosen.

Agents can assist the customer in determining the appropriate amount by going through an analysis of the customer's situation through a variety of available financial evaluation methods. Two of the most commonly used evaluation methods to determine life insurance amounts are the human life value approach and the needs approach.

Human Life Value Approach

The *human life value approach* is an economic estimate of human life value to determine the appropriate amount of life insurance to purchase. This computation does not reflect the value of affection a husband has for his wife, or vice-versa, and does not reflect the amount of love and care a parent has for a child. It's a dollar value that represents the financial loss an income earner's death will cause, based on anticipated earnings over a lifetime, to the income earner's family.

The human life value calculated for this purpose is the present value of the family's share of the deceased income earner's future earnings. The figure computed is basically the amount needed today, if invested at a reasonable, conservative rate, that will yield an annual income equal to the amount the income earner would have contributed to his or her family members' support.

For example, if a 25 year old plans to work until age 65, 40 years of income will be earned. If an average of $30,000 a year is made, this person will earn $1,200,000 over his or her lifetime. Looking at this figure, the human life value approach asks two questions:

- How much of the $1,200,000 ($30,000 for 40 years) will go to family support rather than going to pay for taxes, self-maintenance and insurance premiums?
- What is a reasonable rate of return if a lump sum were provided to family members today that will achieve the income that the deceased would have provided annually to the family members?

VA PPL LH-2_16298

Assume that after consideration, the agent and customer determine that the answer to question 1 is that $20,000 annually goes to family support, and the other $10,000 goes to taxes, insurance and self-maintenance. Assume that the answer to question 2 is that 4% is a reasonable rate of return.

Using a present value table, the number of years to retirement (n = 40) and the rate of 4% (called "the discount rate" in present value calculations), it is determined that $19.80 (rounded) invested today at 4% will yield $1 per year for 40 years. Multiplying $19.80 x $20,000, the family support annual figure, results in $396,000; if the family members received a lump sum of $396,000 today, invested it at 4%, it will provide annual income of $20,000 for 40 years. Therefore, the customer should purchase about $396,000 of life insurance.

# of Payments	Present Value of an Annuity of $1 Per Period for n Periods									
	4%	5%	6%	7%	8%	9%	10%	12%	14%	15%
1	0.9615	0.9524	0.9434	0.9346	0.9259	0.9174	0.9091	0.8929	0.8772	0.8696
2	1.8861	1.8594	1.8334	1.8080	1.7833	1.7591	1.7355	1.6901	1.6467	1.6257
3	2.7751	2.7232	2.6730	2.6243	2.5771	2.5313	2.4869	2.4018	2.3216	2.2832
4	3.6299	3.5460	3.4651	3.3872	3.3121	3.2397	3.1699	3.0373	2.9137	2.8550
5	4.4518	4.3295	4.2124	4.1002	3.9927	3.8897	3.7908	3.6048	3.4331	3.3522
6	5.2421	5.0757	4.9173	4.7665	4.6229	4.4859	4.3553	4.1114	3.8887	3.7845
7	6.0021	5.7864	5.5824	5.3893	5.2064	5.0330	4.8684	4.5638	4.2883	4.1604
8	6.7327	6.4632	6.2098	5.9713	5.7466	5.5348	5.3349	4.9676	4.6389	4.4873
9	7.4353	7.1078	6.8017	6.5152	6.2469	5.9952	5.7590	5.3282	4.9464	4.7716
10	8.1109	7.7217	7.3601	7.0236	6.7101	6.4177	6.1446	5.6502	5.2161	5.0188
11	8.7605	8.3064	7.8869	7.4987	7.1390	6.8052	6.4951	5.9377	5.4527	5.2337
12	9.3851	8.8633	8.3838	7.9427	7.5361	7.1607	6.8137	6.1944	5.6603	5.4206
13	9.9856	9.3936	8.8527	8.3577	7.9038	7.4869	7.1034	6.4235	5.8424	5.5831
14	10.5631	9.8986	9.2950	8.7455	8.2442	7.7862	7.3667	6.6282	6.0021	5.7245
15	11.1184	10.3797	9.7122	9.1079	8.5598	8.0607	7.6061	6.8109	6.1422	5.8474
16	11.6523	10.8378	10.1059	9.4466	8.8514	8.3126	7.8237	6.9740	6.2651	5.9542
17	12.1657	11.2741	10.4773	9.7632	9.1216	8.5436	8.0216	7.1196	6.3729	6.0472
18	12.6593	11.6896	10.8276	10.0591	9.3719	8.7556	8.2014	7.2497	6.4674	6.1280
19	13.1339	12.0853	11.1581	10.3356	9.6036	8.9501	8.3649	7.3658	6.5504	6.1982
20	13.5903	12.4622	11.4699	10.5940	9.8181	9.1285	8.5136	7.4694	6.6231	6.2593
25	15.6221	14.0939	12.7834	11.6536	10.6748	9.8226	9.0770	7.8431	6.8729	6.4641
30	17.2920	15.3725	13.7648	12.4090	11.2578	10.2737	9.4269	8.0552	7.0027	6.5660
40	19.7928	17.1591	15.0463	13.3317	11.9246	10.7574	9.7791	8.2438	7.1050	6.6418
50	21.4822	18.2559	15.7619	13.8007	12.2335	10.9617	9.9148	8.3045	7.1327	6.6605
60	22.6235	18.9293	16.1614	14.0392	12.3766	11.0480	9.9672	8.3240	7.1401	6.6651

If the producer plans to use the human life value approach, there are online calculators and software packages that allow plugging in:

1. Dollar amount of anticipated annual income earned dedicated to family support
2. Number of years until retirement

The calculator or software will provide the suggested amount of insurance based on human value of life. (For example, see: http://www.lifehappens.org/human-life-value-calculator/). The insurer may provide software tools to the producer to assist in providing this analysis.

 VA PPL LH-2_16298

A weakness with this method is that none of the factors in the calculation are absolutely known. Number of years to retirement, amount of anticipated annual income and reasonable rate of return are all based on assumptions and are estimates. However, proponents of this method believe it provides a sound basis for deriving a reasonable amount of insurance that an income earner should purchase to protect a family.

Needs Approach

When determining the amount of life insurance to purchase through the **needs approach**, the producer assists the customer in defining expenditures that will occur throughout life, and then subtracts from that amount the amount of assets available to meet these expenses. As with the human life value approach, there are financial planning software packages that assist in assembling the information needed for this analysis and that will do the "number crunching" necessary to come up with a suggested amount. (Perform the search "how much life insurance do I need" on your favorite internet search engine and many online calculators based on a needs analysis will be found. For example: http://www.life happens.org/life-insurance-needs-calculator/.)

Basically, the needs approach analysis may be accomplished by creating a budget of expenses by category, subtotaling the expenses and then listing offsetting assets.

To exercise due care in this process, factors an agent should consider in this analysis include the following:

Capital Needs for Family Income

Family income needs are considered on a case by case basis when determining life insurance amounts. The number of income earners that are currently supporting the family and will be supporting the family throughout child rearing years is an important difference among families and is crucial to the needs analysis. In some families, two spouses work throughout their lives together. In others, both work until children are born, then one reduces or stops earning income. In still others, one income earner supports the family throughout their lifetimes together. If one income is relied upon and then ceases, experts suggest that most families will be able to maintain their standard of living with about 75% of the former breadwinner's income. However, the ability to live on this reduced income amount may not occur immediately upon the death of the income earner.

There may be a transition period where the surviving spouse must look for a job, or determine what unnecessary expenses to eliminate. This transition period should be considered in the needs analysis.

Capital Needs for Debt Repayment

Typical debts to consider when determining life insurance needs include home mortgages, credit cards, bank loans, business debt, etc. A decision can be made whether the amount of life insurance purchased will be used to eliminate all debt or to set aside some of the life insurance proceeds as a sinking fund, such as placing it in an income producing investment vehicle, to pay off the debt over time.

Other Capital Needs

This might include emergency reserve funds, estimated to be between 50 percent and 100 percent of an income earner's annual after-tax income, and possible college education funds for surviving children.

Capital Needs to Pay for Estate Settlement

Final expenses can be significant. Uninsured medical costs and funeral expenses are one aspect. In addition, there are federal and state death taxes. Although the Economic Recovery Tax Act of 1981 eliminated the federal estate tax on property passed to a surviving spouse, the estate of the second spouse to die may face a large death tax liability on a federal level and state death taxes may apply.

Subtotal These Capital Needs

These capital needs are all totaled to come up with the total capital needs of the family based on the income earners' contribution.

Current Assets Available for Income Production

Subtracted from the total capital needs are the current assets, such as savings accounts, investments, real estate, pension plans, etc., that are

VA PPL LH-2_16298

available for income production or liquidity needs identified in the capital needs analysis thus far.

Net Capital Needs

From this, the agent arrives at the net capital needed to be replaced by life insurance.

Where the capital needs analysis indicate that a $500,000 gap will occur at the death of the income earner(s), the agent's life insurance recommendation should be for $500,000 of life insurance. Anything less could leave the client underinsured. An agent's duty to the customer is to provide sound advice, based on due care such as this type of analysis, concerning real life insurance needs. Lesser amounts may be purchased where the client cannot afford the premiums or makes the choice to carry less. A client, for example, may have chronic health concerns and may need to plan to spend dollars allocated to insurance for higher cost health care or long-term care coverage and so cannot purchase as much life insurance as a client without such health concerns.

On-going monitoring of capital needs is necessary to plan for new client objectives, repositioning of debt, inflation, estate settlement changes and potential health problems that may prohibit coverage in the future.

The needs analysis as described assumes that the average customer buying personal life insurance has or will have a family with children. This is true – the average customer in the personal insurance markets does purchase insurance to provide for that customer's family needs. However, single persons and childless couples also have a need for life insurance. Single persons and childless couples may also support family members, or may have charities that they want to support. They have debt that they do not want others to bear upon their deaths. The needs analysis process may be utilized to determine all customers' needs for personal life insurance coverage. The elements in the analysis and calculation will vary based on the customers' lifestyles.

Lump Sum Life Insurance Needs vs. Income Needs

Life insurance proceeds may be received as a lump sum or may be received over time as income. The best method to receive life insurance proceeds depends on the clients' circumstances. When a person is named as a beneficiary on a life insurance policy, as a beneficiary, the person may select whether the proceeds will be received as a lump sum or as income over time. Only if the owner of the policy sets up certain trusts and places the policy in the trust may the owner dictate the way the policy proceeds are paid to beneficiaries. The owner must define the payout structure at the time of setting up the trust or the owner retains tax liability. Unless such a trust exists, generally, each beneficiary on a life insurance policy determines how his or her share of the proceeds is paid to that beneficiary. This right is given to the beneficiary because the life proceeds are the property of the beneficiary upon the death of the insured, and the beneficiary is liable for tax ramifications, if any, of the payout method chosen.

However, even though the beneficiary chooses the payout option upon death, this does not mean these options shouldn't be discussed prior to the insured's death. Spouses may want to discuss together how the life insurance proceeds will be paid out upon the death of the first spouse to die, based on their lifetime financial goals. Parents may want to discuss this with children, whether minors or adults so that they understand the goals and objectives the parents have in mind when setting up the life insurance plan.

Generally, life insurance death proceeds may be taken as a lump sum immediately upon the death of the insured, may be left on deposit with the insurance company and taken later, or may be taken as income over the lifetime of the beneficiary or for a specified period of time, such as from five to twenty years or more. The lump sum could be placed in another insurance product, or in an investment vehicle. These options should be weighed when determining whether a surviving spouse or dependent will use the death proceeds to pay off debt immediately or over time, whether a college fund will be set up from the proceeds, whether the money will be used to provide retirement income, etc.

 VA PPL LH-2_16298

Retirement Benefits

Retirement benefits must be earned and accumulated in order to provide retirement income for an income earner or surviving beneficiaries. Generally, a surviving spouse is the beneficiary on a qualified retirement plan, such as a 401(k). Only if a spouse waives in writing the right to be named primary beneficiary on qualified retirement plans may a different primary beneficiary be named. In planning for life insurance, an income earner should take into account how much money will be set aside for retirement and how large a retirement account will be available for survivors upon his or her death.

Retirement benefits may generally be paid to retirees in regular monthly payments, or may be taken by withdrawals at times determined by the retiree. A certain amount must be taken annually upon retirement age, generally age 65, as dictated by the qualified retirement plan's legal requirements and plan structure.

If retirement contributions were placed into a qualified plan on a pre-tax basis, such as through salary reduction from each paycheck, when the retirement distributions are made, they are taxable to the retiree. If the retirement vehicle used was a Roth IRA, distributions made from the Roth IRA may be non-taxable to the retiree.

Other Assets and Life Insurance Amounts

Besides Social Security and retirement benefits, the presence of other assets impact the need for life insurance. For example, rental income, income from a court settlement, or income from bonds should be accounted for when determining the need for life insurance. Nonretirement savings accounts, mutual fund accumulations, stocks and other securities should be included as resources that can be used to pay for the support of survivors and to meet financial objectives after an insured passes away.

Suitability Analysis

An important part of the agent's function in underwriting is determining a suitable life insurance product for the client. Many elements are included in determining a client's suitability. These include the age of the client, the tax status of the client, what type of investments the client already owns, the investment objectives of the client and the net worth and overall financial health of the client.

Determining Client Needs – Basic Information

The first part of a needs analysis generally focuses on basic information about the client. The insurer generally provides a needs analysis worksheet to collect this information. The agent will ask for the client's full name, address, occupation, marital status, number and age of minor children, and age of the client, for example. This basic information can help the agent begin to see certain potential needs of the customer. For example:

Marital status	may indicate	financial protection for loved ones
Age	the need	retirement and long term planning
Occupation	for	supplemental health coverage

However, the agent needs more information before the agent may make any judgments about potential product needs.

VA PPL LH-2_16298

Sample Needs Assessment Questionnaire

I. Personal Information

1. Customer Name _____
2. Customer Address _____
3. Customer Phone Number
   Day: _____ Evenings: _____
4. Customer Birth Date _____
5. Customer Occupation _____
6. Customer Marital Status _____
7. Number and Age of Dependent Children Living at Home _____

II. Financial Information

8. Estimated Net Worth (not including primary residence) _____
9. Value of Primary Residence _____
10. Monthly Income from Employment _____
11. Monthly Income from Retirement Plans (Identify Each Source and Amount) _____
12. Other Income: Income Amount and Source _____
13. Marginal Tax Bracket _____

III. Current Savings and Insurance

14. Mutual Funds: Fund Company, Objective, Amount _____
15. Bank Certificates of Deposit: Maturity, Interest Rate and Amount _____
16. Life Insurance in Force: Company, Type of Policy, Face Value and Cash Value _____
17. Annuities in force: Company, Type, Accumulated Value and Yield _____
18. Individual Stocks: Company and Amount _____
19. Individual Bonds: Type and Amount _____
20. Other Investments (e.g., real estate): Type and Value _____
21. Investments previously held but now liquidated: Type, when held, why liquidated _____

IV. Risk Tolerance

22. Able to tolerate significant degree of fluctuation in return for opportunity for high return _____
23. Able to tolerate some fluctuation of principal in return for opportunity for moderate return _____
24. Conservation of principal is primary consideration _____
    Comments: _____

V. Financial Plans

25. Retirement Savings: Type of plan, how long has it been in existence, value, amount and frequency of current contributions, satisfaction level, concerns and questions _____
26. Estate planning: Will? Living Trust? Testamentary Trusts? Key objectives of these tools, satisfaction level, concerns and questions _____

VI. Goals

27. Short-term (1-5 year): Financial goals, amount needed. _____
28. Intermediate term (5-10 year): Financial goals, amount needed _____
29. Long-term (10+): Financial goals, amount needed

COMMENTS: _____

Financial Information

After basic information is gathered from the client, the agent generally asks for financial information from the client. Sometimes a client is hesitant to give this information to the agent. If so, the agent may explain that client information is held confidentially and that the agent has a responsibility to the client to understand his or her financial situation in order to give the best advice possible. The notice of privacy practices is generally provided to a client when the needs analysis is done and helps explain that information is kept confidential. If a client absolutely will not provide financial information, generally the agent should explain to the client that the agent may have to suspend the interview until such time as the client is willing to provide this information. A good insurance decision cannot be made without information about the client's financial situation. Or the agent may have the client sign a statement that the client declined to offer this information and yet wanted to purchase insurance. Trying to assist

VA PPL LH-2_16298

a client with a life insurance product without knowledge of the client's financial situation can compromise the agent's responsibilities to the client, so it is important to ask and to document the results of the question.

Generally, the agent will need to know the client's net worth. The agent may ask for an item-by-item list of the clients' assets and liabilities, or may just ask for a net worth figure from the client. Another critical piece of financial information is the tax status of the client. The agent will generally find out into which tax bracket the client falls.

Current Investments

A third area that the agent may explore is that of the current investments and financial plans of the client. The agent may ask for an inventory of the mutual funds, certificates of deposit, insurance products, individual stocks and bonds, and any other financial products the customer owns. If the agent finds that the client owns any life insurance products, it is important that the agent follow required replacement notice procedures, including providing all appropriate disclosures.

The agent may also ask if there were investments the client previously owned but are currently liquidated. The agent may ask if the client was dissatisfied with these liquidated products, and if so, why? Finding out what type of products a client uses or has used helps the agent to understand the financial experience of the client and the types of products the client will utilize or not utilize.

Related to discovering the types of financial products a client currently owns and has owned is determining the risk tolerance of a client.

Current Plans

The agent may then proceed to asking questions about the kind of financial planning the client has undertaken so far. For example, the agent will ask about retirement plans, estate planning, whether a will is in place, and so on.

Goals

Another area of questioning involves learning about the client's goals, both short-term and long-term.

Short-term goals	Long-term goals
Vacation	College educations
Purchasing home	Retirement Income
Renovating home	Paying off mortgage
Purchasing car or RV	Paying off other debt

Besides discussing goals, the agent will ask whether the client believes major changes in his or her life are coming, such as children getting married, an elderly parent coming to live at the client's home, or the client's own marriage or remarriage.

Providing Product Suggestions

Once the agent has completed the fact-finding process with the client, the agent may be ready to discuss specific products and plans that may meet the client's needs. Or, the agent may want to spend time analyzing the information gleaned from the discussion with the client, and meet with the client in a few days or in the next week to discuss the agent's recommendations. Whenever the agent begins to discuss product and plan options with the client, the agent has a responsibility to provide clear and accurate information about the programs discussed. It is important for the agent to explain both the risks and benefits of any product or plan offered to the client.

Depending upon what product the agent is offering or in what environment the agent works within, the agent may be required to provide specific disclosures to the client regarding the product.

Examples of disclosures	
Solicitation	**Disclosure Types**
Customers of a bank	Insurance products are not FDIC insured
Variable products	Prospectus and notices required by securities regulations
Life insurance with long-term care benefits	Notice of taxes and conditions for long-term care benefits
Life insurance and annuities	Replacement notices if replacement is involved

Documentation

Whether or not the client actually purchases the product offered, the agent should keep a detailed record of the information gathered from meetings with the client, and the documentation, brochures and other information shared with the client about the product. The agent should keep copies of documents noting what product suggestions the agent made that the client declined, in case there is ever a question of whether appropriate product was suggested. Copies of signed disclosures, the application, the fact-finding document, and any other customer-related forms, should be kept on file by the agent. Appropriate copies of documentation must be left with the client, and other copies sent to the insurer, as required by insurer company procedure and the law. The agent's file will not only help the agent should there ever be a question about the suitability of the agent's recommendations by a regulator, the insurer or the client, but will also assist the agent in his or her ongoing relationship with the client.

Business Needs and Life Insurance

Business Continuation and Buy-Sell Agreements

It is the goal of most business owners that their businesses continue.

Owners need financing for businesses to continue ...		
while they are operating them	so that	they can continue to derive revenue and enjoyment from them
after they retire		they can sell them and earn income from the sale, or a relative or loved one can operate them
during an extended sickness or disability		they provide income for their families and employees
after death of all owners		they support beneficiaries or are sustained by surviving owners
after sickness, disability, retirement or death of one owner		remaining owners can continue their operations

Business continuation insurance is insurance that assists a business in meeting this goal of keeping the business going in the face of death, disability or retirement of an owner in the business. The primary method used to meet this goal is through a *buy-sell agreement*, which is an agreement between the owners of a business that addresses the retirement, disability or death, and even the divorce or bankruptcy of an owner, and provides for a method of meeting the financial needs that occur upon any of these events. Both life insurance and disability insurance may be used in conjunction with these agreements.

Another form of insurance that helps a business to continue is known as *key employee* or *key person* insurance. Life insurance is used to provide funds should a key employee, meaning an employee that has a direct impact on the revenues of the business, passes away or becomes disabled. The insurance may even be utilized should the key employee terminate his employment with the firm.

Life Insurance in Business Markets

The primary life insurance tool used in business markets insurance is permanent life insurance that builds cash values. There are several types of permanent life insurance that a business may choose from. The type that is best for the business depends on the objectives the company has for the insurance, such as whether it believes it will access cash values through loans or withdrawals during the life of the policy, or whether the death benefit is the most crucial aspect. The risk tolerance of those making the insurance decision also plays an important role, since some insurance products include non-guaranteed returns.

Buy-Sell Agreements

A buy-sell agreement arranges for the purchase of a deceased, retired or disabled owner's interest in the business by the other owners or principal shareholders. A buy-sell agreement is an agreement, generally between owners or key shareholders of a business, to purchase the interest of the other owners or shareholders should an owner or shareholder die, retire, or become totally disabled. Buy-sell agreements may also address the eventuality of an owner becoming divorced or going bankrupt, the loss of license or professional designation of an owner and partner, or a potential buy-out by a third party. Each of the potential events covered in a buy-sell agreement are known as *trigger events*.

Buy-sell agreements include provisions for determining the value of a business, called valuation provisions. Common valuation provisions in buy-sell agreements provide for:

- Including a specified dollar amount to be paid
- Including a specified method to establish the value of the business
- Using an appraisal to establish the business' value
- Using the capitalization of net earnings method of valuation

Life insurance and disability income are both often used in conjunction with buy-sell agreements. Policies are structured so that the death proceeds can be used to purchase the deceased owner's or shareholder's interest in the business from the deceased's estate, or disability income payments may be used to replace business income generated by the disabled owner. Permanent life insurance is generally used for buy-sell agreements so that the business also has the flexibility to borrow against the policy.

Life Insurance in Buy-Sell Agreements

Life insurance is the primary tool used in buy-sell agreements. Permanent life insurance rather than term is used, so that the business can access the policy's cash values if it needs them. Participating life insurance policies that pay dividends in the form of paid-up additions to coverage may be used, so that the policy coverage amount increases over time to keep up with the value of the business.

Stock Redemption Buy-Sell Agreement

Under a stock redemption buy-sell agreement, also known as an entity purchase buy-sell agreement, a life insurance policy is purchased on the life of each owner. If the owner dies, the life insurance proceeds are used to purchase the shares of the deceased owner from his or her heirs. If the owner retires, or one of the other trigger events in the buy-sell agreement occurs, cash values may be used to supply funds to buy the shares. Under this plan, the insurance is paid for by the business, and the insurance is considered an asset of the business.

Policy Structure:

Owner: Business
Insured: Owner
Beneficiary: Business

Since the business owns the policy, creditors may attach the policy as they could with any other asset owned by the company.

Cross Purchase Buy-Sell Agreement

Under a cross-purchase buy-sell agreement, the owners of the business each purchase a policy on the life of the other owners. Upon the occurrence of a triggering event, the cash values or death proceeds are used by the owner who purchased the policy to purchase the portion of the business owned by the deceased.

Policy Structure:

Owner: Business Owner A
Insured: Business Owner B
Beneficiary: Business Owner A

Because the business owners own the policies, the creditors of the business would generally be unable to attach the policies set up in this manner. However, because business funds are not used to purchase the policies, the premiums are not deductible from the business for tax purposes.

This kind of arrangement is normally best for companies with two or three owners. Otherwise, each owner would have to purchase so many policies that the plan would not be economically or administratively feasible.

No-Sell Buy-Sell Agreements

A no-sell buy-sell agreement may be used in circumstances when the owners do not want the business to be sold upon the death of the owner. Each owner of the business is given one voting share and ninety-nine non-voting shares. In a cross purchase buy-sell agreement, the owners agree that upon the death of an owner, the remaining owners will purchase the voting share, and the remaining shares will be passed on to the owner's heirs.

An irrevocable life insurance trust is also used in this type of arrangement. The owners, the business or both, gift amounts to the trust annually and the trust pays the premium on a policy on the life of that owner equal to the value of the insured owner's share in the business. Upon an owner's death, the life insurance proceeds are paid to his or her beneficiaries.

VA PPL LH-2_16298

Policy Structure:
Owner: Irrevocable Life Insurance Trust
Insured: Owner
Beneficiary: Owner's Heir(s)

If the business pays premiums to the owner who then gifts them to the trust, the premiums may be considered compensation, and are therefore deductible for tax purposes by the business. However, gifts made by the owner to the trust are not deductible to the owner for tax purposes.

Wait and See Buy-Sell Agreement

A wait and see buy-sell agreement provides more than one method of disposing of an owner's shares. A life insurance policy is purchased by the business on the life of each owner. Under this type of agreement, upon an owner's death, the business could use the death proceeds to purchase the deceased owner's share of the business, could loan the proceeds to surviving owners to purchase the deceased owner's share, or could purchase the share's from the deceased owner's estate, through a Section 303 Redemption.

The insurance policy under such a plan may be structured so that a) the business is the owner and beneficiary, or b) the owners purchase policies on the life of the other owners, as under a cross purchase agreement, and upon the death of the insured, could loan the proceeds to the business to fund a purchase of the deceased's shares.

Policy Structure a):
Owner: Business
Insured: Owner
Beneficiary: Business

Policy Structure b):
Owner: Owner A
Insured: Owner B
Beneficiary: Owner A

Third Party Buy-Out Agreement

In some cases, a third party will purchase an owner's shares upon the death of that owner. In this case, a third party buy-out agreement is made. Under this agreement, a life insurance policy is purchased by the third-party on the life of the owner. Upon the death of the owner, the third-party uses the proceeds to purchase the deceased owner's shares.

Third party buy-out agreements are also known as one-way buy-sell agreements, since the third party will be buying the business, but the business will not under any conditions be buying anything from the third party.

Policy Structure:
Owner: Third Party
Insured: Owner
Beneficiary: Third Party

Key Employee or Key Person Insurance

Certain employees or owners have a significant impact on a company's success. Individuals such as key salespeople, the head of research and development or the creator of new technology all fit into this category. Should such a person pass away, the business may suffer significant financial loss due to the loss of their expertise, and often must also spend extensive amounts in order to replace such an individual. Life insurance may be purchased that can protect a business against the financial loss from the death of a key employee.

Many businesses purchase key employee insurance based on the recognition of potential financial loss. Others may have pressure from business relationships to purchase such insurance. *For example, creditors may require that the business purchase this insurance so that loans will be paid off upon the key employee's death. Shareholders or partners may also require that this insurance be purchased in order to protect their investment in the business.*

As with life insurance purchased for buy-sell agreements, permanent life insurance is generally purchased so that the business has the flexibility of accessing cash values, if needed. The amount of insurance purchased depends upon the financial contribution the employee makes, and how long it may take the business to replace the employee. *For example, if a salesperson contributes $1,000,000 in gross revenue annually to the business, and the business assumes it will take up to 24 months to hire and train a replacement, the business may purchase up to a $2,000,000 policy. If the revenue the salesperson brings in is significantly offset by travel and other related expenses, a smaller policy may be appropriate.*

If the key employee to be insured is a technical expert, the amount of insurance needed must take into consideration the loss of revenue from his or her expertise, and the length of time it will take to replace such a person, as well as the length of time it will take the replacement to reach the financial contribution level of the deceased expert.

The policy structure of a key employee policy lists the business as owner and as beneficiary on the policy, and the key employee as the insured. The business pays the premium, which is generally a deductible expense for the business.

Businesses may have more than one key employee. In such a case, first-to-die or joint life insurance may be used. Under this type of policy, two or more insureds are named. Upon the first-to-die of the insureds, the policy pays a death benefit. A guaranteed insurability rider may be added to the policy so that a new policy may be written on the lives of the surviving insureds upon the death of the first-to-die.

Change of Insured Provision

Some joint life policies written for key person purposes also allow the business the option to continue the policy, rather than having the policy pay out at the death of the insured first-to-die. Policies may also include a *change of insured provision*, which allows the business to replace insureds as needed, upon evidence of insurability.

Executive Incentive Plans

An executive incentive plan is utilized to reward and keep employees who command top salaries and who may be wooed by other firms throughout their careers. Executive incentive plans may be in the form of an executive bonus plan, a split-dollar plan, or a deferred compensation plan.

A *split-dollar plan* is an insurance arrangement where two parties, generally employer and employee, split the cost of premiums. Split-dollar arrangements may also include the splitting of cash values, dividends and the death benefit.

Executive Bonus Plans

Executive bonus plans, also known as Section 162 plans, utilize a permanent life insurance policy. The business purchases the policy for the executive through the use of a bonus plan and the executive is named as insured on the policy. The owner of the policy may be the executive or the executive's spouse. The executive names the beneficiaries on the policy.

Because the insurance is purchased through a bonus plan, the payments are considered compensation to the executive. The business may therefore generally deduct these amounts for tax purposes. As compensation, the executive must pay taxes on these amounts as well.

Because permanent life insurance is used, the executive may take loans or withdrawals from the policy. The executive may also take the policy with him or her should the executive leave the firm. Of course, future premium payments are then the responsibility of the executive.

Executive bonus plans are not subject to IRS rules regarding welfare benefit plans, as most employee benefit plans are. This means that the employer need not meet eligibility requirements such as including all employees in the plan, and that the plan does not have caps regarding the amount of bonus that may be paid. The plan also does not have any restrictions regarding what type of product may be used in conjunction with the plan.

Social Security Benefits and Taxation

Social Security was created in 1935 for the purpose of helping a small number of citizens get through hard times. The use of the program has changed markedly since then, so that now Social Security is a major source of income for two-thirds of the elderly and practically the only source of income for the remaining third.

Taxation of social security benefits is calculated by first determining the base amount. The base amount, called provisional income in the IRS regulations, is defined as "adjusted gross income (excluding taxable Social Security benefits) plus tax-exempt interest, certain excluded foreign source income, and one-half of the taxpayer's Social Security benefits." If provisional income is less than a certain amount, no portion of Social Security benefits are taxable. If provisional income falls within a certain range, Social Security benefits are 50% taxable, and if provisional income is above a certain point, Social Security benefits are 85% taxable.

Currently, for a married couple filing jointly, if provisional income is under $32,000, no Social Security benefits are subject to taxation. If provisional income lies between $32,000 and $44,000, up to 50% of Social security benefits are taxable. And up to 85% of social security benefits are taxable if provisional income is over $44,000.

For the individual filing single, generally, if provisional income is less than $25,000, Social Security Benefits are not taxable. If provisional income is $25,000 to $34,000, up to 50% of Social Security Benefits are taxable. If provisional income is over $34,000, up to 85% of Social Security Benefits are taxable.

Placing money in a tax-deferred annuity can reduce provisional income and so reduce tax liability. The effect of placing money in a tax-deferred annuity is most pronounced if the customer's provisional income is reduced so that his exposure to taxation is reduced from 85% of benefits to 50%; or from 50% to 0%.

For example, assume John and Mary Smith receive $12,000 a year in Social Security benefits. None of their investment assets is in tax-deferred annuities; all of their investments are generating taxable or tax-exempt income. Their pensions and investment income total an additional $39,000 each year.

This gives them provisional income of $45,000 ($39,000 plus one-half of $12,000). The Smith's CPA calculated the amount of their Social Security benefits will be included in gross income, and will therefore be subject to income tax, will be $6,850 (85% of this amount will be taxed).

Now, assume instead that John and Mary Smith receive $12,000 a year in Social Security benefits. Their pension and investment incomes total $39,000. They don't need all of their Social Security benefits, pension and investment income to meet their current living expenses. They are able to move $33,333 from a taxable investment earning 6% (equates to $2000/year in income) to a tax-deferred annuity. This leaves them with pensions and investment income of $37,000 a year, making their total provisional income $43,000 ($37,000 plus one-half of

$12,000). The Smith's CPA calculated the amount of their Social Security benefits that will be included in gross income, and will therefore be subject to income tax, will be $5,500 (50% of this amount will be taxed).

Tax Treatment of Insurance Premiums, Proceeds and Dividends
Individual Life Insurance
Cash Value Increases

Earnings that accumulate on a policy's cash value are not taxable while they remain in the policy. If withdrawn, however, they are taxable. Generally, life insurance policy withdrawals are considered to be comprised of cost basis prior to earnings for tax purposes.

Dividends

Generally, dividends from life policies are considered a return of excess premium paid, and are therefore not taxable. If interest is earned on dividends, such as when they are accrued during the year, held by the insurance company and paid out annually, the interest is taxable.

Loans

Loans from non-MEC policies are not taxable. Interest on policy loans is not deductible if the loan is from a policy issued under a personal or non-business situation. In some cases, policy loan interest may be deductible for a trade or business of if loan proceeds are used for an investment or passive activity interest.

Surrender of Cash Value

The tax treatment applied to a surrender or withdrawal from a life insurance policy depends on the age of the insurance policy and whether or not a policy is considered a MEC. If a policy is a life insurance policy and is not a MEC, withdrawals are generally received tax-free until the cost basis of the policy has been distributed. In other words, principal in the cash value life insurance policy is considered to be withdrawn before interest. An exception to this general rule occurs when a withdrawal causes a reduction in the face amount or death benefit and the withdrawal and reduction occur within fifteen years of policy issue. Under such circumstances, the withdrawal will be treated as consisting of interest, and therefore is taxable, up to a ceiling amount found in the IRS Code.

A MEC is a life insurance policy that does not meet the *seven-pay test* found in Internal Revenue Code Section 7702, or is a policy received in exchange for a MEC. Withdrawals and surrenders from MECs are taxed as being made up of earnings prior to cost basis.

Taxation of Accelerated Death Benefit Riders and Viatical Settlements

Certain amounts paid as accelerated death benefits under a life insurance contact or a viatical settlement before the insured's death are excluded from income if the insured is terminally ill or chronically ill. This gives these accelerated death benefits the same tax treatment as a life insurance death benefit, which is generally not taxable to the beneficiary who receives the death benefit.

If the insured meets the definition of chronically ill, the accelerated death benefits paid on the basis of costs incurred for qualified long-term care services are fully excludable from income for tax purposes. If the accelerated death benefit is paid on a per day basis, such as $125 per day as long as the insured meets the payment trigger requirements in the contract, the amounts are excludable up to a limit.

Qualified long-term care services means necessary diagnostic, preventive, therapeutic, curing, treating, mitigating, and rehabilitative services, and maintenance or personal care services, which are required by a chronically ill individual, and are provided pursuant to a plan of care prescribed by a licensed health care practitioner.

The definitions of terminally ill and chronically ill as found in IRS Publication 554, *Tax Guide for Seniors*, is the same definition provided in the course within the topic "Accelerated Death Benefits" within the chapter "Policy Riders, Provisions, Options and Exclusions."

Personal care is a form of long-term care that is on-medical care consisting of helping with personal needs such as bathing, dressing, walking, and assistance with other ADLs. It is also known as *custodial care.*

Amounts Received by the Beneficiary

General Rules and Exceptions

In general:
- life insurance death benefits are received tax-free to beneficiaries;
- earnings in life insurance policies grow tax-deferred;
- loans may be received tax-free from life insurance policies; and
- accumulated earnings in deferred annuity death benefits are taxable to the beneficiary.

However, there are many exceptions to these general statements. The structure of the policy – both in terms of the ownership construct and the premiums paid in relation to the death benefit amount – determines the policy's tax treatment.

Settlement Options

Death benefits from life insurance policies may be received in a lump sum by beneficiaries upon the insured's death or via a settlement option that pays the lump sum at a later date, that pays interest only or that provides income for the life of the beneficiary. Other options include installments for a fixed period, or as a fixed amount. The tax ramification arising from each of these options is slightly different. As each of the settlement options are described next, the settlement option's tax treatment, including exceptions, is explained.

Lump Sum at Insured's Death

A death benefit paid upon the insured's death to a beneficiary is excluded from the gross income of the beneficiary for tax purposes. If there is any interest paid to the beneficiary that accrued after the insured's death, the interest is taxable to the beneficiary. *For example, assume a death benefit of $100,000 is payable upon the insured's death to his daughter. The date of death was May 1. The insurer, due to the time it takes to submit and process the death claim, cuts the check to the daughter on August 1 of the same year. The insurer pays 4% interest on the $100,000 death benefit for the period from May 2 through August 1, resulting in a little over $650 in interest earnings that are taxable to the daughter as beneficiary.*

Lump Sum at a Later Date

A beneficiary may decide to leave a lump sum death benefit on deposit with a life insurance company to be taken at a later date. This is not uncommon when a beneficiary wants to delay making a decision about what to do with the insurance benefit while adjusting to the death of the insured. The interest earned while the money is on deposit with the insurer is taxable to the beneficiary and the policy death benefit is excludable from the beneficiary's income, regardless of when it is received.

Interest Only

A death benefit or settlement option available to a beneficiary is to take interest only from a death benefit and leave the death benefit proceeds on deposit with the insurance company. Interest is taxable as earned on the deposited amount. When the death benefit amount is taken by the beneficiary, it is not taxable.

Life Income

Another settlement option available to a beneficiary is to have the death benefit payable in installments over his or her life. When installment payments are made, a formula found in the Internal Revenue Code is used to determine the excludable amount of each payment. The includable amount is the portion of each payment that is attributable to the earnings on the death benefit.

Basically, the formula used to determine the taxable and non-taxable portion of each payment first involves calculating the amount held by the insurer, which under a settlement option is generally the amount of the death benefit, and dividing that amount by the expected return to be paid by the insurer. This calculation results in the *exclusion ratio*. The second step of the formula is to calculate the number of years in the payment period, which under a life installment option is the life expectancy of the beneficiary. The third step of the calculation involves multiplying the exclusion ratio by the installment payment amount. The result is the non-taxable, or excludable, amount of each payment. This calculation is also used for annuity income payments to determine taxable amounts.

If the beneficiary outlives the payment period based on life expectancy, payments become all interest, and therefore are taxable. If the beneficiary chooses a life income with refund installment option and does not outlive the life expectancy payment period, the amount of the death benefit that has not been paid out will be paid to the secondary beneficiary as a tax-free death benefit.

Fixed Period

A fixed period settlement option pays out the death benefit in installments over a fixed period, and if the beneficiary dies during that period, will continue payments for the period to the secondary beneficiary. Note that who that secondary beneficiary is depends on the beneficiary structure determined by the policyholder. It is possible the primary beneficiary may name his or her own beneficiary, or that the terms of the contract require the payments to be made to a secondary beneficiary already specified by the beneficiary structure in place at the time of the insured's death. The taxable and non-taxable portion of each payment is determined as described earlier, except that the number of years in the payment period will be equal to the fixed period rather than the beneficiary's life expectancy. The earnings portion of each payment is taxable to the person entitled to receive it: the primary beneficiary during his or her life, or the secondary beneficiary should the primary beneficiary pass away during the fixed payment period.

Fixed Amount

Under a fixed amount settlement option, the beneficiary requests a fixed amount, and based on that amount, the amount of the death benefit, and the rate of return paid by the insurance company, the number of payments are determined. The taxable and non-taxable portion of each payment is determined using these figures in the IRS prescribed formula. If the beneficiary dies during the period in which payments are guaranteed, the secondary beneficiary will receive the fixed amount payments. The portion subject to taxation of each payment to the secondary beneficiary continues to be the same as that which was subject to taxation when paid to the primary beneficiary.

Group Life Insurance

Group Term Life Insurance

Group term life insurance premiums are subject to special tax treatment if the group sponsor is an employer. For federal tax purposes, an employer can generally deduct premiums for up to $50,000 of insurance on employees. The premiums paid by the employer are not considered taxable income to the employee. The employer sponsored coverage must meet non-discrimination rules to be eligible for this tax treatment.

If the employee is covered by more than $50,000 of group term life insurance, and the employer pays premium, the employer must include, for tax purposes, the cost of insurance for each $1000 in coverage in excess of $50,000. The IRS provides a table that gives the monthly cost of insurance for employer sponsored group term life coverage for employees based on age. The employer uses this table to determine the amount that must be included in wages. *For example, if an employer paid for $100,000 in insurance on a 41 year old employee, the employer must, for tax purposes, include $60 in the employee's taxable wages (50 [number of $1000 units above $50,000] x .10 [from table] x 12 [months])*

Cost Per $1000 of Protection for 1 Month

Age	Cost
Under 25	$ .05
25 through 29	.06
30 through 34	.08
35 through 39	.09
40 through 44	.10
45 through 49	.15
50 through 54	.23
55 through 59	.43
60 through 64	.66
65 through 69	1.27
70 and older	2.06

(From IRS Publication 15-B)

Group Ordinary Life Insurance

When an employer pays premium for group ordinary life insurance, the employer generally pays the deductible cost of insurance portion of the premium, and the employee pays the remainder. If the employer pays more than the cost of insurance, the employee must be taxed on the amount paid by the employer in excess of the cost of insurance.

Modified Endowment Contracts versus Life Insurance

Seven-Pay Test

A life insurance product that passes the *seven-pay test* is a life insurance contract under the law and retains the tax free loan treatment. Any life insurance product that does not pass the seven-pay test is treated for tax purposes as a modified endowment contract and tax free loans are not allowed. Under the seven-pay test, generally, if the calculated net level premium during the first seven years of the contract, which is calculated based on assumptions in the IRS code, is less than the amount paid in the first seven years of the contract, the contract is considered a MEC. The seven-pay test applies to life insurance policies issued after June 20, 1988, a life insurance policy exchanged for another policy after June 20, 1988, and to policies that undergo a *material change*.

If a policy fails the seven-pay test at policy inception or when it is exchanged, or if a policy undergoes a material change that requires it to be subject to the seven-pay test and the policy then fails the test, it is considered a MEC. Once a contract is classified as a MEC it cannot be reclassified at a later date as a non-MEC. Material changes that can cause an existing policy to undergo the seven-pay test include:

- certain increases in the death benefit;
- a term policy's conversion to a permanent insurance policy; and
- an exchange of one policy for another.

Distributions

The tax treatment of withdrawals from MEC policies requires that withdrawals be considered as being made up of earnings prior to cost basis (cost basis is also known as *principal*, so MECs are treated as though earnings are distributed before principal). Loans are treated as withdrawals from these contracts for tax purposes.

Premature withdrawals are withdrawals from MEC policies that occur prior to the owner's age 59 ½. Premature withdrawals are subject to an addition 10% tax on the earnings included in the withdrawal, unless the withdrawal meets an exception to the 10% tax. The exceptions to the tax include attaining age 59 ½, withdrawals attributable to the owner's disability and payments based on the life or life expectancy of the contract holder or the joint life expectancies of the contract holder and beneficiary.

VA PPL LH-2_16298

Death benefits from a MEC upon the insured's death are treated like other life insurance death benefit proceeds and are generally tax-free to the beneficiary.

VA PPL LH-2_16298

Section IV Review

1) Of the following, which "person" cannot be named an insured?
   a. A grandchild of the policy owner
   b. A child of the policy owner
   c. An employee of a business, when the business is the policy owner
   d. A business that is also the policy owner

2) Under group term insurance:
   a. each group member is named in the master policy.
   b. each group member is given a certificate of coverage.
   c. five year level renewable term policies are generally used.
   d. the amount of coverage is mandated by state law.

3) Qualified distributions from Roth IRAs are:
   a. taxable
   b. non-taxable
   c. subject to required minimum distribution rules
   d. tax-deductible

4) Ed put $4000 in his Roth IRA on March 10, 2010. He was 56 at the time. When can he distribute that money as a qualified distribution?
   a. September 10, 2013
   b. March 10, 2013
   c. March 10, 2015
   d. September 10, 2016

5) Withdrawals from Roth IRAs are not taxable as long as the money has been in the plan for at least 5 years, and the owner is at least age:
   a. 65
   b. 59 ½
   c. 71
   d. 55

6) A 401(k) plan is a type of:
   a. private retirement plan
   b. IRA plan
   c. defined contribution plan
   d. defined benefit plan

7) The method of determining the appropriate amount of life insurance to obtain that calculates the present value of a family's share of a deceased income earner's future earnings is:
   a. the needs approach
   b. the human life value approach
   c. the income earner's approach
   d. the estimated value approach

8) A _____ is the type of buy-sell agreement under which the owners of the business each purchase a policy on the life of the other owners. Upon the occurrence of a triggering event, the cash values or death proceeds are used by the owner who purchased the policy to purchase the portion of the business owned by the deceased.
   a. Cross-Purchase Buy-Sell Agreement
   b. Wait and See Buy-Sell Agreement
   c. Third Party Buy-Out Buy-Sell Agreement
   d. Stock Redemption Buy-Sell Agreement

9) Joint life insurance may cover:
   a. only two insureds.
   b. multiple insureds.
   c. a husband and wife only.
   d. related insureds only.

10) Policy loans:
   a. are never treated as taxable distributions.
   b. are always treated as taxable distributions.
   c. are a feature of all cash value life insurance policies.
   d. are subject to surrender charge fees from the insurance company.

Section V: Virginia Statutes and Requirements Pertinent to Life Insurance Only

Insurance law and regulation applicable to life insurance is explored in this section. Topics include:

- Life insurance and annuity marketing practices
- Suitability in annuity transactions
- Replacement
- Accelerated benefits
- Group life
- Policy loans
- Viatical settlements
- Military sales

Life Insurance and Annuity Marketing Practices

Life insurance and annuity products are subject to marketing practices laws. The Virginia Administrative Code contains advertising requirements for these products in 14VAC 5-14-10 through 160. The purpose of these regulations is to set forth minimum standards and guidelines to assure a full and truthful disclosure to the public of all material and relevant information in the advertising of life insurance policies and annuity contracts.

Insurers are responsible for their advertising, regardless of who wrote, created, designed or presented it. Insurance agents are also responsible for advertising they create or present.

14VAC 5-41-10

Definition of Advertisement

For the purpose of these regulations, advertisement means "any marketing communication that is oral, printed, written, or other material of any type from any source that is used by an agent or insurer and that is designed to create or has the effect of creating public interest in life insurance or annuities, or induces or tends to induce the public to purchase, increase, modify, reinstate, borrow on, surrender, replace, or retain a policy including, but not limited to:

1. Printed or published material, audiovisual material, mailing envelopes, or descriptive literature of an insurer or agent used in direct mail, newspapers, magazines, radio, telephone and television scripts, billboards or similar displays, websites and other Internet displays or communications, social media, or other forms of electronic communications;
2. Descriptive literature and sales aids of all kinds, authored by the insurer, its agents, or third parties, issued, distributed, or used by an insurer or agent including but not limited to circulars, booklets, illustrations, form letters, pamphlets, brochures, and books or portions thereof;
3. Materials, statements, or communications of any type used for the recruitment, training, and education of an insurer's sales personnel and agents that are designed to be used or are used to induce the public to purchase, increase, modify, reinstate, borrow on, surrender, replace, or retain a policy; or
4. Prepared or extemporaneous sales talks, presentations, and material for use or used by agents."

None of the following are considered advertisements, and so are not subject to the standards and guidelines contained in these regulations:

1. Communications or materials used within an insurer's own organization that are not used as a sales aid, and not intended to be disseminated to the public
2. Communications with policyholders other than material urging them to purchase, increase, modify, reinstate, borrow on, surrender, replace, or retain a policy
3. A general announcement from a group or blanket policyholder to eligible individuals on an employment or membership list that a policy or program has been written or arranged, as long as the announcement clearly indicates that it is preliminary to the issuance of a booklet explaining the proposed coverage

14VAC 5-41-20

Advertising Requirements

Many insurance advertising methods are prohibited because they are deceptive. In some cases, they also constitute unfair trade practices in the business of insurance as defamation, illegal inducement and material misrepresentation.

No Hiding Insurance Solicitation

No advertisement may be combined or included with an advertisement of a product or service that is not life insurance or an annuity where the nature of the advertisement is disguised, misleading, miscommunicated or minimized.

Complete, Accurate and Clear

Advertisements must be truthful and not misleading in fact or by implication. The form and content must be sufficiently accurate, complete and clear in order to avoid deception. Advertisements may not have the capacity or tendency to mislead or deceive. The Commission determines whether an advertisement has the capacity or tendency to mislead or deceive from the overall impression that the advertisement may be reasonably expected to create within the segment of the public to which it is directed.

No Material Omissions

An advertisement may not omit material information. It may not use words, phrases, statements, references, or illustrations if the omission or use has the capacity, tendency, or effect of misleading or deceiving purchasers, prospective purchasers or policyowners as to:

- the nature of their relationship with the insurer; or
- the nature or extent of any policy benefit, loss covered, premium payable, or state or federal tax consequences.

The fact that a policy is made available to a prospective insured for inspection prior to consummation of the sale, or an offer is made to refund the premium if the purchaser is not satisfied, does not keep misleading statements from being a violation of Virginia insurance regulations.

No Unfair Policy or Insurer Comparisons

Advertisements may not make unfair, inaccurate, or incomplete comparisons of policies, benefits, dividends, or rates of other insurers. They may not disparage or falsely or unfairly describe other insurers, agents, policies, services, or methods of marketing.

Prohibited Terms

An advertisement may not use the terms in connection with a policy in a context or under circumstances or conditions as to have the capacity or tendency to mislead a purchaser or prospective purchaser or a policy to believe that:

- he or she will receive; or
- it is possible that he or she will receive:
  - something other than a policy; or
  - some benefit not available to other persons of the same class and equal expectation of life.

Specific terms that are prohibited for use in life insurance advertising as misleading are:

- investment
- investment plan
- founder's plan
- charter plan
- expansion plan
- profit
- profits
- profit sharing
- deposit
- interest plan
- savings
- savings plan
- retirement plan
- private pension plan

No Implication of Special Privileges

An advertisement of a particular policy must not state or imply that prospective insureds will be or become members of a special class, group or quasi-group and as such enjoy special rates, dividends, or underwriting privileges, unless that is fact.
14VAC 5-41-30

General Disclosure Requirements

Advertisements must contain certain disclosures if certain terms or product features are contained within them. When an advertisement contains a required disclosure, the disclosure may not be minimized, rendered obscure or presented in an ambiguous fashion or intermingled with the text of an advertisement to confuse or mislead.

"Nonmedical" and "No Medical Examination" Disclosure

When an advertisement uses the terms "nonmedical," "no medical examination required," or similar terms when issue of the insurance policy is not guaranteed, these terms must be accompanied by further disclosure that explains that issuance of the policy may depend upon the answers to health questions contained in the application. The disclosure must be of equal prominence and placed next to these terms.

Statistical Information and Dollar Amounts

Advertisements may not contain figures, dollar amounts, or statistical information unless it accurately reflects recent and relevant facts. The source of any figures, dollar amounts, or statistics used in advertisements must be identified within the advertisement.

Benefit Limitations

An advertisement for a life insurance policy that contains graded or modified benefits must prominently display any limitation of benefits. If the premium is level and coverage decreases or increases with age or duration, that fact must be disclosed.

An advertisement of a life insurance policy under which the death benefit varies with the length of time the policy has been in force must accurately describe and clearly call attention to the amount of minimum death benefit under the policy.

Universal Life Policies

Any advertisement that mentions or refers to universal life insurance premiums must indicate that it is possible that coverage will expire when either no premiums are paid following the initial premium, or subsequent premiums are insufficient to continue coverage, if this is true of the policy.

Incontestability Period for Suicide

An insurer or agent must advise a prospective applicant who is considering replacing a policy

that under the existing policy the period of time during which the existing insurer could contest the policy or deny coverage for death caused by suicide may have expired or may expire earlier than it will under the proposed policy.

Preneed Funeral Contracts

An advertisement for life insurance or an annuity that is to be used to fund a preneed funeral contract must disclose that fact. An advertisement of a life insurance policy or annuity that will not fund a preneed funeral contract and that includes a listing, summary, description, or comparison of actual or estimated costs of funeral goods or services must contain the following disclosure:

> "This (life insurance or annuity) does not specifically cover funeral goods or services, and may not cover the entire cost of your funeral at the time of your death. The beneficiary of this (life insurance or annuity) may use the proceeds for any purpose, unless otherwise directed."
>
> *14VAC 5-41-40*

Premiums

When an advertisement refers to an amount that is a premium for a policy, it may use only the word "premium." Other terms, such as "deposit," "deposit premium," "investment" or other misleading or confusing terminology are specifically prohibited to be used.

Advertisements must not contain a statement or representation that premiums paid for a policy can be withdrawn under the terms of the policy. An advertisement may refer to amounts paid into an advance premium fund, which are intended to pay premiums at a future time, to the effect that they may be withdrawn under the conditions of the prepayment agreement. Reference may also be made to withdrawal rights under any unconditional premium refund offer.

An advertisement for a policy with nonlevel premiums must prominently describe the premium changes.

An advertisement in which the insurer describes a policy that reserves the right to change the amount of the premium during the policy term must prominently describe this feature.

An advertisement for a policy with pure *endowment* benefits payable within the premium paying period must contain information regarding the premium charged in a clearly identified separate amount. The specific amount of each separate endowment must be shown in dollar amounts only. An advertisement may not represent a pure endowment benefit as a "profit" or "return" on the premium paid, rather than a policy benefit for which a specified premium is paid.

An endowment policy is a life insurance policy that pays the face amount at the end of a specified period or at a specified age of the insured. An endowment benefit pays a death benefit if the insured dies prior to the end of the specified period or specified age.

An advertisement must not imply the existence of an actuarial relationship between a specific premium or a specific benefit provided under a policy where, in fact, none exists. No premium or a portion of a premium may be represented as an "additional," "separate," or "special" premium unless there is an actuarial relationship between the premium and some specifically identifiable benefit.

No artificial relationships among premiums, interest rates, and benefits or portions may be implied or created.

An advertisement may not represent that premium payments will not be required for every year of the policy in order to maintain the illustrated death benefits, unless that is the fact.

An advertisement may not use certain terms to describe a plan using nonguaranteed elements to pay a portion of future premiums. Prohibited terms are:

- vanish;
- vanishing premium; and
- similar terms that imply the policy becomes paid-up.

14VAC 5-41-50

Nonguaranteed Policy Elements

Advertising nonguaranteed interest rates, benefit amounts and premium levels can be very misleading if the audience does not understand that they are NOT guaranteed. Because of their capacity to be misleading, there are special disclosure requirements when an advertisement refers to nonguaranteed policy elements.

Dividends

An advertisement must not utilize or describe nonguaranteed policy elements in a manner that is misleading or has the capacity or tendency to mislead. In this connection, analogies and comparisons between dividends payable on shares of stock and dividends payable under a policy are prohibited unless the advertisement fully, clearly, and accurately describes the differences.

An advertisement must not state or imply that dividends are other than mainly a refund or return of part of the premium paid or that dividends are guaranteed. An advertisement may state or imply that dividends are dependent on the investment earnings, lapse experience, mortality experience, and expense experience of the insurer, if true.

An advertisement must not refer to dividends as "tax free" or use words of similar import, unless the tax treatment of dividends is fully explained and the nature of the dividend as a return of premium is indicated clearly.

If a dividend illustration is determined in a manner involving substantial deviation from the contribution principle, an advertisement showing illustrated dividends must prominently display the following caution:

> "The illustrated dividends for this policy were determined in a manner inconsistent with generally accepted practices."

Illustrations

An advertisement may not state or imply that the payment or amount of nonguaranteed policy elements is guaranteed. If nonguaranteed policy elements are illustrated, they must be based on the insurer's current scale, and the illustration must contain a prominent statement to the effect that the nonguaranteed policy elements are not to be construed as guarantees of amounts to be paid in the future.

Paid-up Policies

An advertisement must not state or imply that illustrated dividends or other nonguaranteed policy elements under either or both a participating policy or pure endowment will be or can be sufficient at any future time to assure without the future payment of premiums, the receipt of benefits, such as a paid-up policy, unless the advertisement clearly and precisely explains the benefits or coverage provided at that time and the conditions required for that to occur.

Benefits Outside of the Policy

An advertisement must not state or imply that a prospective policyholder will receive dividends or other nonguaranteed benefits, or special or favored treatment in the allowance or payment of amounts or other monetary benefits not expressly provided in the policy.

14VAC 5-41-60

Disclosure of Policies and Benefits
Clear Labeling of Policy Type

An advertisement must not use as the name or title of a policy any phrase which omits the words "life insurance" or "annuity," as appropriate, unless accompanied by other language clearly indicating the policy is life insurance or an annuity. Advertisements must also clearly and prominently describe the true nature or type of policy advertised.

No Representation of Benefits Not Provided

An advertisement must not state, represent or imply that a prospective or current policyholder will receive the right to benefits that are not a part of the policy and approved by the Commission.

An advertisement must not state or imply that a policy contains features or benefits that are not found in other policies, unless that is true.

No Representation of Nonexistent Group

An advertisement must not represent, directly or indirectly, that a policy may be sold only to certain persons because of their occupation, association, age, sex, or other condition unless it can be shown that the policy advertised is, in fact, sold only to those persons.

No Representation of Referral Compensation

An advertisement must not contain statements indicating that because a prospect has agreed to furnish names of potential purchasers, he is entitled to any specific benefits not available to all policyholders generally.

No Misrepresentation of Increasing or Additional Insurance

An advertisement must not represent an increasing or other term insurance provision as a return of premium, a cash surrender value, or anything other than a guaranteed insurance benefit for which a premium is charged.

No Misrepresentation of Premium Allocation

In any advertisement, the basic death benefit must be shown as a single amount, not arbitrarily or deceptively split into two or more parts, implying that there is a relationship between some part of a premium or other policy amount and some part of the death benefit, unless that is the fact, and provided the relationship is not for the purpose of, or may likely have the effect of, misleading or deceiving.

Illustration of Nonforfeiture Values

If nonforfeiture values are shown in any advertisement, the values must be shown either for the entire amount of the basic death benefit or for each $1,000 of initial death benefit.

No Misrepresentation of Death Benefit

An advertisement must not state or imply that on the death of an insured, the beneficiary will receive, or should have received, the cash value of a policy in addition to the face amount, unless the policy so provides.

No Misrepresentation of Responsibility to Repay Policy Loans

An advertisement must not state or imply in any way that interest charged on a policy loan or the reduction of death benefits by the amount of outstanding policy loans is unfair, inequitable, or in any manner an incorrect or improper practice.

No Misuse of Banking or Investment Terms for Insurance Benefits

The use of savings "passbooks" and similar misleading techniques to show a policy's cash

VA PPL LH-2_16298

value is prohibited. Analogies between a policy's cash values and savings accounts or other investments and between premium payments and contributions to savings accounts or other investments must be complete and accurate. The analogy must make clear that the representation is an analogy only and that cash values and premium payments are not identical to a savings account or other investments and contributions.

No Mischaracterizing Endowment Benefit as Earnings on Premiums

An advertisement must not represent a pure endowment benefit as earnings on premiums paid or represent that a pure endowment benefit in a policy is other than a guaranteed benefit for which a specific part or all of the premium is being paid by the policyholder. Coupons or other devices for periodic payment of endowment benefits are included within the phrase "a pure endowment benefit."

14VAC 5-41-70

Policy Costs and Cost Comparisons

Deceptive marketing of insurance through incomplete, inaccurate or misleading communication of policy costs is also prohibited. The following advertising of policy costs and comparisons are all prohibited under Virginia insurance regulations:

"No Cost"

The words "free," "no cost," "without cost," "no additional cost," "at no extra cost," or words of similar import may not be used with respect to any benefit or service being made available with a policy unless true. If there is no charge to the insured, then the identity of the payor and the amount of the payment must be prominently disclosed. An advertisement may specify the charge for a benefit or a service or may state that a charge is included in the premium or use other appropriate language.

"Inexpensive"

An advertisement of a particular policy must not use the phrase "inexpensive," "low cost" or any similar term unless that fact is capable of being demonstrated to the satisfaction of the Commission.

Twisting

An advertisement must not imply or state that all older policies are more or less costly than newer policies.

Incomplete Package Cost Information

An advertisement of two or more policies sold as a "package" or other combination is prohibited from directing attention improperly at the cost competitiveness of one part of the "package" when the cost competitiveness of that part is not indicative of the cost competitiveness of the "package" as a whole.

Incomplete Policy Cost Information

An advertisement of a single policy may not direct attention improperly at the cost competitiveness of a part of the policy when the cost competitiveness of that part is not indicative of the cost competitiveness of the entire policy.

Misrepresentation of Underwriting Factors

An advertisement of a policy at a particular issue age, sex, or amount must not lead prospective policyholders to believe that the cost competitiveness of the policy is similar at other issue ages, sex, or amounts unless that is a fact.

Misrepresentation of Earnings Basis

An advertisement containing a cost comparison of two or more policies with nonguaranteed policy elements in which the method of investment income allocation differs between or among the policies must state that fact and must contain a brief explanation of the implications of the cost comparison.

14VAC 5-41-80

Insurer Identity and Representations

Several advertising practices related to insurer and identity and representations are also prohibited:

Misleading Financial Information

An advertisement may not contain statements, pictures, comparative financial ratios, or illustrations that are false, misleading, or irrelevant with respect to the assets, liabilities, insurance in force, corporate structure, financial condition, age, or relative position of the insurer in the insurance business or with regard to affiliates or subsidiaries of the insurer.

Unfounded Endorsements

An advertisement must not contain a recommendation by any commercial rating service unless it clearly defines the scope and extent of the recommendation.

Misrepresentation of Earnings

An advertisement must not state or imply that a purchaser of a policy will share in or receive a stated percentage or portion of the earnings on the general account assets of the insurer unless that is a fact.

Insurer Identification

The name of the insurer must be clearly identified in all advertisements about the insurer or its products, and if any specific policy is advertised it must be identified either by its form number or other appropriate description. If an application is a part of the advertisement, the name of the insurer must be shown on the application.

Misrepresentation of Insurer Identity

An advertisement may not use a trade name, an insurance group designation, name of the parent company of the insurer, name of a particular division of the insurer, a reinsurer of the insurer, service mark, slogan, symbol, or other device or reference without disclosing the name of the insurer if the advertisement would have the capacity or tendency to mislead or deceive as to the true identity of the insurer, or create the impression that a company other than the insurer would have any responsibility for the financial obligations under a policy.

Misrepresentation of Government Insurance

An advertisement must not use any combination of words, symbols, or physical materials that by their content, phraseology, shape, color, or other characteristics are so similar to a combination of words, symbols, or physical materials used by a governmental program or agency or otherwise appear to be of a nature that they tend to mislead prospective insureds into believing that the solicitation is in some manner connected with a governmental program or agency.

No Coercion

An advertisement may not use any combination of words, symbols, or physical materials that by their content, phraseology, shape, color, or other characteristics are so similar to a combination of words, symbols, or physical materials used by a noninsurance company with whom the prospective insured has a financial relationship or otherwise appear to be of a nature that it tends to mislead or deceive the prospective insured into believing that the purchase of insurance is required by the company.

False Financial Information

An advertisement may not represent that the mere size of an insurer or its total insurance in force necessarily affects either the solvency of the insurer or the reliability of the policies issued by the insurer.

Misrepresentation of Stock Benefits

An advertisement may not contain any statement that would lead a prospective buyer or policyholder of life insurance or annuity to believe that he is acquiring stock in an insurer by purchasing the life insurance or annuity.

An advertisement may not contain any statement that creates an inference that policyholders are entitled to benefits or profits on the same basis as stockholders.

Misrepresentation of Compensation

An insurer or agent may not use the terms "financial planner," "investment advisor," "financial consultant," "financial counseling" or other similar terms in a way that implies that the person who is engaged in the business of insurance, is generally engaged in an advisory business in which compensation is unrelated to sales unless that is actually a fact.

Misrepresentation of Planner or Advisor Status

No person engaged in the business of insurance may hold himself out, directly or indirectly, to the public as a "financial planner," "investment advisor," "financial consultant," "financial counselor" or any other specialist engaged in the business of giving complete financial planning advice relating to investments, insurance, real estate, tax matters, and trust and estate matters unless that person in fact is engaged in that business and renders those services.

VA PPL LH-2_16298

Not included in "services" is the presentation of computer printouts that fall into the category of advanced programming for the purpose of selling a policy.

Misrepresentation of Policy Costs

An advertisement of a policy marketed by direct response techniques may not state or imply that because there is no insurance agent or commission involved there will be a cost savings to prospective purchasers unless that is the fact.

A *direct response solicitation* occurs when a person sees or hears public advertisements for an insurance company and requests an application based on those advertisements. In contrast to direct response solicitation, an *agent solicitation* is a solicitation of insurance that occurs when an insurance agent or producer offers to sell an insurance policy to a potential customer.

Deception through Combined Information

An insurer or agent must not use materials, statements, or communications of any kind that when used alone are not misleading, but become deceptive or misleading when combined.

Illegal Inducements

An insurer or agent may not offer or provide to a proposed insured or other person a gift of substantial value if an application, inquiry card, or reinstatement application is returned within a specified period of time. However, a nonmonetary gift valued at $25 or less is not considered a "gift of substantial value."

14VAC 5-41-90

Testimonials

A testimonial, appraisal, analysis, or endorsement used in an advertisement must:

- be genuine;
- represent the current opinion of the author;
- be applicable to the policy advertised, if any; and
- be accurately reproduced with sufficient completeness to avoid misleading or deceiving prospective insureds as to the nature or scope of the testimonial, appraisal, analysis, or endorsement.

In using testimonials, appraisals, analyses, or endorsements, the insurer or agent makes as its own all the statements contained within them, and these statements are all subject to the advertising regulations found in *14VAC 5-41-10* and following.

Disclosure of Interest in the Insurer

If the individual making a testimonial, appraisal, analysis, or endorsement has a financial interest in the insurer or a related entity as a stockholder, director, officer, employee, or otherwise, that fact must be clearly and prominently disclosed in the advertisement.

If the entity making the endorsement or testimonial is owned, controlled, or managed by the insurer or receives any payment or other consideration from the insurer for making the endorsement or testimonial, that fact must be disclosed in the advertisement.

An advertisement must not state or imply that an insurer or a policy has been approved or endorsed by a group of individuals, society, association, or other organization unless that is the fact and unless any proprietary relationship between an organization and the insurer is disclosed.

Disclosure of Compensation

If an individual receives any financial benefit directly or indirectly, greater than required union scale wages, that fact must be clearly and prominently disclosed in the advertisement by language identical or substantially similar to the following:

THIS IS A PAID ENDORSEMENT

(14VAC 5-41-100)

Introductory, Initial or Special Offers

Advertisers know that people are more likely to buy when they believe a product is limited or that the good deal they see today will not be available tomorrow. Insurance products are subject to rate regulation and financial solvency standards that disallow "specials," "limited time offers" or "clearance sales." The Virginia insurance regulations specifically prohibit advertising practices that lead the consumer to believe that an insurance purchase is a special offer when this is not the case.

An advertisement of one policy or combination of policies may not state or imply that the policy or combination of policies is an introductory, initial, or special offer, or that applicants will receive substantial advantages not available at a later date, or that the offer is available only to a specified group of individuals, unless that is the fact.

An advertisement may not describe an enrollment period as "special" or "limited" or use similar words or phrases in describing it when the insurer uses successive enrollment periods as its usual method of marketing its policies.

An advertisement may not state or imply that only a specific number of policies will be sold, or that a time is fixed for the discontinuance of the sale of a particular policy because of special advantages available in the policy.

Reduced Initial Premium Rates

An advertisement may not offer a policy that utilizes a reduced initial premium rate in a manner that overemphasizes the availability and the amount of the reduced initial premium. When an insurer charges a reduced initial premium that differs in amount from the amount of the renewal premium payable on the same mode, all references to the reduced initial premium must be followed by an asterisk or other appropriate symbol that refers the reader to the specific portion of the advertisement that contains the full rate schedule for the policy.

Enrollment Period

An enrollment period during which a particular policy may be purchased on an individual basis may not be offered within this Commonwealth unless there has been a lapse of not less than six months between the close of the immediately preceding enrollment period for the same or substantially similar policy and the opening of a new enrollment period. The advertisement must specify the date by which the applicant must mail the application, that may be not less than 10 days and not more than 40 days from the date on which the enrollment period is presented for the first time in the advertisement.

This regulation applies to all the affiliated companies of a group of insurance companies under common management or control. It does not apply to the use of a termination or cutoff date beyond which an individual application for a guaranteed issue policy will not be accepted by an insurer in those instances where the application has been sent to the applicant in response to his request. It is also inapplicable to solicitations of employees or members of a particular group or association that otherwise would be eligible under specific provisions of the Code of Virginia for group, blanket, or franchise insurance. In cases where a policy is marketed on a direct response basis to prospective insureds by reason of some common relationship with a sponsoring organization, this regulation applies separately to each sponsoring organization.
14VAC 5-41-110

Policies Sold to Students

There are special advertising regulations when insurance is marketed to or for students. The envelope in which advertisement material is contained may be addressed to the parents of students. The address may not include any combination of words that imply that the correspondence is from a school, college, university, or other education or training institution nor imply that the institution has endorsed the material or supplied the insurer with information about the student unless that is a fact.

All advertisements must be clearly identified as coming from an insurer or agent, if that is the case, and these entities must be clearly marked as such. The return address on the envelope may not imply that the soliciting insurer or agent is affiliated with a university, college, school, or other educational or training institution unless that is a fact.
14VAC 5-41-120

Individual Deferred Annuity Contracts or Deposit Funds

Any illustrations or statements containing or based upon nonguaranteed interest rates in annuity contracts must provide with equal prominence comparable illustrations or statements containing or based upon the guaranteed accumulation rates. The nonguaranteed interest rate may not be greater than those currently being credited by the company unless the nonguaranteed rates have been publicly declared by the company with an effective date for new issues not more than three months after the date of declaration.

If an advertisement for a particular annuity or advance premium fund states the accumulation interest rate based on net contributions, it must also disclose in close proximity and with equal prominence, the accumulation interest rate based on gross contribution and the relationship between gross and net contributions.

An advertisement may not state or imply that annuities or advance premium funds are accorded preferential tax treatment unless the advertisement describes the tax consequences of purchasing an annuity or making payments into an advance premium fund, including tax consequences on surrender and on death.

If the contract does not provide a cash surrender benefit prior to commencement of payment of annuity benefits, an illustration or statement concerning the contract must prominently state that cash surrender benefits are not provided.

Any illustrations, depictions, or statements containing or based on determinable policy elements must set forth with equal prominence comparable illustrations, depictions, or statements containing or based on guaranteed policy elements.

14VAC 5-41-130

Jurisdictional Licensing

Insurance advertising may cross state lines through the radio, television, or over the internet. The insurer may not be authorized in all the states in which the advertising is seen, or may not have the product it is advertising approved in all these states. For this reason, insurers must follow certain practices when advertising across state lines.

An advertisement that is intended to be seen or heard beyond the limits of the jurisdiction in which the insurer or agent is licensed may not imply licensing beyond those limits. An advertisement may state that an insurer or agent is licensed in the state where the advertisement appears, as long as it does not exaggerate that fact or suggest or imply that competing insurers or agents may not also be licensed.

An advertisement may not create the impression that the insurer, its financial condition or status, the payment of its claims, or the merits, desirability, or advisability of its policy forms or kinds of plans of insurance are recommended or endorsed by any governmental entity. However, where a governmental entity has recommended or endorsed a policy form or plan, that fact may be stated if the entity authorizes its recommendation or endorsement to be used in an advertisement.

An advertisement may not represent or imply that any financial ratio, illustrative material or advertisement, including pictures, diagrams, charts, projections, or other material, has been approved or sanctioned by the Commission, unless that is a fact.

14VAC 5-41-140

Approval and Records Maintenance Requirements

Insurer Approval Required

The insurer must approve all advertisements written, created, designed, or presented by an agent or other party responsible for advertisement.

Each insurer must inform its agents of the requirements of this regulation.

System of Control over Advertisements

Each insurer must establish and at all times maintain a system of control over the method of dissemination, content, and form of all advertisements of its policies. A system of control must include regular and routine notification to agents, brokers, and others authorized by the insurer to disseminate advertisements of the requirement and procedures for company approval prior to the use of any advertisement that is not furnished by the insurer.

Advertisement File

Each insurer must maintain at its home or principal office a complete file containing:

- a specimen copy of every printed, published, or prepared advertisement of its individual policies;
- specimen copies of typical printed, published, or prepared advertisements of its blanket, franchise, and group policies disseminated in Virginia;
- a notation indicating the manner and extent of distribution and the form number of any policy referred to in any advertisement.

The file is subject to inspection by the Commission.

All advertisements must be maintained in the file for a period of five years after discontinuance of their use or publication.

Submission of Advertisements to the Commission

If the Commission finds that it may be in the best interests of the public, at the Commission's specific request, it may require particular insurers or agents to submit all or part of their advertisements to the Commission for review or approval prior to use.
14VAC 5-41-150

Suitability in Annuity Transactions

Virginia insurance regulations, in *14 VAC 5-45-40*, requires insurance agents to have reasonable grounds to believe that a recommendation of an annuity is suitable for the individual. These reasonable grounds must be based on an inquiry into the individual's financial status, investment objectives and other relevant information. The insurer and producer must also establish and maintain a system to monitor recommendations made to determine that recommendations are made to achieve compliance with the suitability rules.

The suitability rules apply to any purchase or exchange of an annuity.
VA Regulation 14VAC 5-45-10

Recommendation

The insurance regulations defines an annuity "recommendation" as "advice provided by an agent, or an insurer where no agent is involved, to an individual consumer that results in a purchase or exchange of an annuity in accordance with that advice."
VA Regulation 14VAC 5-45-20

Suitability Inquiry

Before the purchase or exchange of an annuity that results from a recommendation, the agent, or when no agent is involved such as through direct mail or internet marketing, the insurer, must make reasonable efforts to obtain information concerning:

- the consumer's financial status;
- the consumer's tax status;
- the consumer's investment objectives; and
- other information the producer or insurer determines is reasonable to obtain in order to make a recommendation that is suitable for the consumer.

VA Regulation 14VAC 5-45-40

No Obligation to Determine Suitability

The producer or insurer has no obligation to make a reasonable determination of suitability when a consumer:

- refuses to provide relevant information requested by the insurer or insurance agent;
- decides to enter into an insurance transaction not based on a recommendation of the insurer or insurance producer; or
- fails to provide complete or accurate information.

VA Regulation 14VAC 5-45-40

Supervisory System

The system required to be established and maintained to monitor compliance with the suitability regulation includes:

- maintaining written procedures; and
- conducting periodic reviews of its records that are reasonably designed to assist in detecting and preventing violations.

This type of system is to be established by the insurer and adopted by general agents and independent agencies to supervise insurance producer recommendations. An insurer may utilize a third party to establish and maintain this system, but must take steps to make sure the third party is in compliance with the suitability regulations. These steps include:

- annually obtaining a certification from a third party senior manager who has responsibility for the delegated functions that the manager has a reasonable basis to represent and does represent, that the third party is performing the required functions; and

- periodically review the third parties to determine whether they are performing the required functions.

VA Regulation 14VAC 5-45-40

Replacement

The Virginia Insurance Regulations includes replacement rules that establish minimum standards of conduct on the part of agents and insurers which must be observed in replacement in order to protect purchasers. These protection standards have been developed to:

- regulate the activities of insurers and agents with respect to the replacement of existing life insurance and annuities; and
- protect the interests of life insurance and annuity purchases.

14 VAC 5-30-10

"Replacement" means a transaction in which a new policy or contract is to be purchased, and it is known or should be known to the proposing agent, or the proposing insurer if there is no agent, that by reason of the transaction, an existing policy or contract has been or is to be:

- Lapsed, forfeited, surrendered or partially surrendered, assigned to the replacing insurer, or otherwise terminated;
- Converted to reduced paid-up insurance, continued as extended term insurance, or otherwise reduced in value by the use of nonforfeiture benefits or other policy values;
- Amended to effect either a reduction in benefits or in the term for which coverage would otherwise remain in force or for which benefits would be paid;
- Reissued with any reduction in cash value;
- Used in a financed purchase.

14VAC 5-30-20

Some replacement transactions are exempt from the rules, including transactions involving:

- Group life insurance or group annuities when there is no direct solicitation
- *Credit life* insurance (which is term insurance with a benefit that is based on the balance of a loan)
- Group life insurance and annuities used to fund prearranged funeral contracts
- An application to the existing insurer that issued the existing life insurance:
  - because a contractual change or a conversion privilege is being exercised; or
  - when the existing policy or contract is being replaced by the same insurer pursuant to a plan filed and approved by the commission; or
  - when a term conversion privilege is exercised among corporate affiliates
- Proposed life insurance to replace life insurance under a binding or conditional receipt with the same company
- Policies or contracts used to fund qualified retirement plans and nonqualified deferred compensation arrangements
- A life insurance policy that is paid for solely by an employer or an association of which the insured is a member
- Existing life insurance that is a nonconvertible term life insurance policy that will expire in five years or less and cannot be renewed
- Immediate annuities purchased with proceeds from an existing contract
- Structured settlements

14 VAC 5-30-30

Duties of Agents in Replacement

An agent or broker who solicits a life insurance application must submit to the insurer a statement signed by the applicant and the agent as with or as part of each application as to whether replacement of existing life insurance or annuity is involved.

14 VAC 5-30-40.A.

Provision of "Important Notice" Regarding Replacement

If the applicant has an existing policy or contract, the agent must present and read a notice regarding the replacement of life insurance or annuities. The notice must be presented and read not later than at the time of taking the application. The content must be presented in the following form, or in a similar way approved by the Commission:

IMPORTANT NOTICE: REPLACEMENT OF LIFE INSURANCE OR ANNUITIES

This document shall be signed by the applicant and the agent and a copy left with the applicant.

You are contemplating the purchase of a life insurance policy or annuity contract. In some cases this purchase may involve discontinuing or changing an existing policy or contract. If so, a replacement is occurring. Financed purchases are also considered replacements.

A replacement occurs when a new policy or contract is purchased and, in connection with the sale, you discontinue making premium payments on the existing policy or contract, or an existing policy or contract is surrendered, forfeited, assigned to the replacing insurer, or otherwise terminated or used in a financed purchase.

A financed purchase occurs when the purchase of a new life insurance policy involves the use of funds obtained by the withdrawal or surrender of or by borrowing some or all of the policy values, including accumulated dividends, of an existing policy, to pay all or part of any premium or payment due on the new policy. A financed purchase is a replacement.

You should carefully consider whether a replacement is in your best interest by reviewing questions on page 2 of this form. You will pay acquisition costs and there may be surrender costs deducted from your policy or contract. You may be able to make changes to your existing policy or contract to meet your insurance needs at less cost. A financed purchase will reduce the value of your existing policy and may reduce the amount paid upon the death of the insured.

We want you to understand the effects of replacements before you make your purchase decision and ask that you answer the following questions and consider the questions on the back of this form.

1. Are you considering discontinuing making premium payments, surrendering, forfeiting, assigning to the insurer, or otherwise terminating your existing policy or contract? ___ YES ___ NO

2. Are you considering using funds from your existing policies or contracts to pay premiums due on the new policy or contract? ___ YES ___ NO

If you answered "yes" to either of the above questions, list each existing policy or contract you are contemplating replacing (include the name of the insurer, the insured, and the contract number if available) and whether each policy will be replaced or used as a source of financing:

	CONTRACT OR POLICY #	INSURED	REPLACED (R) OR FINANCING (F)
1.			
2.			
3.			

Make sure you know the facts. Contact your existing company or its agent for information about the old policy or contract. If you request one, an in-force illustration, policy summary or available disclosure document must be sent to you by the existing insurer. Ask for and retain all sales material used by the agent in the sales presentation. Be sure that you are making an informed decision.

The existing policy or contract is being replaced because _____

_____

_____

I certify that the responses herein are, to the best of my knowledge, accurate:

_____ _____

Applicant's Signature and Printed Name Date

_____ _____

Agent's Signature and Printed Name Date

I do not want this notice read aloud to me. _____ (Applicants must initial only if they do not want the notice read aloud.)

Page 2

A replacement may not be in your best interest, or your decision could be a good one. You should make a careful comparison of the costs and benefits of your existing policy or contract and the proposed policy or contract. One way to do this is to ask the company or agent that sold you your existing policy or contract to provide you with information concerning

VA PPL LH-2_16298

your existing policy or contract. This may include an illustration of how your existing policy or contract is working now and how it would perform in the future based on certain assumptions. Illustrations should not, however, be used as a sole basis to compare policies or contracts. You should discuss the following with your agent to determine whether replacement or financing your purchase makes sense:

PREMIUMS: Are they affordable?
Could they change?
You're older – are premiums higher for the proposed new policy?
How long will you have to pay premiums on the new life insurance policy?
On the old life insurance policy?

POLICY VALUES: New policies usually take longer to build cash values and to pay dividends.
Acquisition costs for the old policy may have been paid, and you will incur costs for the new one.
What surrender charges do the policies have?
What expense and sales charges will you pay on the new life insurance policy?
Does the new life insurance policy provide more insurance coverage?

INSURABILITY: If your health has changed since you bought your old policy, the new one could cost you more, or you could be turned down.
You may need a medical exam for a new policy.
Claims on most new policies for up to the first two years can be denied based on inaccurate statements.
Suicide limitations may begin anew on the new coverage

IF YOU ARE KEEPING THE OLD POLICY AS WELL AS THE NEW POLICY:
How are premiums for both policies being paid?
How will the premiums on your existing policy be affected?
Will a loan be deducted from death benefits?
What values from the old life insurance policy are being used to pay premiums?

IF YOU ARE SURRENDERING AN ANNUITY OR INTEREST SENSITIVE LIFE PRODUCT:
Will you pay surrender charges on your old annuity contract?
What are the interest rate guarantees for the new annuity contract?
Have you compared the annuity contract charges or other life insurance policy expenses?

OTHER ISSUES TO CONSIDER FOR ALL TRANSACTIONS:
What are the tax consequences of buying the new life insurance policy?
Is this a tax-free exchange? (See your tax advisor.)
Is there a benefit from favorable "grandfathered" treatment of the old life insurance policy under the Internal Revenue Code?
Will the existing insurer be willing to modify the old policy?
How does the quality and financial stability of the new company compare with your existing company?

Form 30-A
14 VAC 5-30-40.B

Signature of Attestation in the Notice

The notice must be signed by both the applicant and the agent attesting that the notice has been read aloud by the agent, or that the applicant did not wish the notice to be read aloud and that a copy of the notice was left with the applicant.
14 VAC 5-30-40.B.

List of Existing Contracts in the Notice

The notice includes a section where all life insurance or annuities that the applicant currently holds that are proposed to be replaced are properly identified by the name of the insurer, the insured or annuities, and policy or contract number. If a policy or contract is not to be replaced or will be used as a source of financing the new policy, this must also be stated.
14 VAC 5-30-40.C.

Copies of Sales Material

The agent must leave with the applicant at the time an application for a new policy or contract is completed the original or a copy of all sales material. A copy of electronically presented sales material is provided to the policyholder in printed form no later than at time of policy and contract delivery.
14 VAC 5-30-40.D.

The producer must also submit to the insurer to which an application for a policy or contract is presented a copy of each required document, a statement identifying any preprinted or electronically presented insurer-approved sales materials used, and copies of any individualized sales materials including any illustrations related to the purchased policy or contract.

14 VAC 5-30-40.E.

Replacement through 1035 Exchanges

A 1035 exchange is an exchange involving insurance policies that meets the requirements of Internal Revenue Code Section 1035. Under this section, certain exchanges may be made without incurring a tax liability. Section 1035 exchanges are not considered distributions under the tax laws. Exchanges that qualify for such tax treatment include an exchange of:

- a life insurance policy for a life insurance policy;
- a life insurance policy of an endowment contract;
- an endowment contract for another endowment contract;
- an endowment contract for an annuity contract; and
- an annuity for another annuity.

Internal Revenue Code Section 1035 very simply states as follows:

(a) General rules

No gain or loss shall be recognized on the exchange of –

    (1) A contract of life insurance for another contract of life insurance or for an endowment or annuity contract; or

    (2) A contract for endowment insurance

        (A) For another contract of endowment insurance which provides for regular payments beginning at a date not later than the date payments would have begun under the contract exchanged, or

        (B) For an annuity contract; or

        (C) For a qualified long-term care insurance contract; or

    (3) An annuity contract for an annuity contract or for a qualified long-term care insurance contract; or

    (4) A qualified long-term care insurance contract for a qualified long-term care insurance contract.

The law goes on to define annuity contract:

For the purpose of this section… an annuity contract is a contract to which paragraph (1) applies but which may be payable during the life of the annuity only in installments. For purposes of the preceding sentence, a contract shall not fail to be treated as an annuity contract solely because a qualified long-term care insurance contract is a part of or a rider on such contract.

These exchanges must be done directly between insurance companies. Each insurer and the producers involved must follow disclosure and record-keeping regulations related to replacing insurance contracts when 1035 exchange transactions occur.

Insurer Duties in Replacement

Insurers that use agents must maintain a system to ensure compliance with the replacement requirements. The insurer's system must include, at a minimum, a process of:

- informing its agents of the replacement requirements and incorporating them into producer training manuals prepared by the insurer.
- providing each agent a written statement regarding the insurer's position for the acceptability of replacement and including guidance to its agents as to the appropriateness of the transactions.
- reviewing the appropriateness of each replacement transaction that the agent does not indicate is in accordance with the insurer's replacement guidelines.
- confirming that the rule's requirements have been met.
- detecting transactions that are replacements of existing policies or contracts by the existing insurer but that have been reported by the applicant or agent.

The insurer may use any of the following means to accomplish this replacement monitoring system:

 VA PPL LH-2_16298

- customer surveys
- interviews
- confirmation letters
- programs of internal monitoring

14 VAC 5-30-60.A.

Monitoring Replacements

Insurers with agents must have the capacity to monitor each producer's life insurance and annuity replacements for that insurer. The replacement records must be available to the insurance division upon request. Capacity to monitor includes the ability to produce records for each agent's:

- life replacements, including financial purchases, as a percentage of the agent's total annual sales for life insurance;
- number of lapses of policies by the producer as a percentage of the agent's total annual sales for life insurance;
- annuity contract replacements as a percentage of the agent's total annual contract sales;
- number of transactions that are unreported replacements of existing policies or contracts by the existing insurer detected by the insurer's monitoring systems; and
- replacements, indexed by replacing agent and existing insurer.

If an application does not meet the replacement notice rules, the insurer must notify the agent and the applicant and fulfill the outstanding requirements.

14 VAC 5-30-60.B. to G.

Replacing Insurers

Replacing insurers that use agents must verify that the required forms are received and are in compliance with the replacement regulations. They must also notify any other existing insurer that may be affected by the proposal replacement within five business days of receipt of a completed application indicating replacement or when the replacement is identified and not indicated on the application, and mail a copy of the available illustration or policy summary for the proposed policy or available disclosure document for the proposal contract within five business days of a request from an existing insurer. The replacing insurer must be able to produce copies of the notification regarding replacement, indexed by producer, for at least five years.

For example, an applicant completes the "Important Notice; Replacement of Life Insurance or Annuities" and discloses within it that she has two life insurance policies. One is a whole life, cash value policy and the other is a term policy. She also has an existing deferred annuity. The applicant is 68 and has had the annuity for 12 years. She wants to replace this annuity with the product the agent is offering because the yield is better on it. She has taken no withdrawals from her current annuity and has additional savings and receives more retirement income from her qualified plans than she uses for expenses. The three policies are listed in the notice and it is indicated in the list that she will be replacing the annuity. The application and replacement documents are received by the insurer on April 5, 2013. The replacement is finalized and occurs on May 15, 2013. The replacing insurer must be able to produce copies of the replacement notice for the entire time the annuity owner keeps the contract through 5 years after it is fully distributed. The insured must also be able to produce copies of the notification, indexed by producer, until at least May 15, 2018.

The insurer must also provide to the policy or contract owner notice of the right to return the policy or contract within 10 days of the delivery of the contract and receive an unconditional full refund of all premiums or considerations paid on it including any policy fees or charges or, in the case of a variable deferred annuity, or payment of the cash surrender value plus the fees and other charges deducted from the policy or contract.

14 VAC 5-30-51.

Duties of Existing Insurer

The existing insurer must retain and be able to produce all replacement notifications received, indexed by replacing insurer, for at least five years. It must also send a letter to the policy or contract owner notifying the owner of the right to receive information regarding the existing policy or contract values including a notice that an existing policy or contract is being replaced. The information must be provided within five business days of receipt of the request from the policy or contract owner. Upon receipt of a request to surrender or withdraw any annuity values, the insurer must send the applicant a notice, advising the policyowner that the release of policy values may affect the guaranteed elements, nonguaranteed elements, face amount or surrender value of the policy from which the values are released. This notice must be sent separately from the check if the check is sent to anyone other than the policyowner.

14 VAC 5-30-55.

Insurers Using Direct-Response Solicitations

When applications are initiated as a result of a direct-response solicitation, and the applicant indicates a replacement or change is not intended or if the applicant fails to respond to the questions regarding existing policies and replacement, the insurer must include the following notice, or a substantially similar one approved by the Commission:

NOTICE REGARDING REPLACEMENT
REPLACING YOUR LIFE INSURANCE POLICY OR ANNUITY?

Are you thinking about buying a new life insurance policy or annuity and discontinuing or changing an existing one? If you are, your decision could be a good one – or a mistake. You will not know for sure unless you make a careful comparison of your existing benefits and the proposed policy or contract's benefits.

Make sure you understand the facts. You should ask the company or agent that sold you your existing policy or contract to give you information about it.

Hear both sides before you decide. This way you can be sure you are making a decision that is in your best interest.

If the insurer has proposed the replacement or if the applicant indicates a replacement is intended and the insurer continues with the replacement, the insurer must provide the applicants or prospective applicants with the policy or contract the replacement notice, or other substantially similar form. This notice is almost identical to the one used when an agent is involved in the replacement. A minor difference in the two forms is that the section for listing the policies or contracts has minor changes in wording:

Please list each existing policy or contract you are contemplating replacing (include the name of the insurer, the insured, and the contract number if available) and whether each policy will be replaced or used as a source of financing:

	CONTRACT OR POLICY #	INSURED	REPLACED (R) OR FINANCING (F)
1.			
2.			
3.			

The other difference is that only the applicant's signature is required on the form, since there is no agent.

The insurer's obligation to obtain the applicant's signature is satisfied if it can demonstrate that it has made a diligent effort to secure a signed copy of the notice. This requirement is satisfied if the insurer includes in the mailing a self-addressed, postage prepaid envelope with instructions for the return of the signed notice.

14 VAC 5-30-70.

Accelerated Benefits

Virginia insurance law and regulation allow life insurance policies to include an accelerated payment of benefits provision. The conditions for payment of the benefit during the lifetime of the insured are:

- If a qualified health care provider or court of competent jurisdiction has determined that the insured is no longer able to perform two of the following activities of daily living:
  - bathing;
  - dressing;
  - continence;
  - eating;
  - toileting; or
  - transferring; or
- If a qualified health care provider or court of competent jurisdiction has determined that the insured requires substantial supervision by another person to protect the health and safety of the insured or any other person.

VA Code §38.2-3115.1

Definition of Accelerated Benefits

Accelerated benefits are defined under the Virginia insurance regulations as "benefits payable under a life insurance contract:

- to a policyholder or certificateholder, during the lifetime of the insured, in anticipation of death or upon the occurrence of specified life-threatening or catastrophic conditions as defined by the policy or rider;

VA PPL LH-2_16298

- which reduce the death benefit otherwise payable under the life insurance contract; and
- which are payable upon the occurrence of a single **qualifying event** which results in the payment of a benefit amount fixed at the time of acceleration."

14VAC 5-70-40

Qualifying Events

Qualifying events that may trigger an accelerated death benefit are:

- A medical condition which would result in a drastically limited life span as specified in the contract, for example, 24 months or less;
- A medical condition which has required or requires extraordinary medical intervention, such as a major organ transplant or continuous artificial life support, without which the insured would die;
- Any condition which usually requires continuous confinement in an eligible institution as defined in the contract if the insured is expected to remain there for the rest of his or her life;
- A medical condition which would, in the absence of extensive or extraordinary medical treatment, result in a drastically limited life span. Such conditions may include, but are not limited to, one or more of the following:
  - coronary artery disease resulting in an acute infarction or requiring surgery;
  - permanent neurological deficit resulting from cerebral vascular accident;
  - end stage renal failure;
  - Acquired Immune Deficiency Syndrome; or
  - other medical conditions which the Commission approves for any particular filing;
- A condition where a qualified health care provider or court of competent jurisdiction has determined that the insured is no longer able to perform at least two of the following activities of daily living:
  - bathing;
  - dressing;
  - continence;
  - eating;
  - toileting; or
  - transferring;
- A condition for which a qualified health care provider or court of competent jurisdiction has determined that the insured requires direct supervision by another person during the majority of each day to protect the health and safety of the insured or any other person; or
- Other qualifying events which the Commission approves for any particular policy.

(14VAC 5-70-40)

Payment Conditions

The accelerated benefit must allow the insured to authorize a lump sum payment. The payment may not be made as an annuity contingent upon the insured's life. The insurer may not place restrictions on the use of the payment proceeds.

If a policy has an accidental death provision, such as a double indemnity provision, this provision must remain in force as long as there is any death benefit remaining in the policy after the payment of an accelerated benefit.

14VAC 5-70-70

Disclosures

The accelerated benefit provision in a policy or rider must have a title that includes the term "accelerated benefit."

Tax Disclosure

If there is an accelerated benefit provision in a policy or rider, a disclosure statement is required at the time of application and at the time the accelerated benefit payment request. The disclosure must state that the benefits may be taxable and that assistance should be sought from a tax advisor. The disclosure must be prominently displayed on the first page on the first page of the policy or rider and any other related documents.

Benefit Disclosure

In addition, a written disclosure must be given to the applicant. The disclosure must include a brief description of the accelerated benefit and definitions of the conditions or occurrences triggering payment of the benefits must be given to the applicant. The description must include an explanation of any effect of the payment of a benefit on the policy's cash value, accumulation account, death benefit, premium, policy loans and policy liens.

Illustration

If there is a premium or cost of insurance charge for the accelerated benefit, the insurer must give the applicant a generic illustration that numerically demonstrates any effect of the payment of a benefit on the policy's cash value, accumulation account, death benefit, premium, policy loans and policy liens.

The benefit disclosure and illustration must be given to the applicant by the agent at time of application, or at policy delivery along with a notice of the right to return policy for a full refund during the free look period if the policy was sold by direct response. If a group policy, the benefit disclosure and illustration must be part of the certificate of coverage or a related document provided to the certificateholder by the insurer.

Administrative Expense Charges

The insurer must disclose to the policyowner any administrative expense charge. For group policies, the insurer must make a reasonable effort to assure that the certificateholder is aware of any administrative expense charges that the certificateholder is required to pay.

Effect of Payment

When a policyowner or certificateholder requests an acceleration, the insurer must send a statement to the policyowner or certificateholder and irrevocable beneficiary showing any effect that the payment of the accelerated benefit will have on the policy's cash value, accumulation account, death benefit, premium, policy loans and policy liens. The statement must disclose that receipt of accelerated benefit payments may adversely affect the recipient's eligibility for Medicaid or other government benefits or entitlements. In addition, receipt of an accelerated benefit payment may be taxable and assistance should be sought from a personal tax advisor.

When the insurer agrees to accelerate death benefits, the insurer must issue an amended schedule page to the policyholder or notify the certificateholder under a group policy to reflect any new, reduced in-force face amount of the contract. *14VAC 5-70-80*

Effective Date of Accelerated Benefits

The accelerated benefit provision must be effective:
- for accidents, on the effective date of the policy or rider.
- for illness, no more than 30 days following the effective date of the policy or rider.

14VAC 5-70-90

Waiver of Premium

The insurer may offer a waiver of premium for the accelerated benefit provision. At the time the benefit is claimed, the insurer must explain any continuing premium requirement to keep the policy in force.
14VAC 5-70-100

Discrimination

Insurers must not unfairly discriminate among insureds with differing qualifying events covered under the policy or among insureds with similar qualifying events covered under the policy. Insurers may not apply conditions on the payment of the accelerated benefits other than those conditions specified in the policy or rider.
14VAC 5-70-110

Group Life

Eligible Groups

In Virginia, groups that may issue life insurance include:

Employer Groups

A group policy may be issued to an employer, or to the trustees of a fund established by an employer, which employer or trustees must be deemed the policyholder, to insure employees of the employer for the benefit of persons other than the employer, subject to the following requirements:
- The employees eligible for insurance under the policy must all be employees of the employer.
- The premium for the policy must be paid either from the employer's funds or from funds contributed by the insured employees, or from both.

Creditor Groups

Policies may be issued to creditors to insure the life of debtors of the creditor that is the policyowner of the policy. The premium for the policy must be paid either from the creditor's funds, or from charges collected from the insured debtors, or from both. The amount of the insurance on the life of any debtor may never exceed the greater of the scheduled or actual amount of unpaid indebtedness to the creditor.

Labor Unions

Group policies may also be issued to a labor union, or similar employee organization to insure members of such union or organization for the benefit of persons other than the union or organization or any of its officials, representatives, or agents. The premium for the policy must be paid either from funds of the union or organization, or from funds contributed by the insured members specifically for their insurance, or from both.

Associations

An association or a trust or the trustees of a fund established, created, or maintained for the benefit of members of one or more associations may be issued group life insurance. To qualify as a group for insurance purposes, the association or associations must:

- have a minimum of 100 persons;
- have been organized and maintained in good faith for purposes other than that of obtaining insurance;
- have been in active existence for at least five years; and
- have a constitution and bylaws which provide that:
- the association or associations hold regular meetings not less than annually to further purposes of the members;
- except for credit unions, the association or associations collect dues or solicit contributions from members; and
- the members have voting privileges and representation on the governing board and committees.

The premium for the policy may be paid from funds contributed by the association or associations, or by employer members, or by both, or from funds contributed by the covered persons or from both the covered persons and the association, associations, or employer members.

Credit Unions

A group policy may be issued to a credit union or to a trustee or trustees or agent designated by two or more credit unions, which credit union, trustee, trustees, or agent must be deemed policyholder, to insure members of such credit union or credit unions for the benefit of persons other than the credit union or credit unions, trustee or trustees, or agent or any of their officials. The premium for the policy must be paid by the policyholder from the credit union's funds and generally must insure all eligible members.

Associations that Provide Funeral Plans and Insurance

A policy issued to an incorporated association whose principal purpose is to assist its members in financial planning for their funerals and burials and obtaining insurance for the payment, in whole or in part, for funeral, burial and other expenses. The association is the policyholder and insures the members of the association for the benefit of persons other than the association. A policy may not be issued to an association in which membership is conditioned upon the member's designation at any time of a specific funeral director or cemetery as the beneficiary under the insurance, so as to deprive the representatives or family of the deceased member from, or in any way control them in, obtaining funeral supplies and services in an open competitive market.

VA Code §38.2-3318.1

Conversion Privileges

Termination of Employment or Membership in a Group

All group life insurance policies must contain a provision that if the insurance, or any portion of it, on a person covered under the policy, other than a minor child, ceases because of termination of employment or of membership in the class or classes eligible for coverage under the policy, the person must be entitled to have the insurer issue him without evidence of insurability an individual policy of life insurance, without disability or other supplementary benefits, subject to the following:

- Application for the individual policy must be made within 31 days after the termination
- The first modal premium paid to the insurer within 31 days after the termination
- The individual policy may be any of the policies customarily issued by the insurer, except term insurance, at the insured's option and subject to the insurer's customary age and amount requirements
- The amount of the individual policy must not exceed the amount of terminated group life insurance less the amount of any group life insurance that the person is or becomes eligible for within 31 days after the termination
- The premium on the individual policy must be at the insurer's then current rate applicable to the form and amount of the individual policy, to the class of risk to which the person then belongs, and to the person's age on the effective date of the individual policy

VA Code §38.2-3332

Termination of Group Policy or Class of Insureds

Each group life insurance policy must contain a provision that if the group policy terminates or is amended so as to terminate the insurance of any class of insured persons, every person, other than a minor child whose insurance terminates and who has been insured for at least five years prior to the termination date is entitled to have the insurer issue him an individual life insurance policy. The group policy may contain a provision that the amount of the individual policy will not exceed the smaller of:

- the amount of the person's life insurance protection ceasing because of the termination or amendment of the group policy, less the amount of any life insurance for which he is or becomes eligible under any group policy issued or reinstated by the same or another insurer within 31 days after the termination; or
- $10,000.

VA Code §38.2-3333

Death during Conversion Eligibility Period

Each group life insurance policy must contain a provision that if a person insured under the group policy dies during the period within which he is entitled to have an individual policy issued to him and before the individual policy has become effective, the amount of life insurance that he would have been entitled to have issued to him under an individual policy must be payable as a claim under the group policy, whether or not application for the individual policy or the payment of the first premium was made.

VA Code §38.2-3334

Policy Loans

Individual life insurance policies must include a policy loan provision that allows policy loans once the policy has been in force for three years. The loan value allowed by the insurer may be equal to or less than the cash surrender value. A policy loan provision is not required in term insurance policies. Policies issued after July 1, 1981 must contain a policy loan interest rate provision that permits either:

- a maximum fixed interest rate of not more than eight percent per year; or
- an adjustable maximum interest rate established from time to time by the insurer as permitted by law.

The policy may provide that if the interest on the loan is not paid when due, it will be added to the existing loan and will bear interest at the same rate as currently applied to the loan.

The insurer must:

- notify the policyowner of the initial interest rate at the time a cash loan is made;
- notify the policyowner of the initial interest rates on a premium loan as soon as it is reasonably practical to do so after making the loan; and
- send reasonable advance notice of any increase in the rates to policyowners with loans.

Except when policy loans are made to pay premiums, the insurer may defer issuing the loan for up to six months after the date on which the loan is applied.

VA Code §38.2-3308

Military Sales

Sales and solicitations to persons in the military are subject to special insurance regulations. Virginia insurance administrative code 14VAC 5-420 contains these regulations. This code section has the purpose of setting forth standards to protect active duty service members of the United States Armed Forces from dishonest and predatory insurance sales practices by prohibiting certain false, misleading, deceptive or unfair acts and practices.

14VAC 5-420 applies only to the solicitation or sale of life insurance or annuity products by an insurer or insurance agent to an **active duty service member of the United States Armed Forces.**

14VAC 5-420-10

Existing Insurance Programs for Service Members

Certain armed forces personnel have special life insurance available to them through two programs, the Servicemembers' Group Life Insurance program (SGLI) and the Veterans' Group Life Insurance (VGLI). According to the National Association of Insurance Commissioners:

"SGLI is a program of low cost group term life insurance automatically available to all servicemembers on active duty, active duty for training or inactive duty for training and members of the Reserves. This policy is automatically activated for a coverage amount of $400,000, the maximum amount of coverage, unless the servicemember opts out in writing. In addition, designated beneficiaries now receive an additional payment of $100,000 if a servicemember dies while on active duty. Coverage is available for spouses; dependent children are automatically insured for $10,000. When released from active duty or the Reserve, members with full-time SGLI coverage can convert their coverage to Veterans Group Life Insurance or to an individual commercial life insurance."

Since SGLI and VGLI coverage may be sufficient for many service members, insurers and insurance agents are not allowed to solicit insurance to active duty service members in the same manner that is allowed when soliciting to the general public.

Soliciting Face-to-Face on a Military Installation

The following acts or practices when committed on a military installation by an insurer or insurance agent through in-person, face-to-face solicitation of life insurance are prohibited:

- Knowingly soliciting the purchase of any life insurance product door to door or without first establishing a specific appointment for each meeting with the prospective purchaser
- Soliciting service members in a group or mass audience or in a captive audience where attendance is not voluntary
- Knowingly making appointments with or soliciting service members during their normally scheduled duty hours
- Making appointments with or soliciting service members in barracks, day rooms, unit areas, or transient personnel housing or other areas where the installation commander has prohibited solicitation
- Soliciting the sale of life insurance without first obtaining permission from the installation commander or the commander's designee
- Posting unauthorized bulletins, notices or advertisements
- Failing to present DD Form 2885, *Personal Commercial Solicitation Evaluation*, to service members solicited, or encouraging service members solicited not to complete or submit a DD Form 2885
- Knowingly accepting an application for life insurance or issuing a policy of life insurance on the life of an enlisted member of the United States Armed Forces without first obtaining a completed copy of any required form that confirms that the applicant has received counseling or fulfilled any other similar requirement for the sale of life insurance established by regulations, directives or rules of the Department of Defense (DoD) or any branch of the Armed Forces

14VAC 5-420-40

Other Insurance Practices on a Military Installation

The following acts or practices when committed on a military installation by an insurer or insurance agent are prohibited:

VA PPL LH-2_16298

- Using DoD personnel, directly or indirectly, as a representative or agent in any official or business capacity with or without compensation with respect to the solicitation or sale of life insurance to service members
- Using an insurance agent to participate in any United States Armed Forces sponsored education or orientation program

14VAC 5-420-40

Prohibited Practices of Insurers and Agents and Military Regardless of Location

The following acts or practices by an insurer or insurance agent are considered to be corrupt practices, improper influences or inducements that are prohibited regardless of location:

- Submitting, processing or assisting in the submission or processing of any allotment form or similar device used by the United States Armed Forces to direct a service member's pay to a third party for the purchase of life insurance, including using or assisting in using a service member's MyPay account or other similar internet or electronic medium for such purposes
- Knowingly receiving funds from a service member for the payment of premium from a depository institution with which the service member has no formal banking relationship
- Employing any device or method or entering into any agreement whereby funds received from a service member by allotment for the payment of insurance premiums are identified on the service member's Leave and Earnings Statement or equivalent or successor form as "savings" or "checking" and where the service member has no formal banking relationship
- Entering into any agreement with a depository institution for the purpose of receiving funds from a service member whereby the depository institution, with or without compensation, agrees to accept direct deposits from a service member with whom it has no formal banking relationship
- Using DoD personnel, directly or indirectly, as a representative or agent in any official or unofficial capacity with or without compensation with respect to the solicitation

or sale of life insurance to service members who are junior in rank or grade, or to the family members of such personnel
- Offering or giving anything of value, directly or indirectly, to DoD personnel to procure their assistance in encouraging, assisting or facilitating the solicitation or sale of life insurance to another service member
- Knowingly offering or giving anything of value to a service member for his attendance to any event where a life insurance application is solicited
- Advising a service member to change his income tax withholding or state of legal residence for the sole purpose of increasing disposable income to purchase life insurance

14VAC 5-420-50

Prohibited Acts Related to Sponsorship of and Affiliation with an Insurer

The following acts or practices by an insurer or insurance agent lead to confusion regarding source, sponsorship, approval or affiliation and are prohibited.

Confusing Titles

It is prohibited for an insurer or insurance agent to make any representation, or use any device, title, descriptive name or identifier that has the tendency or capacity to confuse or mislead a service member into believing that the insurer, insurance agent or product offered is affiliated, connected or associated with, endorsed, sponsored, sanctioned or recommended by the U.S. Government, the United States Armed Forces, or any state or federal agency or government entity.

Examples of prohibited insurance agent titles include, but are not limited to "Battalion Insurance Counselor," "Unit Insurance Advisor," "Servicemen's Group Life Insurance Conversion Consultant" or "Veteran's Benefits Counselor."

Use of Third Party

Insurers and insurance agents may not solicit the purchase of any life insurance product through the use of or in conjunction with any third party organization that promotes the welfare of or assists members of the United States Armed Forces in a manner that has the tendency or capacity to

VA PPL LH-2_16298

confuse or mislead a service member into believing that either the insurer, insurance agent or insurance product is affiliated, connected or associated with, endorsed, sponsored, sanctioned or recommended by the U.S. Government or the United States Armed Forces.

14VAC 5-420-50

Prohibited Acts Related to Premiums, Costs or Investment Returns

The following acts or practices by an insurer or insurance agent lead to confusion regarding premiums, costs or investment returns and are prohibited:

- Using or describing the credited interest rate on a life insurance policy in a manner that implies that the credited interest rate is a net return on premium paid
- Excluding individually issued annuities, misrepresenting the mortality costs of a life insurance product, including stating or implying that the product costs nothing or is free

14VAC 5-420-50

Prohibited Acts Related to SGLI and VGLI

The following acts or practices by an insurer or insurance agent regarding SGLI or VGLI are prohibited:

- Making any representation regarding the availability, suitability, amount, cost, exclusions or limitations to coverage provided to a service member or dependents by SGLI or VGLI that is false, misleading or deceptive
- Making any representation regarding conversion requirements, including the costs of coverage, or exclusions or limitations to coverage of SGLI or VGLI to private insurers that is false, misleading or deceptive
- Suggesting, recommending or encouraging a service member to cancel or terminate his SGLI policy or issuing a life insurance policy that replaces an existing SGLI policy unless the replacement will take effect upon or after the service member's separation from the United States Armed Forces

14VAC 5-420-50

Prohibited Practices Related to Disclosure

The following acts or practices by an insurer or insurance agent regarding disclosure are prohibited:

- Deploying, using or contracting for any lead generating materials designed exclusively for use with service members that do not clearly and conspicuously disclose that the recipient will be contacted by an insurance agent, if that is the case, for the purpose of soliciting the purchase of life insurance
- Failing to disclose that a solicitation for the sale of life insurance will be made when establishing a specific appointment for an in-person, face-to-face meeting with a prospective purchaser
- Excluding individually issued annuities, failing to clearly and conspicuously disclose the fact that the product being sold is life insurance
- Failing to make, at the time of sale or offer to an individual known to be a service member, the written disclosures required by §10 of the Military Personnel Financial Services Protection Act
- Excluding individually issued annuities, when the sale is conducted in-person, face-to-face with an individual known to be a service member, failing to provide the applicant at the time the application is taken:
- an explanation of any free look period with instructions on how to cancel if a policy is issued
- either a copy of the application or a written disclosure

The copy of the application or the written disclosure must clearly and concisely set out the type of life insurance, the death benefit applied for and its expected first year cost. A basic illustration is sufficient to meet this requirement for a written disclosure.

14VAC 5-420-50

Prohibited Acts Related to Certain Life Insurance Products

The following acts or practices by an insurer or insurance agent with respect to the sale of certain life insurance products to those in the military are prohibited:

- Recommending the purchase of any life insurance product, other than an individual annuity, that includes a side fund to a service member unless the insurer has reasonable grounds for believing that the life insurance death benefit, standing alone, is suitable.
- Offering for sale or selling a life insurance product that includes a side fund to a service member who is currently enrolled in SGLI, is presumed unsuitable unless, after the completion of a needs assessment, the insurer demonstrates that the applicant's SGLI death benefit, together with any other military survivor benefits, savings and investments, survivor income, and other life insurance are insufficient to meet the applicant's insurable needs for life insurance. For the purposes of this subdivision:
  - "Insurable needs" are the risks associated with premature death taking into consideration the financial obligations and immediate and future cash needs of the applicant's estate, survivors or dependents.
  - "Other military survivor benefits" include, but are not limited to:
    » the death gratuity;
    » funeral reimbursement;
    » transition assistance;
    » survivor and dependents' educational assistance;
    » dependency and indemnity compensation;
    » TRICARE healthcare benefits;
    » survivor housing benefits and allowances;
    » federal income tax forgiveness; and
    » Social Security survivor benefits.
- Excluding individually issued annuities, offering for sale or selling any life insurance contract that includes a side fund:
- unless interest credited accrues from the date of deposit to the date of withdrawal and permits withdrawals without limit or penalty;
- unless the applicant has been provided with a schedule of effective rates of return based upon cash flows of the combined product; and
- which by default diverts or transfers funds accumulated in the side fund to pay, reduce or offset any premiums due.
- Excluding individually issued annuities, offering for sale or selling any life insurance contract that after considering all policy benefits, including but not limited to endowment, return of premium or persistency, does not comply with standard nonforfeiture law for life insurance.
- Selling any life insurance product to an individual known to be a service member that excludes coverage if the insured's death is related to war, declared or undeclared, or any act related to military service except for an accidental death coverage, e.g., double indemnity, which may be excluded.

14VAC 5-420-50

VA PPL LH-2_16298

Section V Review

1) When a life insurance advertisement uses the phrase "no medical examination required" when issue of the policy is not guaranteed, the advertisement:
   a. is illegal.
   b. must be approved by the Commission.
   c. must be advertising a life insurance policy with a death benefit that is $25,000 or lower
   d. must include further disclosure that plainly explains that issuance of the policy may depend on the answers to heath questions contained in the application

2) If a life insurance policy requires regular modal premiums to be made to age 100 or until the death of the insured in order for the coverage to remain in force:
   a. an advertisement may not include premium requirements.
   b. an advertisement for it may not represent that premium payments will not be required for every year of the policy.
   c. an advertisement for it may use the phrase "vanishing premium."
   d. an advertisement for it may use the phrase "premiums vanish."

3) If an annuity customer gives a licensed agent the names of friends and family who might be interested in an annuity, the customer:
   a. may be credited with a higher interest rate on his annuity for up to one year.
   b. may have withdrawal charges waived on his annuity.
   c. may not receive any benefits not available to all policyholders generally.
   d. may have up to a $1000 additional contribution made by the insurer to his annuity.

4) Under what circumstances must the phrase "this is a paid endorsement" be used in a life insurance advertisement?
   a. Whenever a testimonial is used in a life insurance advertisement.
   b. When a person endorses the life insurer in the advertisement and that person receives a financial benefit greater than required union scale wages.
   c. Whenever a paid actor is used in a life insurance advertisement.
   d. Whenever statistics are used in a life insurance advertisement.

5) When an insurer operates in several states and creates advertising that crosses state lines, for example through television or the internet, generally, its advertising must follow the licensing laws of:
   a. each state in which the insurance is being advertised
   b. its state of domicile, where it is a domestic insurer
   c. the federal government
   d. the state with the largest population in which it advertises

6) Under the suitability laws, advice provided by an agent, or an insurer where no agent is involved, to an individual consumer that results in a purchase or exchange of an annuity in accordance with that advice is a:
   a. recommendation
   b. proposal
   c. suggestion
   d. coercive action

7) If a life policy is replaced by a life policy from the same issuer, generally, replacement requirements:
   a. do not apply
   b. apply
   c. partially apply
   d. none of the above

8) In Virginia's required disclosure, the "Important Notice, Replacement of Life Insurance or Annuities", if a new life policy is purchased and premiums are no longer made on an existing life policy and it is surrendered:
   a. the new sale may not be made
   b. replacement is considered to be present
   c. replacement is not considered to be present
   d. no regulatory provisions apply

9) One of the conditions for payment under an accelerated payment of benefits provision is the inability to perform two of six defined activities of daily living, which are bathing, dressing, continence, toileting or:
   a. ambulating
   b. transferring
   c. rotating
   d. moving

10) Which of the following is an allowable payout option from an accelerated death benefit on a life insurance policy?
    a. A lump sum payment
    b. A period certain and life annuity
    c. A straight life annuity
    d. A joint and survivor life annuity

11) What types of groups are NOT eligible for group insurance?
    a. Creditor Groups
    b. Individual employer groups
    c. Labor unions
    d. A neighborhood group formed just to obtain group insurance

12) To exercise a conversion privilege on a group life policy, the application for the individual policy and the first modal premium must be paid to the insurer within:
    a. 10 days after the termination
    b. 31 days after the termination
    c. 40 days after the termination
    d. 60 days after the termination

13) An individual life insurer receives a policy loan request on May 1 for a policy that has been in force for ten years. The loan amount is to be paid to the policyowner. By what date must the insurer issue the policy loan?
    a. May 31
    b. June 30
    c. August 31
    d. November 1

14) A viator opened a life insurance policy 18 months ago. It is the first life insurance coverage he has ever had. He discovered he is terminally ill two days ago. Under Virginia law:
    a. He must wait for 6 months before he can exercise a viatical settlement.
    b. He can never exercise a viatical settlement.
    c. He can exercise a viatical settlement according to state law.
    d. He must exercise a viatical settlement to prevent seizure of his assets.

15) To catch the attention of military personnel, an agent that markets product to a military base adds a logo to his fliers that is similar to the Department of Veteran's Affairs (the VA) logo. This logo:
    a. is a legal, innovative marketing technique.
    b. is allowed as long as it is not identical to the VA's logo.
    c. is an illegal insurance advertising practice under state law because it is deceptive.
    d. is illegal because the agent markets near a military base.

HEALTH

Section VI: Types of Health Policies

This section focuses on types of health insurance policies. Topics include:

- Disability income insurance
- Accidental death and dismemberment coverage
- Medical expense insurance
- Medicare supplement insurance
- Group insurance
- Long-term care insurance
- Limited benefit plans

Health insurance is also known as accident and sickness insurance. *Accidental injury* is generally defined in this insurance as injury to the body as a result of an accident and *sickness* is generally defined as illness or disease.

Disability Income Insurance

Disability income insurance, or DII, is insurance that provides protection against financial loss due to the inability to earn income because of disability. DII provides a stated income to the insured, and pays benefits due to illness (sickness) or injury (accident).

Statistically, it is more likely for a person to become disabled prior to retirement than to die. Disability may not be permanent, but lack of income for a period of several weeks or months is financially difficult for many individuals or families to manage. Still, people are often unprotected from this financial risk. The disability income insurance agent can provide a valuable service to clients by educating them about disability protection and offering coverage to them.

Defining Disability and Benefits

Disability income policies pay benefits when the insured's condition meets the definition of a covered disability under the policy. Disability policies may define disability based on being able to work in *any gainful occupation* or in the insured's *own occupation*. In some cases, disability policies use both of these definitions, and pay benefits for a specified period if the insured is unable to work in his or her own occupation. In other policies, a loss-of-income definition is used, and benefits are paid based on the insured losing income because of a covered accident or illness.

Total Disability

One of the circumstances that cause a disability income policy to pay benefits occurs when the insured meets the policy's definition of total disability. Generally, *total disability* is defined to mean that the insured is unable to perform the duties of his or her own regular occupation, or any gainful occupation, is under a doctor's care, and the insured is not working.

Partial Disability

Partial disability is generally defined to mean the inability to perform some, but not all, of the important duties of the insured's regular occupation. A specified percentage of time the insured is able to work in the occupation may also be included in the partial disability definition, such as "the insured's inability to engage in his or her regular occupation for longer than 50% of the time normally spent in performing the usual duties of the regular occupation."

The payment amount for partial disability is generally some percentage of the total benefit amount, such as 50% of the benefit amount for total disability.

Temporary Disability

Total and partial disabilities may be temporary, and often are. Benefits for total and partial disabilities generally continue while the insured is disabled, or for the policy's benefit period, whichever is shorter.

Presumptive Disabilities

Some conditions are automatically considered total disabilities under DII policies. The policy will pay benefits for these conditions on the basis of them being total disabilities. These conditions are known as *presumptive disabilities*, and may include loss of sight in both eyes, loss of hearing in both ears, loss of both hands, loss of both feet, and loss of one hand and one foot. Some policies require the loss to be by severance, which means having been severed

VA PPL LH-2_16298

or cut off from the limb. Other policies pay based on the loss of use of these body members.

Disability Due to Sickness

Disability due to sickness is covered in disability income policies. In many policies, the sickness must manifest itself during the policy period in order for the disability to be covered. *For example, if Joe had a diagnosed heart condition prior to purchasing a disability income policy, and six months later had a heart attack during the policy period that left him disabled, the disability would probably be excluded from coverage.*

In individual policies, disabilities from sicknesses manifesting themselves within five years of the inception of coverage are generally excluded. In group disability income policies, disabilities from sicknesses manifesting themselves or treated within one year of inception of coverage are generally excluded.

Disability Due to Accidents

For disability benefits to be paid, older policies may require that bodily injury must have occurred by accidental means. Today, the definition used to trigger benefits is disability due to accidental bodily injury, meaning that the result, which is the bodily injury, must be accidental.

Individual Disability Income Insurance

Individual disability income policies are marketed primarily to the self-employed and high-income executives, professionals and businessowners. Individual disability income coverage often has high total disability benefits, is more likely to include an own occupation total disability definition, and may include long-term benefits lasting to age 65 or for life. High-income policies are generally only affordable by professionals such as surgeons or lawyers, or by entertainers or athletes.

Types of Disability Benefits

Disability income insurance policies may include different methods or calculations for determining the amount of disability benefits. One method pays a stated percentage of gross earnings once it is determined the insured is totally disabled. Another method, used often for partial disabilities, but in some policies for all types of disabilities, is to pay a pro-rata benefit based on loss-of-income. The third calculation type is also a loss-of-income method, and is found commonly in policies with an occupation related disability definition. The third calculation type is known as a residual disability benefit.

Stated Percentage of Gross Earnings – Total Disability

For total disability, some disability income policies pay a stated percentage of gross earnings. When the insured purchases the policy, the stated percentage is selected, and may be 50%, 75%, 80% or some other percentage. Most policies do not allow insureds to be paid a benefit that exceeds 70% to 80% of gross earnings.

The gross earnings of the insured are evaluated at the time of disability. The average earnings of the prior six to twelve months may be used to determine the gross earnings amount. *For example, Sam purchases a disability income policy that will pay 75% of his gross earnings, up to a maximum benefit of $4,000, should he become totally disabled. He earns an average of $5,000 over the six months immediately preceding his total disability. The policy pays Sam $3750 a month (75% x $5,000) for the benefit period of the policy, or for as long as the total disability lasts, whichever is shorter.*

Income Benefits – Monthly Indemnity – Partial and Total Disabilities

For partial disabilities, a loss-of-income calculation may apply in policies that use a stated percentage for total disabilities. In addition, some policies do not define total disability, but simply look at loss of income for all types of disabilities. Under the loss-of-income approach, benefits are paid on a pro-rata basis if earnings are reduced due to a covered disability. *For example, if the maximum monthly policy benefit is $4,000, and the insured's income is reduced by 60%, the policy will pay $2,400 a month, or $4,000 x 60%. For those policies that use this approach for total disability, if total disability occurs, the policy will pay $4,000 per month, or 100% of the monthly maximum benefit.* Some policies consider a loss of income of 85% or more as automatically equivalent to total disability, so will pay 100% of the monthly benefit if the disability causes the insured to lose 85% or more in income.

VA PPL LH-2_16298

Residual Benefits – Partial Disability

Insurers want to encourage insureds to return to work. However, under older policies, an insured could lose all disability benefits if he or she returned to work, because the insured would no longer meet the policy's definition of total disability. Recognizing that relying solely on the definition of total disability as the basis for paying benefits could cause a disincentive to returning to work, insurers began offering *residual disability* benefits. Residual benefits are paid when insureds return to work, but do not return to their full earning capacity.

Residual benefits pay a pro-rata amount of the policy benefit based on the loss of income due to an accident or sickness. Requirements of residual benefit payments may include that:

- The insured is unable to perform one or more of the important daily business duties of the insured's occupation; or
- The insured is unable to do usual daily business duties for as long as the insured would normally be able to do them; and
- The loss of income is at least 25% of the insured's prior monthly earnings; and
- The insured is under the care of a physician.

Other policies that use residual benefit provisions may have simpler requirements, such as only requiring that loss of income be at least 20% of prior earnings, due to an injury or sickness.

Recurring Disabilities and Benefits

Disability income policies also vary regarding their coverage of *recurring disabilities*. One type of provision treats a second total disability due to the same or related condition within six months of a prior total disability, as the same disability. This means the waiting period is waived for the second disability that meet this criteria, and the benefit period is considered to have begun at the time benefits began for the first total disability. If the second total disability occurs over six months after the first one, it is treated as a separate disability, so the waiting period must be satisfied before benefits begin.

Other recurring disability provisions treat a total disability recurring three months after a prior total disability due to the same cause as the same

disability for the purpose of applying the waiting and benefit periods. Some individual policies for professionals waive the *elimination period* for periods of disability that occur within five years of one another and that are from the same cause.

The *elimination period* is the waiting period after a health insurance policy goes into effect and before benefits begin. The elimination period may vary based on the type of benefit to be paid.

Elimination and Benefit Periods
Benefit Periods

The benefit period of disability income policies may vary by type of policy and type of disability benefit. *Short-term disability* policies pay benefits for a maximum of 26, 52 or 104 weeks. *Long-term disability* policies may have benefit periods of 2, 5, or 10 years, through age 65, or for life.

A policy that pays benefits for life may vary the amount of the benefit based on the age of the insured at the time the disability commences. Such a provision may be stated as follows:

> If the insured becomes totally disabled before age 65 and remains continuously so disabled to the end of the benefit period, the insurer will pay a percentage of the monthly disability benefit each month for the rest of the insured's life while the insured is totally disabled.

A table is included with this type of provision that lists the percentage of benefits that will be paid, based on the insured's age.

Waiting or Elimination Periods

The waiting period, also known as the elimination period, is the length of time after which disability occurs before benefits will be paid. Waiting periods may be 30, 60, 90, 180 or 365 days.

Longer waiting periods can make a policy less expensive to purchase. A policy with a 180-day waiting period can have significantly lower premiums than that same policy with a thirty-day waiting period. The applicant must consider whether savings or sick leave pay can provide sufficient income to merit the reduction in premium that comes from the selection of a longer waiting period.

Policies can also vary regarding whether or not the elimination period must be satisfied in consecutive days. Under some policies, the insured must be disabled for the entire waiting period in consecutive days. In others, the days of disability do not have to be consecutive. Under this type of policy, if an insured is disabled for a two-week period, then later for three days, and then for seven days, the insured has satisfied 24 days of the elimination period.

Waiver of Premium

The waiver of premium provision found in many disability policies waives premium once the insured has been determined to be totally disabled for a specified period of time, such as 90 days. Premiums paid during the specified waiting period are often refunded once the insured qualifies for the waiver of premium.

Guaranteed Renewable Contracts

Most disability income policies issued today are *guaranteed renewable* contracts. Guaranteed renewable contracts are renewed as long as premium is paid. Premium rates can only be increased if premiums are increased for an entire class of insureds. The insurer may not raise premiums just on a single insured's policy.

Noncancellable Contracts

Noncancellable contracts guarantee that the premium on a contract will never go up at renewal, up through a specified period or age. Because this type of policy provision is difficult to manage from a risk standpoint, few disability income policies issued today are noncancellable.

Optionally Renewable

Optionally renewable contracts may be non-renewed at any renewal period by the insurer. Optionally renewable contracts are uncommon.

Conditionally Renewable

Conditionally renewable contracts include some provisions that give the insurer the right to non-renew a policy. For example, a policy may be conditionally renewable at the insured's age 65. If the insured is still employed full-time, the insurer will renew the contract, if the insured continues to work. If the insured stops working at age 65 or thereafter, the policy will not renew.

An example of a conditionally renewable provision is as follows:

> After the insured is age 65, the insured may renew the policy at the end of each renewal period as long as the insured is at work full time. But, the insured must be at work at least thirty hours each week for at least ten months each year.

Unique Aspects of Individual Disability Underwriting

Disability income insurance is a form of health insurance, but includes important factors not relevant in other forms of health insurance. Disability income insurance provides payment if the insured becomes disabled as defined under the policy. Underwriting in disability income insurance does not just look at the current health and health history of an insured, but also attempts to determine less easily documented risk characteristics related to the motivation of an insured to return to work should a disability occur.

Disability income insurance applications generally include the following items:

- Age of the insured
- Sex of the insured
- Occupation of the insured, including details regarding the insured's position
- Medical history
- An explanation of medical conditions, including their frequency, severity and likelihood of recurrence
- Height and weight of the insured
- Blood pressure and other health indicators
- Financial information such as the applicant's income, unearned income and net worth
- Mental health history
- Treatment for drug or alcohol use
- Prior coverage history
- Claims history

Disability income insurance applications include information regarding the medical history and current health conditions of an applicant that is similar to that found on other health insurance applications. However, disability underwriters are more concerned about whether or not a medical condition will lead to disability than are underwriters of other forms of health insurance.

Disability income insurance applications also include information regarding the financial status of an applicant that is not found in other forms of health insurance. This is because disability underwriters attempt to issue policies with benefit levels that do not encourage an insured to submit claims in order to better their financial position. Even the most generous disability income benefits are generally designed to meet basic income needs of the insured, not to give an insured a higher income than he or she would have had if the insured had been able to keep working.

Disability income policies also include information regarding the position of the insured within a business. Individual disability income policies are often marketed to owners of businesses, professionals or key executives. One reason that disability insurers look for such individuals to purchase their policies is that such individuals are generally highly motivated to return to work, meaning that disability income payments may not continue as long as they would for someone with less motivation to return to work.

Underwriting Factors

Underwriting for all disability income policies includes consideration of all the following items. However, for higher-limit policies, the insurer may require more documentation and do a more thorough check on each underwriting factor than if lower benefit limits were involved.

Age

Age is an important factor in individual disability income insurance underwriting. Younger females statistically file more disability claims than males of the same age. The risk of disability increases with age, so the risk increases. Because of this increase in risk, most long-term disability policies, including high-limit policies, cease coverage at age 55 or later, and often reduce benefits payable at older ages.

Occupation

Occupation is one of the pivotal underwriting factors in disability income insurance. Insurers generally file rates for disability coverage in four to six categories, with each occupation assigned a certain risk category. High-limit policies often include occupations in the highest risk categories.

Medical History

Medical history is also an important underwriting factor in disability insurance. A limited paramedical exam or a full medical exam may be required, depending on the type of policy written and its limits.

Certain preexisting conditions are excluded from coverage, at least for a specified period. Certain chronic conditions could keep an applicant from being insurable.

The mental health history of an applicant may also play a factor in an applicant's insurability and premium charged. The likelihood of an emotional or mental disability is analyzed by the underwriters.

Earnings

The financial situation of the applicant is also an important consideration for the disability income insurance underwriter. The earnings of the applicant must generally be documented, and the applicant's unearned income and net worth are also taken into consideration. For high-limit policies, the insurer will require significant financial information.

Moral Hazards

Insurance policy terms and underwriting standards consider *hazards* that may be present in the type of insurance being issued. A hazard increases the chance of loss. Disability income pays benefits when an individual is not working. The *moral hazard* imbedded in this feature is that the insured may take the view that he or she is being paid not to work. The attraction of being paid to work can lead an insured to dishonestly mischaracterize his or her condition in order to continue to collect benefits.

One way that this moral hazard is addressed in disability income policies is through the waiting period. Today, long-term disability policies are rarely sold that have waiting periods of under 30 days. When a longer waiting period is selected, premiums decrease. One of the reasons for the premium decrease is that many disabilities do not last long, so an extended waiting period means that the policy will not need to pay for these shorter disabilities. Another reason the premium is decreased is because the risk of this moral hazard decreases as the waiting period is extended. It becomes more expensive to the insured to pretend to be disabled if the policy does not pay benefits for several weeks.

Unforeseen Increase in Risk

Disability is being defined in broader and broader terms. The passage of the Americans With Disabilities Act, for example, has brought into the courts many plaintiffs asking the court to consider conditions as qualifying for disability that were not previously generally considered disabling conditions. Obesity and emotional disorders may now be considered as disabilities. Pressure is placed on insurers to cover such conditions under their existing disability policies.

Because of these changes, it can be difficult for insurers to accurately measure the risks they are covering. This has led to more expensive policies, with shorter benefit periods and more strictly defined provisions than policies of the past.

Motivation to Return to Work

Disability insurers do not want to insure people who do not want to return to work. A few decades ago, statistics indicated that professionals such as surgeons and attorneys tend to return to work faster than less-skilled workers. Insurers wrote many liberal, high-limit policies on individuals in these types of professions.

However, in the past several years, insurers discovered that a type of profession does not always mean a greater likelihood of returning to work. Doctors today are less satisfied with their work than were doctors several years ago. This has been blamed on the lack of control many doctors have over their own patients. Many attorneys do not make the high incomes they had hoped for, in part because there are so many attorneys.

Society as a whole has seemed to have had a change in the attitude it takes toward disability. It is more socially acceptable today than in the past to stop working and remain on disability. This attitude is found in all income levels.

Benefit Limits

Because of factors like these, insurers found that the liberal policies written for the higher income professional market were causing losses for them. Today, high-limit policies are much more restricted in their provisions than several years ago. Benefit limits are not as high as they once were, and insurers may require more medical-related documents and medical examinations than in the past to verify disability as long as benefits are being paid.

However, policies are still available to meet the needs of high-income or high-risk individuals. The applicant for this type of policy should expect to undergo rigorous underwriting and to provide significant amounts of documentation upon submitting a claim.

Business Overhead Expense Insurance

Another way disability income insurance is used in a business setting is to provide income during periods of temporary disability. Businesses have fixed expenses that must be paid, whether the business is making money or not. If an owner or other key employee becomes disabled, the business may suffer a reduction of income, and have difficulty paying these overhead expenses. A disability income policy, known as *business overhead expense insurance*, or BOE, can be purchased on the owners and key employees. The policy will pay a monthly benefit to the business so that the business can meet its ongoing overhead.

Amount of Coverage

The types of expenses that the owner should consider when determining the amount of coverage to purchase to protect against this risk include:

- Mortgage or rent
- Electricity, heat, water
- Telephone
- Mailing and shipping
- Employee's salaries and benefits
- Property taxes
- Accounting and legal expenses
- Dues and subscriptions
- Depreciation of owned equipment and business premises

VA PPL LH-2_16298

- Insurance premiums, such as malpractice insurance or health coverage
- Other fixed expenses

The owner should consider his or her share of these expenses to determine the appropriate coverage amount for a BOE policy.

Business Overhead Expense Insurance Features

Benefit Amounts

BOE insurance pays benefits based on covered overhead expenses. The policy defines what items are covered and what items are excluded. The items listed above in the discussion of the "Amount of Coverage" are generally covered by BOE policies.

Exclusions from coverage under a BOE policy may include:

- Cost of goods sold
- Additions to inventory
- Wages or other compensation to the insured
- Wages or other compensation for an individual hired to perform the functions of the insured
- Wages or other compensation to a family member, unless the family member was working for the business prior to the disability for at least a specified period of time, such as 12 months

The policy will generally only pay a benefit amount equal to the actual covered expenses incurred, up to the maximum monthly benefit of the policy.

BOE Feature	Explanation
Renewability	Guaranteed renewable through specified age; may be noncancellable
Definition of total disability	Insured unable to perform main duties of regular occupation due to injury or sickness and under a doctor's care
Guaranteed insurability benefit	Gives specified times during the policy life that benefits may be increased; increase may require evidence of insurability and financial underwriting in order to be approved
Partial disability benefit	Pays the amount of covered overhead expenses that exceed the gross income of the business during the insured's partial disability

Accumulation of Benefits

Since a BOE policy may only pay benefits equal to covered overhead expenses, some policies include an accumulation of benefits provision. Under this type of provision, when covered expenses are less than the monthly maximum payment, unused amounts of the monthly benefit can be carried over to a future month when expenses exceed benefits, or to extend the benefit period.

For example, CBD Industries has a BOE policy that pays up to $8,000 monthly upon the owner's total disability. The owner becomes totally disabled, and benefits commence under the policy in January. Covered overhead expenses total $6,000 in January, $5,800 in February and $8,900 in March. Because covered overhead expenses in January and February were under the maximum benefit of $8,000, there were $4,200 ([$8,000-$6,000] + [$8,000-$5800]) in carryover benefits. Therefore, the full $8,900 of covered expenses in March are paid by the policy and $3,300 ($4,200-$900) of accumulated benefits still remain.

Disability Buy-Sell Agreements

The terms of the sale of the shares of the deceased or disabled owner are made under a buy-sell agreement. The buy-sell agreement sets the specific terms of the sale. The method that will be used to value the business at the time of an owner's death or disability is included in the agreement. Also included are provisions concerning:

- Who will buy each owner's shares
- Under what circumstances, or trigger events, the shares will be sold. Trigger events may include:
  - Death
  - Disability
  - Retirement
  - Divorce
  - Signed agreement by all owners (e.g. if an owner wants to sell his or her shares in order to move, or take his or her share of the profits)

There are four basic types of buy-sell agreements: stock redemption, cross purchase, wait and see, and third-party buy-out.

Stock Redemption Plans

Under a stock redemption plan, the business buys the deceased or disabled stockholder's shares. This type of plan is also known as an entity purchase plan, since the entity, the business, purchases the shares. The plan includes a formula for determining the value of the shares to be purchased at the time of disability, death or other trigger event. The insurance used to fund a stock redemption plan is structured so that the business purchases a life and a disability policy on each major shareholder and the benefit is used to pay for the shares upon death or disability.

Cross Purchase Plans

A cross purchase plan sets up an agreement for the remaining partners or owners to buy the deceased or disabled owner's share of the business. Each owner or partner is the beneficiary on a life policy and the payee of a disability policy on the other owners or partners.

For example, assume STS Construction has four partners: Ed, Joe, Ralph and Tom. Ed is the owner and beneficiary of three life insurance policies, where Joe is the insured on one, Ralph is the insured on another and Tom is the insured on the third. Ed is also the owner and payee on three disability policies, and the three partners are each an insured on one of the three disability policies. Ed pays the premiums for all the policies on which he is an owner. In like manner, each of the other partners own life and disability policies on the other three partners. If Ed becomes totally disabled, the three disability policies on which he is the insured will pay lump sum amounts to the remaining three partners. The partners use these proceeds to buy Ed's share of the business, giving Ed needed financial resources and allowing the business to continue.

Wait and See Plans

A wait and see buy-sell agreement gives options to the business and shareholders in the business to buy the deceased or disabled insured's shares. Because of IRS rules, these agreements need to give the option to buy in a specified order. The entity has the first option to buy. If the entity does not buy all the shares, the remaining shareholders may purchase the shares. Any remaining shares must be purchased by the entity.

Insurance under a wait and see plan can be structured in more than one way. The corporation could purchase insurance on each of the shareholders and then use the proceeds of the

policy to pay the deceased or disabled shareholder for the affected shares. If the corporation opts not to buy all the shares, the remaining insurance proceeds can be loaned to the remaining shareholders so that they can purchase them. Or, the shareholders could purchase insurance on one another as is done under a cross purchase plan, and if the remaining shareholders opt not to buy all the shares, they could loan the insurance proceeds to the corporation for the purchase.

Third-Party Buy-Out

A third-party buy-out plan provides for a specified named party to purchase the deceased or disabled individual's share of the business. The third-party owns and is named beneficiary or payee on the insurance, and the current owner is the insured.

Planning Before Death or Disability

It is important that a buy-sell agreement be put into place before an owner's death or disability occurs. Without a buy-sell agreement and the purchase of insurance to fund it, several outcomes are likely:

- The business suffers financially or must be dissolved in order to pay the deceased's estate for the owner's share of the business
- The business suffers financially or must be dissolved because a key shareholder or owner is disabled and cannot provide important functions and resulting income to the business
- The deceased or disabled owner's spouse or children try to take over the deceased or disabled owner's job functions and are often unqualified to do so
- The deceased or disabled owner's spouse puts pressure on the remaining owners to sell the business in order to provide income
- The deceased or disabled owner's spouse or children sell the business at a much decreased price, due to the pressure of needing money, or due to lack of knowledge about the market
- The deceased or disabled owner's spouse or children sell the owner's share of the business to a person or entity unsatisfactory to the rest of the owners, perhaps even to a competitor.

VA PPL LH-2_16298

By determining who will buy the business prior to death or disability, the owners are protecting their surviving spouse, family and other dependents, the other owners of the business, and is also ensuring the business will be able to continue with a minimum of disruption.

Disability Buy-Out Policy Features

Disability insurance used to fund buy-sell agreements is known as *disability buy-out insurance*.

Disability Buy-Out Features	Explanation
Benefit trigger conditions	Insured totally disabled, buy-sell agreement is in effect and purpose of buy-sell is the disability
Definition of Total Disability	Insured is unable to perform substantial and material duties of insured's regular occupation, is under the care of the physician, and is not working in any position for the firm
Benefit payments	Option 1 – Lump sum
	Option 2 – Monthly payments for 12 - 24 months
	Option 3 – Smaller lump sum with continued monthly payments
Renewability	Guaranteed renewable through certain age – may decrease benefits at later ages
Guaranteed insurability	As business value increases may purchase more insurance without evidence of insurability
Waiver of premium	Premium waived when insured is totally disabled for a specified period of time, such as 90 days – premiums paid during the specified period may be refunded once the insured qualifies for the waiver of premium
Survivorship benefit	Besides lump sum at death pays a survivorship benefit to a surviving spouse or other dependent – generally 2 or 3 times the monthly benefit
Legal and accounting fees benefit	Pays an additional few thousand dollars for legal and accounting fees associated with exercising buy-sell agreement upon the disability of the insured

Group Disability Income Insurance

Group disability policies are marketed through associations to the self-employed, such as associations for engineers, accountants or computer analysts. They may also be available through clubs and fraternal organizations. Most commonly, group policies are issued through employers.

Self-Employed Group Plans

Purchasing group disability income provides a method for self-employed individuals to obtain disability income coverage on a more affordable basis than if an individual disability income policy were purchased. Often, the best way for a self-employed individual to find group disability income insurance is to join an association that offers group disability income insurance to members. Otherwise, individual policies can be purchased by the self-employed. Benefit amounts and length of waiting periods can be adjusted to make the individual plans more affordable.

Disability Income as an Employee Benefit

Group disability income is often offered through an employer to employees. Premiums may be paid solely by the employer, paid by the employee, or shared by the employer and employee.

Group disability income coverage offered by employers has some differences from individual DII:

Feature	Individual Disability Insurance	Group Disability Insurance
Benefit Amounts	Often high, for high-income earners	Variety of income and benefit levels in the employer group
Waiting/Elimination Periods	Insured selects waiting period at application	Employees may or may not have right to select waiting period*
Eligibility	Must pass health underwriting standards	May be guaranteed issue, regardless of health status
Benefit Periods	Long term, such as 2 years	Short-term or long-term plans may be available

If employees may select the waiting period, shorter periods will require higher premiums than longer periods.

Short-Term Disability Plans

Short-term disability plans generally pay benefits for periods of 13 weeks to 2 years. A common benefit period in plans today is 26 weeks. Short-

VA PPL LH-2_16298

term disability plans generally have very short waiting periods, from one to seven days for sicknesses, and first day coverage for accidents.

Partial disability is not normally covered under group short-term disability plans. The employee must be totally disabled, which is generally defined to mean that the employee cannot perform the duties of his or her occupation.

Most short-term disability plans pay benefits of 50%-70% of earnings. Preexisting conditions are often covered, and many employer sponsored short-term disability plans cover disability due to drug or alcohol abuse and mental disorders. The maximum benefit under a short-term disability plan is normally relatively low, such as $2,000/month.

Short-term disability coverage generally only applies to employees who work a certain minimum number of hours per week, such as 20 or 30 hours.

Long-Term Disability Plans

Long-term disability employer plans pay benefits for two years, up to age 60 or age 65. If the worker continues to work full time after the normal maximum age, benefits may still be payable, but often with a reduced maximum benefit amount.

A combination of total disability definitions are often used in long-term group plans. An own occupation disability income definition may be used for the first two years of disability, and an any gainful occupation definition is used for benefits to continue after the initial two year period.

Long-term disability plans typically pay maximum benefits of 50% to 65% of the employee's earnings. Maximum benefit amounts may be $2,000, $3,000 or $4,000. This maximum benefit cap can cause a disability coverage gap for highly paid employees. *For example, an executive who earns $10,000 a month may be capped at a $4,000 disability income benefit. His or her lifestyle and monthly bills are likely to require the $10,000 per month earned prior to disability, and savings can be eaten up pretty quickly with a shortfall of $6,000 per month.*

Even if an employee is receiving Workers Compensation or Social Security Disability benefits, long-term disability plans may continue to pay benefits. However, benefits are generally reduced by the amounts received under these social insurance plans.

Workers Compensation Insurance is a form of insurance that covers employer risks such as injury, disability or death that occurs to employees while on the job.

Special provisions of employer long-term disability plans may include survivor benefits, a pension accrual benefit, rehabilitation benefits, waiver of premium and convertibility.

Common Benefits in Employer Long-Term DI Plans	
Benefit	**Explanation**
Survivor Benefits	Benefit to survivor often 3 times monthly total disability benefit – only paid if deceased was receiving or eligible for total disability benefits
Rehabilitation Benefits	Generally paid if insurer finds employee good candidate for rehabilitation for specified period such as 36 months – disability payments continue during rehabilitation
Convertibility	Employer coverage may be converted to individual coverage under circumstances such as termination of plan or termination of employment
Waiver of Premium	While employee is receiving disability benefits premium does not have to be paid by employee or employer – premium may be refunded for the elimination period when waiver of premium is triggered

Pension Accrual Benefits

Pension accrual benefits make a contribution to an employee's pension plan while the employee is disabled. The amount of the contribution may be both the employee's contribution and the employer-matching amount. *For example, an employer may offer a retirement plan that allows the employee to contribute up to 10% of his or her earnings, and the employer will match up to 6% of the employee's contribution. Jill, an employee, has been making contributions equaling 8% of her earnings. Jill becomes totally disabled, and the disability plan will make a retirement plan contribution equaling her 8% pre-disability contributions, plus the 6% employer match, while she is totally disabled.*

VA PPL LH-2_16298

Business Disability Insurance

Disability insurance can be used to help a business from suffering financial loss due to the disability of a key owner, partner or shareholder. Disability insurance is used in business continuation plans, and as business overhead protection.

Key Employee Disability Income

Disability insurance is an essential component of business continuation plans. A business continuation plan addresses the risk that a businessowner, a *key employee*, a partner or a stockholder in a closely held corporation dies or becomes disabled. Without this individual contributing to the workplace, the business suffers significantly, or may not even be able to continue. The business continuation plan provides the steps that will be taken to ensure a business will continue when an owner, partner or shareholder leaves the enterprise.

Life and disability insurance are generally purchased to fund business continuation plans. In the case of death or long-term disability, insurance proceeds can be used by the remaining partners, stockholders or a potential buyer, to purchase the deceased or disabled owner's share of the business. The big differences in the disability insurance used to fund a business continuation plan and the types of disability insurance discussed so far in this course is that this insurance makes a lump-sum payment, or pays over a 12- to 24-month period, and can be written for amounts as high as several million dollars.

The business owns the policy, the key employee is the insured, and the business is the beneficiary on a key employee policy.

Accidental Death and Dismemberment

Accidental Death and Dismemberment insurance, or AD&D insurance, pays a lump-sum benefit in the case of accidental death or in the event of the loss of body members due to accidental injury. This form of insurance may be part of a disability insurance plan, may be sold as a stand-alone policy, or may be part of a group plan.

Benefits

The payment for accidental death is referred to as the *principal sum* under an AD&D policy. For example, an AD&D policy may be purchased with a $50,000 principle sum, which is the amount paid for accidental death, and is the maximum the policy will pay. The principal sum may also be paid for a severe injury, such as loss of two limbs or loss of sight in both eyes.

The payment amount for other coverages under the policy is known as the *capital sum*. The amount paid varies depending on which body member is lost, or what type of accidental injury occurs. The capital sum payments are expressed as a percentage of the principal sum.

Examples of Capital Sum Payments	
Loss of one hand	50% of Principal Sum
Loss of sight in one eye	33 1/3 % of Principal Sum
Loss of one thumb or finger	25% of Principal Sum

Definition of Accident

In AD&D policies, a key definition is accident. Some older AD&D policies only cover death, injury, or loss due to an injury caused by external, violent and accidental means. This is more restrictive than today's policies that use a definition that covers *accidental bodily injury*. Today's policies require that only the bodily injury be accidental, not also the means that led to the bodily injury.

Medical Reimbursement Benefit (Non-Disabling Injury)

Disability income policies may include a provision or a rider that will provide reimbursement for medical expenses related to a non-disabling injury or accident. The limit for this reimbursement is generally a specified percentage of the monthly benefit stated in the policy.

Medical Expense Insurance

Medical expense coverage is provided through various types of insurers, health plans and managed care providers.

 VA PPL LH-2_16298

Basic Hospital, Medical and Surgical Policies

A basic medical expense coverage policy pays for services of physicians, hospitals and nurses, and pays for expenses such as:

- Hospital room and board
- Hospital related expenses
- Surgical expenses
- Anesthesia expenses
- Treatment for nervous disorders
- Accidental injury expenses
- Maternity health care expenses
- Physical exams
- Second surgical opinions
- Outpatient surgery
- Home care
- Hospice care
- Screening exams for disease
- Prescriptions
- Certain dental care expenses
- Certain vision care expenses

Some basic medical expense coverage pays benefits based on an expense-incurred basis. As health care services are required, the insurer or plan reimburses the health care provider or insured for the cost of care. These plans are indemnification plans that indemnify as expenses are incurred. They include maximum indemnification amounts that vary based on the service provided, e.g. a plan might pay up to $500 per day for hospitalization expenses.

Some medical expense coverage plans, such as Blue Cross and Blue Shield plans, are prepaid services plans. In return for the amounts paid by members or insureds, they receive care in hospitals that are part of the plan or they receive surgical care by physicians that are part of the plan. Blue Cross provides coverage for hospital expenses, outpatient expenses such as x-rays and tests and supplemental benefits such as nursing care while Blue Shield covers surgical expenses, medical expenses and other services associated with surgical procedures.

Another way medical expense coverage is provided is through managed care organizations, such as Health Maintenance Organizations (HMOs) or Health Insuring Corporations (HICs), Physician Hospital Organizations (PHOs),

Preferred Provider Organizations (PPOs) and similar entities. The services from these plans are paid through capitation. The health care providers are paid a certain amount per member from member premiums, and the providers give services as stated in the plan agreement.

Managed care refers to any health delivery system that includes the utilization of a network of providers and a process of overseeing the types of care and services provided by the physicians and other parties supplying health care inside of the network.

Network refers to the physicians, hospitals, clinics, group practices and other health care providers participating in the managed care plan.

Capitation means to number by the head. It refers to the practice of paying for patient care based on the number of patients under the care of a physician.

Limited and Comprehensive Health Coverage Plans

Limited accident and sickness policies are offered that cover loss due to injury due to only certain accidents or sickness only due to certain diseases. For example, there are policies that cover loss due to cancer only or that cover care resulting from airline travel accidents only. Another form of limited policy is a *dread disease* policy. This provides coverage if the insured must receive medical treatment due to cancer, polio, meningitis, hepatitis, encephalitis and certain other serious diseases.

There are also limited policies that cover only certain services, such as hospital indemnity policies. A hospital indemnity policy pays a specified benefit on a daily or monthly basis when an insured is confined to a hospital.

Major Medical Insurance

Major medical insurance provides broad coverage and typically pays benefits for hospital room and board, hospital extras, nursing services in the hospital or at home, blood, oxygen, surgery, ambulance and other associated fees. To avoid small claims, major medical coverage includes two important features – the deductible and coinsurance. These two features make it possible for insurance companies to offer coverage at reasonable rates.

Deductible

The *deductible* is the portion of medical expenses that must be paid by the insured before the insurance company starts paying benefits. There are different kinds and amounts of deductibles required by insurance companies. In major medical policies there is usually a flat deductible. This amount is payable in full before the insured is paid anything by the insurance company.

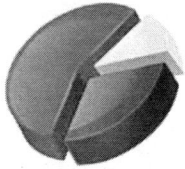

For example, a policy requires a $250 deductible before any benefits are paid. With a $5,000 claim, the insured is responsible for the first $250. The remainder of the claim would be covered by the insurance company, less any applicable coinsurance amount.

Coinsurance

Coinsurance represents a certain portion of the net amount of the claim after the deductible is paid that is also payable by the insured while the insurance company pays their share of the remaining claim.

For example, using the prior example, assume again that the total claim was $5,000. After the deductible is paid by the insured there is a balance of $4,750. If the coinsurance feature is 20%, the insured will have to pay 20% of the remaining $4,750, or $950, while the insurance company pays the remaining 80% or $3,800.

Stop Loss Feature

Some major medical policies have a *stop loss* provision which provides that after the insured pays out a certain amount of out of pocket expenses, the company will pay 100% of all eligible expenses after that during that calendar or plan year.

For example, the coverage includes a $250 deductible with an 80-20% coinsurance feature. Now let's add a $2,000 stop loss feature. Assume the insured has now paid $250 plus $950 or $1,200 out of pocket expenses. If the insured pays $800 more, then the insurance company will be liable for 100 % of all future expenses, during the remainder of the plan year.

Pure comprehensive major medical plans today usually are structured in the following manner:

- The insured pays an initial deductible (i.e. $100, $200, etc.).
- There is a coinsurance feature such as a 20%/80% feature in which the plan pays 80% of the covered expenses remaining after the deductible while the insured pays the balance due on some specified dollar amount (i.e. $5,000 out of pocket).
- After the out of pocket dollar amount indicated above is reached the insurer pays 100% of the remaining balance up to the lifetime maximum benefits allowed.

For example: A plan requires a $100 deductible per covered person per year, and has a coinsurance feature of 20%. After $5,000 out of pocket expenses, the insurer will pay 100% of covered expenses. If the total covered expenses for the year, including the insured's deductible, was $10,000, the insured pays $1,100:

- *the $100 deductible, plus*
- *20% of the first $5,000 of covered expenses which is $1,000.*

The Affordable Care Act ("Obamacare") has restrictions on limiting benefits for essential health care services, so we will see limit provision changes in health plans covered by this Act.

Health Maintenance Organization (HMOs)

Preventing illness by encouraging people to have healthier life styles is the concept behind managed care. It is an approach to health care financing and delivery that promises access to comprehensive and coordinated services while keeping costs under control. Many businesses, government agencies, nonprofit organizations, associations and self-employed persons are learning the value of managed care programs, which involve regular checkups, cholesterol testing, cancer screening and prenatal education programs.

One form of managed care plan is the health maintenance organization. The name health maintenance organization, or HMO, was created by the Nixon administration when the Health Maintenance Organization Act was passed. HMOs select the doctors, hospitals and other medical professionals used to care for its members. The HMO authorizes and arranges the care provided to

 VA PPL LH-2_16298

its members. HMOs differ from traditional health insurance plans because the care provided is managed by the HMO, and is not based on the decisions of an individual physician or physicians. Another key difference is the way care professionals are paid. HMOs collect a monthly premium, which along with a *copayment*, is all the member pays. The physicians within the plan are generally paid by the HMO a flat fee per month for each of the physician's patients under the plan; although a variety of compensation packages are used within HMOs today.

Preferred Provider

In return for joining an HMO care network, providers have the opportunity to increase the number of patients they see. A *preferred provider* is one chosen by the managed care network or managed care sponsor (such as an employer) to provide the health care services outlined in the managed care plan. The services provided by such health care providers are offered on a discounted basis as compared to services from providers outside of the plan.

Primary Care physician

Under an HMO and most managed care plans, each member must select a *primary care physician*. The primary care physician gives most of the care to a patient. A primary care physician is typically a family doctor, pediatrician or other non-specialist.

Gatekeeper

One of the most important functions the primary care physician performs is the role of **gatekeeper** for the managed care organization. Under most plans, the primary care physician determines when a patient should go to a specialist or should be given certain types of medical tests. Because this physician either opens or closes the door to these services, he or she is called a gatekeeper.

Referral

The method used by a primary care physician to give permission to a patient within the managed care network to receive medical care not provided by the primary care physician is known as a *referral*. Under most managed care plans, unless a primary care physician gives a referral in accordance with the process required by the plan, if a patient goes to a specialist, the managed care plan will not pay for the care received.

Specialist

A **specialist** is a physician who specializes in an area outside of primary care. The specialist has advanced training in his or her specialty field. During the 60's and 70's, the high-cost of medical care was blamed in part to the large number of doctors who came out of medical school as specialists, giving them the ability to charge higher fees than the general practitioner. The gatekeeper system was established to provide a way to restrict the overuse of specialists. Today, specialists may agree to discounted fees in return for receiving additional patients through a managed care system.

Case Management

Under some HMOs and other managed care plans, the overall care of certain patients is subject to oversight and coordination by various health care providers through the process of case management. Generally, case management is utilized when a patient needs care from different types of caregivers. For example, a victim of a serious accident may need hospital care, home health care and rehabilitative care. The managed care plan seeks to provide this care for the most reasonable cost by coordinating the care through the process of case management.

Copayment

A *copayment* is a small amount paid by patients in a managed care system for the services received. For example, a patient may pay $5 to $10 each time the patient is seen by the primary care physician.

Coinsurance

Coinsurance is not generally a requirement under care supplied through a managed care network. Rather, it is used in health plans utilizing fee-for-service payment arrangements. Under such health plans, the plan will pay for 50% to 80% of the cost of health services. The patient must pay for the other 20% to 50%. The amount the patient must pay is called *coinsurance*. Some health plans combine managed care with traditional fee-for-service options. Under such plans, the care given outside of the managed care network is generally subject to coinsurance requirements.

Under *fee-for-service plans*, every time a physician provides a service, the physician is paid a fee.

Deductible

Traditionally, managed care plans often do not utilize deductibles; deductibles are found more commonly in plans that reimburse fee-for-service care. However, as health care evolves, these distinctions are less clear-cut and it is possible a managed care plan may require an annual deductible amount to be paid before the plan will pay for covered benefits.

Enrollment Area

Managed care plans generally provide care for residents within a certain geographic area. This geographic area is called the **enrollment area**.

Open Enrollment Period

HMO plans include a period of time in which a new member may enroll. This period of time is called the *open enrollment period*. Generally, this is just prior to the beginning of the plan year, which often coincides with the beginning of the calendar year. People who are newly employed or new members of a sponsoring HMO organization can also generally sign up for the plan at the time of joining the business or sponsoring organization.

Network

Network refers to the physicians, hospitals, clinics, group practices and other health care providers participating in the HMO managed care plan. Care provided within the network is subject to the rules of the plan in order for the plan to pay for the care.

Preventive Care

HMO and other managed care plans generally cover a wide variety of preventive care. Immunizations, screening tests such as mammograms, pap smears and those for prostate cancer, cholesterol levels and blood pressure, as well as care used to manage chronic conditions such as diabetes or asthma, are generally covered.

Plans vary regarding how often tests are covered, for what age groups they are covered, and other criteria that might have to be met in order for various preventive care treatments to be covered. The ACA now requires that many preventive care services be covered by health plans.

Other ways managed care plans may provide preventive care is through the holding of classes or seminars that provide instruction in weight management, smoking prevention, stress management, and management of conditions such as diabetes, high blood pressure or asthma.

Emergency Care

Managed care plans generally divide emergency care into two classifications: **urgent** and **life-threatening**. **Urgent** refers to conditions that need immediate attention, but are not life-threatening. Such conditions may include a broken ankle or broken arm, a severe cut that requires stitches, an extremely high fever perhaps accompanied by a sore throat, or continuous vomiting.

Life-threatening refers to conditions that could result in death, serious disability, disfigurement, or a long-term medical problem. Many managed care plans require that they be notified within 24 to 48 hours of the member's treatment for a life-threatening condition.

Away From Home Care

Managed care plans also have differences regarding how they cover care received out of the area in which the member resides and out of the service area of the managed care organization. Generally, emergency care is treated by managed care plans in the same manner whether the care is provided within the network or out of the area. Rules regarding away from home hospitalization or non-emergency care can vary greatly from plan to plan.

Routine care is unlikely to be covered by the managed care plan if performed out-of-the-area. However, some plans cover such care for college students away from home and covered by the plan. Care for conditions such as the flu or serious cold may also be covered if a member calls the managed care organization prior to treatment for approval.

VA PPL LH-2_16298

Care from Specialists

Managed care plans also vary regarding the methods under which care from specialists is covered. Some plans require a referral from the primary care physician in order for the plan to cover care from a specialist. Other plans allow the member to go to specialists without a referral, but may not cover all the costs of such care.

Managed care plans may include specialists within the plan network, or the plan may refer patients to specialists outside the plan. Plans may also vary regarding what type of physician is considered a specialist.

Hospital Care

Hospital care must generally be authorized by the managed care organization and/or the primary physician. The plan may require that the member attend a specific hospital, or may have a choice of hospitals from which the member may receive care.

Under some managed care plans, hospitalization is subject to a utilization review. This review may include both whether hospitalization is necessary and a determination of how long the patient should remain in the hospital. Under other plans, the hospital medical staff will coordinate care with the primary care physician and this team will determine when a patient should be discharged.

Plans can differ regarding which hospitalization services are covered and which are not. For example, private rooms may not be covered, or covered only under certain circumstances. Television provided in the room and other non-medical services may or may not be covered by the plan.

Maternity Care

Because managed care plans focus on preventive care, they provide coverage for prenatal and maternity care. Generally, HMO and other managed care plans cover all checkups during pregnancy, necessary tests and child birthing, breast-feeding and newborn care classes. The plan will also cover care needed during labor and delivery. Once the baby is born, managed care plans cover immunizations and well-baby checkups.

Some plans will allow the mother to continue to receive care from a previous physician if the mother becomes a member while she is pregnant. Others require that the mother choose a physician within the plan's network. Some plans will cover the use of a midwife.

Pediatric Care

As mentioned, managed care plans cover immunizations for children. They also cover visits to the physician for treatment for earaches, colds, sore throats, the flu, diarrhea, scrapes and bruises and other common childhood ailments. As children get older, plans offer services such as classes or counseling on drug prevention, smoking prevention and other issues affecting teenagers.

Senior Health Care

Managed care plans include many benefits for people as they age. Many cover annual checkups for people in or past their middle years for items such as:

- Breast cancer
- Prostate cancer
- Colorectal cancer
- Blood pressure levels
- Cholesterol levels

Care for conditions commonly associated with aging is also covered by HMO and other managed care plans. Care can be received for diabetes, osteoporosis, arthritis, hearing loss, strokes, incontinence, digestive problems, Alzheimer's disease, and other conditions, whether easily treatable or serious. Some plans also cover care given to treat mental health conditions such as depression and anxiety. Classes and seminars may also be provided through the plan which covers topics of interest to patients in or entering their senior years.

The need for prescription drugs often increases with age and prescription coverage is offered by managed care plans, although the coverage may require payment of additional premium. Many plans include provisions enabling the review of the prescriptions prescribed by physicians within the network to ensure safety in the prescriptions' use.

Primary care physicians can often meet the care needs of aging patients, but those with certain conditions may need to see specialists or select a new primary care physician with experience in geriatrics or other relevant area. It is also important to remember that managed care plans do not provide long-term care benefits. Long-term care insurance policies may be an additional form of insurance that aging adults require to meet health care needs.

Long-term care insurance is private insurance designed to aid individuals in paying for long-term care. Care may be received in the home, in a community facility, or in a residential facility, depending on the policy.

Women's Health

Women have special health care needs. Women may require care related to menstruation, fertility, reproduction, childbirth, menopause, breast cancer, cervical cancer and other conditions related to their gender. Some managed care plans include women's health clinics as part of their network of providers. A gynecologist may be a primary care physician.

Mental Health and Substance Abuse Care

Managed care plans vary in the scope and depth of coverage for mental health and substance abuse related care. The ACA requires that mental health services be provided as part of essential health benefit services. Essential health benefit services must be included in the insurance products offered through state insurance exchanges created under the ACA's requirements.

Some plans may cover such care for a certain number of visits. For example, a plan may cover up to three visits to a psychologist for marital counseling, or may cover drug abuse therapy up to a certain maximum dollar amount of services. A plan may also cover only assessment services.

Plans may allow a member to self-refer to a mental health or substance abuse emergency center. Others allow self-referrals for non-emergency mental health care, especially if mental health care providers are a part of the plan's network. Some require a referral from a primary care physician for such services.

Plans that provide coverage for substance abuse and mental health care differ regarding whether the patient may select their own therapist, whether a therapist will be selected by the plan, or whether care is covered if provided by a therapist outside the plan network.

Some plans may offer group counseling or programs for conditions such as eating disorders or coping with abuse, or other mental health conditions that can be improved by such programs. Other plans do not offer group counseling for these conditions.

Prescription Drugs

Prescription drug coverage is generally offered by managed care plans for additional premiums or member fees. Some plans cover prescriptions filled by network pharmacies only and others have no restrictions regarding where prescriptions must be filled in order to be covered. Of course, prescriptions are generally covered only if written by a primary care physician or other authorized physician under the plan.

It is not uncommon for managed care plans to cover prescriptions based on a *formulary*. A formulary is a list of medications that are used to treat various conditions and is used by physicians within a plan as a guide for prescribing medication appropriate to a patient's condition. Generally, if medications are prescribed according to the formulary, the managed care plan will cover these medications at a higher level than medications not on the list.

As with other services covered, managed care plans cover prescription drugs considered medically necessary. Experimental drugs and drugs used for cosmetic purposes are not covered.

Prescription drug coverage often has associated with it a separate premium or different copayment amount than other care covered under a plan. Drugs may be covered on a percentage of cost basis rather than on a copayment basis. Prescription drugs may also be subject to a specified annual coverage limit separate from other coverage limits.

Other Managed Care Benefits

Other care that may be covered under managed care plans can include dental, hearing and vision care. Plans may categorize this care as **medically necessary, preventive** and **not-medically necessary**.

Medically necessary dental, hearing and vision care includes care such as that required after an accident, or care required due to an infection. Preventive care includes care such as teeth cleaning or routine hearing and vision examinations. Non-medically necessary care may include items such as dentures, hearing aids and corrective lenses.

Some managed care plans offer no coverage or limited coverage for preventive vision, dental or hearing care. Coverage for routine dental examinations may be limited to patients under the age of 12. It is not unusual for preventive vision care not to be covered under low-fee managed care plans.

Preferred Provider Organizations (PPOs)

Professionals and hospitals under contract to a *Preferred Provider Organization* (PPO) are called *Preferred Providers*. Unlike HMOs which compensate physicians on a capitation basis, PPOs compensate health care providers by compensating through a fee schedule.

Typically, PPOs charge a lower monthly membership fee per participant than traditional fee-for-service health care coverage. The types of benefits provided by PPOs are similar to those provided under comprehensive major medical plan with cost containments.

Open Panel PPO

One form of PPO allows access to specialists without requiring a referral from a primary physician. Plans that allow this access are known as open panel or open access plans. The form of preferred provider organization that is open panel is known as an IPA, or independent practitioners association. The IPA may have the responsibility of coordinating care for HMO members and overseeing the care given by the IPA physicians. Members of the HMO-IPA choose a primary care physician from among the many independent

practitioners. The independent practitioners also see fee-for-service patients.

The structure of an IPA is generally as follows, although contractual arrangements vary:

1. The HMO capitates, or pays a monthly fee, to the IPA.
2. The IPA subcapitates, or pays a smaller monthly fee, to the primary care physicians within the IPA.
3. The IPA deposits the remainder of the fees received from the HMO in a risk pool. The risk pool is to be used to pay for specialists, hospital care and other services.
4. Annually, the money left in the risk pool, if any, is shared among the IPA's physicians and the HMO. If a loss occurs, the HMO also has some share in the loss.

Because of the deposits into the risk pool to pay for specialists, IPAs allow access to specialists without a referral, and members are allowed open access to specialist care.

Closed Panel PPO

Closed panel PPOs do not allow access to specialists without a referral, but require patients to obtain a referral from their primary care physician before it will pay for care received by a specialist.

Point of Service Plans

Point of Service Plans, or POS plans, are plans that allow for the use of both HMO and non-network providers. They were created in response to members' desire to have greater choice regarding the care they receive. Under a POS, the HMO coverage generally applies only to the care given by a physician who is part of the HMO network, for emergency care, and for approved care from an outside specialist. If care is provided by a non-network provider or outside of the rules of the HMO plan, it is covered by a traditional health plan, involving deductibles and coinsurance requirements. Because POS plans cover out-of-network providers, they are known as open ended HMOs.

POS plans require referral of a primary care physician for specialist care under the HMO coverage, but no referral is required for coverage

VA PPL LH-2_16298

for out-of-network specialist care under the traditional health care plan coverage that applies to the non-HMO care.

POS plans meet the needs of consumers who do not want to switch doctors in order to be covered by an employer's health plan or who want the freedom to utilize services outside the network and still enjoy coverage. POS plans generally have higher premiums than HMO plans, and the coordination of care that occurs under an HMO form of managed care may be more difficult to arrange under a POS, since both network and non-network providers may be involved in the care of a patient.

Managed Care (PPO, EPO, POS, IPA, HMO)	Fee-For-Service Care
Members receive care from the health care providers within the network.	Patient selects any physician or provider.
Plans include coverage for routine and preventive care, along with care for treatment of illness or accident.	Plan generally covers treatment of illness or accident, not routine or preventive care.
Any necessary care from a Specialist or through a hospital is generally authorized by a primary care physician and arranged by the HMO.	Although insured may have to notify an insurer in advance of specialty or hospital care, traditional fee-for-service plans do not place restrictions on this care.
Managed care plans generally include no deductible nor coinsurance requirements for care given within the plan's network.	Fee-for-service plans include deductibles and coinsurance requirements.
Managed care plans cover most or all of the care provided within the network, but do not cover care outside of the network.	Under fee-for-service plans there is no *inside of network, outside of network* issue. All care provided is subject to the same rules contained in the health plan.
Under many managed care structures, the plan arranges for and is responsible for the care given the patient.	Under fee-for-service plans, the physicians and health care providers are responsible for the care given to a patient. The insurer is not involved.
Managed care plans do not involve paperwork for the patient; there are no claims forms.	Under traditional health plans, the physician or patient must complete claims forms in order to receive reimbursement from the insurer.
Premiums are generally lower in managed care plans, particularly HMOs, than under fee-for-service based plans.	Premiums in fee-for-service plans are commonly 20% higher than in HMO plans.

Flexible Spending Accounts (FSA)

Another type of plan that can be used as a consumer driven health plan is a *flexible spending arrangement* (FSA). An FSA is a benefit plan established by employers that allows employees to set aside pre-tax dollars to pay for certain expenses.

A health FSA allows for contributions by the employer, and salary reduction contributions by the employee. The plan must specify that these contributions be made by the employer in order for employer contributions to be allowable. As unreimbursed qualified medical expenses are incurred, the employee is reimbursed for them from the FSA. Distributions made for this purpose are tax-free.

A health FSA allows for contributions by the employer, and salary reduction contributions by the employee. The plan must specify that these contributions be made by the employer in order for employer contributions to be allowable. As unreimbursed qualified medical expenses are incurred, the employee is reimbursed for them from the FSA. Distributions made for this purpose are tax-free.

Contribution Election

The amount placed in an FSA is based on the amount of unreimbursed qualified medical expenses the employee expects to incur in that year. Amounts not distributed from an FSA at the end of the plan year are normally forfeited. The employee does not want to place too much in the FSA, because the employee will lose the amount not used. The employee notifies the employer how much the employee would like placed in the FSA at the beginning of the plan year, and the employer deducts this amount, before taxes, from the employee's paycheck and places it in the FSA. The amount may be deducted each paycheck, or periodically during the plan year, such as once a month. The employer may contribute some or all of the employee's elected amount if the employer's plan allows it.

Contribution Amounts

For plan years that began after December 31, 2012, salary reduction contributions to a health FSA cannot be more than $2,500 a year. This amount is indexed for inflation and may change from year to year. In 2015, this amount has been adjusted to $2550. The plan established by the employer must designate either a maximum dollar amount, or a maximum percentage of compensation that may be made to the FSA, within legal maximums.

Distributions

Distributions from FSAs are paid to reimburse the employee for qualified medical expenses that were incurred during the plan year. The maximum tax-free amount that can be distributed from the FSA is the amount the employee elected to contribute to the health FSA for the year.

In order for amounts to be distributed from an FSA, the employee must submit written documentation to the FSA plan administrator that shows that the medical expense has been incurred, and the amount of the expense. The employee must also state in writing that the expense has not been paid or reimbursed through other health plan coverage.

In some cases, the employee is provided a debit card, credit card, or stored value card with which to pay medical expenses from the FSA. In this case, the employee may be able to use the card at the health care provider's office, the pharmacy, or other dispenser of qualified medical services. The card may be set up to digitally provide the necessary written documentation to the FSA plan administrator. Or, the employee may be able to use the card for FSA reimbursements, and then be required to provide whatever supplemental documentation is necessary for the plan administrator.

Health FSAs cannot be used to pay for health insurance premiums, long-term care coverage premiums and expenses, or for amounts covered under another health plan.

Grace Period

An FSA plan can allow for up to a 2 ½-month grace period in order for the employees to use funds remaining in the FSA to pay for qualified medical expenses. For example, if the plan year is from January 1 to December 31, the plan can provide that employees have until March 15 of the following year in which to submit reimbursement of funds from the FSA balance in the prior year for expenses incurred to March 15 of the current year.

Prescribed Drug Reimbursement

Prior to the Affordable Care Act's provisions that were effective in 2011, it was possible to be reimbursed for over-the-counter medicine or drug that was not prescribed by a physician through an FSA. After December 31, 2010, as explained in IRS Revenue Notice 2010-59, "expenses incurred for a medicine or a drug shall be treated as a reimbursement for medical expenses only if such medicine or drug is a prescribed drug (determined without regard to whether such drug is available without a prescription) or is insulin. Thus, under new Section 106(f) [of the Internal Revenue Code], expenses incurred for medicines or drugs may be paid or reimbursed by an employer-provided plan, including a health FSA or HRA, only if (1) the medicine or drug requires a prescription, (2) is available without a prescription (an over-the-counter medicine or drug) and the individual obtains a prescription, or (3) is insulin."

Unused Amounts and Carryover Rules

For plan years after December 31, 2012, plans may allow up to $500 of unused amounts remaining at the end of the plan year to be paid or reimbursed for qualified medical expenses incurred in the following plan year. The plan may specify a lower dollar amount as the maximum carryover amount. If the plan permits a carryover, any unused amounts in excess of the carryover amount are forfeited. The carryover does not affect the maximum amount of salary reduction contributions that an employee is permitted to make. *A plan may allow either the grace period or a carryover, but it cannot allow both.*

VA PPL LH-2_16298

Health Savings Accounts (HSAs) and Health Reimbursement Arrangements (HRAs)

High deductible health plans (HDHPs) are used with tax advantaged plans such as *Health Savings Accounts* (HSAs), and Health Reimbursement Arrangements (also known as Health Reimbursement Accounts) (HRAs). These plans have a deductible that is much higher than in traditional group health plan coverage. If an HDHP is used with an HSA as a tax-qualified HDHP, it has mandated annual deductible limits and out-of-pocket maximums.

These plans are designed to provide catastrophic health care coverage, with the insured paying for more routine health expenses.

Creation of HSAs

The first legislation passed concerning HDHPs created Medical Savings Accounts (MSAs), and was enacted in 1996. MSAs were later renamed Archer MSAs in honor of Representative Bill Archer, who was key in developing the MSA legislation. MSAs were created for a rather limited use – for employees of small employers and the self-employed not otherwise covered by insurance. A Medicare MSA program was also passed at this time.

Then, the Federal Congress expanded the use and loosened the deductibility limits of a similar health savings account program and created Health Savings Accounts (HSAs). The HSA legislation encourages the use of HDHPs by providing for contributions to be made to savings accounts on a tax deductible basis for the use of paying for qualified medical expenses. The money in the savings accounts can be used to pay routine medical expenses and other costs of care not covered by the HDHP.

Rules for HSA Plans

Health savings accounts (HSAs) are tax-exempt trusts or custodial accounts used to pay or reimburse certain medical expenses incurred by the employee. They are established in conjunction with a high deductible health plan. They are basically a savings account to pay for qualified medical expenses.

Contributions are made to the HSA. The contributions can be made by the employer and the employee, and are subject to annual maximum limits, depending on the type of coverage. In addition, an HDHP is established. Money from the HSA is used to pay for the deductible and can be used to pay for most health expenses not covered by the HDHP. The contributions made to the HSA are tax deductible to the employee if the employee makes the contributions, and are tax deductible to the employer if the employer makes the contributions. Earnings on money in the HSA are not taxable, and distributions made to pay for qualified medical expenses are tax-free. The HSA belongs to the employee, so if the employee leaves employment, the HSA stays with the employee.

Eligibility

In order to have an HSA, the individual, who can be an employee, must:

- Have an HDHP, on the first day of the month
- Generally, have no other health coverage
- Not be enrolled in Medicare
- Not be claimed as a dependent on another person's income tax return

Other Health Coverage

In order to be eligible for an HSA, neither the employee or the employee's spouse can have health coverage that is not an HDHP, if the non-HDHP plan covers the employee. If the spouse has a non-HDHP, but that plan does not cover the employee, the spouse's plan does not stop the employee from being eligible for an HSA.

The employee can be covered by some limited forms of health insurance that provide the following benefits, and still be eligible for an HSA:

- Liabilities incurred under Workers Compensation laws, tort liabilities, or liabilities related to ownership or use of property
- A specific disease or illness (for example, there are health insurance policies that cover care for cancer, only)
- A fixed amount per day (or other period) of hospitalization

The employee can also have coverage for the following and still be eligible for an HSA:

- Accidents
- Disability
- Dental care
- Vision care
- Long-term care

High Deductible Health Plans and HSAs

HSA provisions include regulated minimum limits for the annual deductible for the HDHP that must be established with the HSA. Each type of plan coverage, self-only and family, has a regulated minimum annual deductible limit. The regulations also include a maximum annual deductible and other *out-of-pocket* expenses for these two coverage types.

The maximum out-of-pocket expense is the maximum dollar amount a group member is required to pay out of pocket during a year. Until this maximum is met, the plan and group member shares in the cost of covered expenses. After the maximum is reached, the insurance carrier pays remaining covered expenses for the year.

A HDHP under a HSA must meet these minimums and maximums, in 2016 and 2017:

Type of Coverage	Minimum Annual Deductible	Maximum Deductible and Out-of-Pocket Expenses
2016		
Self-Only Coverage	$1,300	$6,450
Family Coverage	$2,600	$12,900
2017		
Self-Only Coverage	$1,300	$6,550
Family Coverage	$2,600	$13,100

Self-only coverage is coverage through an HDHP that covers only an eligible individual. Family coverage is through an HDHP that covers an eligible individual and at least one other individual.

Contributions

The eligible individual, whether an employee, self-employed or unemployed, can make contributions to the HSA. The employee's employer can make contributions to the employee's HSA as well. In addition, family members or any other person can make contributions on behalf of eligible individuals.

The limits on contributions are established annually and increase with the cost of living. Eligible individuals can contribute up to the annual maximum amount, regardless of the amount of their plan deductible, as long as the plan and the individual meet the other HSA requirements. Individuals age 55 and older can make additional catch-up contributions of $1,000.

The annual amounts are announced as of June 1 of each year by the U.S. Treasury department.

2016 and 2017 HSA Contribution Limits

Type of Coverage	Contribution Level	Contribution Level 55+
2016		
Self-Only Coverage	$3,350	$4,350
Family Coverage	$6,750	$7,750
2017		
Self-Only Coverage	$3,400	$4,400
Family Coverage	$6,750	$7,750

Contribution Deadlines

Contributions can be made to an HSA for a calendar year up to the tax filing date of the following year.

HSA Distributions

Distributions may be made from HSAs to pay for or be reimbursed for qualified medical expenses. The expenses must be incurred after the establishment of the HSA. Distributions that meet these standards are tax-free. Distributions for HSAs that do not meet these standards are subject to income taxation, and may be subject to an additional 20% tax.

Qualified Medical Expenses

Qualified medical expenses include fees paid to physicians, for prescription medicines, and for necessary hospital services not paid for by insurance.

These medical expenses must be incurred by:

VA PPL LH-2_16298

- The HSA eligible individual and spouse
- Dependents of the HSA eligible individual that are claimed on the tax return

Insurance Premiums

Most payments for insurance premiums are not qualified medical expenses under HSA rules. There are some exceptions to this general rule, however. Premiums paid for the following insurance types can be reimbursed by or paid from an HSA, as qualified medical expenses:

- Long-term care insurance
- Health care coverage paid for while receiving unemployment benefits
- Health care continuation coverage that is required under federal law (such as COBRA)
- Medicare premiums and out-of-pocket expenses, including deductibles, co-pays, and coinsurance for:
  - Part A (hospital and inpatient services)
  - Part B (physician and outpatient services)
  - Part C (Medicare HMO and PPO plans)
  - Part D (prescription drugs)

Non-Qualified Distributions

If distributions are made that aren't made for qualified medical expenses, the distributions are taxable, and if the person is under 65, an additional 20% tax penalty applies. The 20% penalty does not apply to non-qualified distributions after the person becomes age 65, or becomes disabled. *(See IRS Publication 969)*

HSA Beneficiaries

A beneficiary may be named on the HSA. If the named beneficiary is the eligible individual's spouse, upon the death of the eligible individual, the HSA will be treated as belonging to the spouse.

If the beneficiary is not the spouse, upon the eligible individual's death, the account stops being treated as an HSA, and the fair market value of the HSA is taxable to the beneficiary.

Health Reimbursement Arrangement Rules

Health reimbursement arrangements (HRAs) are plans established by employers to reimburse employees for qualified medical expenses. The employees are provided a stated maximum amount that will be reimbursed through the plan if the employee incurs qualified medical expenses.

HRAs are funded solely through the employer. No contributions are made by employees or others. The employer funds the amounts for each participating employee. Unused amounts may be rolled over for use as reimbursements in future years.

Eligibility

HRAs are employer benefit plans and the employer must provide benefits to comply with accident and health plan requirements. HRAs do not require the establishment of an HDHP, although many employers do establish HDHPs as a complement to the use of HRAs. Employers may establish any type of health coverage plan that meets state and federal requirements along with an HRA, but, the employer does not have to establish any other health plan or coverage in order to offer an HRA to employees.

Contributions

Contribution amounts are determined by the HRA plan established by the employer. The contributions are tax-deductible to the employer, if the employer's plan meets tax-qualified requirements. The amounts contributed on behalf of an employee are not taxable to the employee.

Distributions

Distributions may only be made from HRAs to reimburse the employee for qualified medical expenses incurred by the employee or covered family member or dependent. The employee may be issued a debit card, credit card or stored value card to use to reimburse the employee for qualified medical expenses.

Allowable Distributions

Distributions from HRAs may be made to reimburse any of the following:

- Current and former employees
- Spouses and dependents of those employees
- Any person that could be claimed as a dependent on the employee's return, unless:
  - The person filed a joint return

VA PPL LH-2_16298

- The person had gross income of $3,800 or more (this figure is subject to adjustment for inflation annually)
- The employee, or the employee's spouse if filing jointly could be claimed as a dependent on someone's tax return

Taxable Distributions

If a distribution is made, or could be made, for any purpose other than to reimburse the employee for qualified medical expenses, any amount distributed from the HRA in the current tax year is included in gross income.

Medicare Supplement Policies

Medicare Supplement policies, or *Medigap* insurance policies, are designed to fill the gaps Medicare coverage leaves. These policies are structured to pay items such as Medicare coinsurance amounts and Medicare deductibles and to provide coverage for services not paid for by Medicare. Some Medigap policies will pay for the amount charged for services above the Medicare-approved amount. Medigap insurance policies vary in the scope of coverage they provide. Premiums for Medigap insurance are generally more expensive than premiums required for Medicare managed care plans, and the broader the coverage the Medigap policy provides, the more expensive the premium.

OBRA Medigap Legislation

The Omnibus Budget Reform Act of 1990 (OBRA '90) included legislation to prohibit the practice of any insurer from offering any policy that duplicates Medicare coverage. This practice was prohibited because it resulted in the insured paying premiums to the insurer for coverage he or she would receive through Medicare. Therefore, Medigap policies do not duplicate Medicare benefits, but pay amounts not covered by Medicare

OBRA '90 also changed the structure under which commissions are paid on Medigap policies. First year commissions on Medigap policies may not be greater than twice the second year's commissions, and the second through fifty year commission must be equal. States may also have additional regulations regarding Medigap policy commissions. If a Medicare recipient is enrolled in a Medicare managed care plan, the recipient may keep any Medigap policy he or she has. The Medigap policy only applies when a recipient is on the original Medicare plan.

Medigap Plans A – N

There were twelve basic Medigap policies, identified as plans A to L. As of June 1, 2010, two additional Medigap policies became available, plans M and N. At that same time, policies E, H, I and J were no longer available for purchase.

Policies issued to residents of Minnesota, Massachusetts and Wisconsin are exempt from the requirements of the standardized plans. These states had Medigap plans in place prior to the passing of federal regulations that the regulators determined did not have to change.

High Deductible Plan F

Plan F can be purchased as a high deductible health plan. If this option is selected, the insured pays for Medicare-covered costs up to the deductible amount before Medicare will pay for anything.

 VA PPL LH-2_16298

Medigap Benefits	Medigap Plans									
	A	B	C	D	F*	G	K	L	M	N
Part A coinsurance and hospital costs up to an additional 365 days after Medicare benefits are used up	Yes	Yes	Yes	Yes	Yes	Yes	Yes	Yes	Yes	Yes
Part B coinsurance or copayment	Yes	Yes	Yes	Yes	Yes	Yes	50%	75%	Yes	Yes***
Blood (first three pints)	Yes	Yes	Yes	Yes	Yes	Yes	50%	75%	Yes	Yes
Part A hospice care coinsurance or copayment	Yes	Yes	Yes	Yes	Yes	Yes	50%	75%	Yes	Yes
Skilled nursing facility care coinsurance	No	No	Yes	Yes	Yes	Yes	50%	75%	Yes	Yes
Part A deductible	No	Yes	Yes	Yes	Yes	Yes	50%	75%	50%	Yes
Part B deductible	No	No	Yes	No	Yes	No	No	No	No	No
Part B excess charges	No	No	No	No	Yes	Yes	No	No	No	No
Foreign travel exchange (up to plan limits)	No	No	Yes	Yes	Yes	No	No	No	Yes	Yes
Out of pocket limit**	N/A	N/A	N/A	N/A	N/A	N/A	Yes	Yes	N/A	N/A

* Plan F also offers a high-deductible plan.

** After the out-of-pocket yearly limit and yearly Part B deductible is met, the Medigap plan pays 100% of covered services for the rest of the calendar year. See www.medicare.gov for annual out-of-pocket limits.

*** Plan N pays 100% of the Part B coinsurance, except for a copayment for some office visits and a higher copayment for emergency room visits that don't result in inpatient admission.

Source: www.medicare.gov

Additional Benefits in Medigap Plans

An insurer may offer additional benefits in a Medigap standardized policy. According to federal law, an insurer may add new and innovative benefits to a Medicare Supplement Plan. Additional benefits must be:

- cost-effective,
- not otherwise available in the marketplace, and
- offered in a manner that is consistent with the goal of simplifying Medigap insurance.

Medicare SELECT Policies

Medicare SELECT policies are very similar to the standard Medigap policies. The important difference between SELECT policies and Medigap policies is that the insurer offering the plan requires that the insured must use specific hospitals, and in some cases, specific doctors, in order to be covered by the insurance. Because SELECT policies use preferred providers the insurance premiums may be lower than comparable Medigap policies.

Group Insurance

Many employers offer group medical expense insurance, commonly known as group health insurance. Some employers make all the premium payments for their employees; others require that the employee pay some or all of the plan's premium.

Under federal regulations, a group health plan is a plan maintained by an employer or employee organization to provide health care to individuals who have an employment-related connection to the employer or employee organization or to their families.

Most group health insurance is sponsored by employers. However, other groups may sponsor group health insurance, such as an association of professionals, a fraternal society, a cost club and other groups approved by the state.

Group Conversion

Group health plans generally allow the insureds to convert to an individual policy when the insured leaves the group, and/or prior to a certain age,

VA PPL LH-2_16298

without having to demonstrate insurability. The premiums for the individual policy are offered based on attained age at time of conversion. For example, if the insured were 45 when leaving the group, the premium rates for the individual policy would be based on the insured's age 45. The option to convert may only be available up to a specified age. Some groups are subject to COBRA and HIPAA rules which provide for continuation or conversion of group coverage under certain circumstances.

COBRA stands for the federal *Consolidated Omnibus Budget Reconciliation Act of 1985*, and includes requirements for group health plans regarding health care continuation.

HIPAA stands for federal Health Insurance Portability and Accountability Act of 1996. It includes employer group health insurance portability requirements and privacy protections for certain health information.

Group Contract or Master Policy

Group insurance is issued through a master policy. The *master policy* is a contract between the employer, or other sponsoring group, and the insurance company. Some group policies may include a provision that allows the insurer to cancel the policy if the number of employees it covers falls below a certain level. Individual employees are not named in the master policy.

Certificates

Each covered employee is issued a certificate of coverage. The certificate outlines the basics of the coverage – the amount of insurance, the coverage benefits, definition of terms and conditions in the policy, the name of the insureds, and the named beneficiary or beneficiaries, if applicable (e.g. for AD&D insurance death benefits). In addition to the certificate, the group health certificateholder will normally be provided with a health plan benefits packet from the plan, which will include the benefits schedule, list of providers in the network, if applicable, claim forms, telephone numbers, website address and email addresses of the plan, and similar information.

Group Health Plan Rating

In setting group health plan rates, insurers are required to give due consideration to past and prospective loss experience, to the type and scope of hazards, to a reasonable profit margin, to past and prospective expenses and to any special assessments when setting rates.

Experience Rating

When an insurer sets rates based on experience rating, the insurer looks at the loss experience of the group. For example, the insurer will look at the number of claims, the amount paid out under the claims, and the reason for the claims to determine the risk category of the group. Based on the risk category and the coverage plan, the insurer assigns a rate to the group.

Community Rating

Under a pure community rating system, all insureds in a group health plan are charged basically the same rate per unit of the same coverage. The only variance allowed in premium rates are for businesses in different geographic areas and for size of family. Varying premiums based on age or gender is prohibited. Modified community rating does not allow insurers to base rates on health status, but does allow variances for items such as gender and age. The reasoning behind community rating is that it believed that this rating system is a fair one that ensures that those in poor health will be covered.

A *unit* is a measurement used to determine pricing in insurance policies. It varies based on the type of risk being insured. A unit may be referred to as an amount of the death benefit in life insurance, e.g., one unit = $1000 of death benefit. A unit of health insurance may equal $1000 in policy benefits.

Types of Eligible Groups

There are several different categories of group health plan sponsors. Each is defined in a state's insurance laws. Some of these categories are defined in basically the same way as groups that sponsor life insurance plans.

Employer Sponsored Plan

Many group health plans are sponsored by employers. Participation requirements for

VA PPL LH-2_16298

employee group plans may include that the employee be full time (which may be defined as working 30 hours a week or more), have been employed longer than an initial probationary period, such as 90 days, be actively working and apply for the coverage during the plan's enrollment period.

Employer sponsored plans may allow for spouses and dependents to be covered under the plan as well.

Multiple Employer Trust (MET)

Multiple Employer Trusts (METs) are generally found in the small business market. When a small business has not been able to obtain acceptable group insurance rates it can enter into a MET with other similar types of businesses for purposes of forming a large group insurance trust.

The MET sponsor, usually an insurance company, defines the nature and class of the group to be served and create a separate trust to purchase group health coverage for employers in that class who wish to participate. The small businesses in the same class can join with other small businesses and be included in the trust to negotiate together for more liberal benefits, provisions and costs. The resulting MET may not only save the small group money but also provide a broader range of services which would not be available in a plan for a single small business.

Self-insured METs may also be formed, but may have difficulty maintaining sufficient reserves to pay all coverage obligations. Small businesses should investigate the financials of the MET prior to joining one. It is also recommended that a thorough review of premiums and claims experience of the trust be undertaken.

METs are only available for single employer groups.

Multiple Employer Welfare Association (MEWA)

The MEWA is similar to a Multiple Employer Trust but is a self-insured association. By jointly paying bills and sharing the risks small companies can better afford health benefits for their employees. As with METs, it is important for the business to thoroughly investigate a MEWA before joining.

Association Group Sponsors

Associations may also sponsor group health policies. Associations include groups of professionals, alumni and industries.

Debtor or Creditor Groups

Group insurance may be sponsored by creditors. For example, a lending institution may offer borrowers credit health insurance such as accidental death and dismemberment coverage. The policy will pay off the loan or retail credit card upon the death of the insured.

Labor Union Group Sponsors

Labor unions may also sponsor group health plans. The requirements to be an insured under these policies are generally that the insured be a member of the sponsoring union. Spouses and dependents may be allowed to be covered by the union sponsored insurance as well.

Credit Union or Credit Union Trust Group Sponsors

Credit union group insurance is issued to a credit union or credit union trust and covers members of the group, or persons who are or become borrowers from the credit union.

Employer Group Health Insurance

Employers are the largest source of group health care coverage. Providing group health coverage is a valuable benefit to employees.

Differences Between Individual and Group Contracts

Group medical expense coverage plans, when compared to individual coverage plans, generally have certain advantages:

- They are generally less expensive than individual plans.
- An individual or family member that may have difficulty receiving medical coverage will generally be accepted under a group coverage plan.
- The employee portion of the premium payments is often made as a payroll deduction, so the employee will not

 VA PPL LH-2_16298

accidentally cancel coverage through non-payment of premium.

Insurer Underwriting Criteria of Groups
Characteristics of Group

When an insurer underwrites an employer group, it evaluates the characteristics of the group to determine the risk level and premium to charge the group. Characteristics that may be evaluated include:

- Age;
- Sex;
- Health and health history;
- Industry and type of work performed by the group;
- Location;
- Geography of the job sites and office locations;
- Personal habits of the group such as smoking or drinking alcohol;
- Size of the policy;
- Benefits to be offered; and
- Current insurance in force, such as disability or AD&D coverage.

When a small firm offers health coverage, it generally has to pay more than large businesses to provide the same benefits. To keep expenses down, plans offered by smaller firms generally provide fewer features and benefits, or have larger deductibles or lower maximum benefit amounts than those provided by larger firms. The small employer and his or her employees cannot afford the same levels of coverage as the large employer.

The reasons for the higher relative costs to small employers may have to do with ratings of smaller groups due to rating bands. Rating bands allow insurers, within limits, to base health coverage premiums on factors such as the health of the group's employees and dependents, and to take into consideration age, type of business, the group size, gender, geography, location, and so forth. There are limits on the variances in rates based on these factors. Higher costs for small business health coverage may also be due to the costs small employers pay for administration of the plans

State health insurance exchange programs which are to be implemented under the Affordable Care Act across the nation are intended to help small businesses obtain more affordable health coverage.

Private insurers will offer the same menu of coverage plans to small businesses so the pool of insureds will be larger. Creating larger pools of insureds will allow for lower premium rates.

Plan Design Factors

Underwriting group health insurance involves evaluating risk based on the coverage to be provided within the plan. A plan with broad coverage and extensive benefits will be more expensive for the employer and/or employees because of the benefits. Plans with fewer benefits will be less expensive for the same group.

Plan design impacts the underwriting decision and the cost of the coverage to the employer and employees.

In designing a plan, different levels of coverage may be offered to employees who then select the level of coverage. *For example, bronze level may be the basic health plan, and silver, gold, and platinum levels respectively add more coverage benefits. To keep costs down for the employer, the employer pays for bronze level coverage for all and individual employees pay extra amounts for additional coverage above the bronze level.*

Costs can also be reduced through plan design by the employer choosing higher annual deductibles and selecting lower benefit amounts, as allowed under the law.

Another plan design variant is unbundled benefits. When an employer unbundles benefits, the employer allows employees to choose which benefits they want, in conformance with applicable law. Under unbundled plans, the employer can allot a certain dollar amount the employer will pay for health coverage. An employee can choose basic health coverage for that amount and pay for other benefits himself or herself. When benefits are unbundled, an employee may choose among dental coverage, vision coverage, non-preferred provider coverage, or a group of additional medical benefits in addition to or instead of a basic health coverage option.

Eligibility for Coverage

When an employee joins a medical expense plan through an employer, the employee becomes part of a group coverage plan. All employees of a business or several businesses may comprise a group.

Employee Eligibility

Employees are generally eligible if they meet the plan's requirements for number of hours worked and are a certain age. For example, the plan may require eligible employees to work at least 30 hours a week and be age 19.

Annual Enrollment Period

An employee may join a health care plan through an employer when hired, although there may be a waiting period, such as 90 days. New members can also join during the annual open enrollment period. Once an employee is enrolled, if the employee is responsible for all or a portion of the premium payment, the payment will generally be deducted from his or her paycheck at least monthly, and be remitted to the plan.

Dependent Eligibility

If the plan includes dependent coverage, the employee's children, spouse and other dependents are enrolled when the employee is hired or during the annual enrollment period. Newborn children are automatically covered for the period mandated by law, or longer period, and coverage continues for them when the plan is notified within established timeframes. Adopted children are covered when the adoption placement is established. Dependents are covered through a specified age. Under the ACA, health plans must cover dependents to age 26.

Change of Insurance Companies or Loss of Coverage

Coinsurance and Deductible Carryover

Many group health plans have a plan year coinsurance amount and/or deductible. For example, a plan may have a $750 deductible and then pays most benefits for covered care on an 80/20 coinsurance basis, where the insured pays 20% and the insurer pays 80%. Some plans include a carryover into the first three months of the next plan year of the deductible if it has not yet been met by the insured.

When a carryover provision is in place, it works as follows:

Assume that the plan year is from January 1 to December 31. The insured has paid $600 of the $750 annual deductible as of December 31. The plan has a 20% coinsurance requirement. If the insured incurs $1000 of costs in February of the following year, the insured will have to pay a $150 deductible ($750 total deductible less a carryover of $600 from the prior year) plus 20% of the remaining $850 of covered care, or $170.

COBRA

The Consolidated Omnibus Budget Reconciliation Act was enacted in 1986. It provides for continuation of group health care benefits when an employee separates from service and other specified events. Employers with 20 or more employees, and plans offered by state and local governments are generally required to comply with the provisions of COBRA. Plans sponsored by the Federal government or by churches for their employees and plans that are maintained solely to comply with applicable Workers Compensation, unemployment or disability laws are not subject to COBRA's provisions.

Events That Trigger the Offer of Coverage

COBRA requires that covered employees, their spouses, their former spouses, and dependent children be offered continuation coverage when their group health coverage would be terminated, but for the continuation coverage. The qualifying events that trigger the offering of the coverage are:

- Death of the covered employee
- Termination
- Reduction in hours of a covered employee's employment for reasons other than gross misconduct
- Divorce or legal separation from a covered employee
- A covered employee becoming eligible for Medicare
- A child's loss of dependent status under the plan

Costs to Individuals for Continuation Coverage

When individuals elect to continue coverage under COBRA, they must pay the full cost of the coverage, plus a 2% administrative charge. The cost for coverage is generally more than when the employee was covered by the employer's plan, because the employer generally pays for part of the coverage for employees in the plan. The individual under continuation coverage pays all the coverage costs. However, continuation coverage is usually cheaper than an individual policy.

Qualifying Events

When certain qualifying events for continuation coverage occur, the employer must notify the plan. The employer must notify the plan if the qualifying event is:

- termination or reduction in hours of employment of the covered employee
- death of the covered employee
- the covered employee becomes entitled to Medicare
- the employer becomes bankrupt

The employee or qualified beneficiary must notify the plan if any of the following qualifying events occur:

- divorce
- legal separation
- a child's loss of dependent status under the plan

Once the plan receives notice of a qualifying event, the plan gives the qualified beneficiaries an election notice. The election notice describes to the beneficiaries their rights to continuation coverage and information about the coverage and how to elect the coverage.

Continuation Coverage Periods

Continuation coverage must last for 18 or 36 months, depending on the situation. Plans can allow coverage to continue for a longer period, however.

18 Month Coverage

The law requires 18 months of coverage if the qualified event is the covered employee's termination of employment, or reduction in hours of employment.

36 Month Coverage

Thirty-six month coverage is required when the other qualifying events occur. Also, if the qualifying event is the end of employment or reduction of the employee's hours, and the employee became entitled to Medicare less than 18 months before the qualifying event, COBRA coverage for the employee's spouse and dependents can last until 36 months after the date the employee becomes entitled to Medicare.

Termination before the End of the Period

The continuation coverage may terminate prior to the end of the period if:

- premiums are not paid in full on a timely basis
- the employer ceases to maintain any group health plan
- a qualified beneficiary begins coverage under another group health plan after electing continuation coverage, as long as the new plan does not impose an exclusion or limitation affecting a preexisting condition of the qualified beneficiary
- a qualified beneficiary becomes entitled to Medicare benefits after electing continuation coverage
- a qualified beneficiary engages in conduct that would justify the plan in terminating coverage of a similar situated participant or beneficiary not receiving continuation coverage

Generally defined, a *preexisting condition* is a health condition or problem that existed before a health care policy or contract was effective and for which medical advice, diagnosis, care, or treatment was recommended. Each health insurance policy or contract will define preexisting condition in its' policy terms and state the applicable time periods coverage is excluded for preexisting conditions, as allowed under the law.

ERISA

The Employee Retirement Income Security Act of 1974, commonly known as ERISA, regulates pension and welfare employee benefit plans established by private employers, unions, or both, to provide benefits to their workers and dependents. ERISA defines employee welfare benefit plans as those that provide "through the purchase of insurance or otherwise...medical, surgical, or hospital care or benefits, or benefits in the event of sickness, accident, disability, or death."

HIPAA Amendments to ERISA

In 1996, the Health Insurance Portability And Accountability Act (HIPAA) amended ERISA to require portability, nondiscrimination, and renewability of health benefits provided by group health plans and group health insurers. ERISA plans are generally covered under the HIPAA regulations for health plans.

ERISA governs various aspects of employee benefit programs, including pension plans and health insurance coverage. One of the key provisions of ERISA affecting group health plans is its preemptive provision. This provision excludes self-funded health plans from state regulation, and places self-funded plans under ERISA's regulations. This means that many state mandated benefits that do not mirror Federal laws do not apply to self-funded plans.

Larger plans can afford to self-fund, and smaller plans generally cannot. So, the preemption provision of ERISA tends to benefit larger plans, and negatively impact small plans, especially because of the many state mandated benefits in place today. Some states have enacted provisions for the benefit of small employers and their employees that allow them to offer health plans without mandated benefits, because of the concern that mandated state benefits are pricing small employer group health plans out of the market. Other states allow small employers to offer high deductible health plans with limited coverage.

Fiduciary Responsibilities

ERISA requires plans to disclose plan information to plan participants. These disclosures include information about plan features and plan funding. It also makes clear that plan sponsors have *fiduciary* responsibilities in meeting the terms of the plan, such as acting in the best interest of the participants in carrying out duties under the plan. Participants are also given a procedure for making grievances and appeals for benefits under the plan. Participants also have a right to sue for benefits and breaches of fiduciary duties.

Several amendments have been made to ERISA since its passage. HIPAA is an amendment to ERISA, as is the Consolidated Omnibus Budget Reconciliation Act (COBRA). Other amendments to ERISA include the Newborns' and Mothers' Health Protection Act, the Mental Health Parity

Act, and the Women's Health and Cancer Rights Act.

Reporting and Disclosures

ERISA requires that certain disclosures be made to benefit plan participants. These include:
- A written plan summary
- Rules for obtaining benefits
- Plan restrictions and limitations
- Guidelines for obtaining benefits, such as obtaining referrals in advance for surgery or doctor visits

A written policy is required to be established regarding how claims are to be filed. This policy must include a written appeal process for claims that are denied.

In addition, the plan must also give participants a summary annual report. This report is also provided to the Department of Labor through Form 5500.

Preexisting Conditions and Waiting Periods

An insured should consider how a new policy will treat preexisting conditions. A preexisting condition is a health condition or problem that existed before a given health care policy or contract was effective and for which medical advice, diagnosis, care, or treatment was recommended. Certain health insurance contracts define preexisting conditions that are excluded from coverage and will also define time periods that apply for conditions that are covered by the policy after a waiting period.

Many years ago, preexisting conditions of all types were allowed to be excluded or limited under health insurance contracts. However, state and federal regulation has reduced and eliminated many conditions for which coverage can be permanently excluded from health care coverage, even if these conditions are preexisting conditions. Regulation also has limited the time period for which allowable preexisting conditions may be excluded from coverage.

HIPAA and Preexisting Conditions

The Health Insurance Portability and Accountability Act of 1996 (HIPAA) regulates group health plans. Many of HIPAA's provisions apply to large employers (those with over 50 employees), but some also apply to small employers. A small employer is defined in HIPAA as an employer who employed an average of at least two, but not more than fifty employees on business days during the preceding calendar year, and who employs at least two employees on the first day of the plan year.

HIPAA contains several provisions with which group health plans must comply. These include provisions that:

- Limit exclusions for preexisting medical conditions – this provision does not apply now that the ACA applies to group health plans that HIPAA defined; ACA qualified plans do not allow preexisting conditions to be included in coverage.
- Provide credit against maximum preexisting condition exclusion periods of prior health coverage (which is known as *creditable coverage*) – HIPAA creditable coverage is no longer necessary to calculate to ensure preexisting conditions are not applied under new coverage because the ACA does not allow preexisting conditions to apply to employer group health plans.
- Provide a process for providing certificates that show periods of prior coverage to a new health plan or health insurance issue (*creditable coverage certificates*) – Health plans still issue coverage certificates to provide proof of coverage and termination for COBRA continuation purposes.
- Allow individuals to enroll for health coverage when they lose other health coverage, get married or add a new dependent
- Prohibit discrimination in enrollment and in premiums charged to employees and their dependents based on health status-related factors
- Guarantee the availability of health insurance coverage for small employers and renewability of health insurance coverage for both small and large employers

Under HIPAA's rules, a preexisting condition exclusion was "any limitation or exclusion of benefits for a health condition because it was present before coverage begins, regardless of whether any medical advice, diagnosis, care or treatment was recommended or received before that day."

The only allowable type of preexisting condition exclusion under HIPAA could relate to a condition for which medical advice, diagnosis, care or treatment was recommended or received during the six-month period prior to an individual's enrollment date in the plan. The maximum period a preexisting condition may be applied to an individual is generally 12 months, beginning on the individual's enrollment date in the plan.

There were prohibited preexisting condition exclusions under HIPAA. A preexisting condition exclusion could not be applied to pregnancy, whether or not the woman had previous coverage. Other prohibited preexisting condition exclusions applied to:

- A newborn
- An adopted child under age 18
- A child under age 18 placed with a family or individual for adoption, as long as the child became covered with creditable coverage within thirty days of birth, adoption or placement for adoption and does not incur a subsequent 63-day break in coverage
- Genetic information in the absence of a diagnosis of a condition

Waiting Periods and Preexisting Condition Exclusions

A waiting period is not the same as a preexisting condition exclusion (e.g., the six month period before a preexisting condition will be covered by the plan). A waiting period is a period of time before individuals become eligible for all plan benefits. For example, new employees may have to wait 90 days before they are covered by the group health plan. If a plan has a waiting period, the period for any preexisting condition exclusion must begin when the waiting period begins. For example, if the preexisting condition exclusion period is six months (180 days) and the waiting period is 90 days, the preexisting condition exclusion extends 90 days past the waiting period.

Creditable Coverage

HIPAA creditable coverage is coverage that reduces the period of any preexisting condition exclusion because the individual had this coverage prior to being covered by the current group health plan.

HIPAA creditable coverage included:

- A group health plan
- Health insurance coverage
- Medicare
- Medicaid
- CHAMPUS
- A medical care program of the Indian Health Service or of a tribal organization
- A state health benefits risk pool
- A health plan offered under Chapter 89 of title 5 United States Code (which is a section of law that governs health plans for federal government employees)
- A public health plan
- A health benefit plan under Section 5(e) of the Peace Corps Act

An individual's creditable coverage was generally documented for the group health plan by a certificate issued by the creditable coverage plan. Upon receipt of this certificate, the group health plan had to reduce any preexisting condition exclusion period by the length of time of the creditable coverage. *For example, the group health plan had allowable preexisting condition exclusions that apply for 12 months. The individual provided the group health plan with a certificate of creditable coverage of two years. The individual's preexisting condition exclusion period was reduced to zero.*

Affordable Care Act and Preexisting Conditions

The Patient Protection and Affordable Care Act (ACA) was signed into law on March 23, 2010. This Act is implemented over several years, beginning in 2010, and most provisions will be implemented by 2015.

The primary purpose of the ACA is to ensure that no one has to be uninsured. It combines reforms to both public and private health care systems with the aim to provide an affordable, accessible health care system for all. The ACA expands Medicaid so that previously uncovered, lower income segments of the population who are unable to obtain or cannot afford private coverage are provided with health care coverage. *Medicaid* is a joint federal and state program that helps with medical costs for some people with low incomes and limited resources. Medicaid programs vary from state to state.

The ACA also creates health insurance exchanges to provide access to coverage for those who are not eligible for Medicaid and do not have employer sponsored coverage. In addition, it penalizes employers with more than 50 employees who do not provide affordable health coverage in accordance with the ACA. Individuals who do not have health coverage by 2014 will pay a penalty for their lack of coverage.

Under the ACA, as of September 23, 2010, existing group health plans and all new plans issued must cover children under 19, regardless of preexisting conditions. *Grandfathered* individual health plans are not required to include this provision. If a new individual health plan is purchased to replace an existing one, children of the insured under 19 must be covered, regardless of preexisting conditions.

Also under the ACA, as of January 1, 2014, insurers and health plans may not refuse to renew policies or sell coverage because of preexisting conditions. Because of this, HIPAA creditable coverage certificates no longer need to be issued. However, for other purposes, such as to enable COBRA continuation eligibility, proof of coverage certificates or documents are still issued by health plans.

Benefits, Limitations and Exclusions

Although denial of coverage due to preexisting conditions has been restricted by HIPAA and the ACA, coverage for certain conditions is allowed to be excluded in health insurance policies. The types of care that a plan does not cover will be included in the general exclusions section of the health care coverage agreement or contract. Depending on the plan, exclusions may include:

- Acupuncture
- Admission prior to coverage
- Alcoholism and related conditions
- Chemical dependency and related conditions

- Cosmetic or reconstructive surgery
- Custodial care
- Dental procedures
- Experimental procedures
- Hearing aids
- Infertility
- Lifestyle modification
- On-the-job injuries covered by Workers Compensation
- Orthotic devices
- Outpatient treatment for mental or nervous disorders
- Services covered through city, county, state or federal law
- Sexual disorders
- Sterilization and related conditions
- Vision services
- War-related conditions

As the ACA's provisions are implemented, some of these exclusions are being restricted. For example, although conditions resulting from alcoholism may be excluded from coverage if a preexisting condition, the ACA requires preventive services to include alcohol screening and counseling. This means care related to alcohol abuse will be provided.

Long-Term Care (LTC) Policies
Contract Terms

Long-term care insurance is an insurance product designed specifically to help reduce the financial drain on individuals or families trying to meet long-term care expenses. It pays for long-term care services that are not covered by health insurance plans or Medicare. Long-term care insurance policies vary regarding the types of long-term care covered, although state law closely regulates their coverage provisions. These insurance policies also vary in the benefit amounts applying to home health care, other community based care and skilled nursing care, within state regulated bounds.

Long-term care coverage is issued through individual insurance policies, group policies and riders to life insurance and annuity policies. Individual policies tend to provide the broadest coverage, and are generally more expensive than riders and group policies. Group coverage and coverage through riders is more limited in scope.

Long-term care is distinguished from other health care which is given to treat those with *acute* rather than *chronic conditions*. An acute condition, according to the National Association of Insurance Commissioner's Long-Term Care Model regulation, means that "the individual is medically unstable. Such an individual requires frequent monitoring by medical professionals, such as physicians and registered nurses, in order to maintain his or her health status." An acute condition is one that is serious but not normally long-lasting, such as pneumonia, appendicitis or a broken hip. A chronic condition is one that is long lasting and often progressive in nature, such as diabetes.

Another common reason long-term care is needed is cognitive impairment, which includes conditions such as Alzheimer's disease. The Model Regulation defines *cognitive impairment* as "a deficiency in a person's short or long-term memory, orientation as to person, place and time, deductive or abstract reasoning, or judgment as it relates to safety awareness."

Individual Long-Term Care Contracts

Conditions that must be met before a long-term policy pays benefits are known as benefit triggers. Generally, policies include triggers related to activities of daily living (ADLs), medical care certification, and specified conditions, such as cognitive impairment.

Activities of Daily Living

Lack of ability to perform a specified number of ADLs is a common trigger in long-term care policies. For example, a policy may state that benefits will be paid if the insured is unable to perform two of six ADLs as defined in the policy.

Activities of Daily Living include:
- Bathing: Washing oneself by sponge bath, or in either a tub or shower, including the task of getting into or out of the tub or shower.
- Continence: The ability to maintain control of bowel and bladder function; or when unable to maintain control of bowel and bladder

VA PPL LH-2_16298

function, the ability to perform associated personal hygiene (including caring for catheter or colostomy bag).

- Dressing: Putting on and taking off all items of clothing and necessary braces, fasteners or artificial limbs.
- Eating: Feeding oneself by getting food into the body from a receptacle (such as a plate, cup or table) or by a feeding tube or intravenously.
- Toileting: Getting to and from the toilet, getting on and off the toilet and performing associated personal hygiene.
- Transferring: Moving into or out of a bed, chair or wheelchair.

Medical Care Certification

Medical care certification is a trigger that requires a physician to certify that treatment is necessary and that the insured's medical condition will deteriorate if the care is not provided. Certification may also be performed by a case manager, rather than a physician, under some policies.

Specified Conditions

Certain conditions can automatically trigger benefit payment in long-term care policies. For example, cognitive impairment, which includes Alzheimer's disease, is a specified condition that triggers benefit payment.

Levels of Care

Nursing Care

There are three levels of nursing care that long-term care policies cover: skilled, intermediate and custodial.

Skilled Care

Skilled care is care provided by or under the supervision of skilled medical personnel that includes 24-hour nursing or rehabilitative care.

Intermediate Care

Intermediate care is also provided by or under the supervision of skilled medical personnel, but is not around-the-clock nursing care. Intermediate skilled nursing care is occasional nursing or rehabilitative care.

Custodial Care

Custodial care can include some health related care, but no skilled medical care. This type of care is assistance with ADLs – eating, toileting, transferring, bathing, dressing and continence.

In most states it is required today that all levels of care – skilled, intermediate and custodial – are covered on an equal basis in long-term care policies that provide skilled nursing coverage. In addition, most states prohibit policies from requiring that skilled or intermediate care be given prior to covering custodial care. It is also prohibited to require a three-day hospital stay prior to covering nursing home care, as many older long-term care policies did.

Community Based Benefits

Community based benefits include home health care, care given in adult day health care, hospice facility care, assisted living care, personal care and homemaking or chore services.

Community care services can also be placed in the categories of skilled, intermediate and custodial.

Nursing Facility Benefits and Assisted Living / Alternate Facility Benefits

Assisted living facilities, also known as alternate facilities or residential care facilities, are facilities for the elderly or disabled that do not provide skilled nursing on a 24-hour basis. They may be large retirement communities, small group homes, or of a size somewhere in between. They provide personal care services, and chore aid services such as shopping, housekeeping and transportation. Nursing facility benefits in a long-term care policy generally apply to nursing care given in assisted living facilities, although benefits are normally paid at a maximum specified percentage such as 60% or 70% of the nursing facility benefit.

Home Health Care

A variety of health care services may be provided in the home. Long-term care insurance contracts today cover many care services provided in the home. Services provided may include nursing services, physical therapy, speech therapy, occupational therapy, respiratory therapy, nutritional services, medical services, social

VA PPL LH-2_16298

services and medical supplies and equipment services.

Home health care may also include services given by a home health aide. A home health aide may not provide medical treatment, but may monitor a patient's medical condition, by taking his or her temperature, for example. Generally, a home health aide's duties are focused on personal care, such as bathing and dressing, and on performing chores, such as cleaning, doing laundry, cooking and other household chores.

Home Care

Home care is non-medical care. It refers to assistance with chores and personal care. *Home health care* includes medical care, or monitoring of medical care. A policy that covers home health care may not cover home care.

Respite Care

Respite care provisions are for the benefit of the caregiver and the insured. They pay for the insured to be put in a nursing home for a period of days each year to give the caregiver a break. This type of provision is a benefit before the elimination period is met, but once the elimination period is met, the respite care would generally be covered under the other provisions of the policy.

Benefit Periods

Benefit periods dictate the length of time the policy will pay benefits. The policy may have a daily benefit as well as maximum lifetime benefits.

Daily Benefits

Daily benefits may be from $50 to $500. The insured can generally select a daily maximum benefit amount within this or a similar range. The policy will generally pay the daily maximum or the actual cost of care, whichever is less.

Maximum Lifetime Benefits

A maximum lifetime benefit is included in long-term care policies. There may be a different lifetime benefit for different types of care. For example, there may be a two and one-half year maximum benefit period for community based care, and a five-year maximum benefit for nursing home care.

Some policies have a one-time maximum benefit, and others have a maximum benefit per confinement period. If a policy includes a new maximum benefit period per confinement period, it may require that each confinement period have a specified period in between confinements, such as six months.

For example, Jed has a long-term care contract that has a maximum benefit of $125,000 per confinement period. A confinement period is defined as the period beginning when the insured meets the benefit eligibility requirements until the time when the insured no longer meets these requirements, or 24 months, whichever is longer. After a period of at least 9 months without utilizing policy benefits, a new confinement period may begin upon the insured's eligibility for benefits and the maximum benefit of $125,000 is again payable.

Benefit Amounts

Indemnity vs. Actual Cost of Care Policies

Long-term care policies may calculate benefits as indemnity or actual cost of care contracts. Indemnity contracts pay a fixed amount per day, or the actual cost of care, whichever is lower. Actual cost of care contracts pay for the actual cost of care, up to specified limits. Premiums for indemnity policies are affected by the benefit amount selected. This can make them easier to adjust for affordability purposes than actual cost of care policies.

Optional Benefits

Guarantee of Insurability for Additional Coverage

Guarantee of Insurability for Additional Coverage Benefits	
Guaranteed Increase Option (GIO)	*Guaranteed Purchase Option (GPO)*
Allows purchase of additional coverage without evidence of insurability	Allows purchase of additional coverage without evidence of insurability
Offer made periodically, such as every 3 years	Offer made periodically, such as every 3 years
Offers continue even if insured declines to purchase	Offers end if insured declines to purchase a specified number of times
Purchase increase percentages vary among contracts, e.g. 3% or 5% of existing benefits or pool of money	Purchase increase percentages vary among contracts, e.g. 3% or 5% of existing benefits or pool of money
Offer may end at specified age, such as age 90	Offer may end after one or two refusals, or at specified age, whichever occurs first

 VA PPL LH-2_16298

Return of Premium

Return of premium provisions allow a beneficiary to be paid a return of premium benefit if the amounts paid under the policy while the insured was living is greater than the benefits paid out. For example, a return of premium provision may provide that if an insured dies prior to age 65, the named beneficiary receives a benefit equal to total premiums paid, less benefits paid from the policy.

Qualified and Non-Qualified Policies

There is a category of long-term care policy that receives federal tax advantages. These policies are called *qualified long-term care policies*. Most policies offered and sold are qualified policies. However, the policy must clearly and prominently state whether it is or is not intended to be a qualified policy.

A significant benefit of qualified long-term care contracts are the tax advantages. These advantages may not be important to an individual who does not itemize his federal taxes. Most financial professionals recommend that only qualified long-term care benefits be deducted from income under the unreimbursed medical expenses rules. Premiums are not deductible unless the policy is a qualified long-term care policy.

Long-Term Care Policy Exclusions

Certain conditions are excluded from long-term care policy coverage. States prohibit insurers from excluding certain conditions, such as Alzheimer's or other cognitive disorders.

Generally, the only limitations or exclusions allowed in a long-term care policy are:

1. Preexisting conditions or diseases (but generally only for a period of six months);
2. Mental or nervous disorders, however, this does not permit the exclusion or limitation of benefits on the basis of Alzheimer's Disease;
3. Alcoholism and drug addiction;
4. Illness, treatment or medical condition arising out of:
   a. War or act of war (whether declared or undeclared)
   b. Participation in a felony, riot or insurrection

   c. Service in the armed forces or units auxiliary thereto
   d. Suicide (sane or insane), attempted suicide or intentionally self-inflicted injury; or
   e. Aviation (this exclusion applies only to non-fare-paying passengers.)
5. Treatment provided in a government facility (unless otherwise required by law), services for which benefits are available under Medicare or other governmental program (except Medicaid), any state or federal Workers Compensation, employer's liability or occupational disease law, or any motor vehicle no-fault law, services provided by a member of the covered person's immediate family and services for which no charge is normally made in the absence of insurance;
6. Expenses for services or items available or paid under another long-term care insurance or health insurance policy;
7. In the case of a qualified long-term care insurance contract, expenses for services or items to the extent that the expenses are reimbursable under the Social Security Act or would be reimbursable if a deductible or coinsurance amount did not apply.

The NAIC Model Regulations permit exclusions and limitations for payment for services provided outside the United States and legitimate variations in benefit levels to reflect differences in provider rates.

Deficit Reduction Act of 2005 (DRA)

Federal Act including provisions to expand state "Long-Term Care Partnership" programs, previously only in California, Indiana, New York and Connecticut
DRA allows states to disregard assets equivalent to qualified long-term care expenses paid by LTC Partnership Insurance Policies from Medicaid eligibility and estate recovery amounts
Medicaid asset disregard previously illegal under OBRA '93
Allowing Medicaid asset disregard motivates middle income persons to purchase LTC insurance
Increased purchase of Partnership LTC policies reduces states' financial burden related to LTC Medicaid expenses

Underwriting Considerations

The common underwriting factors included on a long-term care insurance application are the following:

- Age
- Sex
- Medical History, including
  - Heart attack
  - Diabetes
  - Cancer
  - High Blood Pressure
  - Arthritis
  - Renal disease (kidney failure)
  - Respiratory distress that requires oxygen use
  - Schizophrenia
  - Dementia
  - Spinal cord disorders
  - Multiple strokes
  - Systemic lupus
  - Most recipients of transplants
  - Tuberculosis
  - Multiple episodes of fainting
  - Severe growths or tumors
  - Current medical condition
- Whether the insured has undergone drug or alcohol abuse treatment
- Family medical history
- Occupation

Long-term care insurance underwriting, as a form of health insurance, involves reviewing medical and health factors. Reports from the MIB and attending physicians will be utilized. Statistics related directly to long-term care are used to evaluate each risk and establish rates. For example, the sex of the applicant is important because women, due to having a longer life expectancy than men, are more likely to need some type of long-term care services.

Group Long-Term Care Contracts

Filing requirements of group long-term care insurers vary by state. Generally, it is required that prior to an insurer or similar organization offering group long-term care insurance to a resident of a respective state under its Long-Term Care Act, the insurer must file with the state commissioner evidence that the group policy or certificate has been approved by a state having statutory or regulatory long-term care insurance requirements substantially similar to those adopted in the state. This regulation allows a state to only allow insurers who have an approved group long-term care product with provisions that would meet substantially all this state's requirements, to file a group contract in the state.

Continuation or Conversion of Coverage

Group long-term care contracts must provide covered individuals with a basis for continuation or conversion of coverage. If a group policy requires that benefits or services be given through only certain providers or facilities, or has incentives, such as covering a higher amount of services given, if certain providers or facilities are used, the continuation coverage may include these same requirements or incentives, or those that are substantially equivalent. The Commissioner of Insurance makes the determination regarding whether continuation benefits are substantially equivalent. *For example, the existing group long-term care plan offered by an employer uses health care providers affiliated with Monolith Hospitals and Clinics as "preferred providers." When an employee leaves the company, the employee may opt to convert the policy to an individual plan that uses an independent physicians and clinics association as preferred providers. The Commissioner of Insurance determined that the benefits offered through the continuation coverage were substantially equal to those of the employer's group plan.*

In order to be eligible for continuation or conversion of coverage, the group member must have a basis for conversion of coverage. The requirements of this basis are that:

- the individual has been continuously insured under the group policy (including a group policy which it replaced) for at least six months immediately prior to termination; and
- the policy has a provision that states that an individual whose coverage under the group policy would otherwise terminate or has been terminated for a reason, including discontinuance of the group policy in its entirety or with respect to an insured class is entitled to the issuance of a converted policy by the same insurer, without evidence of insurability.

For example, Muriel is covered by a long-term care contract which was offered through her employer. She is given notice that her position, which she has occupied for five years, is being eliminated. She is given the option to convert her group coverage to an individual contract

VA PPL LH-2_16298

with the same insurer without having to have any physical examination or other proof that she is insurable.

A converted policy is defined in the Model Regulation as "an individual policy of long-term care insurance providing benefits identical to or benefits determined by the Commissioner to be substantially equivalent to or in excess or those provided under the group policy from which conversion is made."

Time-Frame of Continuation

The written application for a converted policy must be made and the first premium due, if applicable, and payable as the insurer directs no later than 31 days after termination of coverage under the group policy. The converted policy must be issued effective on the day following the termination of coverage under the group policy and must be renewable annually.

Conversion at Issue Age or Attained Age

Issue Age Conversion	Attained Age Conversion
Premium at conversion calculated based on insured's age at issue of group policy	Premium at conversion calculated based on insured's age at time of conversion
If converted group contract had replaced a prior group policy so that there was no break in coverage, premium is based on age at issue of original group policy	

For example, Jay opened a long-term care contract through his employer's group coverage when he was 37, and the premium he paid is based on his age at issue. If he converts to a long-term care contract because the current contract is terminated by the employer, Jay, who is now 43, is given the option to convert to a different long-term care contract with premiums based on his age 37.

Mandatory Continuation of Coverage or Issuance of a Converted Policy

Generally, the requirement that an insured under a group long-term care contract be offered continuation or conversion coverage is mandatory except under the following circumstances:

- Termination of group coverage resulted from an individual's failure to make the required payment of premium or contribution when due.

- The terminating coverage is replaced not later than 31 days after termination by group coverage effective on the day following the termination of coverage. The replacing coverage must include the following:
  1. provide benefits identical to or benefits determined by the Commissioner to be substantially equivalent to or in excess of those provided by the terminating coverage;
  2. the premium is calculated as required based on either issue age or attained age.

Other Conversion Rules

More Than One Contract/Other Insurance	If an insured converts a group LTC policy and has another LTC policy that pays on an actual cost of care basis, the converted policy may include a reduction of benefits provision that reduces benefits if the 2 policies would pay more than 100% of the cost of care without the reduction, as long as premiums are reduced commensurately
Maximum Benefits Payable	Converted policy may provide that its benefits, together with the benefits payable under the group policy from which conversion is made, may not exceed those that would have been payable under the group policy if it had remained in effect.
Continuation of Coverage by Spouses or Family Members	If an individual is a LTC group member based upon the individual's relationship to another person, the individual can convert to an individual LTC policy if the relationship terminates due to death or divorce

Discontinuance and Replacement

Another required consumer protection provision that applies to group long-term care partnership contracts states that if a group long-term care policy is replaced by another group long-term care policy issued to the same policyholder, the succeeding insurer must offer coverage to all persons covered under the previous group policy on its date of termination. *For example, if an employer's current long-term care group plan covers all employees who work at least 30 hours per week and are at least age 22; a succeeding insurer's group plan must cover at least all employees with those same characteristics. The coverage and premium charged to persons under the new group policy may not:*

- result in an exclusion for preexisting conditions that would have been covered under the group policy being replaced; or
- vary or otherwise depend on the individual's health or disability status, claim experience or use of long-term care services.

Limited Benefit Plans

State insurance laws and regulations generally define each type of health insurance policy and health coverage plan offered within the state. These insurance regulations describe the scope of coverage and minimum coverage benefits for each type of plan. The NAIC's model Accident and Sickness Minimum Standards Act and Regulation are used as the basis for many state's laws. The model law and regulation includes these categories of accident and sickness coverage:

- Basic hospital expense
- Basic medical-surgical expense
- Hospital confinement indemnity
- Major medical expense
- Disability income protection
- Accident-only
- Specified disease
- Specified accident
- Limited benefit insurance

Not all states define their accident and sickness policies as falling within these exact categories. However, many of the disclosure and minimum standard provisions from the NAIC's model law and regulation are generally included in each state's individual health insurance laws as they are applicable to the policies issued in the state.

Limited health coverage policies are not required to follow the provisions of the ACA.

Limited Health Policy Types

- Accident-only
- Specified disease
- Specified accident
- Vision only policies
- Dental only policies
- Supplemental plans that cover deductibles and coinsurance

Policies that are not limited policies, such as hospital expense, medical surgical expense, major medical expense and disability income policies, have statutorily defined minimum benefit amounts and periods. Limited policies have benefit amounts, scope and periods that are lower or smaller than the policies that are not limited policies.

It is suggested that existing health insurance policies be reviewed before a consumer purchases a limited benefit policy. It is possible that adequate coverage is being supplied by a comprehensive health insurance policy or a Medicare Supplement policy. It is important that an applicant understand the provisions of a limited policy, its scope of coverage, limitations, exclusions and benefits, before purchase.

Cancer or Specified Dread Disease

One limited policy type is specified dread disease coverage. Specified dread disease coverage covers loss due to disease or sickness caused by sickness or disease named in the policy. These policies do not cover injuries or loss resulting from accidents.

Characteristics of Specified Dread Disease Policies	
Waiting periods	Sickness or disease covered if diagnosed after a specified period, e.g. 30 or 90 days, from policy inception
Terminal Disease	Benefits may only apply if insured survives a specified period of time after diagnosis
Diseases Covered	One diseases only, e.g. cancer, or several named diseases, such as coronary disease, cancer, stroke, kidney failure, multiple sclerosis and payment for organ transplants
Medical and hospital expense coverage	May include related care in hospital and medical expense coverage
Other indemnity coverage	May include indemnity insurance (e.g. $200/day) for hospitalization and/or for disability
Lump sum benefit	Generally pay a lump sum at time of diagnosis
Cancer coverage	Benefits may include prosthetics and bone marrow transplants as well as pay for radiation and chemotherapy treatments
Exclusions	Certain forms of disease may be excluded, e.g. in a cancer policy, skin cancer may not be covered
Policy types	Usually group policies, offered to employees and executives

VA PPL LH-2_16298

Critical Illness Plans

Critical illness insurance pays a lump sum benefit upon diagnosis of a critical illness. The purpose of the lump sum benefit is to pay for:

- uncovered health care expenses;
- deductibles and coinsurance in other health coverage;
- planning and legal expenses that may now be necessary due to the diagnosis;
- ongoing expenses such as a mortgage, car payments, and insurance because earning capacity may be impacted by the illness;
- taking a trip or vacation to fulfill a lifelong dream or visit friends and relatives;
- childcare, custodial care or chore aid services needed due to the illness; and
- transportation to and from health care facilities.

These plans are often offered on a group basis and marketed to employees of a business. The types of illnesses covered by this insurance include:

- heart attack
- stroke
- end-stage renal failure
- coma
- organ transplant
- paralysis / paraplegia
- Alzheimer's disease
- blindness, deafness
- coronary artery bypass graft
- HIV (medical personnel only)
- aortic surgery
- angioplasty
- heart valve surgery
- loss of sight/speech/hearing
- severe burns
- cancers that have spread
- cancers that have not spread

Worksite Limited Benefit Plans

Scheduled Benefit or "Mini-Med" Plans

Scheduled benefit plans provide a limited menu of benefits that are paid on a per visit or per day basis. These plans are also referred to as mini-med plans because they provide the types of benefits of a medical expense plan, but with much lower limits. They also pay on an indemnification basis rather than a reimbursement basis. For example, a mini-med plan may pay $1000 per accident, $300 per day for hospitalization, $50 for a physician office visit and three $50 visits annually for preventive care.

The primary reason for these mini-med plans has been to provide more affordable health insurance coverage for those who cannot afford higher premium plans. Mini-med plans are offered to employees by companies such as fast-food corporations who have a relatively young and lower-paid work force. The groups that purchase this coverage either do not need the high coverage limits of major medical plans or are unwilling or unable to pay for them, and so opt for more limited plans.

These plans are currently undergoing industry and regulatory scrutiny and may be required to increase their limits in order to conform to federal health insurance laws. Under federal law, most of these plans will be required to remove their annual benefit limits by 2014.

Hospital Income or Indemnity Coverage

Hospital income or indemnity coverage provides benefits, generally on a daily basis, for hospital confinement. Some policies pay a lump sum upon confinement rather than a daily benefit.

Daily benefit amounts vary from as low as $50 per day to $250 per day or higher. The benefit period varies as well. Some plans offer benefit periods of 365 days, others have 2 year benefit periods. Those with higher daily benefit amounts may limit the benefit period to a shorter time frame, such as 30 or 180 days annually.

These policies may include optional provisions that can be purchased. A rider may be purchased to provide a lump sum amount upon hospital confinement of an amount from $250 to $5000, for example. Some policies offer riders to pay additional amounts if placed in ICU. Others offer an optional lump sum amount if diagnosed with cancer, a heart attack, stroke or coma.

Dental Coverage

Dental insurance provides coverage for ongoing dental care and dental care needed due to accident or injury. Generally, dental insurance provides benefits based on a class or category of service. Diagnostic and preventive services are covered as a separate class of services from orthodontics, for example, where diagnostic and preventive services may be covered on an 80/20 coinsurance basis and orthodontics on a 50/50 coinsurance basis.

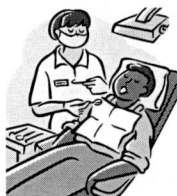

Diagnostic and Preventive Services

Periodic teeth cleaning	Sealants to prevent cavities
X-rays on an annual basis	Emergency examinations
Topical fluoride treatments	
Generally in the highest coverage category (e.g. covered 100% or 80/20 coinsurance)	

Restorative Services

Restorative services that are generally in the highest coverage category (e.g. 100% or 80/20 coinsurance)	
Filling cavities	Adding material to weak teeth to strengthen them
Services that are considered major or special restorative services (e.g. 50/50 coinsurance)	
Crowns	Bridges

Oral Surgery Services

Oral surgery services include extracting teeth and pre-operative and post-operative care. Oral surgery services include anesthesia.

Endodontic Services

Endodontic services include root canals. The word endodontic comes from the Greek, where endo means inside and odont means tooth. Endodontic services deal with the inside of the tooth, the tooth's pulp. Some endodontic treatments are performed by specialists, called endodontists. Pediatric dentists are generally also endodontists.

A dental plan may categorize some endodontic services as basic and some as specialty services, and apply different coinsurance or copayments to them based on service level.

Periodontics

Periodontic services include care for the gums and bone structure supporting the teeth.

Category of service depends on severity of condition, kind and length of treatment
Cleaning the area near the gum line (scaling) to remove plaque hardened into tartar (May be a basic service – e.g. covered 80/20 coinsurance)
Treating gum disease – includes scaling, more regular hygienic exams and cleaning (May be basic or special service – e.g. 80/20 or 50/50 coinsurance)
Treating severe gum disease – includes deeper scaling, may need gum and bone tissue surgery or replacement (Likely to be 50/50 coinsurance)

Prosthodontic Services

Prosthodontic services is a type of dentistry dealing with prosthetics, such as implants and dentures. Prosthodontics is a dental specialty. Besides constructing and fitting implants and dentures, prosthodontists also provide therapy and care for TMJ (temporomandibular joint disorder). As a specialty service, a dental plan will normally assign higher copayments or coinsurance requirements for this care.

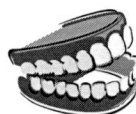

Orthodontic Services

Orthodontic services involve treatment for putting teeth in proper alignment. Orthodontists are specialists who use braces, retainers and other appliances to straighten or otherwise put teeth and jaw in their proper positions.

Orthodontics may not be covered under a basic dental insurance plan. When covered by insurance, orthodontic services are generally subject to a high coinsurance requirement and a capped benefit amount.

Dental Indemnity Plans

Choice of Providers

Indemnity plans are dental plans that are paid for on a fee-for-service basis. Generally, an indemnity plan allows the insured to choose the provider. No referral is required for services from a specialist in order for the plan to cover care.

Scheduled Versus Nonscheduled Plans

A scheduled indemnity plan will pay for services based on a pre-determined fee. The insurer will reimburse the insured for services based on this fee, regardless of how much the dentist or specialist charges. Scheduled plans may include a copayment. They will not pay more than the dentist charges.

A nonscheduled plan will pay for services based on the amount the dentist or specialist charges, subject to limits of insurance. Preventive care is generally paid at the highest level, such as up to 100%. Major and specialty care may be paid at 50% to 80% of cost of care, depending on the service provided. Nonscheduled plans generally include coinsurance and deductibles.

Benefit Categories

Indemnity plans generally categorize services into diagnostic/preventive services, basic services and major services.

Diagnostic/Preventive Services

Diagnostic/preventive services include periodic routine examinations, cleanings, and x-rays.

Basic Services

Basic services generally include:

- Restorative services such as filling a cavity,
- Endodontics such as performing root canals,
- Oral surgery such as pulling wisdom teeth,
- Periodontics, such as periodic teeth scaling for adults

Major Services

Major services generally include specialty restorative services, such as crowns that are not made of basic amalgam or resin materials, prosthodontics and orthodontics.

Deductibles and Coinsurance

Indemnity plans vary concerning the amount of deductible and coinsurance. There may be no deductible applicable to preventive and diagnostic services, or a single deductible may apply to all services provided under the plan.

Coinsurance amounts vary based on the category of service. Diagnostic and preventive services may have from 0% to 20% coinsurance requirements. Basic services may have a 10% or 20% coinsurance requirement, and major services may require the insured to pay 50% of the cost.

Integrated Deductible and Stand-Alone Plans

When employers offer a dental plan along with a health plan, the dental plan may be subject to the same deductible as the health plan, with just one deductible for both plans, or the dental plan may be a separate, distinct stand-alone plan. *For example, employees may be covered by a group health preferred provider plan that includes dental coverage and that has an integrated deductible. The employee's coverage is subject to a $1000 annual deductible, regardless of whether medical expense, hospitalization or dental care services are received through the plan.*

If the dental plan is a stand-alone plan, it will have its own deductible, or if a managed care dental maintenance organization plan (a DMO), it will have its own copayment schedule for services. For example, the employer may offer a preferred provider plan for medical expense and hospitalization coverage and a DMO plan. The medical expense and hospitalization coverage is subject to a $750 annual deductible. The DMO plan has no deductible, but employees pay a copayment for all services received.

Combination Plan

Some insurers provide combination plans. These plans combine an indemnity plan with a managed care plan. The insureds may select a provider within the managed care plan, and will receive coverage based on paying a copayment for services received. Or insureds may choose care outside the network, and pay for it based on the fee-for-service indemnity plan's coinsurance and deductibles.

Exclusions

Dental plans may cover just diagnostic, preventive and basic services and exclude major services. Those that cover all these levels of service may exclude coverage for any care that is cosmetic only.

Other exclusions may include:

- Services covered by Workers Compensation
- Congenital or developmental malformations other than those related to cleft palate
- Restoring teeth structure lost due to wear
- Hypnosis or other alternative medicine treatments
- Prescription drug expenses
- Hospitalization
- Tissue grafts
- Speech therapy

VA PPL LH-2_16298

- Replacement of lost, stolen or damaged appliances
- Services covered by Medicaid

Limitations

Covered dental services are subject to limitations. For example, teeth cleaning may be limited to once or twice annually. Replacement of oral devices may be limited to once every three or five years. Benefit amounts are generally subject to annual maximum limits.

Predetermination of Benefits

A plan may require that it approve services above a certain dollar amount, such as $1000. If so, the insured is required to submit the dentist's or specialist's plan of treatment, including x-rays and justification of treatment, to the plan prior to providing the services. The plan must then approve the services and cost before it will reimburse the insured for their cost.

Vision Care

Vision care plans cover eye examination and prescription lenses. Generally, these are group policies. A wide variety of plan options are available. An annual or biannual eye exam is provided along with coverage for prescription lenses. Plans may require that a copayment be paid for lenses. Some plans pay for frames and prescription lenses for glasses with no copay, but charge a copy for contacts. Other plans pay the full amount for either glasses or contacts, up to a certain dollar limit. Others allow the participant to choose whether to purchase glasses, contacts, or both, up to a certain dollar limit. Some plans provide discounts for Lasik surgery.

Vision care plans may allow members to visit any optometrist and any retailer to purchase the prescription lenses. Others have a network of optometrists and retailers from which the member can receive these services.

Section VI Review

1) "Injury to the body as the result of an accident" is a definition in health insurance policies for the term:
   a. accidental injury
   b. sickness
   c. bodily injury
   d. personal injury

2) Joe has a disability income policy that uses a loss of income approach to calculating disability benefits. A pro-rata amount of the maximum benefit is paid for loss of income under 80%. Loss of income of 80% or more is treated as total disability, and 100% of the maximum benefit is paid. The maximum amount the policy will pay is $4000 per month. Joe's disability has caused him to lose 25% of his pre-disability income. The policy will pay:
   a. $4000 per month
   b. $2000 per month
   c. $1000 per month
   d. $0 per month

3) The type of disability insurance policy that provides insurance to pay for certain expenses of the business should a business owner become disabled is called:
   a. Cost of Living Adjustment Insurance
   b. Hospitalization Benefit insurance.
   c. Business Overhead Expense insurance.
   d. Short-term Disability insurance.

4) Medical expense plans generally pay for care such as:
   a. long-term skilled nursing care
   b. orthodontic care
   c. adult day care
   d. physical exams

5) The type of health policy that pays a specified benefit on a daily or monthly basis when an insured is confined to a hospital is:
   a. a dread disease policy
   b. a comprehensive health coverage policy
   c. a medical expense policy
   d. a hospital indemnity policy

6) As the name "primary care physician" suggests, under managed care plans, this physician is likely to provide the member with _____ medical care the member requires, unless the member needs largely specialized health care.
   a. all of the
   b. most of the
   c. none of the
   d. the most expensive

7) As pertains to emergency care, conditions that could result in death, serious disability, disfigurement, or a long-term medical problem is:
   a. life-threatening emergency care
   b. urgent emergency care
   c. necessary emergency care
   d. essential emergency care

8) In dental, vision and hearing health care plans, _____ care is generally defined in managed care plans to include care such as that required after an accident, or care required due to an infection.
   a. medically necessary
   b. preventative
   c. non-medically necessary
   d. personal

9) Amy has a high-deductible health plan through her employer, and is covered by a low-deductible health plan through her husband's employer. Amy:
   a. cannot establish an HSA
   b. can establish an HSA but cannot make contributions to it
   c. can establish an HSA and an HRA
   d. can establish an HRA

10) As pertains to health savings accounts, if a medical expense is covered by insurance:
    a. it is a "qualified medical expense" according to HSA rules
    b. it is not a "qualified medical expense" according to HSA rules
    c. it is a "qualified medical expense" according to HDHP rules
    d. the employee can be reimbursed for it through an HRA

11) HRA plan distributions can be made to:
    a. current employees only
    b. current employees and their spouses only
    c. current and former employees and their spouses only
    d. current and former employees, spouses and dependents of those employees, and spouses and dependents of deceased employees

12) Which Medigap Plan includes the same benefits as Plan A and pays 50% of the Medicare Plan A deductible and includes coverage for the skilled nursing facility care coinsurance amount?
    a. Plan E
    b. Plan K
    c. Plan L
    d. Plan M

13) A business approaches an insurer about participating in a MET. The insurer determines that the business is related to other businesses in the same trade and that are under control of another business. There are five businesses within this same control group and they are commonly controlled. The insurer tells the business it cannot be part of a MET. Which of the following characteristics of a MET prohibits this business from participating in a MET?
   a. METs are only available for single employer groups
   b. METs are formed with groups of similar businesses
   c. METs are made up of groups of employers
   d. METs are separate trusts that purchase group health insurance

14) The group health insurance plan has a $1200 annual deductible. It has no coinsurance, so the plan pays 100% of covered expenses after the deductible is met. The plan year for this plan is January through December. In December, a member has paid $900 of the deductible. In January of the following year, she incurs covered medical expenses of $400. The insurance company properly pays $100 of these expenses incurred in January. This payment demonstrates that the health insurance plan:
   a. has a coordination of benefits provision
   b. has an annual enrollment period
   c. has a deductible carryover provision
   d. has a copayment provision

15) The reason creditable coverage certificates are not necessary to ensure that preexisting conditions are not unlawfully applied when a group employer plan member moves to a new employer plan is because the Affordable Care Act does not allow a group health plan to:
   a. Charge deductibles
   b. Impose preexisting condition restrictions
   c. Allow employees to select group coverage plans only
   d. Be offered through an employer if it is an HMO plan

16) The type of long-term care that provides assistance with ADLs, and includes no medical care is:
   a. skilled care
   b. intermediate care
   c. custodial care
   d. ADL care

17) A long-term care policy will pay for the actual cost of care, up to a $200,000 life of policy limit, and $50,000 annual limit. This type of long-term care policy is:
   a. illegal
   b. an indemnity policy
   c. a low premium policy
   d. an actual cost of care policy

18) The type of dental care that includes extracting teeth and pre-operative and post-operative care and includes anesthesia is:
   a. restorative services
   b. oral surgery services
   c. endodontic services
   d. diagnostic and preventive services

19) Nonscheduled dental plans:
   a. pay a flat fee for a service, regardless of what the dentist charges.
   b. never include deductibles.
   c. pay for services based on the amount the dentist charges and generally include coinsurance and deductibles.
   d. generally pay a greater percentage of specialty care than for preventive care.

20) The ACA is being implemented over several years, with most provisions implemented by the year:
   a. 2015
   b. 2013
   c. 2012
   d. 2011

VA PPL LH-2_16298

Section VII: Policy Provisions, Clauses and Riders

Mandatory Provisions

The NAIC's Uniform Policy Provisions Model Law, which specifies provisions found in individual accident and sickness insurance policies, has been adopted by all fifty states. It includes mandatory provisions for these policies, as well as optional provisions. Virginia's Code includes these provisions in VA Code §38.2-3503 (mandatory provisions) and §38.2-3504 (optional provisions). As the ACA's provisions are implemented in 2014 and beyond, changes may occur in these contract terms.

Entire Contract and Changes Clause

One of these provisions is the *entire contract* and changes clause. This clause states that the policy is the entire contract of insurance and that no changes may be made unless it is approved by the insurer and an endorsement of the change is attached to the policy. An agent may not change the policy or waive any of its provisions.

Time Limit on Certain Defenses Clause

Another mandatory provision found in individual health policies is the time limit on certain defenses or *incontestability* clause. Under this clause, a limited period of time is provided for an insurer to challenge a contract or deny a claim. This provision limits the period of time that nondisclosures and misstatements, unless fraudulent, may be used to void the policy or deny a claim. In most states, this period is limited to two years, but some states allow three years. This provision also prohibits the insurer from denying a claim based on preexisting conditions after two or three years, unless the condition was specifically excluded under the coverage.

Misstatements	
Once the policy has been issued, the insurer may not void the policy or deny a claim for loss or disability due to misstatements in the application unless fraudulent ...	...in Virginia after 2 years
Preexisting Conditions	
Once the policy has been issued, the insurer may not deny a claim based on preexisting conditions unless the condition was specifically excluded under the coverage...	...in Virginia after 1 year

Grace Period

Under the mandatory *grace period* provision, the policyholder has seven additional days to pay premium if the policy has a weekly premium payment schedule, ten additional days to pay premium if the policy has a monthly premium payment schedule, and thirty-one additional days to pay premium for policies with any other premium payment schedule.

Reinstatement

Under the *reinstatement* provision, if a policy has lapsed and a new application is not required, the acceptance of overdue premium by the insurance company will reinstate the policy. If an application is required with premium, reinstatement is effective as of the date the application is approved. If an application is required and not approved, and if the insurer does not notify the applicant of its disapproval in writing within forty-five days of accepting the overdue premium, the policy must be reinstated. The reinstated policy will cover loss resulting from accidental injury immediately upon reinstatement, but will not cover loss due to sickness that begins ten days or less after reinstatement.

Notice of Claim

Under the Notice of Claim mandatory provision, a policyholder must give the insurer or the insurer's representative notice of a claim within twenty days, or as soon as possible after a loss covered by the policy. If the claim is for payments to be made for at least two years, such as for disability benefits, the insurer may require that a notice of a continuation of the condition be made to the insurer at least every six months, unless the policyholder is legally incapable of doing so.

Claim Forms

Under the *claims forms* provision, the insurer must furnish claim forms to the claimant within fifteen days of notice of the claim. If the insurer does not furnish the claim forms within this time frame, the claimant fulfills the requirement to provide proof of loss by providing written proof covering the occurrence, the character and event of the loss for which the claim is made.

Proof of Loss

The *proof of loss* mandatory individual health insurance policy provision places a time limit upon the period in which a proof of loss form is given to the insurer. Under the provision, the proof of loss must be filed within ninety days of loss, or if the loss is a continuing loss, the proof of loss must be given within ninety days after the period for which the insurer is liable. If it is not reasonably possible for the claimant to furnish the proof of loss within that time period, it must be submitted no later than within one year, except due to legal incapacity.

Time of Payment of Claims

The *time of payment of claims* provision requires the insurer must generally pay claims immediately upon receipt of written proof of loss. An insurer may have up to thirty days after receipt of proof of loss to pay certain claims, such as periodic payment claims.

Payment of Claims

Under the *payment of claims* provision, any death benefits payable will be paid to a named beneficiary on the policy, or to the estate of the insured if a beneficiary is not named. Any other payment will be made to the insured.

Physical Examination and Autopsy

The *physical examination and autopsy* provision allows, in the event of death, the insurer to examine the person of the insured and to make an autopsy where allowed by law. The insurer performs the examinations or the autopsy at its own expense.

Legal Actions

Under the *legal actions* provision, boundaries are set upon the time period during which legal action may be sought. This provision states that legal action to collect from a claim must not begin for at least sixty days from the time a proof of loss form is filed with the insurer, and must be taken in a period no longer than three years from that time.

Change of Beneficiary

Under the mandatory *change of beneficiary* provision, the owner of a policy that includes a death benefit has the right to change the beneficiary without the consent of the beneficiary, unless an irrevocable beneficiary has been named.

Misstatement of Age

If the age of an insured is misstated on the application, the coverage under the plan will be adjusted to reflect the appropriate amount of coverage based on the correct age. Additional premium due must be paid to the insurer if owed due to the age misstatement, or premium must be refunded to the insured, as applicable

Optional Provisions

Individual accident and sickness policies may also include optional provisions. If the insurer offers such provisions in its policy, the state may specify that the insurer must follow the wording in the NAIC's model law, or must provide benefits more favorable to the insured or beneficiary. The states have minor variations in terms of which optional provisions are specifically included in state law, but generally, these optional policy provisions are allowed in all states and governed by the NAIC's model language.

Change of Occupation

This optional provision provides the terms for changing premium rates based on a change of occupation. If an insured is injured or contracts sickness after having changed his or her occupation to one that is classified by the insurer as more hazardous than the one stated in the policy or while working in a more hazardous occupation, the insurer will pay benefits equal to the amount that would have been purchased at the premium rate and policy limits the insurer would have charged for the rating class in which the more hazardous occupation lies.

If the insured changes his or her occupation to one that is classified as less hazardous than that stated in the policy, the insurer, upon receipt of proof of the change, will reduce the premium rate from that stated in the policy, and will return the excess unearned premium on a pro-rata basis from the date of the change of occupation or form the policy anniversary date immediately preceding receipt of the proof, whichever is more recent.

Other Insurance with Insurer

This provision deals with the payment of benefits when the insured has another policy or policies which include accident and/or sickness benefits with the same insurer. A maximum indemnity amount is stated in the policy applicable to various coverages in the accident and sickness contract. Any excess indemnity amount about the maximum stated becomes void and the excess premium related to this excess indemnity amount is returned to the insured or to his or her estate.

For example, Dwayne's individual accident and sickness policy has a specified dread disease rider that states: "If an accident or sickness or accident and sickness policy or policies previously issued by the insurer to the insured be in force concurrently herewith, making the aggregate indemnity for benefits as stated in this rider in excess of $2,000,000, the excess insurance shall be void and all premiums paid for such excess shall be returned to the insured or to his estate." While this policy is in force, Dwayne is diagnosed with cancer. When his family accesses his insurance policies to check his coverage, they find he also has a limited benefit policy with the same insurer with substantially the same additional coverage for cancer as the rider to his accident and sickness policy. The limited policy has a $1,000,000 lifetime maximum benefit applicable to cancer care. The limited benefit policy bears a pro-rata share, with his accident and sickness coverages, of Dwayne's health care expenses related to cancer. The individual accident and sickness insurance carrier will pay, in addition to care covered through the accident and sickness policy outside of the rider, cancer care up to $2,000,000, and return the excess premium paid for the $1,000,000 in coverage above the insurer's liability limit of $2,000,000, to Dwayne.

Alternatively, an individual accident and sickness policy may include the following provision to explain what happens when an insured has more than one policy with the same insurer: "Insurance effective at one time on the insured under a like policy or policies in this insurer is limited to the one such policy elected by the insured, his beneficiary or his estate, as the case may be, and the insurer will return all premiums paid for all other such policies."

For example, assume Dwayne had three limited benefit policies with the same insurer that covered his cancer. One had a maximum limit of cancer care benefits of $1,000,000, the second had a limit of $1,500,000 and the third had a limit of $500,000. Dwayne could elect to apply the coverage under just one of these policies, such as the one with the $1,500,000 limit, and keep it in force to cover his care. The other two policies will no longer be

in force and the premium for them would be refunded to Dwayne.

Insurance with Other Insurers

The insurance with other insurers applies to the situation when a policy pays on an expense incurred basis (rather than paying a stated benefit per day of care), and the insurer is not notified of other coverage in force with other insurers that also cover the accident or sickness or an expense-incurred basis. The liability of the individual accident and sickness insurer is limited to its proportionate share of the expenses incurred. The insurer will return the portion of premiums paid that exceed the pro rata portion of the insurer's liability.

Insurance with Other Insurers – Other Than Expensed Incurred Basis

Another optional provision in individual health policies is used when the benefits are not paid on an expense-incurred basis. The insurer's liability is limited to its proportionate share of the expenses incurred if other coverage is in force and the insurer is not notified of it until after the commencement of the policy.

Relation of Earnings to Insurance

The relation of earnings provision limits the insurer's liability of the amount payable when all coverage applicable to a disability exceeds the insured's monthly earnings. This reduces the risk that an insured is more likely to file a claim because the insurance benefits exceed a reasonable indemnification amount; i.e., it reduces the risk that an insured will file a claim in order to experience a gain due to disability.

If the total of all coverage payable at time of disability:

- exceeds the monthly earnings of the insured at the time the disability commenced; or
- exceeds the insured's average monthly earnings for the period of two years immediately preceding the disability, whichever is greater;

then, the insurer's liability is its proportionate amount of the benefits under the policy as the insured's earnings bears to the total monthly benefit payable by all coverage. Excess premiums paid will be refunded to the insured.

For example, the insured's monthly earnings at the time of disability, which are greater than the average of income over the past two years, are $5000/month. He has three policies that cover the disability, and each would pay a $2000 monthly benefit for the disability if no limit applied, for a total of $6000. The $6000 total benefit exceeds the insured's monthly earnings amount, so the relation of earnings provision applies. The relation of the insured's earnings to the monthly benefit is $5000/$6000, or 5/6. The disability insurer will pay 5/6 of the $2000 monthly benefit, due to the relation of earnings to insurance provision.

Unpaid Premium

If there is unpaid premium due at the time of a claim paid, the insurer can deduct the premium due from the amount payable.

Conformity with State Statutes

The conformity with state statutes optional provision removes conflict in the policy's language with state laws. It amends any provision in the policy on the issue date that is in conflict with a state statute so that it conforms with state law.

Illegal Occupation

The illegal occupation provision states that the insurance does not pay for losses when:

- a contributing cause was the insured's commission of or attempt to commit a felony; or
- to which a contributing cause was the insured's being engaged in an illegal occupation.

Intoxicants and Narcotics

The optional provision concerning loss involving intoxicants or narcotics specifies that the insurer will not be liable for any loss sustained or contracted in consequence of the insured's being intoxicated or under the influence of any narcotic unless administered on the advice of a physician.

Cancellation

The insurer may cancel an accident or sickness policy at any time by written notice delivered to the insured, or mailed to his last address as shown by the records of the insurer. The effective cancellation date may not be less than as specified as the period of days in the policy after the mailing or delivery of the letter.

Once the policy has been continued beyond its original term, the insured may cancel it at any time by written notice delivered or mailed to the insurer. The cancellation may be effective upon receipt by the insurer or on a later date specified in the notice of cancellation.

In the event of cancellation, the insurer must promptly return any unearned portion of the premium.

Other Provisions and Clauses

Insuring Clause

The insuring clause in a health policy generally states that the policy provisions, benefits and terms will apply to the named insured as stated in the policy, declarations page and schedule of benefits.

Free Look

Insurance contracts provide policyholders with the ability to review them for a specified period after delivery and return them to the insurer or the insurer's agent to receive a full refund. Generally, this period is 10 days. The contract normally contains a notice on the front page of the policy that discloses to the policyholder the time frame in which this right may be exercised.

Consideration Clause

The consideration clause provides the premium payment requirements to keep the policy in force. The clause generally states that the premium must be timely paid to maintain the policy, and references the grace period provision applicable to late payments.

Probationary Period

A *probationary* or *waiting period* is the period of time from policy inception before a sickness will be covered. Coverage for care due to accidents is not subject to a waiting period. Different probationary periods may apply depending on the condition. For example, a policy may not allow any probationary period for care due to pneumonia that is diagnosed a week after the policy is issued, but may apply a six month probationary period for care due to a condition such as a hernia or varicose veins.

Elimination Period

An elimination period is the period of time from the insured's condition meets qualifications for coverage before the condition will be covered by the policy. Elimination periods generally apply to disability income benefits and to hospital confinement coverage. A policy often offers two or three elimination periods to select from. The longer the elimination period, generally, the lower the premium for the policy.

Waiver of Premium

Waivers of premium provisions waive the policy premium if the insured has certain conditions. Normally, waiver of premium applies to disability. The waiver of premium provision may have a waiting period before the premium will be waived. For example, the provision may state that the premium will be waived once the insured meets the policy's definition of totally disabled for three months, and will be waived until the insured's condition no longer meets this definition.

Exclusions

Policy exclusions are specific conditions or circumstances for which the health insurance policy or plan will not provide benefits. Policy exclusions are limited by state and federal laws. Common allowable exclusions include:

- Loss sustained or expenses incurred while on active duty as a member of the armed forces of any nation, or losses sustained or expenses incurred as a result of act of war whether declared or undeclared;
- Aviation hazards except while flying on a fare-paying passenger on a commercial airline
- Participation in a riot or insurrection;
- Cosmetic surgery, except when necessitated by covered sickness or injury;
- Specifically named hazardous occupations;
- Specifically named hazardous sport or hobbies;
- Sickness or injury covered by any Worker's Compensation Act or Occupational Disease Law or by U.S. Longshoreman's Harbor Worker's Compensation Act;

- Sickness or injuries to the extent that any covered person under the policy is eligible to receive benefits under Medicare;
- Sickness or injuries to the extent that any covered person under the policy is eligible under specifically named national, state or other government plans; and
- Sickness or injuries sustained during the commission of or attempt to commit, a felony.

Preexisting Conditions

Health policies may include restrictions on benefits based on preexisting conditions. A preexisting condition is a limitation or exclusion of health benefits based on the fact that a physical or mental condition was present before the first day of coverage. Preexisting condition provisions in health insurance and plans are limited by federal HIPAA and ACA laws and under state laws.

Recurrent Disability

A recurrent disability benefit defines when a covered disability is considered the same disability or a different disability in terms of the application of benefits. Disability benefits last for a specified period, and have waiting or elimination periods. Whether or not a disability is considered distinct from a prior disability impacts the length of the waiting and benefit period applicable to the disability benefits.

For example, a policy applies a 90 day waiting period to each disability prior to paying benefits. The policy will pay benefits for 365 days. An insured severely hurts his arm and is considered disabled under the policy. The policy starts paying benefits 90 days after the insured is found to be disabled due to his arm injury. After 120 days, the insured no longer meets the definition of disability and the policy stops paying benefits based on the arm injury. 60 days later, the insured is unable to use his arm again and his physician determines the cause is related to the original injury to his arm. The insured again meets the definition of disabled under the policy. If the policy treats the second disability as a new disability, the policy will not pay benefits for 90 days from the date the arm is again determined to be a disability and a new benefit period will apply to the disability. If the policy treats the second disability as a recurrent disability, the policy will begin paying benefits immediately upon the diagnosis from the physician that meets the policy's definition of disability, and the 365 day benefit period

 VA PPL LH-2_16298

applicable to the disability will be reduced by the 120 days of benefits that have already been paid.

Generally, state laws do not allow a recurrent disability provision to consider a disability the same disability as a prior disability covered under the policy if the period of time since the prior disability occurred was greater than six months.

Coinsurance

Coinsurance is the percentage of allowable charges for health care expenses that the insured pays after meeting any applicable deductible. For example, the insurer may pay 80% of the allowed charges and the insured is responsible to pay 20%. If the policy includes a limit on out-of-pocket payments for the insured, the deductible and the coinsurance amounts paid by the insured count towards the out-of-pocket limit.

Deductibles

The deductible is the amount the insured must pay before the insurer will begin paying its share for services received. A health insurance plan may require that an annual deductible amount be paid before receiving benefits payable by the insurer. Different or separate deductibles may apply to certain benefits.

Eligible Expenses

Health insurance plans base benefit payments on eligible expenses. Eligible expenses are expenses for health care services, including charges for certain medical equipment and supplies that are covered under the policy. When a policy has a coinsurance provision where the insured pays 20% and the insurer pays 80%, this means the insurer will pay 80% of eligible expenses under the policy.

Copayments

A copayment is a specified dollar amount the insured is required to pay each time a health care service is received. For example, a dental plan may require a $15 co-pay each dental appointment and a $10 co-pay for each cleaning.

Co-payments may be applied toward the required annual deductible or maximum out-of-pocket expenses for the insured, depending on the terms of the health plan.

Pre-Authorization and Prior Approval Requirements

Some health plans require that certain services are pre-authorized by the plan in order for payment to apply. For example, a managed care plan may require that a visit to a specialized by authorized by the primary care physician before the specialist is seen in order to pay for the specialist's care.

A plan may also require that a course of care be pre-approved prior to agreeing to pay for the care. *For example, a physician may need to write up a plan of care for an insured needing a knee replacement, including pre-surgery care, surgical care, post-surgical care and rehabilitation and submit it to the health plan prior to providing and ordering these services. The health plan will then approve the care treatment plan for the knee surgery and pay for these services according to the coverage terms of the policy.*

Usual, Reasonable and Customary Charges

When a policy bases payments on standards such as **usual and customary charge**, (UCR) or **reasonable and customary**, or words of similar import must include an explanation of these terms. Generally, a policy that basis payments on a UCR standard utilizes a schedule of fees charged by similarly situated providers rendering the same services in a given locality, region, or area. Under some plans, providers that give health services agree to accept the UCR as the total payment for a service. Under other plans, the insured is responsible to pay the provider the difference between the UCR amount paid by the insurer and the provider's charge.

Lifetime, Annual or Per Cause Maximum Benefits

Prior to the passage of the ACA, any health plan could include lifetime and annual maximum benefit limits. For example, the policy could have a calendar year annual benefit limit of $750,000 and a lifetime maximum benefit limit of $2,000,000.

Maximum benefits could also be applicable to certain conditions or causes. For example, a policy could provide that mental health care may has a specified maximum lifetime limit of $500,000 and an annual limit of $100,000.

However, the ACA includes provisions that disallow lifetime maximum limits on essential health benefits in policies subject to the ACA.

Lifetime and Annual Limits – Virginia Law

The Virginia Code §38.2-3440 addresses lifetime and annual limits on essential health benefits in group and individual health plans and is effective as of January 1, 2014, as follows:

- Notwithstanding any provision of § 38.2-3406.1, 38.2-3406.2, or 38.2-3418.5, or any other section of this title to the contrary, a health carrier offering group or individual health insurance coverage shall not establish a lifetime limit on the dollar amount of essential health benefits for any covered person.
- A health carrier shall not establish any annual limit on the dollar amount of essential health benefits for any covered person.
- The provisions of this section shall not prevent a health carrier from placing annual or lifetime dollar limits for any covered person on specific covered benefits that are not essential health benefits to the extent that such limits are otherwise permitted under applicable federal or state law.
- This section shall apply to any health carrier providing individual or group health insurance coverage, except that the prohibition and limits on annual limits shall not apply to a grandfathered plan providing individual health insurance coverage.

What Are Essential Health Benefits? – Virginia Law

The Virginia Bureau of Insurance provided the following explanation of what are considered *essential health benefits* under the ACA in its *Essential Health Benefits Guidance* published in April 2013 for insurance companies. This Guidance is subject to change as the ACA is more fully implemented in the Commonwealth:

The Patient Protection and Affordable Care Act ("ACA") requires that all non-grandfathered individual and small group health insurance plans sold in the Commonwealth of Virginia ("Commonwealth"), beginning January 1, 2014, cover certain delineated essential health benefits ("EHBs"). In a 2011 bulletin and a final rule released in February of 2013, the United States Department of Health and Human Services ("HHS") provided states with the option to choose a plan from a range of existing health insurance plans to serve as an EHB benchmark plan, which ultimately defines the standard set of benefits that must be covered by plans in the individual and small employer group markets in each state.

The EHB benchmark plan chosen by the Commonwealth is Anthem PPO KeyCare 30, the small group health plan with the largest enrollment in the state and the Medicaid CHIP (SMILES) plan for pediatric dental. The default plan for pediatric vision is the Federal Employee Plan (FEP) Blue Vision plan.

The Guidance provides detailed benefit information related to EHBs. The Guidance may be accessed at the website of the Virginia Bureau of Insurance. (For more information, also see: https://www.cms.gov/cciio/resources/data-resources/ehb.html#Virginia)

Riders

Impairment/Exclusions

Riders may be used to exclude coverage for certain impairments or conditions. For example, if an applicant recently had surgery on his right shoulder two weeks prior to applying for health coverage and is still in rehabilitation, an individual health policy may exclude coverage for treatment required due to the shoulder surgery for six months, through a rider.

Guaranteed Insurability

A disability income policy may have a guaranteed insurability provision or may have one added through a rider, which can be important for disability coverage for those with interest in a business that increases in value over time. The guaranteed insurability provision allows coverage to be increased without the insured having to prove insurability.

Multiple Indemnity

A *multiple indemnity provision* or rider states that a benefit under a policy will be increased by a stated multiple, such as double or triple the normal benefit amount.

Accidental Death and Dismemberment Rider

Accidental Death and Dismemberment insurance, or AD&D insurance, pays a lump-sum benefit in the case of accidental death or in the event of the loss of body members due to accidental injury. This form of insurance may be added as a rider to a health policy.

Accidental Death (Double or Triple Indemnity) Rider

Another rider that can be added to a health policy is the accidental death rider. This rider pays double or triple a stated amount of the AD&D benefit if death occurs as a result of an accident. The definition of accident under these riders does not include disease and death must be the direct result of accidental injury. The rider also specifies that death must occur within a specified number of days from the accident, generally from 90 to 120 days. The coverage from this type of rider generally ends at a specified age, such as age 70.

Rights of Renewability

Noncancellable Contracts

Noncancellable contracts guarantee that the premium on a contract will never go up at renewal, up through a specified period or age, generally age 65.

Cancelable Contracts

Cancelable contracts may be cancelled at any time by the insurer or the insured. The insurer is required to give written notice to insureds prior to cancelling their contracts.

Nonrenewable or Cancelable Contracts

Another form of cancelable contract is the nonrenewable health plan. A nonrenewable health plan is a short-term coverage plan, and is also known as cancelable or term coverage. This type of health plan provides coverage for 6 to 12 months.

Nonrenewable health coverage may be purchased by those who, for example:

- need short term coverage because they don't want to pay for coverage under COBRA during a short period of employment when switching employers;

- are moving and plan to obtain long-term coverage once settled in at their new location; or
- lose health benefits when there is short-term employment shut down, such as a shut down due to a strike.

Nonrenewable policies may include the most commonly used benefits normally found in traditional long-term plans, such as preventive care, emergency medical care, lab work, and so on. These plans cannot be renewed after their term.

Guaranteed Renewable Contracts

Guaranteed renewable contracts are renewed as long as premium is paid. Premium rates can only be increased if premiums are increased for an entire class of insureds. The insurer may not raise premiums just on a single insured's policy.

Conditionally Renewable

Conditionally renewable contracts include some provisions that give the insurer the right to non-renew a policy. For example, a policy may be conditionally renewable at the insured's age 65.

Optionally Renewable

Optionally renewable contracts may be non-renewed at any renewal period by the insurer. Optionally renewable contracts are uncommon.

Period of Time for Renewal

Health insurance policies are generally renewed on an annual basis. They may be renewable only up to a certain age. Because people become eligible for Medicare at age 65, many health insurance contracts are renewable only up to age 65. At age 65, those who want individual health coverage along with Medicare will purchase Medicare Supplement Insurance. Some health insurance contracts are renewable only to age 60, with the condition that if the insured does not enroll in Medicare, the contract may be renewed until age 65.

Limited benefit policies may be renewable up to ages lower than 60 or 65.

VA PPL LH-2_16298

Section VII Review

1) In individual health insurance policies, the clause that provides that the policy and application constitute the entire contract is the:
   a. entire contract clause
   b. incontestability clause
   c. misstatement of age clause
   d. only contract clause

2) _____ are the type of policies to which the Uniform Provisions Model Law developed by the NAIC applies:
   a. Group health insurance policies, also known as accident and sickness group policies
   b. Individual health insurance policies, also known as accident and sickness policies
   c. Limited benefit group health insurance policies
   d. Disability income policies

3) The "time limit on certain defenses," "grace period," and "reinstatement clauses" are mandatory provisions for:
   a. disability income policies
   b. individual health insurance policies
   c. accident-only insurance policies
   d. life insurance policies

4) An individual health insurance policy was reinstated on July 14. The insured was diagnosed with pneumonia on July 16. Care for this bout of pneumonia:
   a. is covered immediately by the policy
   b. won't be covered by the policy
   c. won't be covered by the policy until July 24
   d. won't be covered by the policy until July 26

5) An individual health insurance policy was reinstated on October 27. The insured was diagnosed a severe influenza on November 7. This bout of influenza:
   a. is covered by the policy
   b. won't be covered by the policy
   c. won't be covered until November 17
   d. won't be covered until November 27

6) On April 10, the insured under an individual health insurance policy is injured while on a ladder in his home, doing some home repairs. He severely injured his shoulder and required several therapy visits and prescription pain medicine in order to recuperate. The last therapy visit was completed on October 15 of the same year the insured was injured. Generally, the insured must submit the proof of loss to the insurer for the care for this injury no later than:
   a. January 13 of the year following the year of the injury
   b. July 10 of the same year in which the injury occurred
   c. April 17 of the same year in which the injury occurred
   d. April 27 of the same year in which the injury occurred

7) An individual health insurance policy has an accidental death and dismemberment rider. The insured dies in a car accident on August 13. The death benefit under the policy:
   a. is automatically paid to the insured's surviving spouse
   b. is automatically paid to the named beneficiary on the policy unless a named beneficiary is not named
   c. is automatically paid to the insured's estate because health policies do not allow for the naming of a beneficiary
   d. is kept by the insurer until the insured's estate goes through the probate process

8) An individual health insurer denied a claim submitted by an insured on July 8, 2013. The proof of loss for that claim was submitted to the insurer on June 18, 2013. The loss occurred on May 1, 2013. The insured may file a legal action in court against the insurer asking for a judgment ordering the insurer to pay the claim up until what date?
   a. August 17, 2016
   b. July 31, 2016
   c. July 8, 2015
   d. May 1, 2016

9) Each of the following are optional provisions for individual health insurance policies, EXCEPT:
   a. "Grace Period"
   b. "Change of Occupation"
   c. "Unpaid Premium"
   d. "Cancellation"

10) An insured has two individual health insurance policies. Both include the provision "Insurance with Other Insurers – Other Than Expense Incurred Basis." Neither insurer was notified by the insured of the other policy's coverage. The insured is hospitalized, and the expenses incurred for hospitalization are $120 per day. Insurance Policy A pays $100 per day for hospitalization and the Insurance Policy B pays $300 per day for this same coverage. How much will each insurer pay for the insured's hospitalization?
   a. Insurer A will pay $30 (1/4 of the cost of care) and Insurer B will pay $90 (3/4 of the cost of care)
   b. Insurer A will pay $100 (policy limit) and Insurer B will pay $20 (as excess)
   c. Insurer A will pay $60 (1/2 of the cost of care) and Insurer B will pay $60 (1/2 of the cost of care)
   d. Insurer A will pay $0 and Insurer B will pay $120 (as primary insurer)

11) If an individual health insurance policy contains any provision that is in conflict with state law, what other provision within the contract brings the contract into agreement with state law?
   a. the "Conformity with State Statutes" provision
   b. the "Illegal Occupation" provision
   c. the "Legal Actions" provision
   d. the "Entire Contract and Changes Clause"

12) An insured under an individual health insurance policy is injured in her home. When examined at the hospital emergency room it was discovered she was injured while under an illegal intoxicant and this was duly reported to the appropriate authorities and recorded. According to state law, the individual health insurance policy:
   a. will cover the emergency room care for her injury and all additional care she requires
   b. will cover the post-emergency room care, but not the emergency room care she requires due to this injury
   c. will not cover the care for her injury because she was under the influence of an illegal intoxicant when the injury occurred
   d. will not cover the care for her injury because she went to the emergency room rather than to a non-emergency facility

13) The individual health insurance policy is in force through age 65 and the premium rate may never change on the policy during this period. This contract is:
   a. guaranteed renewable
   b. noncancellable
   c. optionally renewable
   d. nonrenewable

14) An insured purchased a 6 month health insurance plan to cover a period of time when she was unemployed and waiting to start a new position with a new employer. Once employed, she will be placed under the new employer's group health plan. The health insurance contract is nonrenewable and provides the same coverages normally found in traditional longer-term health insurance contracts. This contract is known as:
   a. a guaranteed renewable contract
   b. a noncancellable contract
   c. an optionally renewable contract
   d. a nonrenewable contract

15) A health policy has an accidental death rider. The coverage within the rider pays multiplies the amount of the accidental death and dismemberment benefit by three times if death occurs:
   a. due to cancer
   b. due to pneumonia
   c. due to a heart attack
   d. due to accidentally falling down a flight of stairs

16) In Virginia, once an individual health insurance policy has been issued, the insurer may not void the policy or deny a claim for loss or disability due to misstatements in the application unless fraudulent, after how many years?
   a. 2 years
   b. 3 years
   c. 4 years
   d. 5 years

17) The Patient Protection and Affordable Care Act (the ACA) disallows lifetime maximum limits on essential health benefits in health policies subject to the ACA. In Virginia:
   a. this removal of maximum lifetime limits on essential health benefits does not apply
   b. this provision of the ACA has been put into law and is effective as of January 1, 2014
   c. there is no definition of essential health benefits in state law yet, so no state law change has been made to remove maximum lifetime limits
   d. this requirement only applies to plans covered by ERISA, such as self-insured plans

18) Essential health benefits are a category of benefits that the Patient Protection and Affordable Care Act (the ACA) requires to be provided without lifetime maximum limits. What entity has published an explanation of essential health benefits under Virginia law and regulation?
   a. The Virginia Bureau of Insurance has explained essential health benefits in a publication called "Essential Health Benefits Guidance," which is for insurance companies.
   b. The Centers for Medicare and Medicaid Services has developed a final rule defining essential health benefits for Virginians
   c. The Department of Labor has developed a final rule defining essential health benefits for Virginians
   d. The Virginia Office of the Attorney General has defined essential health benefits for the insurance companies doing business in Virginia.

Section VIII: Social Insurance

Forms of government insurance are explained in this section. Topics include:

- Medicare
- Medicaid
- Social Security benefits

Medicare

Medicare is a federal health insurance program, primarily for seniors. Medicare is provided to people age 65 and over, people under 65 that have certain disabilities and anyone, regardless of age, with permanent kidney failure that requires dialysis or a kidney transplant.

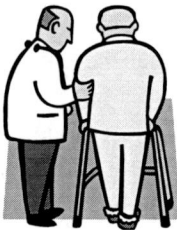

Traditional Medicare is composed of three parts – Part A, Part B and Part D. When Medicare is not provided through managed care plans specially approved by Medicare, it is called Original Medicare. When provided through Medicare-approved managed care plans and through other newer ways established by Congress, it is provided through Medicare Advantage Plans and Medicare Cost Plans. Medicare Part C encompasses these managed care plans.

Primary or Secondary Payor

Persons who are covered by employer group plans and reach age 65 may keep their employer group coverage. The rules regarding whether Medicare coverage is primary or is secondary when employer group health plan coverage applies varies:

- Generally, if an individual is enrolled in Medicare and is covered by an employer plan with fewer than 20 employees, Medicare is primary, i.e., pays first.
- Generally, if an individual is enrolled in Medicare and is under 65 or has Medicare because of a disability, and is covered by an employer plan with fewer than 100 employees, Medicare pays first.
- If an individual is enrolled in Medicare and is covered by a large employer plan, which is a plan sponsored by an employer with 100 employees or more, Medicare pays second.

Under federal regulations, an *employer group health plan* is a plan maintained by an employer or employee organization to provide health care to individuals who have an employment-related connection to the employer or employee organization or to their families

When an individual becomes eligible for Medicare only because of permanent kidney failure, eligibility generally is not effective until the fourth month of dialysis. If the individual is also covered by an employer or union group health plan, the group plan is the only payer until the fourth month. After this initial three month period, the employer becomes the primary payer for a 30 month period, and Medicare is the secondary payer. This 30 month period is referred to as the coordination period. After the cessation of this 30 month period, Medicare pays first, and the group plan pays for services not covered by Medicare, if covered under the provisions of the plan.

Eligibility for Medicare Parts A, B and D

An individual is eligible for premium-free (no cost) Medicare Part A (Hospital Insurance) if:

- He or she is 65 or older and receiving, or is eligible for, retirement benefits from Social Security or the Railroad Retirement Board; or
- He or she is under 65 and has received Railroad Retirement disability benefits for the prescribed time and meets the Social Security Act disability requirements; or
- He or she is the individual's spouse and had Medicare-covered government employment; or
- He or she is under 65 and has End-Stage Renal Disease (ESRD).

If an individual is not eligible for premium-free Medicare Part A, he or she can buy Part A by paying a monthly premium if he or she is:

- age 65 or older; and
- enrolled in Part B; and
- a resident of the United States, and is either a citizen or an alien lawfully admitted for permanent residence who has lived in the United States continuously during the 5 years

VA PPL LH-2_16298

immediately before the month in which the individual applies.

An individual is automatically eligible for Part B (Medical Insurance) if he is eligible for premium-free Part A. He is also eligible for Part B if he is not eligible for premium-free Part A, but is age 65 or older and a resident of the United States or a citizen or an alien lawfully admitted for permanent residency. In this case, he must have lived in the United States continuously during the 5 years immediately before the month during which he enrolls in Part B.

Medicare Part D is the Medicare Prescription Drug Coverage. This coverage may be obtained in a couple of ways:

1. an individual may be covered by a Medicare health insurance plan that has a Medicare compliant Prescription Drug Coverage component. If the individual is enrolled in Medicare and has this coverage, he is enrolled in Medicare Part D; or
2. an individual can enroll in a Medicare Prescription Drug Coverage Plan separately from his or her health coverage.

The premiums for the Drug Coverage vary, based on the type of plan in which the individual enrolls.

Medicare Part A – Hospital Insurance

Part A is hospital insurance. It helps pay expenses for:

- inpatient care;
- skilled nursing facilities;
- hospice care; and
- some home health care services.

Part A requires a monthly premium of over $400. However, most people do not pay this premium because they paid Medicare taxes while working.

Inpatient Care

For inpatient care in hospitals, Medicare Part A helps pay for a semiprivate room, meals, general nursing, and other hospital services and supplies. There is no coverage for private duty nursing, or a private room, unless a private room is medically necessary. Inpatient care in a mental health care facility is limited to 150 days in a lifetime.

There is a deductible in Part A's hospitalization coverage. Many people have Medicare Supplement insurance policies to cover these deductibles and coinsurance.

Skilled Nursing Facility Care

Skilled nursing facility care is covered only if it follows a related three-day inpatient stay in a hospital. The requirement by Medicare for the three-day inpatient stay eliminates coverage in many circumstances, such as if someone has a chronic condition that steadily increases in severity, eventually requiring skilled nursing facility care, but never requiring a three day continuous hospital stay.

The limitations of the Medicare coverage for skilled nursing facility care include that it covers up to 100 days only, and that there is a copayment required in the 21st through 100th day. The care is only covered if the individual needs daily skilled care, which means seven days a week of skilled nursing care, or five days a week of rehabilitative care. Often, people need skilled nursing care less than seven days a week, even though they are in a skilled nursing facility.

Home Health Care

The Medicare home health care coverage applies to reasonable and necessary part-time or intermittent skilled nursing care and home health aide services, as well as to physical therapy, occupational therapy, and speech-language pathology ordered by the patient's doctor and provided by a Medicare-certified home health agency. Medicare does not pay for custodial care, such as assistance with bathing, eating and other activities of daily living.

The primary limitation of the Medicare home health care coverage is that the individual must generally be homebound, and therefore unable to get care services outside the home. The individual must need skilled nurse or skilled physical, speech or occupational therapist care. Home health care for assistance with bathing, toileting, feeding and personal care are covered, if considered home health care, and not simply custodial care.

Hospice Care

The hospice care coverage in Medicare Part A is for people with a terminal illness. Hospice care usually includes services prescribed by the doctor for palliative (comfort) care relating to the terminal illness, such as drugs for symptom control and pain relief and medical and support services from a Medicare-approved hospice. Medicare also covers some caregiver relief services, such as inpatient respite care.

Hospice care coverage is provided only if the individual is expected to live six months or less.

Medicare Part B – Medical Insurance

Medicare Part B requires a monthly premium. Part B also includes a small deductible, and 20% coinsurance for services.

The standard Part B premium is a little over $100 per month, although the premium may be higher for those with modified adjusted gross income above certain levels.

Medicare Part B is medical insurance, and helps cover doctor's care and outpatient services. It covers preventative care, such as screening exams for various conditions. For example, Medicare Part B covers:

- Bone mass measurements
- Cardiovascular screenings
- Colorectal cancer screenings
- Diabetes screening
- Flu shots
- Glaucoma tests
- Hepatitis B shots
- Pap test and pelvic exam
- Pneumococcal shot
- Prostate cancer screening
- Screening mammograms
- A "Welcome to Medicare" one-time physical exam.

Enrollment

Persons not already on Medicare are automatically enrolled as of the first day of the birthday month in the year they turn 65 if they are already receiving Social Security or Railroad Retirement benefits. If an individual receiving Social Security or Railroad Retirement benefits turns 65 on the 1st day of the month, he or she is automatically enrolled as of the month prior.

A disabled person, regardless of age, who has received Social Security disability payments for 24 months is automatically enrolled in Medicare A and B. A person who is not on Social Security or Railroad Retirement benefits may contact the Social Security Administration three months before they turn 65 and enroll in Medicare.

Initial Enrollment Period

Individuals may sign up for Part A and/or Part B during the 7-month period that begins 3 months before the month he or she turn 65, includes the month the individual turns 65, and ends 3 months after the month he or she turns 65.

If the individual signs up for Part A and/or Part B during the first 3 months of the Initial Enrollment Period, generally, coverage starts the first day of the individual's birthday month. However, if his or her birthday is on the first day of the month, coverage will start the first day of the prior month.

For example:

- *Evelyn turns 65 on May 10. If she signs up for Medicare during February, March or April, Medicare coverage will begin on May 1.*
- *Steve turns 65 on May 1. Steve signs up for Medicare on February 5. His coverage is effective April 1.*

If an individual enrolls in Part A and/or Part B the month he or she turns 65 or during the last 3 months of the Initial Enrollment Period, the start date will be delayed.

- *Pat turns 65 on August 8. He does not contact Social Security to sign up for Medicare until August 3. His coverage will not begin on August 1.*

General Enrollment Period

Individuals who did not enroll in Medicare during the initial enrollment period may sign up between January 1–March 31 each year. Coverage for these enrollees begins July 1. Late enrollees may be subject to higher premium rates.

VA PPL LH-2_16298

Special Enrollment Period

Individuals who are covered by an employer group health plan and who did not enroll in Medicare Part A and Part B when first eligible, may enroll

- anytime they are still covered by the group health plan.
- during the 8-month period that begins the month after the employment ends or the coverage ends, whichever happens first.

Medicare Managed Care Plans – Medicare Part C

Managed care plans are also available to Medicare recipients. These plans are known as Medicare Part C, and include Medicare Advantage Plans, Medicare HMOs and Medicare Cost Plans. In order to be able to join a Medicare managed care plan, the Medicare recipient must be enrolled in both Part A and Part B. A recipient who has End-Stage Renal Disease, which has permanent kidney failure with dialysis or a transplant, cannot join a Medicare managed care plan.

Medicare managed care plans must sign a contract with Medicare and agree to continue to offer the Medicare plan for one calendar year. Managed care plans generally charge premiums that the member must pay in addition to the Medicare Part B premiums due.

Medicare Advantage Plan Requirements

Managed care plans approved of by and offered through Medicare are known as *Medicare Advantage* plans. Medicare Advantage plans include:

- Medicare Health Maintenance Organization (HMOs)
- Preferred Provider Organizations (PPO)
- Private Fee-for-Service Plans
- Medicare Special Needs Plans

Conditions to Be a Medicare Advantage Provider

In order to offer Medicare Advantage (MA) plans, an organization must enter into a contract with the *Centers for Medicare & Medicaid Services* (CMS). Eligibility requirements include that the organization must document that it is authorized under state law within the service area in which it is requesting to act as a plan provider to offer health benefits as a risk bearing entity.

Coverage under Medicare Managed Care Plans

There are several positive aspects related to Medicare managed care plans. All care is covered through the plans, not just the care covered through the Original Medicare plan. This may provide the patient with better, coordinated care. Extra services are generally provided as well, including:

- Eye exams
- Discounts for eyeglasses
- Annual well-patient physicals
- Annual mammograms

Some plans also provide basic dental coverage. Besides these advantages, enrollees may be attracted to Medicare managed care plans because the managed care plan screens the physicians who provide care within the plan.

Disadvantages related to Medicare managed care plans include the necessity of getting physician referrals in order to see a specialist. The ability to enroll in a plan and receive treatment may be restricted to a certain geographic territory. In addition, as with all managed care plans, physicians are generally given incentives to see patients as few times as possible.

Medicare Part D – Prescription Drug Coverage

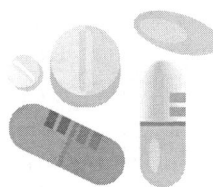

People become eligible for Medicare Part D at the same time they become eligible for Parts A and B. If individuals want to enroll in the Original Medicare Plan, they also need to join a Medicare Prescription Drug Plan. There are stand-alone Prescription Drug Plans that can be joined, or the individual can enroll in a Medicare Advantage or other Medicare Health Plan with prescription drug coverage.

Enrollment Periods

The enrollment period for Medicare Part D is from October 15 through December 7 of each year. If an individual without drug coverage or with drug coverage that does not meet the minimum coverage requirements of a Medicare Prescription Drug Plan, does not enroll during his or her first eligible enrollment period, a premium penalty will be levied upon enrollment. Eligible individuals who wait until after the end of the enrollment period to enroll pay a higher premium. Premiums for the plan will go up at least 1% each month the enrollee waits to join.

Exception to the Premium Penalty

If an individual does not sign up for a Medicare Prescription Drug Plan because at the time of first eligible enrollment period the individual was covered by creditable coverage, such as an employer's prescription drug plan, and then later loses this coverage, there is no premium penalty when enrolling in a Medicare Prescription Drug Plan.

For example, Ralph is a retiree covered by an employer health plan with prescription drug coverage that is creditable coverage. He keeps this coverage when he reaches age 65 in 2014. In 2015, the employer health plan is no longer available. He may enroll in a Medicare Prescription Drug plan with no premium penalty.

Enrollment Materials

At the time of enrollment and annually, enrollees are to be given a Summary of Benefits, Evidence of Coverage, an Abridged Formulary, which is a list of approved prescription drugs (for Medicare Advantage and Medicare Prescription Drug Plans only), an ID Card and a Provider Directory.

Once an individual is enrolled, they will receive a Medicare Prescription Drug card. The Card must meet the National Council for Prescription Drug Program's (NCPDP's) Pharmacy ID Card Standard. The card is used when the enrollee purchases prescription drugs or other covered services.

Medicare Part D Coverage Options

There are several ways individuals can receive Medicare drug plan benefits.

Coverage Through the Original Medicare Plan

Some people are covered solely by Medicare Plan A, Plan B and Plan D.

Coverage through the Original Medicare Plan with a Medigap Policy

People with Medigap policies that include prescription drug coverage have the ability to keep their coverage through the plan, or to purchase a Medicare Prescription Drug Plan. The insured pays the costs of the Medigap drug coverage. Under the Medicare Prescription Drug Plan, the insured pays a monthly premium and then Medicare covers the standard coverage costs in the plan.

Coverage Through Medicare HMOs

Under the Medicare Prescription Drug rules, Medicare HMOs who offer drug coverage must have plans that meet Medicare Part D plan standards. Individuals who have Medicare HMOs have to make a choice about whether they will keep their drug coverage through the HMO or choose another Medicare prescription drug plan.

Medicare Private Fee-For-Service (PFFS) Plans

The insured may get prescription drug coverage through the PFFS, or may obtain a separate Medicare Prescription Drug Plan to add the coverage if it is not part of the PFFS plan.

Medicare Preferred Provider Organization (PPO) Plans

Both local PPOs and regional PPOs could provide Medicare PPO plans. Medicare prescription drug coverage may be included in PPO plans.

Employer and Union Plans

Some people have Medicare health insurance coverage through their employer or union, and may have prescription drug coverage. As long as the employer or union's prescription drug plan is at least as good as the Medicare standard prescription drug coverage, the insured can keep the coverage as long as it is offered by the union or employer. If the coverage ends, the insured will not have to pay a penalty as long as he joins a Medicare drug plan within 63 days after coverage ends.

For example, John is retired. He has prescription drug coverage from his last employer. The employer notifies him that his current drug coverage is at least as good as Medicare prescription drug coverage, and that Medicare will now help pay for the coverage. John has the choice of keeping the employer plan or selecting a Medicare Advantage plan or other Medicare coverage option. He decides to keep his employer plan. If he changes his mind

VA PPL LH-2_16298

at a later date, and enrolls in a Medicare Prescription Drug Plan, he won't have to pay a penalty because his employer plan is at least as good as Medicare Prescription Drug coverage

2016 Medicare Costs
Medicare Part A (Hospital Insurance) Costs
Part A Monthly Premium
Most people don't pay a Part A premium because they paid Medicare taxes while working. If you don't get premium-free Part A, you pay up to $407 each month.

Hospital Stay
You pay:
- $1288 deductible per benefit period
- $0 for the first 60 days of each benefit period
- $322 per day for days 61-90 of each benefit period
- $644 per lifetime reserve day after day 90 of each benefit period (up to a maximum of 60 days over your lifetime)

Skilled Nursing Facility Stay
You pay:
- $0 for the first 20 days of each benefit period
- $161 per day for days 21-100 of each benefit period
- All costs for each day after day 100 of the benefit period

Medicare Part B (Medical Insurance) Costs
Part B Monthly Premium
You pay a Part B premium each month. Most people will pay the standard premium amount. However, if the modified adjusted gross income as reported on an IRS tax return from **2 years ago** is above a certain amount, more premium may be required.

If Your Yearly Income in 2014 (2 years before 2016) was		You pay (2016)
File Individual Return	File Joint Tax Return	
$85,000 or less	$170,000 or less	$121.80
Above $85,000 up to $107,000	Above $170,000 up to $214,000	$170.50
Above $107,000 up to $160,000	Above $214,000 up to $320,000	$243.60
Above $160,000 up to $214,000	Above $320,000 up to $428,000	$316.70
Above $214,000	Above $428,000	$389.80

If you pay a late enrollment penalty, these amounts may be higher. Your monthly premium for Part B may go up 10% for each full 12-month period that you could have had Part B, but didn't sign up for it.

Part B Deductible – $166 per year

Medicare Prescription Drug Plans (Part D) Premiums
The chart below shows the estimated prescription drug plan monthly premium based on income. If the income is above a certain limit, an income-related monthly adjustment amount in addition to the plan premium will be allocated.

If Your Yearly Income in 2014 (2 years before 2016) was		You Pay
File Individual Tax Return	*File Joint Tax Return*	
$85,000 or less	$170,000 or less	Your plan premium
Above $85,000 up to $107,000	Above $170,000 up to $214,000	$12.70 + Your Plan Premium
Above $107,000 up to $160,000	Above $214,000 up to $320,000	$32.80 + Your Plan Premium
Above $160,000 up to $214,000	Above $320,000 up to $428,000	$52.80 + Your Plan Premium
Above $214,000	Above $428,000	$72.90 + Your Plan Premium

2016 Part D National Base Beneficiary Premium – $34.10. This figure is used to estimate the Part D late enrollment penalty and the income-related monthly adjustment amounts listed in the table above. The national base beneficiary premium amount can change each year.

Medicare.gov

VA PPL LH-2_16298

Medicaid

Medicaid is a federal program administered by the states designed to help lower income seniors and others with certain medical and financial needs with medical care. In general, Medicaid pays for hospital, medical, prescription drug and medically necessary nursing home care. Medicaid was designed to provide payment for health care for those with minimal assets. It was established to assist families in crisis and help the medically needy who lack access to medical care. A patient cannot have more than a limited amount of cash or other available assets in order to receive care through Medicaid.

General Eligibility Requirements for Medicaid

Generally, in order to be eligible for services through Medicaid programs, the individual must meet one of the categories of eligibility, which include:

- individuals who are aged (aged means age 65 and older), blind and disabled; and
- certain younger single and married individuals with a temporary disability, limited income or special circumstances such as:
  - under-going drug and alcohol treatment;
  - victim of domestic violence; and
  - caring for a child or disabled person.

The states maintain different types of Medicaid programs. Specific eligibility requirements for these programs vary based on a number of factors.

Social Security Benefits

Social Security was created in 1935 for the purpose of helping a small number of citizens get through hard times. The use of the program has changed markedly since then, so that now Social Security is a major source of income for two-thirds of the elderly and practically the only source of income for the remaining third.

In general, an individual has earned a retirement benefit if he or she: is age 62 (1) is fully insured (worked an adequate number of quarters), and (2) has filed application for retirement benefits.

Age 62 is the earliest age that a retired worker who is fully insured can start to receive retirement benefits. The retirement age when unreduced benefits are available is age 66 for workers reaching age 62 in 2006-2016; will increase by two months a year for workers reaching age 62 in 2017-2022; and will be age 67 for workers reaching age 62 after 2022 (i.e. for those reaching age 67 in 2027).

Amount of a Retirement Benefit

A retirement benefit that starts at Normal Retirement Age equals the worker's PIA (primary insurance amount). A worker who elects to have benefits start before Normal Retirement Age will receive a monthly benefit of only a percentage of the PIA. A person taking reduced retirement benefits before Normal Retirement Age will continue to receive a reduced rate after Normal Retirement Age.

A person's PIA is 90% of the lowest portion of lifetime earnings, plus 32% of the middle portion of lifetime earnings, plus 15% of the highest portion of lifetime earnings.

Survivor's Benefits

Benefits payable to the survivors of a deceased income earner include:

- mother's or father's benefits with children;
- benefits to a surviving spouse of an insured worker;
- benefits to a child of a deceased worker;
- widow(er)'s benefits; and
- a lump sum death benefit of $255.

A surviving spouse will receive Social Security benefits upon a deceased income earning spouse's death. If the surviving spouse then begins to work, he or she may lose Social Security benefits.

Social Security Disability Coverage

Certain individuals with disabilities may qualify for disability payments through the Social Security program. The statutory basis for Social Security Disability payments is found at 42 U.S.C.S. §§401-433. Administrative regulations concerning eligibility are found at 20 C.F.R. Part 404.130

VA PPL LH-2_16298

Work Credits

To qualify for Social Security Disability payments, the individual must have earned a specified number of work credits. Generally, the individual must have earned 40 credits, of which 20 must have been earned in the last ten years. Four credits are the maximum number of credits that may be earned each year.

Definition of Disability

Under Social Security's rules, disability benefits are only paid if the individual is totally disabled. Payments are not made for partial or short-term disability. The disability must be expected to last at least one year, or to result in death. In addition, the individual must be unable to do his or her regular occupation or any other type of work.

The federal Social Security Disability program provides benefits under very limited circumstances. To qualify, an individual must be a worker and meet Social Security's strict definition of disability.

Special Rules

There are some exceptions to this basic determination of disability under Social Security's rules. There are special rules for people who are blind, for widows or widowers who are disabled, and for children who are disabled.

People Who Are Blind

People whose vision cannot be corrected to better than 20/200 in their better eye, or have a vision field of less than 20 degrees or less even with correction, are considered legally blind under Social Security rules. Such individuals automatically qualify under the special rules for people who are blind. Among these rules is an increase in the earnings limit applicable to disability qualification.

Disabled Widows or Widowers

If the worker passes away, Social Security Disability benefits may be payable to a surviving disabled widow or widower. The widow or widower must:

- Be between the ages of 50 and 60
- Meet the definition of disability for adults

- Have a disability that started before the worker's death or within seven years after death

Disabled Children

Disabled children may be eligible for Supplemental Security Income benefits, another Social Security program. To meet the definition of disability to qualify for these benefits, the child must:

- be under age 18;
- have a physical or mental condition that very seriously limits his or her activities, and that condition has lasted, or is expected to last, at least 1 year, or is expected to result in death.

Waiting Period

If an individual qualifies for Social Security Disability payments, the first benefit is paid the sixth full month after the date Social Security finds that the disability began.

Benefit Period

Generally, Social Security Disability payments continue as long as the individual remains disabled. If the person's health improves, and/or they are able to go back to work, benefits will cease.

Family Member Benefits

In some cases, a disabled individual's spouse, divorced spouse or child may receive family member benefits, once that individual qualifies for Social Security Disability income. The maximum disability amount that may be paid to one family is about 150% to 180% of the worker's disability amount.

Spouse

Benefits are payable to a spouse:

- if the spouse is age 62 or older, unless the spouse collects a higher Social Security benefit than the disabled worker, based on the spouse's earnings record. The spouse benefit amount is permanently reduced by a percentage based on the number of months up to his or her full retirement age; or
- if the spouse is caring for the disabled individual's child who is under age 16 or disabled and receiving Social Security benefits.

VA PPL LH-2_16298

Children

Children of a disabled individual may also qualify for benefits if the worker qualifies for Social Security Disability benefits. Eligible children include biological children, adopted children, stepchildren and dependent grandchildren. Qualifications for benefits include that the child:

- be unmarried; and
- be under 18; or
- be 18-19 years old and a full-time student, no higher than grade 12; or
- be 18 or older and have a disability that started before age 22.

Benefits normally terminate at age 18 (other than for a disabled child). If the child is a full-time student at a secondary or elementary school at age 18, benefits continue until the child graduates or 2 months before the child becomes 19, whichever is first.

Divorced Spouse

In some cases, a divorced spouse may receive disability payments based on the disabled worker's records. Qualifications include that the ex-spouse must:

- have been married to the disabled individual for at least 10 years;
- be at least 62 years old;
- be unmarried; and
- not be eligible for an equal or higher benefit on their own Social Security record, or on someone else's Social Security record.

Amount of Social Security Disability Benefits

The average amount of Social Security Disability paid is approximately $1165 per month (and subject to adjustment for inflation annually). This amount is unlikely to cover most people's total monthly expenses. Disability income insurance can provide needed additional income coverage.

Section VIII Review

1) Medicare includes Part A, which is _____ insurance, Part B, which is _____ insurance and Part D which is prescription drug coverage.
   a. medical; long-term
   b. hospital; long-term
   c. hospital; supplementary expense
   d. hospital; medical expense

2) Which of the following services is paid for by Medicare Part A?
   a. Cardiovascular screenings
   b. Hospice care services
   c. Emergency room services
   d. Hearing tests

3) Currently, the maximum number of work credits that may be earned in a year for Social Security Disability Income purposes is:
   a. one
   b. two
   c. three
   d. four

4) The waiting period for Social Security Disability benefits is:
   a. 1 day
   b. 2 weeks
   c. 1 month
   d. 6 months

5) The benefit period for Social Security Disability benefits is:
   a. 1 year
   b. 5 years
   c. 20 years
   d. continues as long as the worker remains disabled, as defined under Social Security Disability income rules

6) Which of the following people are not eligible for Medicare?
   a. A person age 65
   b. A person with permanent kidney failure that require dialysis
   c. A person with permanent kidney failure that requires a kidney transplant
   d. A person age 50 with no disabilities or major health problems

7) John is going to change his Medicare Part D prescription drug coverage insurance plan. He may enroll in the new plan during what time frame?
   a. October 15-December 7
   b. January 1-December 31
   c. June 1-August 31
   d. September 15-November 15

8) June will become eligible for Medicare next August. What type of health insurance policy will she need to purchase to supplement her Medicare coverage?
   a. an ERISA group plan
   b. a traditional, individual health plan
   c. a disability income plan
   d. a Medigap policy

9) Medicare includes health coverage through Part A and Part B. Part A is _____ insurance and Part B is _____ insurance.
   a. hospitalization; medical expense
   b. medical expense; hospitalization
   c. hospital indemnity; major medical
   d. major medical; hospitalization

10) Medicare will pay for assistance with bathing, toileting, feeding and personal care in the home:
    a. only if it is considered home health care and not custodial care
    b. only if it is considered custodial care and not home health care
    c. under no circumstance
    d. if it is required due to frailty

11) Individuals who did not enroll in Medicare during the initial enrollment period may sign up between _____ each year. Coverage for these enrollees begins July 1. Late enrollees may be subject to higher premium rates.
    a. January 1-February 28
    b. January 1-March 31
    c. January 15-April 14
    d. February 1-March 31

12) Edwin is 43 years old, blind and confined to a wheelchair. He was blind since birth and became disabled in his teen years. He was raised as a foster child, and in institutional and assisted living facilities. By the time he reached adulthood, he could perform tasks such as separating machine parts by sense of touch. However, a large manufacturing plant in town which employed him doing this type of work went out of business, and he now is unemployed. For his health care services, Edwin is most likely covered by:

a. Medicare
b. Medicaid
c. Employer group health insurance
d. Individual health insurance

VA PPL LH-2_16298

Section IX: Other Insurance Concepts

Health insurance concepts are discussed in this section. Topics include:

- Total, partial and residual disability definitions
- Policyowner's rights
- Dependent children benefits
- Primary and contingent beneficiaries
- Premium payment modes
- Coordination of benefits
- Occupational and nonoccupational coverage
- Tax treatment of insurance premiums and proceeds
- Managed care
- Workers compensation
- Subrogation

Total, Partial and Residual Disability

Total Disability

Generally, total disability is defined to mean that the insured is unable to perform the duties of his or her regular occupation, or any gainful occupation, is under a doctor's care, and the insured is not working.

Partial Disability

Defined as inability to perform some, but not all, of the important duties of the insured's regular occupation
Definition may include specified % of time insured able to work, e.g. "inability to engage in regular occupation for longer than 50% of time normally spent in performing usual duties of regular occupation"

Residual Disability

Residual benefits are paid when insureds return to work, but do not return to their full earning capacity.

Residual benefits pay a pro-rata amount of the policy benefit based on the loss of income due to an accident or sickness.

Residual Benefit Payments Provision Example 1
Insured unable to perform one or more important daily business duties of insured's occupation; or Insured unable to do usual daily business duties for as long as insured would normally be able to do them; and Loss of income is at least 25% of the insured's prior monthly earnings; and Insured is under the care of a physician
Residual Benefit Payments Provision Example 2
Loss of income is at least 20% of prior earnings, due to an injury or sickness

Owner's Rights

The owner of an individual health insurance contract is often the insured, or one of the insureds, under the contract. However, if health insurance is purchased for a group, the policyowner will be the business, association, or other approved group.

Generally, the owner has the following rights under a health insurance contract, as applicable to the coverage:

- selecting the deductible;
- selecting the elimination period;
- selecting the benefit period;
- selecting the benefits included in the insurance, subject to legal requirements;
- selecting the preferred provider or other providers paid for under the policy;
- appealing denials of coverage;
- adding riders or additional coverages available for additional premium; and
- adding additional insureds under the coverage, such as a spouse and dependent children.

Under group coverage, certificateholders are able to exercise some of these rights. *For example, if an employer sponsors a group health plan, the employer may offer a preferred provider plan and a traditional fee for service plan to eligible employees and their dependents. The employees are able to select which plan they'd like to be insured under and to select their preferred provider or family doctor under the plan. The employees are able to add additional insureds as allowed by the plan, select a deductible and any additional optional benefits. The employee can also appeal coverage denials and add eligible dependent insureds during the enrollment period or as allowed by law.*

   VA PPL LH-2_16298

If the policy pays a death benefit, such as when there is accidental death coverage, the owner or an individual health contract, or the certificateholder of a group contract, names the beneficiary or beneficiaries. If the named beneficiary is not an irrevocable beneficiary, the owner or certificateholder may change the beneficiary at any time.

Dependent Children Benefits

State laws, the ACA, COBRA and HIPAA govern the treatment of dependent children benefits in health insurance plans. The ACA requires that children are covered regardless of preexisting conditions to age 19, and that children to age 26 be allowed to be enrolled in parents' health care coverage. COBRA and HIPAA govern continuation and conversion coverage for dependents. State laws specify additional coverage requirements for dependents.

Dependent Children Coverage – Virginia Law

All group or individual accident and sickness insurance policy contracts delivered or issued for delivery in Virginia that provide that coverage of a dependent child terminates upon the child's attainment of a specified age, must also provide that attainment of the specified age will not terminate the child's coverage while the dependent child is and continues to be both:

1. incapable of self-sustaining employment by reason of intellectual disability or physical handicap; and
2. chiefly dependent upon the policyowner for support and maintenance.

Proof of incapacity and dependency must be furnished to the insurer by the policyowner within 31 days of the child's attainment of the specified age. If the insurer requires such proof after this time, proof may only be required annually after the two-year period following the child's attainment of the specified age.

The insurer may charge additional premium for continuation of coverage beyond the specified age. The additional premium must be determined by the insurer on the basis of the class of risks applicable to the child.
VA Code §38.2-3409

Coverage for Child Health Supervision Services – Virginia Law

In Virginia, generally, all individual or group accident and sickness insurance policy, health services plan certificates of coverage, or evidence of coverage of a health care plan delivered or issued for delivery or renewed, reissued, or extended if already issued, must offer and make available coverage under the policy or plan for child health supervision services to provide for the periodic examination of insured children.

The term child health supervision services means the periodic review of a child's physical and emotional status by a licensed and qualified physician or pursuant to a physician's supervision. This review includes but is not limited to a history, complete physical examination, developmental assessment, anticipatory guidance, appropriate immunizations, and laboratory tests in keeping with prevailing medical standards.

Each policy or plan, offering and making available such coverage, must, at a minimum, provide benefits for child health supervision services at birth, 2 months, 4 months, 6 months, 9 months, 12 months, 15 months, 18 months, 2 years, 3 years, 4 years, 5 years and 6 years of age.

Benefits for coverage for child health supervision services must be exempt from any copayment, coinsurance, deductible, or other dollar limit provision in the policy or plan.
VA Code §38.2-3411.1

The required benefits apply to immunizations administered to each newborn child from birth to 36 months of age.

Adopted Children Coverage – Virginia Law

Individual and group health insurance policies, health plans and HMOs that offer coverage for a family member must also provide that the accident and sickness insurance benefits applicable for children are payable with respect to adopted children of the insured, subscriber, or plan enrollee. The coverage of adopted children must apply in the same manner and extent as to other insureds.

Primary and Contingent Beneficiaries

When a health insurance plan includes benefits payable upon death, beneficiaries are named to receive the death benefit. A named primary beneficiary receives the payment upon the death of the insured. If the primary beneficiary is deceased at the time of the death of the insured, the contingent beneficiary receives the death benefit. More than one primary beneficiary or contingent beneficiary may be named to share the death benefit proceeds. *For example, if a health insurance policy includes an accidental death benefit, the insured/owner may name all three of his children to receive the death benefit in equal shares as primary beneficiaries.*

Modes of Premium Payments

Health insurance policies may allow premium payments to be made annually, quarterly, semi-annually or monthly. It is most common for premiums to be paid monthly.

Most health insurance coverage is provided through employers. Most employer plans provide that premium is paid monthly as a salary reduction amount through payroll.

An insurer or plan may charge administrative fees for the expenses associated with collecting and accounting for premium that become part of the premium paid, or are charged separately to the plan or insured.

Nonduplication and Coordination of Benefits

If people are covered by more than one health coverage plan, the payment of benefits must be coordinated between the plans when more than one plan covers a sickness or injury. If an insured is covered by more than one health insurance policy, one plan becomes the primary, paying claims first; then the second plan pays toward the remaining cost.

Nonduplication of benefits provisions are required by law in some contracts. For example, it is illegal under federal and state law to duplicate benefits provided by Medicare in a health insurance contract.

Circumstances that may result in being covered by more than one health plan include:

- Both spouses being employed and each enrolling the other in their employer-sponsored health plan
- Being involved in an auto accident and the applicable auto insurance providing medical expense coverage
- Being involved in an accident at work where Workers Compensation insurance applies

Occupational vs. Non-Occupational Coverage

Workers compensation and similar government insurance programs cover sickness and injuries that occur in the course of employment in an occupation. Health insurance plans cover non-occupational sickness and injury and exclude from coverage sickness and accidents that are covered through Workers Compensation. Health insurance plans that exclude care covered by Workers Compensation are known as *non-occupational coverage* plans.

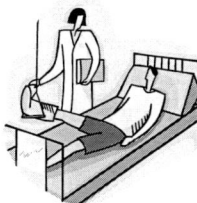

Most disability income policies exclude payment for any condition covered by Workers Compensation. However, there are some disability income policies that provide a supplemental payment if the Workers Compensation payment is not as large as the amount the disability income policy would pay for the same disability. The payment equals the difference between the amount of the Workers Compensation benefit and the amount the disability income policy would pay if the injury or sickness had arisen from a non-occupational cause.

Tax Treatment of Premiums and Proceeds of Insurance Contracts

Disability Income Insurance

When an individual pays for the premiums on a disability income insurance policy, the premium is not deductible and benefits are not taxable.

Medical Expense Insurance

Premiums for medical expense insurance may be included in the medical expense deduction for federal income tax purposes. For purposes of this deduction, premiums paid for medical expense insurance that pays for the following types of care may be included in the medical expense deduction:

- Hospitalization, surgical services, X-rays,
- Prescription drugs and insulin,
- Dental care,
- Replacement of lost or damaged contact lenses, and
- Long-term care (subject to specified limits)

Qualified Long-Term Care Policies

Under the federal Health Insurance Portability and Accountability Act (HIPAA), certain tax advantages were created for long term care contracts that meet federal standards. These contracts are known as **qualified long term care contracts**.

Treated as Accident and Health Insurance

Amounts received under a qualified long-term care contract are treated like amounts received under Accident and Health Insurance contracts. This means they are generally excludable from income, subject to a per-day and annual limit. The taxpayer must itemize his deductions in order to take advantage of this benefit. The amounts received are treated as unreimbursed medical expenses if they meet the IRC's definition of qualified long-term care services. After 2012, generally, unreimbursed medical expenses are deductible if they are at least 10% of AGI, except that in the years 2013–2016, if either the taxpayer or the taxpayer's spouse has turned 65 before the end of the tax year, the increased 10% threshold does not apply and the threshold is 7.5% of AGI. In 2015, the per day limit for deductible amounts received under long term care contracts is $380, and the annual limit is $138,700. These amounts are subject to adjustment for inflation.

Premium Deductibility

Premiums paid for qualified long-term care contracts are deductible, up to certain limits. The amount of premium that may be deducted is known as eligible long-term care premium. The deductibility rules for long-term care premiums

are generally the same as those for unreimbursed medical expenses, except that there is a maximum deductible limit, based on age. For 2014, the premium deductibility limits are as in the following table:

Long Term Care Premium Deductibility Limits (2016)

In the case of an individual with an attained age before the close of the tax year of:	The annual limitation on deductible premiums is:
40 or less	$390
More than 40, but not more than 50	$730
More than 50, but not more than 60	$1,460
More than 60, but not more than 70	$3,900
More than 70	$4,850

Internal Revenue Code Section 213 (d) (10) (A)

Employer Group Health Insurance

Disability Income

General Taxation Rules for Disability Income Insurance	
Premiums not a business expense	*Not deductible*
Premiums a business expense (considered compensation, fringe benefit or wages)	Deductible to the business
Benefits paid from policy with non-deductible premiums	Benefits not taxable
Benefits paid from policy with deductible premiums	Benefits are taxable
General Taxation Rules for Group Employer DII Plan	
Employer pays premium, employee certificate owner and insured and receives benefits	Employer may deduct premiums; Employee benefits are taxable to employee
Employer and employee split premium, employee certificate owner and insured and receives benefits	Employer may deduct amount of premiums paid; Amount of benefits received attributable to the employer-paid premium are taxable to employee

VA PPL LH-2_16298

General Taxation Rules for Bonus Used for DII Policy	
Employer pays a bonus to an employee and bonus used to purchase DII with employee as owner and insured and employee receives benefits	Amount of bonus is taxable to employee; benefits from DII coverage are not taxable to employee

FICA Taxation and Disability Benefits

Disability income payments are paid for both short-term and long-term disabilities. Tax treatment changes when disability payments are made by an employer plan for extended periods of time.

When an employer pays for disability income insurance premiums, when the employee receives benefits, the benefits are considered wages under the Internal Revenue Code, and are taxable as such. Normally, all wages are not just subject to federal and state taxation and withholding requirements, but are also subject to the withholding requirements of FICA. FICA requires withholding a percentage of wages for Social Security and Medicare. These are commonly known as FICA taxes.

FICA withholding must be made from disability income payments paid to an employee while he or she is working for the employer. FICA withholding must also made from disability income payment paid to an employee for the first full six months after the employee no longer works for the employer. However, after the employee has stopped working for the employer for six months, FICA taxes no longer have to be withheld from disability income payment to the ex-employee.

Taxation of Medical Expense Benefits Offered to Employees

Group health plans are subject to Federal taxation rules applicable to accident or health plans. For tax purposes, an accident or health plan is an arrangement that provides benefits for employees, their spouses, and their dependents in the event of personal injury or sickness. The plan may be noninsured or insured.

Not Includable in Wages

The health benefits provided to employees are not included in the wages of employees. Exclusions from wages include:

- Employer contributions to the cost of accident or health insurance
- Contributions to a separate trust or fund that directly or through insurance provides accident or health benefits
- Contributions to HSAs
- Payments or reimbursement of medical expenses
- Payments for specific injuries or illnesses

Deductible for Employers

Contributions and payments made by the employer in accordance with governing law are tax deductible to the employer.

Taxation of Long-Term Care Insurance

Long-term care insurance premiums and benefits are generally treated the same as premiums and benefits from accident and health insurance policies, for tax purposes. Employer paid premiums are deductible to the employer, benefits are **not** taxable to the employee, and if the employee pays any of the premiums, they may be deductible as part of medical insurance expenses on the employee's individual federal tax return.

Key Person Disability Income Taxation

General Taxation Rules for Key Person DII	
Owner: Business Insured: Key Person Benefits paid to: Business	Premiums not deductible to business and benefits are not taxable to business or employee

Business Overhead Expense Disability Income Taxation

General Taxation Rules for BOE DI Policy	
Owner: Business Insured: Owner or Partner or Executive Benefits paid to: Business	Premiums deductible to business and benefits are taxable to business
Note: Benefits will be used to pay for BOE, e.g., electricity and rent, which are deductible to the business	

Taxation of Buy-Sell Agreement Transactions

Premiums paid for disability income or life insurance used for a buy-sell agreement are not tax deductible to the purchaser. Benefits received from the insurance are not taxable.

General Taxation Rules for Buy-Sell DII	
Owner: Business Insured: Owner or Partner or Shareholder Benefits paid to: Business	Premiums not deductible to business and benefits are not taxable to business or insured

Managed Care

Preventing illness by encouraging people to have healthier life styles is the concept behind managed care. It is an approach to health care financing and delivery that promises access to comprehensive and coordinated services while keeping costs under control. The ACA emphasizes preventive care in many of its provisions. Managed care concepts are being utilized in all forms of health care plans today and it will continue to be emphasized in the health coverage requirements under the ACA as a method to control costs and provide superior health care.

Workers Compensation

All states have laws that require the payment of benefits to workers injured on the job or who have an occupational disease or work-related illness. Payments are made for medical expenses, rehabilitation, disability and death. Benefits are payable regardless of who is at fault.

Medical and Rehabilitation Expenses

Medical and rehabilitation expenses covered under Workers Compensation statutes generally include doctor and nursing costs, drugs, specialists, hospitalization, medical equipment, prosthetic devices, psychiatric treatment, and medical rehabilitation. Some states include coverage for a certain amount of vocational rehabilitation as well. Most states do not limit the amount of medical expenses that are recoverable. If medical expenses arise due to an injury or disease covered by Workers Compensation, in most states the medical expenses continue to be covered as long as treatment is required.

Disability Benefits

Disability benefits are generally paid to compensate for loss of wages and for injury sustained. Workers Compensation statutes include four categories of disability, and payments made

vary based on the category of disability under which the injury falls. Generally, the *Workers Compensation categories of disability* are:

1. Temporary Partial Disability
2. Temporary Total Disability
3. Permanent Partial Disability
4. Permanent Total Disability

Temporary Partial Disability

Temporary partial disability is disability that causes the injured employee to be unable to perform the full requirements of his or her usual job for a period of time not expected to be permanent. If a worker is partially disabled, the worker is able to undertake some kind of gainful employment, but is not able to perform the same job as when the worker was not disabled. Temporary partial disability benefits are generally based upon lost wages, but compensation may also be made for loss of future earnings, if such loss can be proven to arise from the covered injury.

Temporary Total Disability

A temporary total disability is a disability that does not allow the worker to perform any kind of work for a period of time not expected to be permanent. Temporary total disability benefits are based on compensation for loss of wages or earnings during the period of disability.

Permanent Partial Disability

A permanent partial disability is a disability that causes the injured employee to be able to perform some but not the full requirements of his or her job, permanently. Benefits are paid based on lost earnings, and may include some amount of compensation for future reduced earning capacity.

Permanent Total Disability

Permanent total disability occurs when a disability results in a worker being unable to perform any kind of work, permanently. Workers Compensation laws also consider certain types of injuries as resulting in permanent total disability, even if the worker is able to obtain some type of gainful employment. For example, the loss of sight in both eyes or the loss of more than one limb may be considered a permanent total disability for the purposes of determining Workers Compensation benefits, even if the worker is able to do some type of work.

Death Benefits

Workers Compensation death benefits are generally determined using a percentage of the deceased worker's average compensation, up to a specified maximum percentage. A surviving spouse is generally entitled to death benefits until and unless the spouse remarries. Other dependents, such as minor children, may also be entitled to compensation under death benefits.

Occupational Disease

All states also include coverage due to occupational disease under Workers Compensation laws.

Workers Compensation Disability Benefits

Generally, Workers Compensation laws automatically assign liability to the employer for injury that arises out of and in the course of employment. Fault or negligence on behalf of the employer does not have to be established in order for the employer to be liable for such injuries.

The employer must pay compensation, but the amount is limited under the Workers Compensation laws, to avoid the situation, as happened during the industrial revolution, where the employer will be put out of business by employee lawsuits. A benefit of Workers Compensation laws for the employee is that he or she does not have to wait for the outcome of a court case in order to be compensated. Workers Compensation payments are generally not made in lump sums, but are set up as periodic payments to the injured worker or survivors.

Paying for Workers Compensation

Workers Compensation is paid for by employers. It is an insurance based system. In a few states, the insurance must be purchased through a state fund. In other states, the employer has a choice to purchase insurance through a private insurer or through the state. The insurer contracts to pay all sums for which the employer is obligated to pay under the law.

Subrogation

Subrogation is a legal concept that puts the insurance company in the place of the insured for purposes of claiming rights to amounts it has paid that should rightfully be paid by another party. To subrogate means to substitute. It can be thought of as "standing in another person's shoes."

When a health insurer is presented with a claim for an accident or sickness, it will ask the claimant whether the insured is covered by any other insurance. It will also ask for the facts surrounding the accident or sickness. If the insurer determines that the accident or sickness is the fault or the responsibility of another party, it may deny the claim and tell the insured the claim is not covered. For example, a health insurer may deny a claim because it is excluded due to coverage by Workers Compensation or due to coverage by another insurer who provides primary coverage.

If a health insurer pays for a claim, and later discovers that another party is responsible or liable for the accident or injury, the insurer has the right to be paid back for the claim by the responsible party. The insured gives the health insurer this right generally through the terms of the health insurance contract. The contract generally includes a provision titled "Right of Reimbursement," "Subrogation," or Right of Recovery," that spells out this right of the insurer. Within this provision, the insured generally gives the insurer the right to recover damages to the extent that they are paid by the insurer when an injury or sickness occurs through the act or omission of another person. In addition, the insured agrees to reimburse the insurer if the insured is paid by both the health insurer and another party for the same injury or sickness in violation of the health insurer's policy.

The common types of insurance from which a health insurer may seek reimbursement after paying a claim on behalf of an insured include:

- Workers compensation coverage
- Uninsured motorist coverage
- Underinsured motorist coverage
- Automobile medical payments coverage
- No-fault insurance coverage
- School insurance coverage

Section IX Review

1) Partial disability is the inability to:
   a. perform the duties of the insured's regular occupation, due to illness or injury
   b. perform some, but not all, of the important duties of the insured's regular occupation, due to illness or injury
   c. perform 50% of the important duties of the insured's regular occupation, due to illness or injury
   d. perform 80% of the important duties of the insured's regular occupation, due to illness or injury

2) If an insured under a group health insurance plan is injured in an auto accident:
   a. she is likely to be covered under more than one insurance policy for her medical expenses.
   b. she may only be covered by one insurance policy for medical expenses and if more than one applies to her bodily injury, she must select which one will cover the expenses.
   c. she will only be covered by auto insurance medical expense coverage, not her group health insurance plan, regardless of who was at fault for the accident.
   d. she will only be covered by the group health insurance policy and any auto insurance medical expense coverage will not apply

3) An insured has group health insurance through his employer and an individual health insurance plan he'd purchased through his business of which he is a self-employed proprietor. He is diagnosed with cancer. His cancer treatment:
   a. will be paid for only by the individual health insurer.
   b. will be paid for by both the individual and group insurance, and the individual policy is probably the primary payor with the employer plan being secondary.
   c. will be paid for by both the individual and group insurance, and the group policy is probably the primary payor with the employer plan being primary.
   d. will be paid for by both the individual and group insurance in equal amounts until the limits of the policy is reached.

4) Premiums for _____ insurance may be included in the medical expense deduction for federal income tax purposes.
   a. individual life
   b. group life
   c. medical expense
   d. disability income

5) The applicant does not normally itemize his taxes. If he purchases a qualified long-term care policy:
   a. He will be able to deduct premiums paid for the policy only if he itemizes his taxes and his unreimbursed medical expenses for the tax year exceed the established percentage of adjusted gross income (7.5% or 10%), under current rules
   b. He will be able to deduct premiums paid for the policy regardless of whether he itemizes his taxes
   c. He will never be able to deduct premiums paid for the policy, under any circumstances
   d. He will be able to deduct benefits received under the policy, but not premiums paid, even if does not itemize his taxes

6) The employer offered a group long-term care plan to its employees. Spouses were also covered by the plan. The employer paid up to $100 of premium monthly for the plan, and employees paid the remaining amount. Which of the following statements is accurate about the taxation of this plan?
   a. the employer paid premium is deductible to the employer
   b. the employee paid premium is not deductible for federal tax purposes
   c. the benefits received by the employee are taxable to the employee
   d. the employer paid premiums are not deductible to the employer

7) The type of coverage that provides financial protection against disability and death due to work-related occurrences is:
   a. Social Security Disability Income
   b. Workers Compensation
   c. Accidental Death & Dismemberment insurance
   d. Short-term disability coverage

8) If the employer pays part of the premium for a group disability income policy that is structured so that the employee is the certificate owner, is the insured on the policy, receives any disability benefits and pays the other portion of the premium for the policy:
   a. benefits are received income tax free by the employee.
   b. benefits are taxable as income to the employee.
   c. benefits are partially taxable as income to the employee.
   d. benefits are received income tax free to the employer.

9) When medical expense insurance is paid for by an employer, benefits from the insurance are:
   a. not taxable as wages to employees
   b. taxable as wages to employees.
   c. not deductible to the employer
   d. taxable to the employer

10) A business purchases BOE disability insurance. The benefits from this insurance:
    a. are not taxable to the business
    b. are taxable to the business
    c. are not paid until accidental death, and are received tax free
    d. are paid directly to utilities and other suppliers of business services, and are taxable to those suppliers

11) When a corporation owns and will receive the benefits from a disability income policy used in a buy-sell agreement:
    a. the premiums are tax deductible and the benefits are not taxable
    b. the premiums are not tax deductible and the benefits are taxable
    c. the premiums are not tax deductible and the benefits are not taxable
    d. the premiums are tax deductible and the benefits are taxable

12) Under a key employee insurance plan:
    a. the employee must pay taxes on the amount of premiums paid for the policy.
    b. the business may deduct premiums paid.
    c. the employee's heirs incur a tax liability for the death benefit paid.
    d. the employee does not incur any tax liability.

13) The categories of disability found in Workers Compensation statutes include all of the following, except:
    a. temporary partial disability
    b. temporary total disability
    c. permanent partial disability
    d. permanent revocable disability

14) Workers Compensation, whether offered through a private insurer or a state fund, generally provides payment for:
    a. death only.
    b. medical and rehabilitation expenses only.
    c. disability expenses only.
    d. death, medical and rehabilitation expenses, disability expenses and occupational disease.

15) Matt is the owner of a health insurance contract. Matt has the ability to do each of the following, EXCEPT:
    a. Select the deductible amount from the offered choices
    b. Select the elimination period from the offered choices
    c. Assign co-pays to benefits
    d. Select a preferred provider from the list of available providers

16) Virginia law requires that accident and sickness policies that covers dependents of a policyholder up to a specified age must continue coverage for dependents who suffer from certain disabling incapacity. The conditions for this continuing coverage on these dependents include each of the following, EXCEPT:
    a. that the dependent is an unmarried child who was covered by the policy prior to reaching age 19.
    b. that the dependent is incapable of self-sustaining employment by reason of intellectual disability or physical handicap.
    c. that the dependent be covered regardless of insurability
    d. that the dependent is chiefly dependent upon the policyholder for support and maintenance.

Section X: Field Underwriting Procedures

Underwriting responsibilities of the health insurance agent are considered in this section. Topics include:

- Completing the application
- Explaining sources of insurability information
- Premium payment and receipt
- Submitting the application
- Policy delivery
- Explaining the policy at delivery
- Replacement
- Contract law

The agent is crucial in the underwriting process. Agents are often referred to as field underwriters, or even simply as underwriters. This is because they gather underwriting information, evaluate risk, often do a preliminary assignment of premium, may authorize preliminary coverage, and may reject applicants on behalf of the insurer. During the underwriting process, the agent is often responsible to gather additional documentation and information to assist the home office underwriting team.

Application Procedures

When making a sales presentation or soliciting business, the agent is responsible for providing required disclosures and using the advertising materials provided by the insurer according to the law and the insurance company's procedures.

Fact-Finding

The producing agent will generally spend the initial period in a customer meeting by finding out the insurance needs of the customer or applicant. This involves asking about the types of coverage the customer currently has, who will be covered by the insurance to be purchased and the coverage needs of these people.

Providing Product Suggestions

Once the agent has completed the fact-finding process with the customer, the agent will be ready to discuss specific products and plans that may meet the customer's needs. Whenever the agent begins to discuss product and plan options with the customer, the agent has a responsibility to provide clear and accurate information about the

programs discussed. It is important for the agent to explain both the risks and benefits of any product or plan offered to the customer.

Taking the Application

If the customer is interested in obtaining health coverage through one of the plans offered by the agent, an application will be taken. The health application requires the applicant to provide medical information and supporting documentation will normally be required if certain medical conditions exist. The agent may also be required to notify the applicant that a paramedical exam will be scheduled if the insurance requires one to meet underwriting standards.

Screening Risk

The agent may be called upon to screen out unacceptable risks for the insurer. The agent may determine that an applicant does not meet minimum underwriting standards. In some cases, the agent must inform the applicant that the insurer will not be able to write a policy for that applicant. Or, the agent may try to work with the applicant to determine if there is another method of covering the risk that will meet minimum underwriting requirements.

Sources of Insurability Information

Underwriting is the process of determining whether an insured is an acceptable risk, and if so, at what rate the insured will be accepted.

Insurers cannot accept every applicant. An insurer has a responsibility to its current policyholders to make sure that it will be able to meet all the contractual obligations of its existing policies. If the insurance company issues policies on applicants that represent risks that are uninsurable or risks that are not properly reflected in premium rates, the insurer's ability to meet its contractual obligations is jeopardized.

On the other hand, an insurer wants to make money and to increase its number of policyholders. No insurer wants to reject applicants unnecessarily. These factors must be taken into consideration in the underwriting process.

Regulation is another important factor in the underwriting process. An insurer is also regulated by the states in which it does business and by certain federal regulations. The lawmakers expect the insurer to establish reasonable, non-discriminatory standards for accepting insureds. Rates for many types of insurance must be approved by the states in which the insurer does business.

The underwriters evaluate basic characteristics of the risk to be insured using the insurance application and data provided through supporting reports and documents. For life and health insurance, information related to the medical history of the insured is weighed, as are the occupation and hobbies of the insured.

Many forms of insurance require financial information to be submitted for the underwriting process. When individuals are covered, personal financial records may be needed. When a business is covered, the business' financial statements are generally submitted. If a professional is covered, both personal and business financials may be requested.

Insurance Applications

The insurance application is a critical underwriting resource. From it, the underwriter finds most of the basic information needed to determine whether to issue a policy, and if so, at what premium and terms.

In underwriting:
1. The application is reviewed for completeness, and to determine whether the application as submitted meets underwriting standards.
2. It is determined whether or not additional documentation is required beyond that which the agent submitted.
3. If additional documentation is required, the underwriter will request documentation directly from the applicant or will notify the agent or agency that these items are needed.
4. Underwriting and policy issue is governed by state regulations and company standards,

so requests for documentation include a date in which compliance must occur.

If the information is not received within the specified time, the application file is generally closed, and any premium received is returned.

Health Insurance Applications

Health insurance is often issued under a group policy through an employer. An application for coverage under a group policy may be simpler than an application for individual coverage, but both individual and group applications ask similar information. Individual applications require supporting reports and health records to be submitted to the insurer that group applications may not. Individual applications generally require a paramedic exam for underwriting purposes.

A group application from an employer will normally include the following elements:
- Employer name
- Employer plan group number
- Employee name
- Employee address and phone number
- Date of hire
- Employee position or title
- Sex of the employee
- Birth date of the employee
- Marital Status
- Whether the employee uses tobacco
- Whether the application for coverage is based on COBRA
- Deductible amount, if any
- Coverage options, such as whether dental coverage or prescription drug coverage is to be included
- Dependent coverage information for spouse and children
- Prior coverage information (this information is necessary to comply with federal health coverage rules for group policies)

If the policy is not a guaranteed issue policy and the application is for a limited health policy or other policy not covered by the ACA's rules, the application contains medical information:
- Height and weight of adults covered
- Whether any insured has had medical treatment for his or her back, colon, liver, kidney, diabetes, intestinal tract, muscular

system, respiratory system, heart or circulatory system, or for any cancer, convulsions, a stroke or mental or emotional issues

- Whether treatment had been received for alcohol or drug use
- Whether the applicant had been diagnosed or treated for HIV, AIDS or ARC
- Whether the applicant or any insured is pregnant
- Whether there has been treatment or diagnosis related to any insured's ear, eye, joint, ulcer, rectal, hernia, allergy, asthma, arthritis, breast, thyroid, prostate, headache, gallbladder, urinary tract, digestive system, reproductive organs, or high blood pressure
- Whether any insured has any other medical condition not included elsewhere in the application
- Request for additional explanation on any medical condition indicated on the application

The information on the health insurance application is necessary for the underwriters to properly underwrite the coverage. In the case of group insurance, the items related to the employer and the employer plan group number is used for the basic purpose of placing the employee within the proper group plan. Date of hire and position in the firm is used to make sure the employee is identified correctly, and because under some benefits programs, the amount the employer pays for health benefits varies based on the length of time an employee is on the job and the position of the employee.

Applications include a question regarding whether the coverage is based on COBRA because COBRA coverage is governed by federal laws. The insurer must make sure that all these laws are complied with if the health coverage does fall under COBRA. Prior coverage information is also important because the appropriate insurance should be charged for care. Optional coverages such as dental and prescription drug impact rates and terms of the coverage applicable to the insured.

Age and use of tobacco are allowed to be used as rate factors under the ACA. Geographical location is also a rating factor under ACA rules. The more detailed health questions are used to determine the

type of health risk the applicant represents for policy types that require health underwriting. Depending upon the answers given, the underwriter may need additional information, such as attending physician statements and other medical reports.

Medical Reports

Besides the application, the underwriters have other resources they may utilize during the underwriting process. For life and certain forms of health insurance, the medical history of the insured must be examined. The application for the policy includes questions pertaining to basic medical information, including age, height, weight and health history of the applicant and the applicant's family.

Besides the application, if the coverage amount requested is above an insurance company's non-medical limit, additional medical information may be requested through a medical report. Generally, a medical report may be completed by a paramedic or a registered nurse. If there is information in the application or medical report that requires further explanation, an attending physician's statement, or APS, may be required. An APS must be completed by a physician who treated the medical condition under question.

Attending Physician Statement (APS)

An APS is a questionnaire sent to the applicant's doctor. The doctor must complete the questionnaire in order for the underwriters to complete the underwriting process. The proposed insured must give his or her permission on the application for the attending physician to provide this information.

An attending physician statement is a relatively simple document. It generally includes:

- Patient's (insured's) name
- Patient's address
- If related to an insured's employment, a statement for the physician to designate whether the patient is able to return to work, and if unable, when it is anticipated the patient will be able to return to work

 VA PPL LH-2_16298

- An area for the physician to indicate the physician's diagnosis and prognosis
- An area for additional remarks for the physician
- The physician's name, license number, address, phone number and signature

Inspection, Consumer and Credit Reports

If an applicant applies for amounts of insurance above certain levels, the insurer may conduct inspection reports and/or acquire credit reports on the applicant. An inspection report is created from interviews with an applicant's neighbors, associates and employees, and sometimes with the applicant. The inspection report and interviews are conducted by national investigative organizations hired by the insurer. Insurance companies request inspection reports in order to get a better understanding of an applicant's overall character, lifestyle, financial situation and risks to which an applicant may be exposed.

Consumer Reports

Credit reports provide information about the financial condition of an applicant. This is important to an insurer because insurance involves a financial commitment from the policyholder. If an insurer accepts policies from people with poor credit, or credit below a certain standard, policy lapses are likely to go up. Lapses cause an increase in expenses to the insurer who has incurred policy issue expenses associated with the policy. In addition, financial problems establish the presence of moral hazard – the applicant may be more likely to submit unfounded claims due to the need for money.

Credit and consumer reports, including investigative consumer reports, are regulated by the Fair Credit Reporting Act.

The MIB

The Medical Information Bureau (MIB) contains information about the medical condition of applicants and insureds. Health insurance applicants must authorize the release of information to the MIB. The information may only be used for underwriting and claims purposes, and medical information is released only to the applicant's physician, or directly to the applicant if the applicant requests.

Initial Premium Payment and Receipt

One of the important duties of an agent related to his or her role as field underwriter is the collection and remitting of premium. Generally, premium handling laws require that agents must place premiums they receive in a trust account for the insurer in a recognized financial institution that is subject to the jurisdiction of the courts within the state in which the agent is doing business. In addition, the account must be insured by an entity of the federal government. The account may be a checking account, a demand account, savings account, or other account with such a financial institution.

Withdrawals from a trust account are limited and generally may be made for the following reasons only:

1. Making payment of premium to the insurance company or other producers.
2. Returning premiums to an insured or other person entitled to them.
3. Withdrawing money the agent had placed in the account on a voluntary basis as additional funds.
4. Transferring interest to another account.
5. Transferring actual or average commissions to another account. If it is common practice to transfer average commissions, the agent must keep on file documentation in the form of a letter signed by each principal regarding the percentage of average commission.
6. Paying of bank fees and charges.
7. Moving funds to another trust account in accordance with the law.

It is generally prohibited for an agent to commingle funds that belong to the insurer with other funds, such as those of an insurance agency. Generally, it is prohibited to treat the funds in a trust account as a personal asset, as collateral for either a personal or business loan, or as a personal asset on a financial statement. The Insurance Commissioner may have a trust account examined and audited at any time.

Submitting the Application

Besides taking the application and screening out unacceptable risks, the agent is responsible to submit documentation that supports the application and is used in the underwriting process. The insurer has standards regarding what type of documentation must be submitted with every application based on product and plan. In order for the application to be processed as quickly as possible, the agent must make sure to obtain and submit this documentation as required.

Other documentation may be asked for by the underwriters after the application is submitted. The agent may have the responsibility to coordinate the collection and submission of such documentation. If so, the agent must do so as promptly as possible to make sure that the underwriting process moves forward.

Whether or not the client actually purchases the product offered, the agent should keep a detailed record of the information gathered from meetings with the client, and the documentation, brochures and other information shared with the client about the product. The agent should keep copies of documents noting what product suggestions the agent made that the client declined, in case there is ever a question of whether appropriate product was suggested. Copies of signed disclosures, the application, the fact-finding documents and any other customer-related forms, should be kept on file by the agent. Appropriate copies of documentation must be left with the client, and other copies sent to the insurer, as required by insurer company procedure and law. The agent's file will not only help the agent should there ever be a question about the suitability of the agent's recommendations, but will also assist the agent in his or her ongoing relationship with the customer.

Requirements at Delivery of Policy

At the time of delivery, a receipt is generally signed by the owner to identify the beginning of the free look period or right to return period, where the applicant may return the contract and receive any premium paid without penalty.

Many producers see the delivery appointment as an opportunity to solidify their relationship with the policyowner. It is a time when any final questions about the contract may be answered and the policyowner's reasons for purchasing the contract may be reaffirmed. The sale is not complete until the delivery is made and the free look period has passed.

Collecting Premium

If additional premium is required at policy delivery, the premium check should be made out to the insurer and a receipt provided to the applicant. If the policyholder pays premium directly to the agent on a periodic ongoing basis after delivery of the contract, the agent must ensure the premium checks are made out to the insurer, and must remit funds to the insurer as required by the insurer's fund handling requirements, and provide a receipt.

Conditional Receipt and the Medical Examination

When premium is provided and accepted at the time of application, a conditional binding receipt or binding receipt may be issued. This *conditional receipt* provides that the coverage will be effective from the date of application, or medical exam, whichever is later, unless the coverage is declined or *rated*, meaning that the insured's risk class is not standard, or issued with riders that exclude coverage.

Premium Collected at Policy Delivery

When premium is not collected at time of application, it must be collected at policy delivery. The policy generally becomes effective when the premium is collected and a statement of good health is signed, unless there is a written agreement with the insurer to make the policy effective under some other condition.

Explaining the Policy at Delivery

When the policy is delivered, its provisions should be reviewed with the policyholder. The policy includes a face page, a copy of the application, and the policy contract.

The face page summarizes key information about the policy:
- The policyholder's name
- The insured's name

- The insured's age at issue
- The premium amount
- The issue date of the policy
- The policy number

Issue Class of Health Insurance

When evaluating applicants for limited health policies and other policies not governed by the ACA, underwriters determine whether insurance on the applicant will be:

- rejected;
- issued on a substandard basis;
- issued on a standard basis; or
- issued on a preferred basis.

Each of these underwriting outcomes is explained in this course within the topic "Risk Classification."

Health Insurance Replacement

When health insurance is replaced, care must be taken to make sure that the insured is not losing important benefits or status under the existing policy and that the insured understands the differences in benefits and features of policies being considered.

Preexisting Conditions and Waiting Periods

An insured should consider how a new policy will treat preexisting conditions. A preexisting condition is a health condition or problem that existed before a given health care policy or contract was effective and for which medical advice, diagnosis, care, or treatment was recommended. Health insurance contracts define preexisting conditions that are excluded from coverage and will also define time periods that apply for conditions that are covered by the policy after a waiting period.

Benefits and Limits

Benefits and their limits that should be considered when evaluating and comparing health plans include:

Deductibles

The deductible is the amount the insured must pay before the health plan pays for covered services. Low deductible plans are plans that range from having no deductible to having about a $500 deductible for individuals and a $1,000 deductible for family coverage. High deductible plans may have deductibles of $1500 to $5,000.

Copayments

Some plans require copayments for each visit. For example, each physician office visit may require a payment of from $5 to $30 at the time of service.

Coinsurance

Coinsurance is the amount the covered person pays after the deductible and any copayments. *For example, a plan may have a $100 annual deductible and a $20 office visit copayment. The insurance covers 80% of the care above this amount, and the individual is responsible for the remaining 20%. The 20% amount is coinsurance.*

Ambulance Care

Health plans often cover transportation via ambulance within certain dollar limits. The plans generally cover ground and air transportation to the nearest facility, or based on prearrangement with a physician or other licensed health provider. The coverage generally only applies to medically necessary or emergency care.

Hospitalization Benefits

Health plans usually cover inpatient hospital care. This may include semiprivate room care and when necessary, private room care, as well as intensive care, operations, treatment and recovery rooms, anesthesia, prescription drugs while in the hospital, lab work, general nursing care, physician services and emergency care. Outpatient surgery is often covered under hospitalization benefits in a plan as well, as is other outpatient care such as therapy, drugs administered during therapy, radiation and chemotherapy, diagnostic services, diabetes self-management, lab work and emergency care.

Emergency Room Services

Emergency room care is covered by health plans. Most plans distinguish between emergency care and urgent care, and may have different payment schedules applied to these two types of care. *Emergency care* is generally defined as necessary care that a person reasonably believes to be

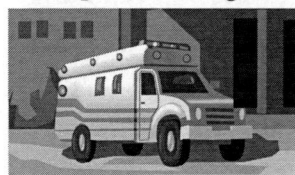

immediately necessary to preserve life, prevent serious impairment to bodily functions, organs or part, or prevent placing the physical or mental health of the individual in serious jeopardy. Plans generally allow for the use of calling 911 and for going to the nearest emergency facility. The ACA prohibits plans from requiring pre-authorization from the health plan in order to cover emergency room care.

Urgent Care

Urgent care is used for conditions that require urgent care, but are not life threatening. Often, plans have required contacting the primary provider or clinic prior to receiving urgent care. In preferred provider plans, there are usually entities designated as urgent care facilities that are to be used to provide urgent care.

Physician Services

Physician outpatient services are also covered by health plans. Generally, all services provided in office visits are covered, which may include x-rays, lab work, surgery, hearing exams, medical supplies, allergy testing and injections, and similar care.

Wellness Care

The ACA requires plans to cover preventive, or wellness care. Wellness care can include routine physical exams, well-child care, immunizations, flu shots, lab and diagnostic imaging, routine hearing exams, prenatal care, and routine eye exams.

Chiropractic Care

Chiropractic care is covered under most health plans. Chiropractic care may be subject to a specified limit of visits or amount covered, and may have its own copay and coinsurance schedule.

Therapy

Health plans cover various types of therapy. Therapy covered may include rehabilitative and habilitative physical therapy, speech therapy, and occupational therapy. It may also include massage therapy that is part of physical or occupational therapy.

Home Health Care

Health plans often cover home health care for terminal illness or rehabilitative purposes. The home health care may have to be administered by certain types of caregivers in order to be covered, and may be subject to a maximum number of visits per plan year.

Mental Health Care

Mental health care may be provided in group health plans. The coverage may be for both inpatient treatment and outpatient treatment. The coverage generally applies only to diagnosable mental health conditions. The ACA also requires expanded coverage of mental health care in plans required to conform to its provisions.

Substance Abuse Treatment

Health plans provide coverage for substance abuse, such as drugs and alcohol. The coverage generally has separate limits for impatient treatment and for outpatient treatment. The coverage is generally subject to a professional diagnosis, and the professional often develops a treatment plan or recommendation for the patient.

Other Benefits

Group health plans may provide a number of other benefits, including:

- Organ, bone marrow and tissue transplants
- Dental care
- Home infusion therapy
- PKU dietary treatment
- Prescription drugs
- Reconstruction surgery
- Family planning services and infertility treatments
- Durable medical equipment, supplies, prosthetics, and orthotics

Replacing Health Insurance Policies and the ACA

Replacing health insurance policies has always required due care on the part of the licensee. Now that the ACA has been passed and is implemented, due care requires a close examination of provisions under both the existing and new policy. There may be many differences in policies because of ACA requirements. Some existing policies are not required to adhere to all the ACA coverage requirements. In other words, the insurer does not have to change the existing policy's terms to meet all the ACA's provisions. However, when a policy

VA PPL LH-2_16298

is replaced, generally, the new policy must meet all of the ACA's coverage requirements. This may mean a change in the available benefits to the insured. Costs and benefits of the existing and replacement policy should still be compared before the replacement occurs. It is possible that the insured has special benefits in the existing policy that are not required under the ACA and that the insured needs and uses. Perhaps an insured should keep that existing policy rather than replace it. Or, perhaps the insured should add riders and optional coverages to an ACA qualified policy. In all replacement situations, careful disclosure and explanation of the consequences of replacement is required.

When replacing individual health coverage, the insured will have to meet the underwriting requirements of the new coverage. An APS, a paramedic exam and explanatory documents concerning medical conditions and past treatment may be required to be submitted to the insurer. When replacing group coverage, the underwriting requirements may not as significant, but they still must be met by the group. Even though federal legislation limits preexisting conditions in health coverage exclusions, the coverage may be significantly more expensive when a new policy is purchased if health has deteriorated since the purchase of the existing coverage.

Contract Law

The insurance relationship occurs under the bounds of contract law. The insurance contract has characteristics that distinguish it from many other contract forms.

Elements of Legal Contracts

In order for a contract to be valid under the law, it must contain four elements: 1) offer and acceptance, 2) consideration, 3) competent parties, and 4) legal purpose.

Offer and Acceptance

Both the insurer and the applicant of an insurance policy can be considered the offeror of a contract. Traditionally, the applicant is considered the offeror by completing the application and disclosing the characteristics of the risk that is to be insured and by submitting premium. The applicant is offering the insurer premium payment if the insurer will agree to accept the risk by authorizing the application and issuing a contract. An insurer may be considered the offeror as well, by advertising its products and offering the terms of coverage to prospects. The applicant is then seen as the party accepting the offer by completing an application and submitting premium.

Counteroffers are made when an insurer offers coverage with conditions and endorsements not included in the initial offer. If the applicant signs the conditional agreements or endorsements, or continues to submit premium when the insurer has issued the policy with the conditions and endorsements, the applicant/insured has accepted the counteroffer.

Consideration

The parties to a contract must each provide valuable consideration in a contractual relationship. The premium is the consideration by the insured and the promise to fulfill policy obligations is the consideration given by the insurer.

The applicant's premium is based on the statements made in the application. The consideration is not commensurate to the insurer's stake in the policy if the applicant makes material misrepresentations or false statements in the application. The insurer can void coverage in certain circumstances when material misrepresentation or false statements are made, or, the insurer may reduce coverage when misstatements are discovered so that the premium reflects the actual cost to the insurer in providing coverage.

Competent Parties

Parties to contracts must be recognized as having the legal ability to enter into them. For example, a party to a contract must generally be of majority age in the state in which the contract is made. Insurance policyholders must be of legal age and must also be considered legally competent to enter into the agreements.

The insurer must be legally authorized to place the insurance business in the state and the producer

VA PPL LH-2_16298

must be licensed in the state in order to be legally competent to enter into the contract.

Legal Purpose

All valid contracts must be made with a legal purpose. A contract between two drug lords to distribute their illegal substances is not valid under the law (although the tax laws may still apply to their activities). The drug lords cannot go to the courts to seek enforcement of their contractual distribution provisions.

Insurable Interest

Insurable interest is a legal concept underlying insurance contracts. It means that the insured or policy owner has to suffer financially or be harmed in another way if a loss occurs in order for insurance to be issued. In other words, the insured or policy owner must have a financial stake or economic interest in the property or person insured. If the insured or owner isn't harmed by a loss, insurance should not be issued.

For example, the spouse and children of an income earner suffers financially if the income earner is in disabled or dies, as do the spouse and children of a non-income earning individual who provides care to the spouse and children. These persons have an insurable interest in the person who may suffer disability of death.

If people without an insurable interest were allowed to purchase insurance, negative consequences can occur:

First, it would make insurance a form of gambling. The purchaser would be hoping for a loss so he could collect his winnings, the policy benefits. This is not in the best interest of the public.

Secondly, an individual without insurable interest is more likely to want to purposefully cause a loss; if insurance were issued without requiring insurable interest, the *moral hazard* is greatly increased.

Insurable interest is closely tied to the **principle of indemnity**. Most insurance contracts are indemnity contracts. This means that the insured can only be compensated for the amount of the loss; he cannot make a profit due to an insured loss. In most contracts, insurance payment cannot exceed the amount of insurable interest in the property, or other item being insured.

For example, if an income earner makes $100,000 per year and has an expected continued work life of 10 years, and were able to purchase a disability income policy that would pay him $1,000,000 for ten years if he becomes disabled, he is in the position of making a profit from his disability since the contract payment exceeds the amount of loss the earner is suffering.

The requirement of insurable interest protects against insurance being used to make a profit.

Representations, Misrepresentations and Warranties

Representations are made prior to or at the same time as the formation of a contract of insurance. Representations are written or oral statement made by the applicant for insurance. These statements are inducements to the insurer to enter into the contract and issue a policy.

A **material fact** is one that, if known to the insurer at time of application, would have caused the insurer to deny coverage or issue coverage under substantially different conditions.

Warranties

Warranties are statements or promises made by an applicant for insurance that are serious or material enough in nature that they must be true or the insurer's liability is ended under the policy. Warranties may be made by agreeing to conditions for coverage under policies.

Concealment

Concealment by the applicant or insured can also cause the denial or loss of insurance coverage. *Concealment* is the intentional nondisclosure of a material fact. Nondisclosure or concealment has the same legal effect as a material misrepresentation. Coverage may be denied based on concealment only if the insured knew the fact to be material and only if the insured intended to defraud the insurer, for most forms of insurance.

Characteristics of Insurance Contracts

Because insurance contracts include a promise to fulfill obligations in the future based on conditional events that may or may not occur, they have unique characteristics.

Conditional Contracts

Insurance contracts are **conditional**. The insurer provides a contract that has terms that give the insured responsibilities or conditions in order for the insurer's ongoing obligations to be fulfilled. All insurance contracts require the insured to pay required premiums for a specified period or until the contract terminates. Insurance contracts also require insureds or policyholders to follow certain rules when claims are made, or the insurer is not required to cover the claim. The policyholder/insured must meet all the policyholder's/insured's responsibilities under these conditions in order for the contract's terms to be fulfilled by the insurer.

Contracts of Adhesion

Insurance contracts are written by the insurer, and the policyholder may only negotiate terms according to the options the insurer gives. This makes them contracts of **adhesion**. For example, an insured may select a deductible level, the elective coverage options offered by the insurer and the amount of coverage or benefits payable. The insurer controls the terms of the contract and the insured adheres to these terms.

Ambiguities in a Contract of Adhesion

If there is a contractual dispute involving the wording or terms of an insurance contract, a court generally rules in favor of the insured because the insured had nothing to do with the construction of the contract's terms. Ruling in favor of the insured is a legal principal followed by courts when interpreting an insurance contract when there is ambiguity because the insurance policy is a contract of adhesion.

Aleatory Contracts

Insurance contracts are **aleatory**. This means that the outcome is affected by chance, and that the values exchanged may not be equal. Only if a peril or other insured cause of loss occurs will payment be made by the insurance company. This is different from a contract for payment for an appliance and its installation, which is known as a **commutative** contract. In a commutative contract, the payment will be made upon installation. There is no chance involved.

Under insurance contracts, if a loss occurs, the premium is much less than the benefit received. The value received is not generally equal to the value paid. With a commutative contract, the value of the appliance and installation is considered to be equal to the amount paid by the purchaser.

Unilateral Contracts

Contracts may be bilateral or unilateral. Bilateral contracts are contracts where the parties exchange a promise for a promise. Commercial contracts are generally bilateral.

Insurance contracts are **unilateral contracts**. The insurer only promises to fulfill the terms of the contract. The insured only promises to pay premium; no other requirements apply to the insured. The insurer can be held in breach of contract by a court of law, whereas an insured may not. An insured may stop paying premium or stop meeting maintenance conditions and the contract is not renewed; the insured isn't sued to require enforcement of these obligations.

Section X Review

1) Which of the following is NOT a duty of a licensed insurance agent that is related to underwriting?
   a. Having a health insurance applicant answer medical and health questions on a health application.
   b. Determining whether an insured is a preferred standard or substandard risk based on the information on the application in order to tell the insured anticipated premium levels.
   c. Rejecting an applicant based on information in the application based on underwriting guidelines provided by the insurer.
   d. Conducting an informational seminar to small businesses concerning new coverages available from health insurers due to changes in state law.

2) Which of the following is NOT a responsibility of an agent when suggesting a health insurance product after the agent has obtained the basic facts surrounding the customer's needs and situation?
   a. Checking the customer's bank records to make sure the customer has sufficient funds to pay premium
   b. Providing clear and accurate information about health plan options
   c. Explaining risks of health plan options
   d. Explaining benefits of health plan options

3) Submitting a complete health insurance application with appropriate documentation helps to avoid:
   a. the agent from practicing misrepresentation
   b. the insurer and agent from committing deceptive advertising practices
   c. the insurer from accepting insureds that do not meet the minimum standards of the insurer
   d. the practice of earning unearned premium

4) Underwriters may require that health insurance applicants provide a statement by the applicant's physician that provides more information about health conditions listed in the application. This statement is called a(n):
   a. Medical Information Bureau statement
   b. Attending physician statement
   c. Inspection report
   d. Consumer report

5) Fernando accepted a health insurance application from Ron. Ron submitted initial premium of $130 with the application. After the application was turned into underwriting, the insurer asked for an attending physician statement regarding diagnosis and treatment for a medical condition listed in Ron's application. Ron's physician refused to provide the information because the insurer did not supply Ron's authorization. The insurer and Fernando asked Ron to authorize the release of the attending physician statement four times over a two month period and Ron refused. What is the insurer most likely to do now?
   a. Issue the policy with an exclusion for any care related to the medical condition for which the report was requested.
   b. Return Ron's premium and close the application file.
   c. Keep Ron's premium and close the application file.
   d. Issue the policy and keep a close eye on Ron's medical care and terminate the policy at renewal if his health is poor.

6) Each of the following are found on an Attending Physician Statement (APS), EXCEPT:
   a. Patient's opinion of his or her health status and treatment
   b. The physician's name, license number, address, phone number and signature
   c. If related to an insured's employment, a statement for the physician to designate whether the patient is able to return to work, and if unable, when it is anticipated the patient will be able to return to work
   d. An area for the physician to indicate the physician's diagnosis and prognosis

7) Generally, all of the following activities are prohibited regarding the trust account used to hold premiums from policy owners to be paid to the insurer, EXCEPT:

    a. commingling the insurer's premiums with the insurance agency's funds

    b. treating the trust account as collateral for a business loan for the agency

    c. putting premium into the trust account that may later be returned to a client if the application is denied by the insurer

    d. treating the trust account as collateral for a personal loan for a licensed agent

8) A _____ is a document required at policy delivery that is used to check on the health status of an insured between the time a health insurance policy was applied for and when it is delivered.

    a. the policy delivery receipt

    b. separate insured statement

    c. Medical Information Bureau report

    d. statement of good health

9) When a health insurance applicant represents a risk that falls outside of the underwriting standards established by the insurance company, the applicant:

    a. is rejected

    b. is issued a substandard policy with higher premiums

    c. is issued a standard policy

    d. is issued a preferred policy

10) Which of the following is the least important factor when comparing policies because an insured is considering replacing a health insurance policy?

    a. policy deductibles, coinsurance and/or copayments

    b. policy benefits and limits

    c. insurer financial strength

    d. whether the insurer is domestic or foreign

11) Necessary care that is reasonably believed to be immediately necessary to preserve life, prevent serious impairment to bodily functions, organs or parts, or prevent placing the physical or mental health of the individual in serious jeopardy is:

    a. urgent care

    b. hospitalization care

    c. emergency care

    d. emergency room care

12) If a minor enters into a contract, the contract is missing a required element for a valid contract. The missing element is:

    a. consideration

    b. assent of both parties

    c. competent parties

    d. legal purpose

13) Susan took out a disability insurance policy that would pay $300 a month upon her total physical disability. However, Susan never became disabled during the policy term and no benefits were ever paid. The fact that Susan ultimately received less in value under the contract than what she paid demonstrates which characteristic of insurance contracts?

    a. Adhesion

    b. Aleatory

    c. Conditional

    d. Unilateral

14) An insurance contract is considered to be a contract of adhesion. All of the following statements about contracts of adhesion are correct EXCEPT:

    a. The parties cannot include endorsements or riders to such policies

    b. The parties do not negotiate the contract's terms

    c. Any ambiguities in the contract's language will typically be interpreted in favor of the insured

    d. The applicant must accept the contract as written and cannot make a counterproposal

15) What is an aleatory contract?

    a. A non-insurance contract

    b. A contract which is written by a certain type of attorney

    c. A contract whose outcome is affected by chance

    d. A commutative contract

Section XI: Virginia Statutes and Regulations Pertinent to Health Insurance Only

This section concentrates on Virginia insurance law and regulation applicable to health insurance. Topics include:

- Medicare supplement policies
- Long term care
- Advertising
- Minimum standards for individual health policies
- HIPAA
- Group health insurance
- Defined groups
- HMOs
- Small employer health plans

Virginia's Medicare Supplement Policies

Open Enrollment Period

When a Medicare Supplement application for a policy or certificate is submitted prior to or during the 6-month period beginning with the first day of the first month in which an individual enrolled for benefits under Medicare Part B, a Medigap plan issuer:

- may not deny or place conditions on a Medicare Supplement policy or certificate available for sale in Virginia; or
- discriminate in the pricing of a policy or certificate because of the applicant's:
  - health status;
  - claims experience;
  - receipt of health care; or
  - medical condition.

Creditable Coverage and Open Enrollment for Medicare Supplement Coverage

If a qualified applicant submits an application during the open enrollment period and, as of the date of application has had a continuous period of creditable coverage:

- of at least 6 months, the Medigap issuer may not exclude benefits based on a preexisting condition.

- that is less than 6 months, the Medigap issuer must reduce the period of any preexisting condition exclusion by the applicable period of creditable coverage.

14VAC 5-170-100

Standards for Marketing

Virginia insurance regulation 14VAC 5-170-180 includes standards for marketing Medicare Supplement policies. These regulations require that a Medigap policy issuer, directly, or through its producers, must:

- Establish marketing procedures to assure that comparison of policies by its producers will be fair and accurate
- Establish marketing procedures to assure excessive insurance is not sold or issued
- Display prominently, on the first page of the policy the following:
  "Notice to buyer: This policy may not cover all of your medical expenses."
- Inquire and otherwise make every reasonable effort to identify whether a prospective applicant or enrollee for Medicare Supplement insurance already has accident and sickness insurance and the types and amounts of this insurance
- Establish auditable procedures for verifying compliance with these regulations

These regulations also state that, in addition to practices prohibited by the Virginia Unfair Trade Practices laws, the following acts and practices are prohibited:

- *Twisting.* Knowingly making any misleading representation or incomplete or fraudulent comparison of insurance policies or insurers for the purpose of inducing, or tending to induce, a person to lapse, forfeit, surrender, terminate, retain, pledge, assign, borrow on or convert an insurance policy or to take out a policy of insurance with another insurer.
- *High pressure tactics.* Employing a method of marketing having the effect of or tending to induce the purchase of insurance through force, fright, threat, whether explicit or

VA PPL LH-2_16298

implied, or undue pressure to purchase or recommend the purchase of insurance.

- *Cold lead advertising.* Making use directly or indirectly of a method of marketing which fails to disclose in a conspicuous manner that a purpose of the method of marketing is solicitation of insurance and that contact will be made by a producer or insurance company.

The terms "Medicare Supplement," "Medigap," "Medicare Wrap-Around" and similar words may not be used unless the policy is issued in compliance with the Medicare Supplement laws and regulations.

14VAC 5-170-180

Virginia Advertising Requirements

An issuer of Medigap policies must provide a copy of any Medicare Supplement advertisement intended for use in Virginia to the Commission. This filing requirement applies to all Medigap policy advertising, whether through written, radio or television medium.

VA Code §38.2-3609

Virginia Requirement for Appropriate Recommendations of Medigap Policies

In recommending the purchase or replacement of a Medicare Supplement policy or certificate, a producer must make reasonable efforts to determine the appropriateness of a recommended purchase or replacement.

No one may make a Medicare Supplement coverage sale that provides an individual more than one Medicare Supplement policy or certificate.

An issuer may not issue a Medicare Supplement policy or certificate to an individual enrolled in Medicare Part C unless the effective date of the coverage is after the termination date of the individual's Part C coverage.

14VAC 5-170-190

Virginia Replacement Requirements for Medigap Policies

Medigap application forms must include the following requirements and questions designed to elicit information as to whether, as of the date of application, the applicant currently has Medicare Supplement, Medicare Advantage, Medicaid coverage, or another health insurance policy or certificate in force or whether a Medicare Supplement policy or certificate is intended to replace any other accident and sickness policy or certificate presently in force.

Required Statements

At application, the application or application forms must include these statements:

- You do not need more than one Medicare Supplement policy.
- If you purchase this policy, you may want to evaluate your existing health coverage and decide if you need multiple coverages.
- You may be eligible for benefits under Medicaid and may not need a Medicare Supplement policy.
- If, after purchasing this policy, you become eligible for Medicaid, the benefits and premiums under your Medicare Supplement policy can be suspended, if requested, during your entitlement to benefits under Medicaid for 24 months. You must request this suspension within 90 days of becoming eligible for Medicaid. If you are no longer entitled to Medicaid, your suspended Medicare Supplement policy or, if the Medicare Supplement policy is no longer available, a substantially equivalent policy will be reinstituted if requested within 90 days of losing Medicaid eligibility. If the Medicare Supplement policy provided coverage for outpatient prescription drugs and you enrolled in Medicare Part D while your policy was suspended, the reinstituted policy will not have outpatient prescription drug coverage, but will otherwise be substantially equivalent to your coverage before the date of suspension.
- If you are eligible for, and have enrolled in a Medicare Supplement policy by reason of disability and you later become covered by an employer or union-based group health plan, the benefits and premiums under your Medicare Supplement policy can be suspended, if requested, while you are covered under the employer or union-based group health plan. If you suspend your Medicare Supplement policy under these

circumstances, and later lose your employer or union-based group health plan, your suspended Medicare Supplement policy (or, if that is no longer available, a substantially equivalent policy) will be reinstituted if requested within 90 days of losing your employer or union-based group health plan. If the Medicare Supplement policy provided coverage for outpatient prescription drugs and you enrolled in Medicare Part D while your policy was suspended, the reinstituted policy will not have outpatient prescription drug coverage, but will otherwise be substantially equivalent to your coverage before the date of suspension.

- Counseling services may be available in your state to provide advice concerning your purchase of Medicare Supplement insurance and concerning medical assistance through the state Medicaid program, including benefits as a Qualified Medicare Beneficiary (QMB) and a Specified Low-Income Medicare Beneficiary (SLMB).

The application or application forms must include the following information and questions:

If you lost or are losing other health insurance coverage and received a notice from your prior insurer saying you were eligible for guaranteed issue of a Medicare Supplement insurance policy, or that you had certain rights to buy such a policy, you may be guaranteed acceptance in one or more of our Medicare Supplement plans. Please include a copy of the notice from your prior insurer with your application.

PLEASE ANSWER ALL QUESTIONS.
Please mark Yes or NO below with an "X"
To the best of your knowledge, did you turn age 65 in the last 6 months?
YES ☐ NO ☐

Did you enroll in Medicare Part B in the last 6 months?
YES ☐ NO ☐
If yes, what is the effective date? _____

Are you covered for medical assistance through the state Medicaid program?
YES ☐ NO ☐
NOTE TO APPLICANT: If you are participating in a "Spend-Down Program" and have not met your "Share of Cost," please answer NO to this question.

If yes, will Medicaid pay your premiums for this Medicare Supplement policy?
YES ☐ NO ☐

Do you receive any benefits from Medicaid OTHER THAN payments towards your Medicare Part B premium?
YES ☐ NO ☐

If you had any from any Medicare plan other than the original Medicare within the last 63 days (for example, a Medicare Advantage plan, or a Medicare HMO or PPO), fill in your start and end dates below. If you are still covered under this plan, leave "END" blank.

START ___/___/____ END ___/___/____

If you are still covered under the Medicare plan, do you intend to replace your current coverage with this new Medicare Supplement policy?
YES ☐ NO ☐

Was this your first time in this type of Medicare plan?
YES ☐ NO ☐

Did you drop a Medicare Supplement policy to enrollment in the Medicare Plan?
YES ☐ NO ☐

Do you have another Medicare Supplement policy in force?
YES ☐ NO ☐
If so, with what company and what plan do you have (optional for Direct Mailers)?
If so, do you intend to replace your current Medicare Supplement policy with this policy?
YES ☐ NO ☐

Have you had coverage under any other health insurance within the past 63 days? (For example, an employer, union, or individual plan)
YES ☐ NO ☐
If so, with what company and what kind of policy?
What are your dates of coverage under the policy (If you are still covered under the other policy, leave "END" blank.)?

START ___/___/____ END ___/___/____

Agents must list on the application form the following health insurance policies they have sold to the applicant:
- Policies sold which are still in force.
- Policies sold in the past 5 years which are no longer in force.

Notice

If a sale involves replacement of Medicare Supplement coverage, an issuer, other than a direct response issuer, or its agent, must furnish the applicant a notice regarding replacement of Medicare Supplement coverage prior to issuance or delivery of the Medicare Supplement policy or certificate. One copy of the notice signed by the applicant and the agent must be provided to the

VA PPL LH-2_16298

applicant and an additional signed copy must be retained by the issuer, except when coverage is sold without an agent. A direct response issuer must deliver to the applicant at the time of the issuance of the policy the notice regarding replacement of Medicare Supplement coverage.

The notice for an issuer must be provided in substantially the following form in at least 12 point type:

NOTICE TO APPLICANT REGARDING REPLACEMENT OF MEDICARE SUPPLEMENT INSURANCE OR MEDICARE ADVANTAGE

(Insurance company's name and address)

SAVE THIS NOTICE!
IT MAY BE IMPORTANT TO YOU IN THE FUTURE.

According to (your application) (information you have furnished), you intend to terminate existing Medicare Supplement or Medicare Advantage and replace it with a policy to be issued by (Company Name) Insurance Company. Your new policy will provide thirty (30) days within which you may decide without cost whether you desire to keep the policy.

You should review this new coverage carefully. Compare it with all accident and sickness coverage you now have. If, after due consideration, you find that purchase of this Medicare Supplement coverage is a wise decision, you should terminate your present Medicare Supplement or Medicare Advantage coverage. You should evaluate the need for other accident and sickness coverage you have that may duplicate this policy.

STATEMENT TO APPLICANT BY ISSUER, PRODUCER (OR OTHER REPRESENTATIVE):
I have reviewed your current medical or health insurance coverage. To the best of my knowledge, this Medicare Supplement policy will not duplicate your existing Medicare Supplement or, if applicable, Medicare Advantage coverage because you intend to terminate your existing Medicare Supplement coverage or leave your Medicare Advantage plan. The replacement policy is being purchased for the following reason(s) (check one):
☐ Additional benefits.
☐ No change in benefits, but lower premium.
☐ Fewer benefits and lower premiums.
☐ My plan has outpatient prescription drug coverage and I am enrolling in Part D.
☐ Disenrollment from a Medicare Advantage plan. Please explain reason for disenrollment (optional only for Direct Mailers.)
☐ Other. (please specify) _____

_____

(Signature of producer or other representative)*

_____

(Typed Name and Address of issuer, producer or other representative)

_____

(Applicant's Signature)   (Date)

* Signature not required for direct response sales.

Additional Statements

The notice must include the following statements, except that clauses (A) and (B), applicable to preexisting conditions, may be deleted by an issuer if the replacement does not involve application of a new preexisting condition limitation:

A. If the issuer of the Medicare Supplement policy being applied for does not, or is otherwise prohibited from imposing preexisting condition limitations, please skip to the next statement below. Health conditions which you may presently have (preexisting conditions) may not be immediately or fully covered under the new policy. This could result in denial or delay of a claim for benefits under the new policy, whereas a similar claim might have been payable under your present policy.

B. State law provides that your replacement policy or certificate may not contain new preexisting conditions, waiting periods, elimination periods or probationary periods. The insurer will waive any time periods applicable to preexisting conditions, waiting periods, elimination periods, or probationary periods in the new policy (or coverage) for similar benefits to the extent such time was spent (depleted) under the original policy.

C. If you still wish to terminate your present policy and replace it with new coverage, be certain to truthfully and completely answer all questions on the application concerning your medical and health history. Failure to include all material medical information on an application may provide a basis for the company to deny any future claims and to refund your premium as though your policy had never been in force. After the application has been completed and before you sign it, review it carefully to be certain

VA PPL LH-2_16298

that all information has been properly recorded. (If the policy or certificate is guaranteed issue, this paragraph need not appear.)

   D. Do not cancel your present policy until you have received your new policy and are sure that you want to keep it.

14VAC 5-170-160

Replacement, Preexisting Condition and Waiting Periods

If a Medicare Supplement policy or certificate replaces another Medicare Supplement policy or certificate, the replacing issuer must waive time periods applicable to preexisting conditions, waiting periods, elimination periods and probationary periods in the new Medicare Supplement policy or certificate for similar benefits to the extent the time was spent under the original policy.

If a Medicare Supplement policy or certificate replaces another Medicare Supplement policy or certificate which has been in effect for at least 6 months, the replacing policy may not provide a time period applicable to preexisting conditions, waiting periods, elimination periods and probationary periods for benefits.

Virginia Medicare Supplement Policy Minimum Benefit Standards

A Medicare Supplement policy will not be approved by the Department of Insurance unless at least the following provisions and benefits are in the policy:

   • A Medicare Supplement policy may not exclude losses incurred more than six months from the effective date of coverage for a preexisting condition. The policy may not define a preexisting condition more restrictively than a condition for which medical advice was given or treatment was recommended by or received from a physician within six months prior to the effective date of coverage.
   • The policy may not cover against losses resulting from sickness on a different basis than losses resulting from accidents.
   • The policy must provide that benefits designed to cover cost sharing amounts under

Medicare are changed automatically to coincide with any changes in the applicable Medicare deductible amount and copayment percentage factors. Premiums may be changed to correspond with such changes.
   • The policy must provide for termination of coverage of a spouse solely because of the occurrence of an event specified for termination of coverage of the insured, other than the nonpayment of premium.
   • The policy must be guaranteed renewable; the insurer is prohibited from cancelling or nonrenewing the policy based solely on health status and may not cancel or nonrenew a policy for any reason other than nonpayment of premium or material misrepresentation.
   • If the policy is terminated by a group policyholder and not replaced by the policyholder, the issuer must offer certificateholders an individual Medicare supplement policy that provides for continuation of benefits contained in the group policy and provides all other benefits as required by the Medicare Supplement insurance laws.
   • If a group certificateholder terminates membership in the group, the insurer must offer the certificateholder the ability to convert to an individual policy or offer to continue the certificateholder's coverage under the group policy.
   • If a group Medicare supplement policy is replaced by another group Medicare supplement policy purchased by the same policyholder, the issuer of the replacement policy must offer coverage to all persons covered under the old group policy on its date of termination. Coverage under the new policy may not result in any exclusion for preexisting conditions that would have been covered under the group policy that was replaced.

Misrepresentation is generally defined as written or oral statements made by the insured, the insurer, or a representative of the insurer, which misstates information regarding the risk, terms, coverages, benefits, returns, or other material fact related to the contract.

VA PPL LH-2_16298

Core Benefits

Every issuer of Medicare supplement insurance benefit plans must make available a policy or certificate including only the following basic core package of benefits to each prospective insured:

- Coverage of Part A Medicare eligible expenses for hospitalization to the extent not covered by Medicare from the 61st day through the 90th day in any Medicare benefit period.
- Coverage of Part A Medicare eligible expenses incurred for hospitalization to the extent not covered by Medicare for each Medicare lifetime inpatient reserve day used.
- Upon exhaustion of the Medicare hospital inpatient coverage, including the lifetime reserve days, coverage of 100% of the Medicare Part A eligible expenses for hospitalization paid at the applicable prospective payment system rate, or other appropriate Medicare standard of payment, subject to a lifetime maximum benefit of an additional 365 days.
- Coverage under Medicare Parts A and B for the reasonable cost of the first three pints of blood.
- Coverage for the coinsurance amount or the copayment amount if applicable, of Medicare eligible expenses under Part B regardless of hospital confinement, subject to the Medicare Part B deductible.
- Coverage of cost sharing for all Part A Medicare eligible hospice care and respite care expenses.

14VAC 5-170-75

Required Disclosures

Renewal Provision

Medicare Supplement policies must include a renewal, continuation, or nonrenewal provision that is consistent with the contract to be issued. The provision must be appropriately captioned, appear on the first page of the certificate, and clearly state the *renewability* period and the term of coverage for which the policy is issued.

14VAC 5-170-150

Prohibited Payment Bases

Medicare supplement policies or certificates are prohibited from providing for the payment of benefits based on standards described as "usual and customary," "reasonable and customary" or words of similar import.

14VAC 5-170-150

Preexisting Conditions Limitations

If a Medicare Supplement policy contains any limitations with respect to preexisting conditions, such limitations appear as a separate paragraph of the certificate and be labeled as "Preexisting Condition Limitations."

14VAC 5-170-150

Outline of Coverage

Insurers issuing Medicare Supplement policies must deliver an outline of coverage to the applicant at the time application is made and, except for the direct response policy, an acknowledgment of receipt or certification of delivery of the outline of coverage must be provided to the insurer.

If an outline of coverage was delivered at the time of application and the certificate is issued on a basis which would require revision of the outline, a substitute outline of coverage must accompany the certificate when it is delivered and must contain the following statement, in no less than 12-point type, immediately above the company name:

"NOTICE: Read this outline of coverage carefully. It is not identical to the outline of coverage provided upon application and the coverage originally applied for has not been issued."

14VAC 5-170-150

Signed Acceptance of Riders That Change Coverage

Riders or endorsements added to a Medicare Supplement policy after the date of issue or at reinstatement or renewal which reduce or eliminate benefits or coverage in the policy require a signed acceptance by the insured, except for riders or endorsements:

- made at the request of the insured, that exercise a specifically reserved right under a Medicare Supplement policy; or
- that are required to avoid duplication of Medicare benefits.

A rider or endorsement which increases benefits or coverage and increases premium must be agreed to in writing signed by the insured, unless:

- the benefits are required by the minimum standards for Medicare Supplement policies; or
- the increased benefits are required by law.

14VAC 5-170-150

Right to Return Notice

Medicare supplement policies and certificates must have a notice prominently printed on the first page of the policy or certificate or attached to it that states in substance that the policyholder or certificateholder have the right to return the policy or certificate within 30 days of its delivery and to have all premiums made for the policy refunded if, after examination of the policy or certificate, the insured person is not satisfied for any reason.

14VAC 5-170-150

Medicare Supplement Buyer's Guide

Insurers issuing accident and health policies delivered or issued for delivery in Virginia which provide hospital or medical expense coverage to a person eligible for Medicare by reason of age, must provide a Medicare Supplement buyer's guide, *Guide to Health Insurance for People with Medicare.* Delivery of the buyer's guide must be made whether or not the policy qualifies as a Medicare Supplement policy. Except in the case of direct response insurers, delivery of the buyer's guide must be made at the time of application, and acknowledgment of receipt of certification of delivery of the buyer's guide must be provided to the insurer. Direct response insurers issuing Medicare Supplement policies must deliver the buyer's guide upon request, but not later than at the time the policy is delivered.

14VAC 5-170-150

Coverage Modification Notice

No later than 30 days prior to the annual effective date of Medicare benefit changes, a Medigap policy issuer must notify its policyholders and certificateholders of modifications it has made to Medicare Supplement insurance policies or certificates. The notice must:

- include a description of revisions to the Medicare Program and a description of each modification made to the coverage.
- inform each policyholder or certificateholder when a premium adjustment will be made due to changes in Medicare.

14VAC5-170-150

Outline of Coverage Contents

The required outline of coverage consists of four parts:

1. a cover page;
2. premium information;
3. disclosure pages; and
4. charts displaying the features of each benefit plan offered by the issuer.

Disclosure of All Medicare Supplement Plans

All Medicare Supplement plans must be shown on the cover page, and the plans that are offered by the issuer must be prominently identified. Premium information for plans that are offered must be shown on the cover page or immediately following and be prominently displayed. The premium and mode must be stated for all plans that are offered to the prospective applicant. All possible premiums for the prospective applicant must be illustrated.

The following items and notices must be included in the outline of coverage, in this order:

1. PREMIUM INFORMATION

    We (insert issuer's name) can only raise your premium if we raise the premium for all policies like yours in this Commonwealth. [If the premium is based on attained age of the insured, include the following information:

    1. When premiums will change;
    2. The current premium for all ages;
    3. A statement that premiums for other Medicare Supplement policies that are issue age or community rated do not increase due to changes in your age; and
    4. A statement that while the cost of this policy at the covered individual's present age may be lower than the cost of a Medicare supplement policy that is based on issue age or community rated, it is important to compare the potential cost of these policies over the life of the policy.].)

VA PPL LH-2_16298

2. DISCLOSURES

   Use this outline to compare benefits and premiums among policies.

3. READ YOUR POLICY VERY CAREFULLY

   This is only an outline describing your policy's most important features. The policy is your insurance contract. You must read the policy itself to understand all of the rights and duties of both you and your insurance company.

4. RIGHT TO RETURN POLICY

   If you find that you are not satisfied with your policy, you may return it to (insert issuer's address). If you send the policy back to us within 30 days after you receive it, we will treat the policy as if it had never been issued and return all of your payments.

5. POLICY REPLACEMENT

   If you are replacing another health insurance policy, do NOT cancel it until you have actually received your new policy and are sure you want to keep it.

6. NOTICE

   This policy may not fully cover all of your medical costs. Neither [the insurance company] nor its producers are connected with Medicare.

   This outline of coverage does not give all the details of Medicare coverage. Contact your local Social Security Office or consult "Medicare and You" for more details.

7. COMPLETE ANSWERS ARE VERY IMPORTANT

   When you fill out the application for the new policy, be sure to answer truthfully and completely all questions about your medical and health history. The company may cancel your policy and refuse to pay any claims if you leave out or falsify important medical information.

Review the application carefully before you sign it. Be certain that all information has been properly recorded.

[Include for each plan prominently identified in the cover page, a chart showing the services, Medicare payments, plan payments and insured payments for each plan, using the same language, in the same order, using uniform layout and format as shown in the charts below. No more than four plans may be shown on one chart. For purposes of illustration, charts for each plan are included in this regulation. An issuer may use additional benefit plan designations on these charts pursuant to *14VAC5-170-85*.]

[Include an explanation of any innovative benefits on the cover page and in the chart, in a manner approved by the State Corporation Commission.] *14VAC 5-170-150*

Permitted Compensation Arrangements

Compensation for the sale of a Medicare Supplement policy or certificate may not have a 1st-year commission or other compensation greater than 200% of the commission or compensation paid for selling or servicing the policy or certificate in the 2nd year or period.

The commission or compensation provided in renewal years must be the same as that provided in the 2nd year or period and must be provided for no fewer than 5 renewal years.

If an existing policy or certificate is replaced, an issuer or other entity may not provide compensation to its producers or its other representatives and a producer may not receive compensation greater than the renewal compensation payable by the replacing issuer on renewal policies or certificates. *14VAC 5-170-140*

Guaranteed Issue

Generally, persons eligible for Medicare due to age are those who are eligible for Medicare Supplement policies.

With respect to eligible persons, a Medigap issuer may not:

- Deny or condition the issuance or effectiveness of a Medicare Supplement policy that is offered and is available for issuance to new enrollees by the issuer.
- Discriminate in the pricing of a Medicare Supplement policy because of health status, claims experience, receipt of health care or medical condition.

- Impose an exclusion of benefits based on a preexisting condition under a Medicare Supplement policy.

14VAC 5-170-105

Virginia Long-Term Care Insurance Laws

Virginia's Long-Term Care Insurance Act is found in the Virginia Code §38.2-5200 through 5210. Regulations for Virginia long-term care insurance are found in 14VAC 5-170 to 201.

Long-Term Care Insurance Definition

The definition of long-term care insurance in the Virginia Long-Term Care Insurance Act is as follows:

"Long-term care insurance means any insurance policy or rider advertised, marketed, offered or designed to provide coverage for not less than twelve consecutive months for each covered person on an expense incurred, indemnity, prepaid, or other basis, for one or more necessary or medically necessary diagnostic, preventive, therapeutic, rehabilitative, maintenance, personal care, mental health or substance abuse services, provided in a setting other than an acute care unit of a hospital. Such term includes group and individual annuities and life insurance policies or riders that provide directly or that supplement long-term care insurance. Such term shall also include qualified long-term insurance contracts. Long-term care insurance may be issued by insurers, fraternal benefit societies, health services plans, health maintenance organizations, cooperative nonprofit life benefit companies or mutual assessment life, accident and sickness insurers to the extent they are otherwise authorized to issue life or accident and sickness insurance. Health maintenance organizations, cooperative nonprofit life benefit companies and mutual assessment life, accident and sickness insurers may apply to the Commission for approval to provide long-term care insurance." [The "Commission" is the Virginia State Corporation Commission. The Bureau of Insurance is under the auspices of the Corporation Commission.]

VA Code §38.2-5200

The definition refers to acute care. Generally, long-term care is needed for chronic conditions as opposed to acute conditions. *Acute conditions* include short term illness or injury which develop rapidly and require intense treatment, such as X-rays or surgery. *Chronic conditions* are long-term or permanent illnesses or conditions such as permanent damage from a stroke or progressively worsening conditions such as diabetes.

Preexisting Conditions Definition

Virginia's definition of preexisting condition in its Long-Term Care Act is the standard for the most restrictive definition that may be used for preexisting conditions in a long-term care insurance policy issued in Virginia. The language defining preexisting condition under Virginia's Act is:

"No long-term care insurance policy or certificate shall use a definition of 'preexisting condition' which is more restrictive than the following: 'preexisting condition' means the existence of symptoms which would cause an ordinary prudent person to seek diagnosis, care or treatment, or a condition for which medical advice or treatment was recommended by, or received from a provider of health care services, within six months preceding the effective date of coverage of an insured person."

Notice that Virginia's Code uses the standard that a preexisting condition may be one that is evidenced by symptoms for which an "ordinary prudent person" would "seek diagnosis, care or treatment. "

VA Code §38.2-5204

Refund of Premium

The Virginia Long-Term Care Insurance Act provides that premium must be returned on a pro-rata basis if a long-term care insurance policy is terminated:

"**§38.2-5202.1. Refund of premium for cancellation or termination of policy.**

"A. Each individual long-term care insurance policy or certificate shall provide for refund of premium in the event of cancellation or termination of coverage. In the event that the policy or certificate is cancelled by the insurer or terminated by the insured, the insurer must, within thirty days of the effective date of such cancellation or termination, return to the insured the unearned portion of any premium paid. The earned premium must be computed on a pro rata basis.

"B. The requirements of this section shall apply to all individual long-term care insurance policies, contracts, and plans delivered, issued for delivery, reissued, renewed, or extended or at any time when any term of any such policy, contract, or plan is changed or any premium adjustment is made. The requirements of this section shall apply to neither group long-term care insurance nor to any individual long-term care insurance policy, contract or plan providing coverage for the duration of the insured's life if the premium for the coverage is paid in a single installment payment."

Prohibited Provisions in Long-Term Care Insurance Contracts

The prohibited provisions for long-term care insurance contracts issued for delivery in Virginia include that no long-term care insurance policy may:

- Be cancelled, nonrenewed, or otherwise terminated on the grounds of the age or the deterioration of the mental or physical health of the insured individual or certificateholder;
- Contain a provision establishing any new waiting period in the event existing coverage is converted to or replaced by a new or other form within the same company, except with respect to an increase in benefits voluntarily selected by the insured individual or group policyholder;
- Provide coverage for skilled nursing care only or provide significantly more coverage for skilled care in a facility than coverage for lower levels of care;
- Be issued based on medical or health status when the policy is issued by an agent or third-party administrator pursuant to the underwriting authority granted to the agent or third-party administrator by the insurer; or
- Provide that an insurer who has paid benefits under a long-term care insurance policy or

certificate may recover the benefit payments in the event that the policy or certificate is rescinded.

VA Code §38.2-5203

Limitations and Exclusions

The only limitations and exclusions to coverage allowed in a long-term care policy are:

1. Preexisting conditions or diseases.
2. Mental or nervous disorders; however, this does not permit exclusion or limitation of benefits on the basis of Alzheimer's disease, senile dementia, organic brain disorder or other similar diagnosis.
3. Alcoholism and drug addiction.
4. Illness, treatment or medical condition arising out of any of the following:
   a. War or act of war (whether declared or undeclared);
   b. Participation in a felony, riot or insurrection;
   c. Service in the armed forces or units auxiliary threats;
   d. Suicide (sane or insane), attempted suicide or intentionally self-inflicted injury;
   e. Aviation (this exclusion applies only to nonfare-paying passengers).
5. Treatment provided in a government facility (unless a charge is made and the insured is legally obligated to pay), services for which benefits are available under Medicare or other governmental program except Medicaid, a state or Federal workers' compensation, employer's liability or occupational disease law or services provided by a member of the covered person's immediate family and services for which no charge is normally made in the absence of insurance.
6. Expenses for services or items available or paid under another long-term care insurance or health insurance policy.
7. In the case of a qualified long-term care insurance contract, expenses for services or items to the extent that the expenses are reimbursable under Title XVIII of the Social Security Act (Medicare) or would be so reimbursable but for the application of a deductible or coinsurance amount.

14VAC 5-200-60

Prior Hospitalization

Virginia's Long-Term Care Insurance Act and Administrative Code includes provisions pertaining to the prohibition against prior hospitalization or institutionalization before the payment of certain benefits. Virginia's Long-Term Care Act states the following:

"§ 38.2-5205. Prior institutionalization.

"No long-term care insurance policy may be delivered or issued for delivery in this Commonwealth if such policy conditions eligibility (i) for any benefits provided in an institutional care setting on the receipt of a higher level of institutional care or (ii) for any benefits on a prior hospitalization requirement."

The Administrative Code adds the following regulations:

"Prior hospitalization. In addition to the provisions of §38.2-5205 of the Code of Virginia, no long-term care insurance policy may be delivered or issued for delivery in the Commonwealth if the policy conditions eligibility for any benefits other than waiver of premium, post-confinement, post-acute care or recuperative benefits on a prior institutionalization requirement.

"A long-term care insurance policy containing a benefit advertised, marketed or offered as a home health care or home care benefit may not condition receipt of benefits on a prior institutionalization requirement."

14VAC 5-200-60

Required Disclosure of Rating Practices

Insurers must provide notice of an upcoming premium rate schedule increase to all policyholders or certificateholders, if applicable, at least **60 days** prior to the implementation of the premium rate schedule increase by the insurer for the policyholder or certificateholder.

14VAC 5-200-75

Post-Claims Underwriting Notice

Virginia's Administrative Code, in 14 VAC 5-200-80 dealing with the prohibition against post-claims underwriting, requires that the following language, or language substantially similar to the following, be set out conspicuously, in bold face type, on the long-term insurance policy or certificate at the time of delivery:

Caution: This policy may not apply when you have a claim! Please read! The issuance of this long-term care insurance [policy] [certificate] **is based upon your responses to the questions on your** [application] [enrollment form]. **A copy of your** [application][enrollment form][is enclosed] [was retained by you when you applied]. **If your answers are incorrect or untrue, the company has the right to deny benefits or rescind your** [policy] [certificate]. **The best time to clear up any questions is now, before a claim arises! If, for any reason, any of your answers are incorrect, contact the company at this address:** [insert address].

Increasing Benefits Disclosure in Outline of Coverage

The Virginia Administrative Code requires that insurers include the following information in or with the Outline of Coverage:

1. A graphic comparison of the benefit levels of a policy that increases benefits over the policy period with a policy that does not increase benefits. The graphic comparison must show benefit levels over at least a 20-year period.
2. Any expected premium increases or additional premiums to pay for automatic or optional benefit increases. If premium increases or additional premiums will be based on the attained age of the applicant at the time of the increase, the insurer will also disclose the magnitude of the potential premiums the applicant would need to pay at ages 75 and 85 for benefit increases. An insurer may use a reasonable hypothetical, or a graphic demonstration, for the purposes of this disclosure.

14VAC 5-200-100

Policies with a Fixed or Limited Premium Paying Period

Under the following circumstances, a contingent benefit on lapse must be triggered for policies with a fixed or limited premium-paying period:

1. An insurer increases the premium rates to a level that results in a cumulative increase of

VA PPL LH-2_16298

the annual premium equal to or exceeding the percentage of the insured's initial annual premium as described in the table below;

2. the policy or certificate lapses within 120 days of the due date of the premium that was increased;

3. the ratio of the number of completed months of paid premiums divided by the number of months in the premium-paying period is 40% or more. *For example, the insured has paid premiums for 60 months and the premium-paying period is 120 months. This results in a ratio of 50%, meaning this ratio meets the qualifications for requiring a contingent benefit on lapse for a fixed or limited premium-paying period long-term care policy.*

The table that triggers the contingent benefit on lapse for a fixed or limited premium-paying policy is as follows:

Triggers for a Substantial Premium Increase

Issue Age	Percent Increase Over Initial Premium
Under 65	50%
65-80	30%
Over 80	10%

Contingent Benefit on Lapse for a Fixed or Limited Premium-Paying Policy

The insurer offering a contingent benefit on lapse for a fixed or limited premium-paying policy must, on or before the effective date of a substantial premium increase:

- offer to reduce policy benefits provided by the current coverage without the requirement of additional underwriting so that required premium payments are not increased;
- offer to convert the coverage to a paid-up status where the amount payable for each benefit is 90% of the amount payable in effect immediately prior to lapse times the ratio of the number of completed months of paid premiums divided by the number of months in the premium paying period. This option may be elected at any time during the 120-day period from the due date of the premium that was increased;
- notify the policyholder or certificateholder that a default or lapse at any time during the 120-day period is deemed to be the election of the offer to convert the policy to a paid-up

status, if the ratio of completed months of paid premiums to the number of months in the premium-paying period is 40% or more.
14VAC 5-200-185

Potential Rate Increase Disclosure Form

Insurers in Virginia must provide long-term care applicants with a Potential Rate Increase Disclosure Form. If the policy is a fixed or limited premium-paying period policy, the disclosure must include the contingent benefit on lapse information applicable to these policies. The content of the disclosure is as follows:

Long-Term Care Insurance Potential Rate Increase Disclosure Form

1. **[Premium Rate] [Premium Rate Schedules]:** [Premium rate] [Premium rate schedules] that [is] [are] applicable to you and that will be in effect until a request is made and [filed] [approved] for an increase [is] [are] [on the application] [$])

2. The [premium] [premium rate schedule] for this policy [will be shown on the schedule page of] [will be attached to] your policy.

3. **Rate Schedule Adjustments:** The company will provide a description of when premium rate or rate schedule adjustments will be effective (e.g., next anniversary date, next billing date, etc.) (fill in the blank):

_____.

4. **Potential Rate Revisions:** This policy **is Guaranteed Renewable**. This means that the rates for this product may be increased in the future. Your rates can **NOT** be increased due to your increasing age or declining health, but your rates may go up based on the experience of all policyholders with a policy similar to yours.

If you receive a premium rate or premium rate schedule increase in the future, you will be notified of the new premium amount and you will be able to exercise at least one of the following options:

- Pay the increased premium and continue your policy in force as is.
- Reduce your policy benefits to a level such that your premiums will not increase. (Subject to state law minimum standards.)

 VA PPL LH-2_16298

- Exercise your nonforfeiture option if purchased. (This option is available for purchase for an additional premium.)
- Exercise your contingent nonforfeiture rights. (This option may be available if you do not purchase a separate nonforfeiture option.)

Availability of New Services or Providers

Long-term care insurers are generally required to notify policyholders of the availability of a new long-term care insurance policy series that provides coverage for new long-term care services or providers, is material in nature, and has not been previously available through the insurer to the general public. This notice is required to be provided within 12 months of the date the new policy series is made available for sale in Virginia. Excepted from this notice requirement are policyholders or certificateholders who are currently eligible for benefits within an elimination period or on a claim, who previously had been in claim status, or who would not be eligible to apply for coverage due to issue age limitations under the policy.

An insurer with a new policy series may require that policyholders or certificateholders meet all eligibility requirements, including underwriting and payment of the premium, to add the new services or providers.

Making Coverage Available

An insurer may make the new coverage available:

1. By adding a rider to the existing policy and charging a separate premium for the new rider based on the insured's attained age;
2. By exchanging the existing policy or certificate for one with an issue age based on the present age of the insured and recognizing past insured status by granting premium credits toward the premiums for the new policy or certificate;
3. By exchanging the existing policy or certificate for a new policy or certificate in which consideration for past insured status will be recognized by granting premium credits for the new policy or certificate at the issue age of the policy or certificate being exchanged; or

4. By an alternative program developed by the insurer that meets the intent of the regulation, if the program is filed and approved by the Commissioner.

Limited Distribution of New Policies

If a new proprietary policy series is created and filed for use in a limited distribution channel, the insurer is not required to notify policyholders or certificateholders. *For example, ABC Insurance developed a long-term care policy offered to scuba diver. ABC Insurance does not have to notify policyholders in the state of this new long-term care contract, since it's for a limited distribution channel.* However, if a new policy is developed for that same limited distribution channel that has material new coverage, the policyholders or certificateholders in that distribution channel must be notified. *For example, ABC Insurance developed a new policy for scuba divers that included expanded home health care coverage benefits. It must notify all policyholders or certificateholders in Virginia of this new policy offering.*

Exchanges

If a new policy is issued under this regulation to provide new services or providers to an existing policyholder, it is considered an exchange, not a replacement, so the replacement regulations do not apply to the transaction.

Right to Purchase New Benefits

An insurer may offer any policy, rider, certificate or coverage change to any policyholder or certificateholder; an offer does not just have to be made in the case of the issuing of a new policy series.

Any policyholder or certificateholder may apply for currently available coverage that includes the new services or providers.

This regulation does not apply to life insurance policies or riders containing accelerated death benefit long-term care benefits.

Notification of Group Certificateholders

If a policy is offered through an employer, labor organization, professional, trade or occupational association, the required notification of the new service or provider is made to the offering entity, e.g., the employer or labor organization. However, if the policy is issued to a certain groups the Commission approves as purchasers of long-term care insurance, the notification is made to each certificateholder.

14VAC 5-200-181

Right to Reduce Coverage and Lower Premium

Virginia's long-term care regulations were amended to add a new right to policyholders that became effective as of September 1, 2007. All long-term care insurance policies and certificates must include a provision that allows the policyholder or certificateholder to reduce coverage and lower the policy or certificate premium in at least one of the following ways:

1. Reducing the maximum benefit; or
2. Reducing the daily, weekly or monthly benefit amount.

For example, the insured has a policy with a $153,300 maximum pool of money benefit amount. It pays a daily benefit for its covered services of $140 on an actual cost of care basis for three years. The insured has the option to reduce the maximum daily benefit on the policy to $110, which, if no benefits have been paid out at the time of the daily benefit reduction, also reduces the pool of money maximum benefit to $120,450. The insured is given a reduced premium by reducing the benefit.

An insurer may also offer other reduction options that are consistent with the policy or certificate design or the carrier's administrative processes. The age used to determine the premium for the reduced coverage is based on the age used to determine the premiums for the coverage currently in force.

The provision must include a description of the ways in which coverage is reduced and also the process for requesting and implementing a reduction in coverage.

An insurer may limit any reduction in coverage to plans or options available for the policy form and to those for which benefits will be available after consideration of claims paid or claims payable.

This right must be included in the notice of lapse that must be provided to insureds at least 30 days before the effective date of a lapse or termination.

This right does not apply to life insurance policies or riders containing accelerated long-term care benefits.

14VAC 5-200-183

Virginia Long-Term Care Partnership Act

The Virginia Administrative Code was amended in September 2007 to incorporate regulations applicable to Long-Term Care Partnership policies. These regulations are found in *14 VAC 5-200-205.*

Virginia Resident

The policy must be issued to a person who was a Virginia resident at the time coverage became effective in order to be recognized as a Partnership policy in Virginia.

Qualified Long-Term Care Contract

Partnership policies must be qualified long-term care insurance contracts, as defined in Internal Revenue Code Section 7702B(b).

Date of Issue

To be a Partnership policy in Virginia, the policy cannot have been issued prior to September 1, 2007.

Compliance with DRA Consumer Protection Provision Requirements

Partnership policies must comply with all the NAIC Model Act and Regulation consumer protection provisions as required in the Deficit Reduction Act.

Inflation Protection

The inflation protection provisions required in Long-Term Care Partnership policies are as follows:

- If the Partnership policy is sold to an individual who has not attained age 61 as of the date of purchase, the policy must provide an inflation protection feature at least equivalent to the following:
  - Increases benefit levels annually, in a manner so that the increases are compounded annually, at a rate not less than 5.0%;
  - Guarantees the insured individual the right to periodically increase benefit levels without providing evidence of insurability or health status, as long as the offer to

increase from the previous period has not declined. The amount of the additional benefit may be no less than the difference between the existing policy benefit and a benefit compounded annually at a rate of at least 5.0% for the period beginning with the purchase of the existing benefit and extending until the year in which the offer is made; or

- Covers a specified percentage of actual or reasonable charges and does not include a maximum specified indemnity amount or limit.
- If the Partnership policy is sold to an individual who has attained age 61, but has not attained age 76 as of the date of purchase, the policy must also provide inflation protection at least equal to that offered to those under age 61.
- If the Partnership policy is sold to an individual who has attained age 76 as of the date of purchase, the policy must also offer at least the same inflation protection as offered to those under 61, and may offer other inflation protection provisions as well.

The Virginia requirement that Partnership policies offer inflation protection apply to all long-term care insurance policies offered in Virginia. All long-term care insurance applicants must be offered inflation protection.

Notice Before Lapse or Termination

All individual long-term care policies or certificates may only be issued after the insured has received from the applicant either:

- a written designation of at least one person, in addition to the applicant, who is to receive notice of lapse or termination of the policy or certificate for nonpayment of premium, or
- a written waiver dated and signed by the applicant electing not to designate additional persons to receive notice.

Designating Another Receiver of Notice

The applicant has the right to designate at least one person who is to receive the notice of termination, in addition to the applicant/insured. The designation does not constitute acceptance of liability on the third party for services provided to the insured. The form used to make the written designation provides space to name at least one additional person, including full name and home address.

If the applicant/insured decides not to designate another person to receive notice, he or she must sign a waiver that states:

"Protection against unintentional lapse. I understand that I have the right to designate at least one person other than myself to receive notice of lapse or termination of this long-term care insurance policy for nonpayment of premiums. I understand that notice will not be given until 30 days after a premium is due and unpaid. I elect not to designate a person to receive this notice."

The insured must have the ability to change the written designation at any time. The insurer must notify the insured of the right to change the written designation, at least once every two years.

Requirements for Notice for Policies Paid for Through a Deduction Plan

When a policy or certificate holder pays premium for a long-term care insurance contract through a payroll or pension deduction plan, the notice does not have to be provided until 60 days after the policyholder or certificateholder is not on the payment plan.

Lapse or Termination for Nonpayment of Premium

A long-term care contract or certificate may not lapse or be terminated for nonpayment of premium unless the insurer gives notice at least 30 days before the effective date of the lapse or termination for the insured and the designated person or persons. Notice may not be given until 30 days after premiums are due and unpaid. The notice is deemed to have been given as of five days after the date of mailing.

For example, Marna has a long-term care contract for which she pays her premium on a quarterly basis. She neglected to pay the premium due on June 30. Her contract will lapse due to this nonpayment. Her insurer must not send her notice before July 30, and if it sends notice then, the policy may not lapse until September 5.

Reinstatement

Long-term care contracts must also include a provision that allows for reinstatement of coverage in the event of lapse if the insurer is provided proof that the policyholder or certificateholder was cognitively impaired or had a loss of functional capacity before the grace period contained in the policy expired. The insured must be able to reinstate the policy under these conditions if requested within five months after termination. The insurer has the right to collect the past due premium, when functional capacity may not be more stringent than the benefit eligibility criteria or cognitive impairment or the loss of functional capacity contained in the policy and certificate.

Provision of Partnership Program Notice

Partnership policy insurers must provide the Notice Regarding Long-Term Care Insurance Partnership Status to the insured at the issuance of a policy intended to be a Partnership policy. It must be provided with the Outline of Coverage.

The Notice is labeled as Form 200-A and is as follows:

Partnership Program Notice

Important Consumer Information regarding the Virginia Long Term Care Insurance Partnership Program

Some long-term care insurance policies [certificates] sold in Virginia may qualify for the Virginia Long Term Care Insurance Partnership Program (the Partnership Program). The Partnership Program is a partnership between state government and private insurance companies to assist individuals in planning their long term care needs. Insurance companies voluntarily agree to participate in the Partnership Program by offering long term care insurance coverage that meets certain sate and federal requirements. Long Term care insurance policies [certificates] that qualify as partnership policies [certificates] may protect the policyholder's [certificateholder's] assets through a feature known as "asset disregard" under Virginia's Medicaid Program.

Asset Disregard means that an amount of the policyholder's [certificateholder's] assets equal to the amount of long term care insurance benefits received under a qualified Partnership Policy [Certificate] will be disregarded for the purpose of determining the insured's eligibility for Medicaid. This generally allows a person to keep assets equal to the insurance benefits received under a qualified Partnership Policy [Certificate] without affecting the person's eligibility for Medicaid. All of the Medicaid eligibility criteria will apply and special rules may apply to persons whose home equity exceeds $500,000. Asset Disregard is **not** available under a long term care insurance policy [certificate] that is not a Partnership

Policy [Certificate]. Therefore, you should consider if Asset Disregard is important to you, and whether a Partnership Policy meets your needs. **The purchase of a Partnership Policy does not automatically qualify you for Medicaid.**

What are the Requirements for a Partnership Policy [Certificate]? In order for a policy [certificate] to qualify as a Partnership Policy [Certificate], it must, among other requirements:

1. Be issued to an individual after September, 2007;
2. Cover an individual who was a Commonwealth of Virginia resident when coverage first becomes effective under the policy;
3. Be a tax-qualified policy under Section 7702(B)(b) of the Internal Revenue Code of 1986;
4. Meet stringent consumer protection standards; and
5. Meet the following inflation protection requirements:

For ages 60 or younger – provides compound annual inflation protection

For ages 61 to 75 – provides some level of inflation protection

For ages 76 and older – no purchase of inflation protection is required

If you apply and are approved for long term care insurance coverage, [carrier name] will provide you with written documentation as to whether or not your policy [certificate] qualifies as a Partnership Policy [Certificate].

What Could Disqualify a Policy [Certificate] as a Partnership Policy? Certain types of changes to a Partnership Policy [Certificate] could affect whether or not such policy [certificate] continues to be a Partnership Policy [Certificate]. If you purchase a Partnership Policy [Certificate] and later decide to make any changes, you should first consult with [carrier name] to determine the effect of a proposed change. In addition, if you move to a state that does not maintain a Partnership Program or does not recognize your policy [certificate] as a Partnership Policy [Certificate], you would not receive beneficial treatment of your policy [certificate] under the Medicaid program of that state. The information contained in this disclosure is based on current Virginia and Federal law. These laws may be subject to change. Any change in law could reduce or eliminate the beneficial treatment of your policy [certificate] under Virginia's Medicaid Program.

Additional Information. If you have questions regarding long term care insurance policies [certificates] please contact [carrier name]. If you have questions regarding current laws governing Medicaid eligibility, you should contact the Virginia Department of Medical Assistance Services.

Partnership Disclosure Notice

A Partnership policy issued or issued for delivery in the Commonwealth of Virginia must include a Partnership Disclosure Notice (Form 200-B). This notice explains the benefits associated with a Partnership policy and indicates that at the time issued, the policy is a qualified state long-term care insurance Partnership policy. The notice also includes a statement that by purchasing the Partnership policy, the insured does not automatically qualify for Medicaid.

A similar notice to the one below may be used by the insurer if the form is filed and approved by the Commission.

Important Information Regarding Your Policy's [Certificate's] Long Term Care Insurance Partnership Status

NOTE: Please keep this Notice with Your Long Term Care Insurance Policy.

Partnership Policy [Certificate] Status. Your long-term care insurance policy [certificate] is intended to qualify as a Partnership Policy [Certificate] under the Virginia Long-Term Care Partnership Program as of your Policy's [Certificate's] effective date.

The long-term care insurance policy [certificate] recently purchased and enclosed qualifies for the Virginia Long Term Care Insurance Partnership Program. Insurance companies voluntarily agree to participate in the Partnership Program by offering long term care insurance coverage that meets certain state and federal requirements. Long Term Care Insurance Policies [Certificates] that qualify as Partnership Policies [Certificates] may protect your assets through a feature known as "Asset Disregard" under Virginia's Medicaid Program.

Asset Disregard means that an amount of the policyholder's [certificateholder's] asset equal to the amount of long term care insurance benefits received under a qualified Partnership Policy [Certificate] will be disregarded for the purpose of determining the insured's eligibility for Medicaid. This generally allows a person to keep assets equal to the insurance benefits received under a qualified Partnership Policy [Certificate] without affecting the person's eligibility for Medicaid. All other Medicaid eligibility criteria will apply and special rules may apply to persons whose home equity exceeds $500,000. **In addition, the purchase of this Partnership Policy does not automatically qualify you for Medicaid.**

What Could Disqualify Your Policy [Certificate] as a Partnership Policy? If you make any changes to your policy [certificate], such changes could affect whether your policy [certificate] continues to be a Partnership Policy [Certificate]. ***Before you make any changes, you should consult with [carrier name] to determine the effect of a proposed change.*** In addition, if you move to a state that does not maintain a Partnership Program or does not recognize your policy [certificate] as a Partnership Policy [Certificate], you would not receive beneficial treatment of your policy [certificate] under the Medicaid program of that state. The information contained in this disclosure is based on current Virginia and Federal law. These laws may be subject to change. Any change in law could reduce or eliminate the beneficial treatment of your policy [certificate] under Virginia's Medicaid Program.

Additional Information. If you have questions regarding long term care insurance policies [certificates] please contact [carrier name]. If you have questions regarding current laws governing Medicaid eligibility, you should contact the Virginia Department of Medical Assistance.

Commissioner Certification of Policy

The DRA requires that a plan amendment be filed for the state's Medicaid program that states that the Commissioner certifies that policies meet the specified consumer protection requirements of the NAIC Long-Term Care Model Act and Regulation. In compliance with this DRA provision, it is required for an insurer to complete a Partnership Certification Form (Form 200-C) that certifies that the policy meets the consumer protection provisions required for Partnership policies in the DRA.

An insurer who requests that a previously approved policy be approved as a qualified state long-term care Partnership policy must submit to the Commission a Partnership Certification Form signed by an officer of the company. A copy of the policy or certificate form must also be submitted, along with the approval date and a bookmark for each of the requirements listed in the form.

Partnership Policy Training Requirements

Insurers who offer Partnership policies must obtain verification that an agent has received required training before the agent is permitted to sell, solicit or negotiate the insurer's Partnership policy.

Agents must undergo an initial training of not less than 8 hours and ongoing training every 24 months thereafter of not less than 4 hours. The training must consist of topics related to long-term care insurance, long-term care services, and qualified state long-term care insurance Partnership programs, including, but not limited to:

- State and federal regulations and requirements and the relationship between qualified state long-term care insurance Partnership programs and other public and private coverage of long-term care services, including Medicaid;
- Available long-term care services and providers;
- Changes or improvements in long-term care services or providers;
- Alternatives to the purchase of private long-term care insurance;
- The effect of inflation on benefits and the importance of inflation protection; and
- Consumer suitability standards and guidelines.

Insurers must maintain records with respect to the training of its agents qualified to sell, solicit or negotiate Partnership policies, to include training received and that the agent has demonstrated an understanding of the Partnership policies and their relationship to public and private coverage of long-term care, including Medicaid, in Virginia. The insurer must maintain these records for a period of not less than five years and must make them available to the Commission upon request.

Reporting to Department of Health and Human Services

Each insurer who issues a Partnership policy must provide regular reports to the Secretary of Health and Human Services in accordance with regulations of the Secretary that include notification of the date benefits were paid, the amount paid, the date the policy terminates, and other information as the Secretary determines may be appropriate to the administration of Partnerships.

Advertising

Virginia insurance regulations in 14VAC 5-90 govern advertising of accident and sickness insurance intended for presentation, distribution or dissemination in Virginia when made by or on behalf of an insurer or insurance agent. Insurers must establish and maintain a system of control over the content, form and method of dissemination of all advertisements of its policies. All advertisements, regardless of by whom written, created, designed or presented, are the responsibility of the insurer whose policies are advertised.
14VAC 5-90-20

Advertisements for accident or sickness insurance must be truthful and not misleading in fact or in implication. Words or phrases the meaning of which is clear only by implication or by familiarity with insurance terminology may not be used.

The format and content of a health insurance advertisement must be sufficiently complete and clear to avoid deception or the capacity or tendency to mislead or deceive. Whether an advertisement has a capacity or tendency to mislead or deceive must be determined by the Commission from the overall impression that the advertisement may be reasonably expected to create upon the segment of the public to which it is directed.
14VAC 5-90-50

For the purposes of accident and sickness insurance advertising, advertisement means

- printed and published material, audio visual material, and descriptive literature of an insurer used in direct mail, newspapers, magazines, radio scripts, television scripts, web sites and other Internet displays or communications, other forms of electronic communications, billboards, and similar displays;
- descriptive literature and sales aids of all kinds issued by an insurer or agent for presentation to the insurance-buying public, including but not limited to circulars, leaflets, booklets, depictions, illustrations, and form letters; and
- prepared sales talks, presentations and material for use by agents. The term advertisement does not include:
  - material used in-house by insurers;
  - communications within an insurer's own organization not intended for dissemination to the insurance-buying public; however, to the extent any communications are in fact disseminated to the insurance-buying

public or utilized in a sales presentation to the insurance-buying public, the materials must be considered to fall within the definition of advertising;

- individual communications of a personal nature with current policyholders other than material urging the policyholder to increase, expand, terminate or purchase new coverages;
- correspondence between a prospective group or policyholder and an insurer in the course of negotiating a group contract other than material urging the policyholder to increase or expand coverages;
- court-approved material ordered by a court to be disseminated to policyholders;
- a general announcement from a group policyholder to eligible individuals on an employment or membership list that a contract or program has been written or arranged, provided that the announcement clearly indicates that it is preliminary to the issuance of a booklet and that the announcement does not describe specific benefits under the contract or program nor describe advantages as to the purchase of the contract or program. This does not prohibit a general endorsement of the program by the sponsor;
- electronic communications devoted to electronic business transactions between existing members, providers, employers, and the insurer containing no materials relating to increasing, decreasing, terminating, or expanding coverages; or
- member newsletters or educational material sent to existing members, providers, or employers containing no materials relating to increasing, decreasing, terminating, or expanding coverages.

14VAC 5-90-30

Advertising Covered Benefits

An advertisement of covered benefits is prohibited from omitting information or using words, phrases, statements, references or illustrations if the omission of the information or the using of words, phrases, statements, references or illustrations has the capacity, tendency or effect of misleading or deceiving as to the nature or extent of any policy benefit payable, loss covered or premium payable. Providing a policy for the purchaser's inspection prior to the sale does not relieve the insurer of the requirement to abide by this advertising regulation.

An advertisement of a benefit for which payment is conditioned upon confinement in a hospital or similar facility may not use words or phrases such as:

- tax free;
- extra cash;
- extra income;
- extra pay; or
- substantially similar words or phrases.

These words and phrases are prohibited because they have the capacity, tendency or effect of misleading the public into believing that the policy advertised will, in some way, enable them to make a profit from being hospitalized.

The words and phrases "all", "full", "complete", comprehensive", "unlimited", "up to", "as high as", "this policy will help fill some of the gaps that Medicare and your present insurance leave out", "this policy will replace your income" (when used to express loss of time benefits), or similar words and phrases may not be used to exaggerate any benefit beyond the terms of the policy. However, they may be used to fairly to describe the benefit.

An advertisement of a hospital or other similar facility confinement benefit is prohibited from advertising that the amount of the benefit is payable on a monthly or weekly basis when in fact, the amount of the benefit payable is based upon a daily pro rata basis relating to the number of days of confinement. When the policy contains a limit on the number of days of coverage provided, the limit must appear in the advertisement.

It is unlawful for an advertisement of a direct response insurance product to state or imply that because "no insurance agent will call and no commissions will be paid to agents" that it is "a low cost plan," or use other similar words or phrases because the cost of advertising and servicing the policies is a substantial cost in the marketing by direct response.

A policy covering only one disease or a list of specified diseases may not be advertised to imply coverage beyond the policy's terms. Synonymous terms may not be used to refer to any disease to imply broader coverage than the policy actually possesses.

14VAC 5-90-60

Disclosing Policy Exceptions, Reductions and Limitations

An invitation to contract must disclose exceptions, reductions, and limitations affecting the basic provisions of the policy.

It is unlawful for an advertisement to contain descriptions of a policy exception, reduction, or limitation worded in a positive manner to imply that it is a benefit, such as describing a waiting period as a "benefit builder" or stating "even preexisting conditions are covered after two years." Words and phrases used in advertisements to describe policy limitations, exceptions, and reductions must fairly and accurately describe the negative features of the limitations, exceptions, and reductions.

When an advertisement refers to any dollar amount, period of time for which any benefit is payable, cost of policy, or specific policy benefit or the loss for which the benefit is payable, it must disclose those exceptions, reductions, and limitations affecting policy provisions as necessary to keep the advertisement from being misleading or deceiving.

When a policy contains a waiting, elimination, probationary or similar time period an advertisement must disclose the existence of these periods.

An advertisement may not use the words "only," "just," "merely," "minimum," "necessary," or similar words or phrases to describe the applicability of any exceptions, reductions, limitations, or exclusions, such as stating: "This policy is subject to the following minimum exceptions and reductions."

An advertisement for a policy providing benefits for specified illnesses only, such as cancer, or for specified accidents only, such as automobile accidents, must clearly and conspicuously state in boldface type and all capital letters the limited nature of the policy. The statement must be worded in language identical to, or substantially similar to, the following:

"THIS IS A LIMITED POLICY"; "THIS IS A CANCER ONLY POLICY"

14VAC 5-90-60

Disclosing Preexisting Conditions in Advertisements

An advertisement must, in negative terms, disclose the extent to which any loss is not covered if the cause of the loss is traceable to a condition existing prior to the effective date of the policy. The term "preexisting condition," without an appropriate definition or description, is prohibited from use.

When a policy does **not** cover losses resulting from preexisting conditions, an advertisement may not state or imply that the applicant's physical condition or medical history will not affect the issuance of the policy or payment of a claim under the policy. It is prohibited to use the phrase "no medical examination required" and similar phrases. If an insurer requires a medical examination for a specified policy, the advertisement must disclose that a medical examination is required.

14VAC 5-90-60

Testimonials

Similarly to advertisements for life insurance, any testimonial, appraisal, analysis, or endorsement used in an accident and sickness insurance advertisement must:

- be genuine;
- represent the current opinion of the author;
- be applicable to the policy advertised; and
- be accurately reproduced.

In using testimonials, appraisals, analyses, or endorsements, the insurer or agent makes as its own all the statements contained within them, and these statements are all subject to the advertising regulations found in 14VAC 5-90-10 and following.

Disclosure of Interest in the Insurer

If the individual making a testimonial, appraisal, analysis, or endorsement has a financial interest in the insurer or a related entity as a stockholder, director, officer, employee, or otherwise, that fact must be disclosed in the advertisement.

If an individual receives any financial benefit directly or indirectly, greater than required union scale wages, that fact must be clearly and prominently disclosed in the advertisement by language identical or substantially similar to the following:

Paid Endorsement

14VAC 5-90-80

Use of Statistics

An advertisement relating to the dollar amounts of claims paid, the number of persons insured, or similar statistical information relating to any insurer or policy may not use irrelevant facts, and may not be used unless it accurately reflects all current and relevant facts. The advertisement may not imply that the statistics are derived from the policy advertised unless that is the fact, and when applicable to other policies or plans must specifically so state.

An advertisement must not represent or imply that claim settlements by the insurer are "liberal" or "generous," or similar terms, or that claim settlements will be beyond the actual terms of the contract. An unusual amount paid for a unique claim for the policy advertised is misleading and is prohibited from being used.

The source of any statistics used in an advertisement must be identified in the advertisement.

14VAC 5-90-90

Insurer Identity

The identity of the insurer must be made clear in all of its advertisements. The name of the actual insurer, the form number or numbers of the policies advertised and the form number of any application must be stated on all invitations to contract. An advertisement may not use a trade name, service mark, slogan, symbol, or other device which has the tendency to mislead or deceive as to the true identity of the insurer.

14VAC 5-90-130

Introductory, Initial of Special Offers

An advertisement of an individual policy is prohibited from representing that:

- a contract or combination of contracts is an introductory, initial or special offer;
- applicants will receive substantial advantages not available at a later date; or
- the offer is available only to a specified group of individuals, unless that is the fact.

An advertisement may not contain phrases describing a "time-limited solicitation period" as "special," "limited," or similar words or phrases when the insurer uses the "time-limited solicitation periods" as the usual method of marketing accident and sickness insurance.

A "time-limited solicitation period" advertised for an individual policy may not be offered and opened in Virginia unless there has been at least 4 months since the end of the immediately preceding "time-limited solicitation period" for the same product.

Use of the words "enrollment" or "enrollment period" in connection with a "time-limited solicitation period" is prohibited unless the insurance product offered will be issued automatically as advertised upon receipt of the application and premium by the insurer or its agent.

It is prohibited to use any statement to the effect that only a specific number of policies will be sold, or that a time is fixed for the discontinuance of the sale of the particular policy advertised because of special advantages available in the policy, unless that is the fact.

An advertisement may not offer a policy that utilizes a reduced initial premium rate in a manner that overemphasizes the availability and the amount of the initial reduced premium.

14VAC 5-90-150

Statements Concerning an Insurer

An advertisement may not contain statements which are untrue in fact, or by implication misleading, with respect to the assets, corporate structure, financial standing, age or relative position of the insurer in the insurance business.

It is prohibited for an advertisement to contain a recommendation by any commercial rating system unless it clearly indicates the purpose of the recommendation, the name and a description of the entity through which the rating is obtained, and the limitations of the scope and extent of the recommendation.

14VAC 5-90-160

Advertising File

Each insurer must maintain at its home or principal office a complete file containing:

- every printed, published, or prepared advertisement of individual policies; and
- typical printed, published, or prepared advertisements of blanket, franchise, and group policies.

There must be a note attached to each advertisement that states the manner and extent of distribution and any advertised policy's form number. The file is subject to regular and periodical inspection by the Commission. These documents must be maintained for a period of the longer of 4 years or until the filing of the next regular report on examination of the insurer.

14VAC 5-90-170

Senior Specific and Professional Designations

The Virginia regulations include special protections for senior solicitation. Seniors are particularly vulnerable to certain misleading sales practices and advertising which the regulations identify. Seniors also generally live on fixed incomes so a financial setback is potentially more devastating for them than for younger persons who have the opportunity of rebuilding assets if they are financially harmed. Seniors become more dependent on government and charitable resources if they are bilked of their assets. No consumer should be misled or deceived, but certain regulations are designed to particularly protect seniors from deceptive advertising practices because of their more vulnerable status.

14VAC5-43 contains standards to protect consumers from misleading and fraudulent trade practices with respect to the use of senior-specific certifications and professional designations in the marketing, solicitation, sale or purchase of, or advice made in connection with, a life or accident and sickness insurance or an annuity product. It applies to any marketing, solicitation, sale or purchase of, or advice made in connection with, a life or accident and sickness insurance policy or annuity product by an insurance agent, whether issued on an individual or group basis, including fixed and variable annuities, long-term care insurance, including long-term partnership plans, Medicare Supplement, Medicare Part C, and Medicare Part D.

14VAC 5-43-10

Senior-Specific Designations

No insurance agent may use a senior-specific certification or professional designation that misleadingly indicates or implies that the insurance agent has special certification or training in advertising or servicing seniors in:

- connection with the marketing, solicitation, sale or purchase of a life or accident and sickness insurance policy or annuity product; or
- the provision of advice as to the value of or the advisability of purchasing or selling:
  - a life or accident and sickness insurance policy; or
  - annuity product.

This prohibition applies to direct or indirect indication or implication through publications or writings, or by issuing or promulgating analyses or reports related to a life or accident and sickness insurance policy or annuity product.

The prohibited use of senior-specific certifications or professional designations includes, but is not limited to:

- use of a certification or professional designation by an insurance agent who has not actually earned or is otherwise ineligible to use such certification or designation;
- use of a nonexistent or self-conferred certification or professional designation;
- use of a certification or professional designation that indicates or implies a level of occupational qualifications obtained through education, training or experience that the insurance agent using the certification or designation does not have; and

- use of a certification or professional designation that was obtained from a certifying or designating organization that:
  - is primarily engaged in the business of instruction in sales or marketing;
  - does not have reasonable standards or procedures for assuring the competency of its certificants or designees;
  - does not have reasonable standards or procedures for monitoring and disciplining its certificants or designees for improper or unethical conduct; or
  - does not have reasonable continuing education requirements for its certificants or designees in order to maintain the certificate or designation.

It is not generally considered a violation of these regulations if the certification or designation does not primarily apply to sales or marketing and when the organization or the certification or designation in question has been accredited by:
- the American National Standards Institute (ANSI);
- the National Commission for Certifying Agencies; or
- any organization that is on the United States Department of Education's list entitled "Accrediting Agencies Recognized for Title IV Purposes."

In determining whether a combination of words or an acronym standing for a combination of words constitutes a certification or professional designation indicating or implying that a person has special certification or training in advising or servicing seniors, factors considered by the regulatory authorities include:
- Use of one or more words such as:
  - senior;
  - retirement;
  - elder; or
- The words above or similar words combined in the name of the certification or professional designation with one or more words, such as:
  - certified;
  - registered;
  - chartered;
  - advisor;
  - specialist;
  - consultant;
  - planner; or
  - similar words; and
- The manner in which these words are combined.

A job title within an organization that is licensed or registered by a state or federal financial services regulatory agency is not a certification or professional designation, unless it is used in a manner that would confuse or mislead a reasonable consumer, when the job title:
- indicates seniority or standing within the organization; or
- specifies an individual's area of specialization within the organization.

The term "financial services regulatory agency" includes, but is not limited to, an agency that regulates insurers, insurance producers, broker-dealers, investment advisers, or investment companies as defined under the Investment Company Act of 1940 (15 USC §80).
14VAC 5-43-20

Minimum Standards for Individual Policies

The Commission has authority to issue rules and regulations to:
- provide reasonable standardization and simplification of terms and coverages of individual accident and sickness insurance policies;
- facilitate public understanding and comparison;
- eliminate provisions contained in individual accident and sickness insurance policies which may be misleading or unreasonably confusing in connection either with the purchase of coverages or with the settlement of claims; and
- provide for full disclosure in the sale of individual accident and sickness policies.

VA Code §38.2-3516

Basic Hospital Expense Coverage

For the purposes of the minimum standards for individual policies, "basic hospital expense coverage" is defined as a policy of accident and sickness insurance providing coverage for a minimum of 31 days during any continuous hospital confinement for each insured person, for expenses incurred for the necessary treatment and services rendered as a result of accident or sickness for at least the following:

- Daily hospital room and board in an amount not less than the lesser of:
  - 80% of the charges for semi-private room accommodations; or
  - $60 per day;
- Miscellaneous hospital expenses for services and supplies which are customarily rendered by the hospital for use during one period of confinement, in an amount not less than either:
  - 80% of the charges incurred up to at least $2,000; or
  - 10 times the daily hospital room and board benefits; and
- Hospital outpatient services consisting of:
  - hospital services on the day surgery is performed;
  - hospital services rendered within 72 hours after accidental injury, in an amount not less than $100; and
  - X-ray and laboratory tests to the extent that benefits for such services would have been provided to an extent not less than $200 if rendered to an inpatient of the hospital.
- These benefits may be provided subject to a combined deductible amount of no more than $200.

Basic Medical-Surgical Expense Coverage

"Basic medical-surgical expense coverage" is a

policy of accident and sickness insurance which provides coverage for each person insured under the policy for the expenses incurred for the necessary services rendered by a physician for treatment of an injury or sickness for at least the following:

- Surgical services:
  - in amounts not less than those provided on a fee schedule based on:
    » the relative values contained in the State of New York certified surgical fee schedule; or

» the 1964 California Relative Value Schedule; or
» other acceptable relative value scale of surgical procedures;
up to a maximum of at least $1,000 for any one procedure; or
- not less than 80% of the reasonable charges.
- Anesthesia services, consisting of administration of necessary general anesthesia and related procedures in connection with covered surgical service rendered by a physician other than the physician (or his assistant) performing the surgical service:
  - In an amount not less than 80% of the reasonable charges; or
  - 15% of the surgical service benefit.
- In-hospital medical services, consisting of physician services rendered to a person who is a bed patient in a hospital for treatment of sickness or injury other than that for which surgical care is required, in an amount not less than:
  - 80% of the reasonable charges; or
  - $10 per day for not less than 31 days during the period of confinement.

Hospital Confinement Indemnity Coverage

"Hospital confinement indemnity coverage" is a policy of accident and sickness insurance which provides daily benefits for hospital confinement on an indemnity basis in an amount not less than $30 per day and not less than 31 days during any one period of confinement for each person insured under the policy.

Major Medical Expense Coverage

"Major medical expense coverage" is defined as an accident and sickness insurance policy which provides hospital, medical, and surgical expense coverage:

- to an aggregate maximum of not less than $25,000;
- copayment by the covered person not to exceed 25% of covered charges;
- a deductible stated on a per person, per family, per illness, per benefit period, or per year basis, or a combination of such bases not to exceed 5% of the aggregate maximum limit under the policy; or

- if the policy is written to complement underlying hospital and medical insurance, the deductible may be increased by the amount of the benefits provided by the underlying insurance up to certain limits.

Disability Income Protection Coverage

"Disability income protection coverage" is defined as a policy which provides for periodic payments, weekly or monthly, for a specified period during the continuance of disability resulting from either sickness or injury or a combination, and that:

- Provides that periodic payments payable after age 62 reduced solely on the basis of age, are at least 50% of amounts payable immediately prior to age 62.
- Contains an elimination period no greater than:
    - 90 days when coverage provides a benefit of one year or less;
    - 180 days when coverage provides a benefit of more than one year but not greater than two years; or
    - 365 days in all other cases during the continuance of disability resulting from sickness or injury.
- Generally, has a maximum period of time for which a benefit is payable during disability of at least six months. However, policies that cover disability arising out of pregnancy, childbirth, or miscarriage may limit the benefit period to one month.
- Does not reduce benefits because of an increase in social security or similar benefits during a benefit period.

Income Replacement Coverage

Income replacement coverage differs from disability income coverage under the Virginia regulations in that it does not pay benefits unless there is loss of income. A disability income policy pays income in circumstances where loss of income does not occur. "Income replacement coverage" means a policy which provides for periodic payments, weekly or monthly, for a specified period during which there is a loss of income resulting from sickness, injury, or a combination which:

- Provides that periodic payments, which are payable after age 62 and reduced solely on the basis of age, are at least 50% of amounts payable immediately prior to age 62.
- Contains an elimination period no greater than:
    - 90 days when coverage provides a benefit of one year or less;
    - 180 days when coverage provides a benefit of more than one year but not greater than two years; or
    - 365 days in all other cases during the continuance of loss of income resulting from sickness or injury;
- Generally, has a maximum period of time for which a benefit is payable during disability of at least six months. However, policies that cover disability arising out of pregnancy, childbirth, or miscarriage may limit the benefit period to one month.
- Does not reduce benefits because of an increase in social security or similar benefits during a benefit period;
- Requires loss of income to be no greater than 80% of pre-disability income in order to pay full periodic benefits; and
- Includes a front page of the policy that must contain the following statements: THIS IS AN INCOME REPLACEMENT POLICY. THE POLICY PAYS NO BENEFITS IF THERE IS NO LOSS OF INCOME. (This notice must be in capital letters and in no less than 14-point type.)

Limited Benefit Health Insurance Coverage

"Limited benefit health insurance coverage" is defined as any policy or contract that:

- does not provides coverage for a category or categories of insurance defined in the regulations; or
- provides coverage for a category or categories of insurance defined in the regulations, but does not meet the minimum standards for the specified category or categories; or
- provides accident only coverage or specified accident only coverage.

All limited benefit policies must be approved by the Commission may not be issued as any other form of policy and must meet disclosure requirements.
14VAC 5-140-70

Disclosure Requirements

Renewal Provision Disclosure

All individual policy of accident or sickness insurance must include a renewal, continuation or nonrenewal provision. The provision must:

- be appropriately captioned;
- appear on the first page of the policy;
- clearly state any limited duration of renewability; and
- clearly state the duration of the policy term and each renewal term.

Signed Acceptance of Coverage Changes

All riders or endorsements added to a policy after the date of issue or at reinstatement or renewal which reduce or eliminate benefits or coverage in the policy require signed acceptance by the policyholder, except when the insurer is fulfilling a request made in writing by the policyholder or there is an exercise of a right under the policy. After the date of policy issue, any rider or endorsement which increases coverage with an accompanying increase in premium must be agreed to in writing by the insured, unless the increased coverage is required by law.

Additional Premium Disclosure

When a separate additional premium is charged for riders or endorsements, the premium charge must be stated in the policy.

Reasonable and Customer Charges Disclosure

A policy which provides for the payment of benefits based on standards described as "usual and customary," "reasonable and customary," or words of similar import must include an explanation of these terms.

Preexisting Conditions Disclosure

If a policy contains any limitations with respect to preexisting conditions these limitations must appear as a separate paragraph of the policy and be labeled as "Preexisting Conditions Limitation."

Reduction in Coverage Due to Age Disclosure

If age is to be used as a determining factor for reducing the maximum aggregate benefits made available in the policy as originally issued, this fact must be prominently set forth in the policy.

Conversion Privilege Disclosure

If a policy contains a conversion privilege, the conversion provision must be communicated according to these guidelines:

- The caption of the provision must be "Conversion Privilege," or words of similar meaning;
- The provision must indicate:
  - the persons eligible for conversion;
  - the circumstances applicable to the conversion privilege, including any limitations on the conversion; and
  - the person by whom the conversion privilege may be exercised;
- The provision must specify the benefits to be provided on conversion or may state that the converted coverage must be as provided on a policy form then being used by the insurer for that purpose.

Disclosure Rules for Limited Benefit Policies Other than Accident Only Policies

All limited benefit policies must adhere to these disclosure requirements:

1. A cover sheet, containing only the following information must be permanently attached to the front of the policy:

COMPANY NAME
LOGO (OPTIONAL)

NOTICE: LIMITED BENEFIT DISCLOSURE FORM. THE POLICY DESCRIBED IN THIS COVER SHEET DOES NOT MEET THE MINIMUM STANDARDS REQUIRED BY THE BUREAU OF INSURANCE, VIRGINIA STATE CORPORATION COMMISSION, FOR INDIVIDUAL ACCIDENT AND SICKNESS POLICIES. (This notice must be in capital letters and in no less than 14-point type.)

Minimum standards were established by the Bureau to insure the availability of health insurance contracts providing a minimum of basic benefits needed for health care. This policy does not meet the Virginia minimum standards for the following reason(s): (A listing of the reason(s) shall be furnished by the Bureau at the time the contract is reviewed and the actual Bureau language shall be used.)

(The following language shall be required for an insurer, other than a direct response insurer.) I have read this cover sheet and realize that this policy does not meet minimum standards required by Virginia law and that it can only be sold as a LIMITED BENEFIT POLICY.

Signature_____

FORM NUMBER xxx This is a disclosure form. It is not part of the policy to which it is attached._____

The cover sheet must contain one duplicate copy to be maintained by the insurance company for the length of time that the policy is in force or for three years, whichever is greater.

Disclosure Rules for Accident Only and Specified Accident Policies

Disclosure requirement for all accident only and specified accident only policies are as follows:

Insurers have the option of

- printing, clearly stamping or printing on gum labels on the first page of the policy;
- attaching a cover sheet to the front of the policy; or
- adding to their outline of coverage attached to the front of the policy: NOTICE: THIS IS A LIMITED BENEFIT POLICY. IT DOES NOT PAY ANY BENEFITS FOR LOSS FROM SICKNESS. THIS POLICY PROVIDES RESTRICTIVE COVERAGE FOR CERTAIN LOSSES WHICH OCCUR AS A RESULT OF (AN ACCIDENT) (A SPECIFIED ACCIDENT) ONLY. (This notice must be in capital letters and in no less than 14-point type.)

14VAC 5-140-80

Requirements for Replacement

Application forms must include a question designed to elicit information as to whether the insurance to be issued is intended to replace any other accident and sickness insurance presently in force.

Upon determining that a sale involves replacement an insurer or its agent must furnish the applicant, prior to policy issue or delivery, a replacement notice. One copy of the notice must be retained by the applicant and an additional copy signed by the applicant must be retained by the insurer. A direct response insurer must also deliver a replacement to the applicant upon issuance of the policy. These notices are not required in the solicitation of accident only and single premium nonrenewable policies.

The content of the required replacement notice for an insurer other than a direct response insurer is as follows:

NOTICE TO APPLICANT REGARDING REPLACEMENT OF ACCIDENT AND SICKNESS INSURANCE

According to your application, you intend to lapse or otherwise terminate existing accident and sickness insurance and replace it with a policy to be issued by (insert Company Name) Insurance Company. For your own information and protection, you should be aware of and seriously consider certain factors which may affect the insurance protection available to you under the new policy.

1. Health conditions which you may presently have (preexisting conditions) may not be immediately or fully covered under the new policy. This could result in denial or delay of a claim for benefits under the new policy, whereas a similar claim might have been payable under your present policy.

2. You may wish to secure the advice of your present insurer or its agency regarding the proposed replacement of your present policy. This is not only your right, but it is also in your best interests to make sure you understand all the relevant factors involved in replacing your present coverage.

3. If, after due consideration, you still wish to terminate your present policy and replace it with new coverage, be certain to truthfully and completely answer all questions on the application concerning your medical/health history. Failure to include all material medical information on an application may provide a basis for the company to deny any future claims and to refund your premium as though your policy had never been in force. After the application has been completed and before you sign it, re-read it carefully to be certain that all information has been properly recorded.

The above "Notice to Applicant" was delivered to me on:

(Date)_____

_____
(Applicant's Signature)

The content of the required replacement notice for a direct response insurer is as follows:

NOTICE TO APPLICANT REGARDING REPLACEMENT OF ACCIDENT AND SICKNESS INSURANCE

According to your application, you intend to lapse or otherwise terminate existing accident and sickness insurance and replace it with the policy delivered herewith issued by (insert Company Name) Insurance Company. Your new policy provides 10 days within which you may decide without cost whether you desire to keep the policy. For your own information and protection, you should be aware of and seriously consider certain factors which may affect the insurance protection available to you under the new policy.

1. Health conditions which you may presently have (preexisting conditions) may not be immediately or fully covered under the new policy. This could result in denial or delay of a claim for benefits under the new policy, whereas a similar claim might have been payable under your present policy.

2. You may wish to secure the advice of your present insurer or its agent regarding the proposed replacement of your present policy. This is not only your right, but it is also in your best interests to make sure you understand all the relevant factors involved in replacing your present coverage.

3. (To be included only if the application is attached to the policy.) If, after due consideration you still wish to terminate your present policy and replace it with new coverage, read the copy of the application attached to your new policy and be sure that all questions are answered fully and correctly. Omissions or misstatements in the application could cause an otherwise valid claim to be denied. Carefully check the application and write to (insert Company Name and Address) within 10 days if any information is not correct and complete, or if any medical history has been left out of the application.

(Company Name)
14VAC 5-140-90

HIPAA

In Virginia, the continuation of coverage provisions found in HIPAA are implemented in Virginia Code §§38.2-3430.1 – 3430.9 and §§38.2-3432.1 – 3232.3.

Eligible Individuals

These laws apply to eligible individuals. Eligible individual means an individual:

- for whom the aggregate of the periods of creditable coverage is 18 or more months;
- whose most recent prior creditable coverage was under individual health insurance coverage, a group health plan, governmental plan, church plan, or a state plan under Title XIX of the Social Security Act, or health

insurance coverage offered in connection with any such plan;
- who is not eligible for coverage under:
  - a group health plan;
  - part A or part B of Title XVIII of the Social Security Act; or
  - a state plan under Title XIX of such Act, or any successor program, and does not have other health insurance coverage;
- with respect to whom the most recent coverage within the coverage period was not terminated based on nonpayment of premiums or fraud;
- who elected continuation coverage under a COBRA continuation provision or under a similar state program;
- who has exhausted such continuation coverage under such provision or program; and
- in the case where individual health insurance coverage is the most recent creditable coverage, the coverage was nonrenewed by the health insurance issuer because the insurer discontinued offering all insurance in Virginia, in which case the aggregate period of creditable coverage required is reduced to 12 months.

Creditable Coverage Period

A period of creditable coverage is not counted with respect to enrollment of an individual under a health benefit plan if, after such period, there was a 63-day period during which the individual was:

- not covered under any creditable coverage; or
- not serving a waiting period for coverage under a group health plan, or for group health insurance coverage; or
- in an affiliation period.

This period begins on the day following an individual's termination of coverage and continues until the date an individual submits an application. When an application is submitted by mail, the date of postmark is considered the date the application is submitted.
VA Code §38.2-3430.2

Guaranteed Availability

All eligible individuals must be provided a choice of all individual health insurance coverage currently being offered by a health insurance issuer and chosen coverage must be issued. This coverage may not impose any preexisting condition exclusion or affiliation period with respect to the coverage. Health insurance issuers are prohibited from imposing any limitations or exclusions based upon named conditions that apply to eligible individuals.

Health insurance issuers must include on all applications for health insurance coverage questions which will enable the health insurance issuer to determine if an applicant is applying for coverage as an eligible individual.

VA Code §38.2-3430.3

Renewability of Individual Health Insurance Coverage

Generally, a health insurance issuer that provides individual health insurance coverage must renew or continue in force such coverage at the option of the individual. However, a health insurance issuer may nonrenew or discontinue health insurance coverage of an individual in the individual market based on one or more of the following:

- the individual has failed to pay premiums or contributions in accordance with the terms of the health insurance coverage or the issuer has not received timely premium payments;
- the individual has performed an act or practice that constitutes fraud or made an intentional misrepresentation of material fact under the terms of the coverage;
- the issuer is ceasing to offer coverage in the individual market;
- in the case of a health insurance issuer that offers health insurance coverage in the individual market through a network plan, the individual no longer resides, lives, or works in the service area, or in an area for which the health insurance issuer is authorized to do business but only if such coverage is terminated uniformly without regard to any health status-related factor of covered individuals; or
- in the case of health insurance coverage that is made available in the individual market only through one or more associations, the

membership of the individual in the association ceases, but only if such coverage is terminated under this section uniformly without regard to any health status-related factor of covered individuals.

VA Code §38.2-3430.7

Renewability for Group Insureds

These renewability provisions are effective as of January 1, 2014: Every health insurance issuer that offers health insurance coverage in the group market in Virginia must renew or continue in force coverage with respect to all insureds at the option of the employer except:

- For nonpayment of the required premiums by the policyholder, or contract holder, or where the health insurance issuer has not received timely premium payments;
- When the health insurance issuer is ceasing to offer coverage in the small group market;
- For fraud or misrepresentation by the employer, with respect to their coverage;
- With regard to coverage provided to an eligible employee, for fraud or misrepresentation by the employee with regard to his or her coverage;
- For failure to comply with contribution and participation requirements defined by the health benefit plan;
- For failure to comply with health benefit plan provisions that have been approved by the Commission;
- When a health insurance issuer offers health insurance coverage in the group market through a network plan, and there is no longer an enrollee in connection with the plan who lives, resides, or works in the service area of the health insurance issuer;
- When health insurance coverage is made available in the group market only through one or more associations, the membership of an employer in the association ceases, but only if such coverage is terminated under this subdivision uniformly without regard to any health status related factor relating to any covered individual;
- When a health insurance issuer decides to discontinue offering a particular type of group health insurance coverage in the group market in this Commonwealth, coverage may

be discontinued by the health insurance issuer only if:

- the health insurance issuer provides notice of the discontinuation to each covered plan sponsor, participant and beneficiary at least ninety days prior to the date of the discontinuation of such coverage;
- the health insurance issuer offers each covered plan sponsor the option to purchase any other health insurance coverage currently being offered by the health insurer to a group health plan in the market; and
- in exercising the option to discontinue coverage of this type and in offering the option of coverage, the health insurance issuer acts uniformly without regard to the claims experience of the sponsors or any health status-related factor relating to any participants or beneficiaries covered or new participants or beneficiaries who may become eligible for such coverage;

- In any case in which a health insurance issuer elects to discontinue offering all health insurance coverage in the group market in Virginia, health insurance coverage may be discontinued by the health insurance issuer only in accordance with the laws of Virginia and if:
  - the health insurance issuer provides notice to the Commission and to each covered plan sponsor of the discontinuation at least 180 days prior to the date of the discontinuation of coverage; and
  - all health insurance issued or delivered for issuance in Virginia in such market is discontinued and coverage is not renewed;
- In the case of a discontinuation in a market, the health insurance issuer may not provide for the issuance of any health insurance coverage in the market and this Commonwealth during the five-year period beginning on the date of the discontinuation of the last health insurance coverage not so renewed;
- At the time of coverage renewal, a health insurance issuer may modify the health insurance coverage for a product offered to a group health plan or health insurance issuer offering group health insurance coverage if modification is consistent with the laws of

Virginia and effective on a uniform basis among group health plans or health insurance issuers offering group health insurance coverage with that product.

VA Code §38.2-3432.1.

Limitation on Preexisting Condition Exclusion Period

As of January 1, 2014, the following preexisting condition exclusion provisions apply to a health insurer offering health insurance coverage. Insurers may, with respect to a participant or beneficiary, impose a preexisting limitation only if:

- for group health insurance coverage, the exclusion relates to a condition for which medical advice, diagnosis, care, or treatment was recommended or received within the six-month period ending on the enrollment date;
- for individual health insurance coverage, the exclusion relates to a condition that, during a 12-month period immediately preceding the effective date of coverage, had manifested itself in a manner as would cause an ordinarily prudent person to seek diagnosis, care, or treatment, or for which medical advice, diagnosis, care or treatment was recommended or received within 12 months immediately preceding the effective date of coverage;
- such exclusion extends for a period of not more than 12 months after the enrollment date; and
- the period of any such preexisting condition exclusion is reduced by the aggregate of the periods of creditable coverage, if any, applicable to the participant or beneficiary as of the enrollment date.

Exceptions to the Preexisting Condition Provision

A health insurance issuer offering health insurance coverage may not impose any preexisting condition exclusion:

- in the case of an individual who, as of the last day of the 30-day period beginning with the date of birth, is covered under creditable coverage unless the individual goes 63-days without being covered under any creditable coverage.

- in the case of a child who is adopted or placed for adoption before attaining 18 years of age and who, as of the last day of the 30-day period beginning on the date of the adoption or placement for adoption, is covered under creditable coverage unless the individual goes 63-days without being covered under any creditable coverage.
- relating to pregnancy as a preexisting condition, except in the case of individual health insurance coverage for a person who is not considered an eligible individual, in which case the health insurance issuer may impose a preexisting condition exclusion for a pregnancy existing on the effective date of coverage.

A period of creditable coverage will not be counted, with respect to enrollment of an individual under a health benefit plan, if, after such period and before the enrollment date, there was a 63-day period during all of which the individual was not covered under any creditable coverage.

Certification of Creditable Coverage

A health insurance issuer offering group health insurance coverage must provide for certification of the period of creditable coverage:

- at the time an individual ceases to be covered under the plan or otherwise becomes covered under a COBRA continuation provision;
- in the case of an individual becoming covered under a COBRA continuation provision, at the time the individual ceases to be covered under such provision; and
- at the request, or on behalf of, an individual made not later than 24 months after the date of cessation of the coverage.

Enrollment Rules

A health insurer offering group health insurance coverage must permit an employee who is eligible, or a dependent of the employee if the dependent is eligible but not enrolled, to enroll for coverage under the terms of a plan if each of the following conditions is met:

- the employee or dependent had health coverage at the time coverage was previously offered to the employee or dependent;
- the employee stated in writing at the time that the existing health coverage was the reason for declining enrollment, but only if the plan sponsor or health insurance issuer required such a statement and provided the employee with notice of the requirement at that time;
- the employee's or dependent's coverage:
  - was under a COBRA continuation provision and the coverage was exhausted; or
  - was not under a COBRA continuation provision and either the coverage was terminated as a result of loss of eligibility for the coverage or employer contributions towards the coverage were terminated; and
- under the terms of the plan, the employee requests enrollment not later than 30 days after the date of exhaustion of coverage, termination of coverage or employer contribution.

Special Enrollment Period for Dependents

A health insurance issuer must provide a special enrollment period for a dependent if:

- a health insurance issuer makes coverage available with respect to a dependent of an individual; and
- the individual is a participant under the plan; or
- the individual has met any waiting period applicable to becoming a participant under the plan and is eligible to be enrolled under the plan but did not enroll during a previous enrollment period; and
- a person becomes a dependent of the individual through marriage, birth, or adoption or placement for adoption.

The dependent may be enrolled under the plan as a dependent of the individual, and in the case of the birth or adoption of a child, the spouse of the individual may also be enrolled as a dependent of the individual if the spouse is otherwise eligible for coverage.

The dependent special enrollment period is not less than 30 days and must begin on the later of:

- the date dependent coverage is made available; or
- the date the marriage, birth, or adoption or placement for adoption.

If an individual enrolls a dependent during the first 30 days of the dependent special enrollment period, the coverage of the dependent becomes effective:

- in the case of marriage, not later than the first day of the first month beginning after the date the completed request for enrollment is received;
- in the case of a dependent's birth, as of the date of such birth; or
- in the case of a dependent's adoption or placement for adoption, the date of such adoption or placement for adoption.

Late Enrollees

A late enrollee may be excluded from coverage for up to 12 months or may have a preexisting condition limitation apply for up to 12 months; however, in no case will a late enrollee be excluded from coverage for more than 12 months. An eligible employee or dependent are not considered late enrollees if all of the conditions set forth below in 1 through 4 are met or one of the conditions set forth below in 5 or 6 is met. (However, such individual may be considered a late enrollee for benefit riders or enhanced coverage levels not covered under the enrollee's prior plan.):

1. The individual was covered under a public or private health benefit plan at the time the individual was eligible to enroll.
2. The individual certified at the time of initial enrollment that coverage under another health benefit plan was the reason for declining enrollment.
3. The individual has lost coverage under a public or private health benefit plan as a result of termination of employment or employment status eligibility, the termination of the other plan's entire group coverage, death of a spouse, or divorce.
4. The individual requests enrollment within 30 days after termination of coverage provided under a public or private health benefit plan.
5. The individual is employed by a small employer that offers multiple health benefit plans and the individual elects a different plan offered by that small employer during an open enrollment period.
6. A court has ordered that coverage be provided for a spouse or minor child under a covered employee's health benefit plan, the minor is eligible for coverage and is a dependent, and the request for enrollment is made within 30 days after issuance of such court order.

VA Code §38.2-3432.3

Group Insurance Continuation

Each group hospital policy, group medical and surgical policy or group major medical policy delivered or issued for delivery in Virginia, or each of these policy types that are renewed, reissued or extended, must provide for continuation of coverage if the insurance on a person covered under a policy ceases because of the termination of the person's eligibility for coverage prior to the person becoming eligible for Medicare or Medicaid coverage. This continuation provision is not applicable if the group policyholder is required by federal law to provide for continuation of coverage under its group health plan pursuant to COBRA.

The present coverage under the policy continues for a period of 12 months immediately following the date of the termination of the person's eligibility, without evidence of insurability, subject to the following requirements:

- The application and payment for the extended coverage is made to the group policyholder within 31 days after issuance of written notice, but in no event beyond the 60 day period following the date of termination of the person's eligibility;
- Each premium for extended coverage is paid on time to the group policyholder on a monthly basis during the 12 month period;
- The premium for continuing the group coverage is at the insurer's current rate applicable to the group policy plus any applicable administrative fee not to exceed 2% of the current rate; and
- Continuation is only available to an employee or member who has been continuously insured under the group policy during the entire 3 months' period immediately preceding termination of eligibility.

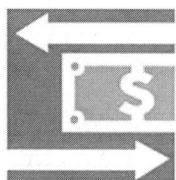

Written Notice

The group policyholder must provide each employee or other person covered under the policy written notice of the availability of the continuation of coverage and the procedures and timeframes for obtaining continuation of the group policy. The notice must be provided within 14 days of the policyholder's knowledge of the employee's or other covered person's loss of eligibility under the policy.

VA Code §38.2-3541

Defined Accident and Sickness Insurance Groups

Virginia insurance law recognizes specified groups that may offer accident and sickness insurance, in VA Code §38.2-3521.1

Employer Groups

An employer group policy is a policy issued to an employer, or to the trustees of a fund established by an employer, which employer or trustees may be an accident and sickness insurance policyholder, to insure employees of the employer for the benefit of persons other than the employer, subject to the following requirements:

- The employees eligible for insurance under the policy are the employees of the employer. The policy may provide that the term employee includes retired employees, former employees and directors of a corporate employer. A policy issued to insure the employees of a public body may provide that the term employee includes elected or appointed officials.
- The premium for the policy may be paid either from the employer's funds or from funds contributed by the insured employees, or from both.
- An insurer may exclude or limit the coverage on any person when evidence of individual insurability is not satisfactory to the insurer.

Creditor Groups

Creditor groups are another authorized group type under Virginia insurance law. A policy may be issued to a creditor or its parent holding company or to a trustee or trustees or agent designated by two or more creditors, where the creditor, holding company, affiliate, trustee, trustees or agent is deemed the policyholder, to insure debtors of the creditor or creditors with respect to their indebtedness, subject to the following requirements:

- the debtors eligible for insurance under the policy are all of the debtors of the creditor or creditors, or all of any class of debtors of the creditor;
- the premium for the policy must be paid either from the creditor's funds, or from charges collected from the insured debtors, or from both.
- An insurer may exclude any debtors as to whom evidence of individual insurability is not satisfactory to the insurer.
- The total amount of insurance payable with respect to an indebtedness may not exceed the greater of the scheduled or actual amount of unpaid indebtedness to the creditor.
- The insurance may be payable to the creditor or any successor to the right, title, and interest of the creditor. Such payment or payments reduce the unpaid indebtedness of the debtor and any excess of the insurance is payable to the insured or the estate of the insured.

Labor Union Groups

Accident and sickness policies may be issued to a labor union, or similar employee organization. The labor union or organization is the policyholder on such a group contract and the policy insures members of the union or organization for the benefit of persons other than the union or organization or any of its officials, representatives, or agents, subject to the following requirements:

- The members eligible for insurance under the policy must all be members of the union or organization, or all of any class or classes thereof.
- The premium for the policy must be paid either from funds of the union or organization, or from funds contributed by the insured members specifically for their insurance, or from both. Generally, a policy on which no part of the premium is to be derived from funds contributed by the insured members specifically for their insurance must insure all eligible members, except those who reject such coverage in writing.

236 VA PPL LH-2_16298

- An insurer may exclude or limit the coverage on any person as to whom evidence of individual insurability is not satisfactory to the insurer.

Association Groups

Association groups may be authorized to issue accident and sickness insurance. The association or associations must:

- Have at the outset a minimum of 100 persons;
- Have been organized and maintained in good faith for purposes other than that of obtaining insurance;
- Have been in active existence for at least five years;
- Have a constitution and bylaws which provide that:
  - the association or associations hold regular meetings not less than annually to further purposes of the members;
  - except for credit unions, the association or associations collect dues or solicit contributions from members; and
  - the members have voting privileges and representation on the governing board and committees;
- Does not condition membership in the association on any health status-related factor relating to an individual;
- Makes health insurance coverage offered through the association available to all members and those eligible through the member, regardless of any health status-related factor;
- Does not make health insurance coverage offered through the association available other than in connection with a member of the association; and
- Meets any additional requirements imposed under the laws of Virginia.

Credit Union Groups

Credit unions may also be approved to offer accident and sickness insurance to members through group policies. A policy may be issued to a credit union, or to a trustee or trustees or agent designated by two or more credit unions, to insure members of such credit union or credit unions for the benefit of persons other than the credit union or credit unions, trustee or trustees, or agent or any of their officials, subject to the following requirements:

- The members eligible for insurance must be all of the members of the credit union or credit unions, or all of any member class or classes.
- The premium for the policy must be paid by the policyholder from the credit union's funds and must insure all eligible members.
- An insurer may exclude or limit the coverage on any person that does not meet the lawful individual insurability requirements of the insurer.

Health Maintenance Organization Groups

Health Maintenance Organizations may also be issue accident and sickness insurance group policies.
VA Code §38.2-3521.1

Health Maintenance Organizations

A health maintenance organization may not be established in Virginia until licensed by the Commission.
VA Code §38.2-4301

Evidence of Coverage

HMOs must provide each subscriber with evidence of coverage under a health care plan. Coverage under HMO plans must be approved by the Commission, and no evidence of coverage, or an amendment, may be delivered or issued for delivery in Virginia unless approved by the Commission. (Note: Medicare HMO coverage through Medicare Part C is subject to different disclosure laws and is not subject to the evidence of coverage laws and regulations applicable to all other HMO coverage in Virginia.)

No evidence of coverage may contain provisions or statements which are unjust, unfair, untrue, inequitable, misleading, deceptive or misrepresentative. It must contain a clear and complete statement if a contract, or a reasonably complete summary if a certificate, of:

- the health care services and any insurance or other benefits to which the enrollee is entitled under the health care plan;
- any limitations on the services, kind of services, benefits, or kind of benefits to be

provided, including any deductible or copayment feature, or both;

- where and in what manner information is available as to how services may be obtained;
- the total amount of payment for health care services and any indemnity or service benefits that the enrollee is obligated to pay with respect to individual contracts, or an indication whether the plan is contributory or noncontributory for group certificates;
- a description of the health maintenance organization's method for resolving enrollee complaints;
- a list of providers and a description of the service area which must be provided with the evidence of coverage, if such information is not given to the subscriber at the time of enrollment; and
- any right of subscribers covered under a group contract to convert their coverages to an individual contract issued by the health maintenance organization.
- the terms and conditions under which coverage may be terminated or rescinded;
- coordination of benefits provisions, if applicable;
- assignment restrictions in the contract;
- the procedure for filing claims;
- the eligibility requirements, including the conditions under which dependents may be added and the limiting age for dependents and subscribers;
- an incontestability clause;
- a provision that the contract or evidence of coverage and any amendments to it constitutes the entire contract;
- except for an evidence of coverage that does not provide for the periodic payment of premium or for the payment of any premium, a provision that the contract holder is entitled to a grace period of not less than 31 days for the payment of any premium due except the first premium; and
- terms and conditions related to the designation of a primary care health care professional.

Schedule of Charges

All schedule of charges for enrollee coverage for HMO health care services must be filed with the Commission. A schedule may not be used or delivered until it has been filed and approved.
VA Code §38.2-4306 and 14VAC 5-211-210

Prohibited Practices

No health maintenance organization or its representative may cause or knowingly permit the use of:

- advertising that is untrue or misleading;
- solicitation that is untrue or misleading; or
- any form of evidence of coverage that is deceptive.

Standards for Determining Untrue, Misleading and Deceptive HMO Advertising

A statement or item of information is deemed to be untrue if it does not conform to fact in any respect that is or may be significant to an enrollee or person considering enrollment in a health care plan.

A statement or item of information is deemed to be misleading, whether or not it may be literally untrue, if the statement or item of information may be understood by a reasonable person who has no special knowledge of health care coverage as indicating:

- a benefit or advantage if that benefit or advantage does not in fact exist; or
- the absence of any exclusion, limitation or disadvantage of possible significance to an enrollee or person considering enrollment in a health care plan if the absence of that exclusion, limitation, or disadvantage does not in fact exist.

In making a determination regarding a misleading statement, consideration is given to the total context in which the statement is made or the item of information is communicated.

An evidence of coverage is deemed to be deceptive if it causes a reasonable person who has no special knowledge of health care plans to expect benefits, services, charges, or other advantages that the evidence of coverage does not provide or that the health care plan issuing the evidence of coverage does not regularly make available for enrollees covered under the evidence of coverage. In making a determination regarding a deceptive evidence of coverage, consideration is given to the evidence of coverage taken as a whole and to the typography, format, and language.

Virginia's unfair trade practices in insurance laws found in VA Code §38.2-500 and following apply to HMOs, health care plans and evidences of coverage, except to the extent that the Commission determines that the nature of health maintenance organizations, health care plans, and evidences of coverage render any of these provisions clearly inappropriate.

HMO Prohibited Words

No health maintenance organization, unless licensed as an insurer, may use in its name, contracts, or literature:

- any of the words "insurance," "casualty," "surety," "mutual"; or
- any other words descriptive of the insurance, casualty, or surety business; or
- any words deceptively similar to the name or description of any insurance or fidelity and surety insurer doing business in this Commonwealth.

Prohibited Discrimination in Selecting Providers

No HMO is allowed to discriminate on the basis of race, creed, color, sex or religion in the selection of health care providers for participation in the organization.

No health maintenance organization may unreasonably discriminate against physicians as a class or against any class of providers or against pharmacists when contracting for specialty or referral practitioners or providers. However, a health maintenance organization may select, based on its judgment, the numbers of providers necessary to render the services offered by it.

No contract between a health maintenance organization and a provider may include provisions which require a health care provider or health care provider group to deny covered services that such provider or group knows to be medically necessary and appropriate that are provided with respect to a specific enrollee or group of enrollees with similar medical conditions.
VA Code §38.2-4312 and 14VAC 5-211-240

Freedom of Pharmacy Choice

No HMO providing health care plans may prohibit any person receiving pharmaceutical benefits from selecting, without limitation, the pharmacy of his or her choice to furnish the benefits. This right of selection extends to and includes pharmacies that are not participating providers under the HMO's health care plan and that have previously notified the health maintenance organization of their agreement to accept reimbursement for their services at rates applicable to pharmacies that are participating providers, including any copayment consistently imposed by the plan, as payment in full.

No HMO may impose upon any person receiving pharmaceutical benefits furnished under a health care plan:

1. Any copayment, fee or condition that is not equally imposed upon all individuals in the same benefit category, class or copayment level, whether or not such benefits are furnished by pharmacists who are not participating providers;
2. Any monetary penalty that would affect or influence any such person's choice of pharmacy; or
3. Any reduction in allowable reimbursement for pharmacy services related to utilization of pharmacists who are not participating providers.

A HMO providing health care plans to select a single mail order pharmacy provider as the exclusive provider of pharmacy services that are delivered to the covered person's address by mail, common carrier, or delivery service. The laws applicable to freedom of pharmacy choice do not apply to such contracts.
VA Code §38.2-4312.1

Emergency Service Access

A health maintenance organization must have a system to provide to its members, on a 24-hour basis:

- access to medical care; or
- access by telephone to a physician or licensed health care professional with appropriate medical training who can refer or direct a member for prompt medical care in cases

where there is an immediate, urgent need or medical emergency.

A HMO must reimburse a hospital emergency facility and provider, less any applicable copayments, deductibles, or coinsurance, for medical screening and stabilization services to meet federal law requirements if:

- the health maintenance organization or its designee or the member's primary care physician or its designee authorized, directed, or referred a member to use the hospital emergency facility; or
- the health maintenance organization fails to have a system for provision of 24-hour access.

Each evidence of coverage provided by a health maintenance organization must include a description of procedures to be followed by the member for emergency services, including:

- the appropriate use of hospital emergency facilities;
- the appropriate use of any urgent care facilities with which the health maintenance organization may contract;
- the potential responsibility of the member for payment for nonemergency services rendered in a hospital emergency facility; and
- the member's covered benefits for emergency services.

VA Code §38.2-4312.3

HMO Solicitation through Life and Health Insurance Agents

HMO enrollee contracts may be solicited only through life and health insurance. Home office salaried officers whose principal duties and responsibilities do not include the negotiation or solicitation of enrollee contracts are not required to be licensed.

VA Code §38.2-4313

Affiliation Period

A health maintenance organization which offers health insurance coverage in connection with a group health plan or group health insurance coverage and which does not impose any preexisting condition exclusion allowed under the Virginia health insurance laws, may impose an affiliation period with respect to any coverage option, but only if:

- the period is applied uniformly without regard to any health status-related factors; and
- the period does not exceed two months (or three months in the case of a late enrollee).

An affiliation period under a plan must run concurrently with any waiting period under the plan.

Affiliation period is defined as a period which, under the terms of the health insurance coverage offered by a HMO, must expire before the health insurance coverage becomes effective. The HMO is not required to provide health care services or benefits during the period and no premium may be charged to the participant or beneficiary for any coverage during the period.

1. Such period must begin on the enrollment date.
2. An affiliation period under a plan must run concurrently with any waiting period under the plan.

VA Code §§38.2-3431 and 38.2-4322

Continuation of Coverage

Generally, an HMO health care plan must offer to its group contract holders, for an enrollee whose eligibility for coverage terminates under the group contract, the option to continue coverage. The member may continue coverage under the existing group contract for a period of at least 12 months immediately following the date of termination of the enrollee's eligibility for coverage under the group contract. Continuation coverage is not applicable if the group contract holder is required by federal law to provide for continuation of coverage under its group health plan pursuant to COBRA. Coverage must be provided without additional evidence of insurability subject to the following requirements:

- the application and payment for the extended coverage is made to the group contract holder within 31 days after written notice and no later than 60-days following the date of the termination of the person's eligibility;
- each premium for the extended coverage is timely paid to the group contract holder on a

monthly basis during the 12-month period; and

- the premium for continuing the group coverage must be at the health care plan's current applicable rate plus any applicable administrative fee not to exceed 2.0% of the current rate.

The group contract holder must provide each enrollee or other person covered under the group contract written notice of the availability of continuation and the procedures and timeframes for obtaining continuation or conversion of the group contract. The notice must be provided within 14 days of the group contract holder's knowledge of the enrollee's or other covered person's loss of eligibility under the group contract.
14VAC 5-211-70

Extension of Benefits for Total Disability

A group contract issued by an HMO must contain a reasonable extension of benefits upon discontinuance of the group contract with respect to members who become totally disabled while enrolled under the contract and who continue to be totally disabled at the date of discontinuance of the contract.

Upon payment of premium, coverage will remain in full force and effect:

- for a reasonable period of time of at least 180 days;
- until the member is no longer totally disabled; or
- until a succeeding carrier elects to provide replacement coverage to that member without limitation as to the disabling condition.

Upon termination of the extension of benefits, the enrollee has the right to convert or continue coverage.
14VAC 5-211-13

Freedom of Choice

At the time of enrollment an enrollee must have the right to select a primary care health care professional from among the HMO's affiliated primary care health care professionals. An enrollee who is dissatisfied with his primary care health care professional has the right to select another primary care health care professional from among

the health maintenance organization's affiliated primary care health care professionals, subject to availability.
14VAC 5-211-140

Basic Health Care Services

An HMO must provide, or arrange for the provision of basic health care services that include the following:

Inpatient Hospital and Physician Services

Inpatient hospital and physician services are defined as medically necessary hospital and physician services affording inpatient treatment to enrollees in a licensed hospital for a minimum of 90 days per contract or calendar year.

Hospital Services		
Room and board	Short-term rehabilitation services	Intensive care unit and services use
General nursing care	X-ray, lab, other diagnostic tests	Medically necessary special duty nursing
Medically necessary special diets	Whole blood, blood plasma administration	Short-term physical therapy, radiation therapy, inhalation therapy
Operating room, related facilities use	Drugs, medications, biologicals, anesthesia, oxygen services	
Physician Services		
Medically necessary health care services		
Performed, prescribed or supervised by physicians		
Provided in hospitals for registered bed patients		

Outpatient Medical Services

Medically necessary health care services for enrollees Performed, prescribed or supervised by physicians			
Provided in:			
Nonhospital based health care facilities	Hospitals	Enrollee's homes	Physician's offices
Include:			
Diagnostic services	Treatment services		Laboratory services
X-ray services	Outpatient surgery		
Short-term physical therapy and rehabilitation services which the HMO determines are expected to result in significant improvement of member's condition within 90 days			

Diagnostic Services

Diagnostic laboratory and diagnostic and therapeutic radiologic services are basic HMO services.

Preventive Health Services

Preventive health services are those required by the ACA to be provided to HMO and accident and sickness policy holders with ACA qualified health plans. These services are found in VA Code §38.2-3442. No cost sharing, e.g., no copayments, deductibles or coinsurance, apply to these services:

Evidence-based items or services that have in effect a rating of A or B in the recommendations of the U.S. Preventive Services Task Force,
Immunizations for routine use in children, adolescents, and adults that have in effect a recommendation from the Advisory Committee on Immunization Practices of the Centers for Disease Control and Prevention with respect to the individual involved
For infants, children, and adolescents, evidence-informed preventive care and screenings provided for in comprehensive guidelines supported by the Health Resources and Services Administration
With respect to women, evidence-informed preventive care and screenings recommended in comprehensive guidelines supported by the Health Resources and Services Administration

In-Area and Out-Of-Area Emergency Services

In-area and out-of-area emergency services are required to be provided by HMOs as basic services and include medically necessary ambulance services, available on an inpatient or an outpatient basis 24 hours per day, seven days per week.

Mental Health and Substance Use Disorder Services

Mental health and substance use disorder services must be provided on parity with the medical and surgical benefits contained in the plan in accordance with the Mental Health Parity and Addiction Equity Act.

Medically Necessary Dental Services as a Result of Accidental Injury

These services are provided regardless of the date of the injury, however, contracts may require that treatment be sought within 60 days of the accident for injuries occurring on or after the effective date of coverage.

14VAC 5-211-160

Preexisting Conditions

In accordance with VA Code § 38.2-3444, HMOs cannot limit or exclude coverage for an enrollee by imposing a preexisting condition exclusion. This provision does not apply to a grandfathered plan as defined under the ACA for individual health insurance coverage.

A waiting period not to exceed 90 days may be allowed for a group health plan or excepted benefits policies or contracts that do not provide for essential health benefits. A waiting period begins on the enrollment date for group coverage or the effective date of the policy, as applicable.

14VAC 5-211-220

Reasons for Termination and Rescission

An HMO may not terminate an enrollee's coverage for services provided under an HMO contract except for one or more of the following reasons:

- Failure to pay the premium required by the contract as shown in the contract or evidence of coverage;
- The policyholder or contract holder has performed an act or practice that constitutes fraud or made an intentional misrepresentation of material fact in connection with the coverage
- The group contract holder has failed to comply with a material plan provision relating to employer contribution or group participation rules; or
- Discontinuance of the group contract under which the enrollee was covered.

Generally, an HMO cannot terminate coverage without giving the subscriber written notice of termination, effective at least 31 days from the date of mailing or, if not mailed, from the date of delivery.

In the case of termination of coverage due to nonpayment of premium, the coverage continues in force during the grace period unless the contract holder has given written notice to the HMO of discontinuance of the contract in advance of the discontinuance. The contract may provide that the

VA PPL LH-2_16298

contract holder must pay a pro rata premium for the time the contract was in force during the grace period.

In the case of termination of coverage due to employer non-payment of premium, the termination cannot occur until the employer has been provided with a written notice of termination. The notice must include a specific date, not less than 15 days from the date of the notice, by which coverage will terminate if overdue premium is not paid. Coverage cannot terminate for at least 15 days after this notice has been mailed. The HMO must reimburse all valid claims for services incurred prior to the date coverage is terminated.

An HMO may not rescind coverage for services provided under a contract unless the enrollee or a person seeking coverage on behalf of an enrollee performs an act, practice, or omission that constitutes fraud, or the person makes an intentional misrepresentation of material fact, as prohibited by the terms of the plan.

14VAC 5-211-230

Unfair Discrimination

An HMO may not unfairly discriminate against an enrollee on the basis of the age, sex, health status, race, color, creed, national origin, ancestry, religion, marital status, or lawful occupation of the enrollee, or because of the frequency of utilization of services by the enrollee.

14VAC 5-211-240

Group Insurance and Small Employer Plans

Small employer groups are subject to the provisions found in Virginia Code §38.2-3431 to 3437. This section has reviewed some of the requirements found in §38.2-3431 to 3437 and will now look at small employer group insurance in more detail.

Small Employer Defined

Small employer means in connection with a group health plan or health insurance coverage with respect to a calendar year and a plan year, an employer who employed an average of at least one but not more than 50 employees on business days during the preceding calendar year and who

employs at least one employee on the first day of the plan year.

VA opted to stay with 50 employees for a small employer and not increase to 100, per PACE.

Each insurer proposing to issue individual or group accident and sickness insurance policies providing hospital, medical and surgical or major medical coverage on an expense incurred basis, each corporation providing individual or group accident and sickness subscription contracts, and each health maintenance organization or multiple employer welfare arrangement providing health care plans for health care services that offers individual or group coverage to the small employer market in this Commonwealth is subject to Virginia Code *§38.2-3431 to 3437.* An issuer of individual coverage to employees of a small employer is subject to these provisions if any of the following conditions are met:

- any portion of the premiums or benefits is paid by or on behalf of the employer;
- the eligible employee or dependent is reimbursed, whether through wage adjustments or otherwise, by or on behalf of the employer for any portion of the premium;
- the employer has permitted payroll deduction for the covered individual and any portion of the premium is paid by the employer, if the health insurance issuer providing individual coverage is registered as a health insurance issuer in the small group market and offers small employer group insurance to the employer; or
- the health benefit plan is treated by the employer or any of the covered individuals as part of a Cafeteria Plan under IRC 125 or Employer Contribution Plan under IRC 106 or 162.

Small Employer Health Coverage Requirements

If accident and sickness coverage is offered in the small employer market, the coverage must be offered and made available to all eligible employees of every small employer and their dependents, including late enrollees, that apply for the coverage. No coverage may be offered only to certain eligible employees or their dependents and no employees or their dependents may be excluded or charged additional premiums because of health status.

All products that are approved for sale in the small group market that the health insurance issuer is actively marketing must be offered to all small employers, and the health insurance issuer must accept any employer that applies for any of those products. Coverage offered cannot exclude an employer based solely on the nature of the employer's business.

A health insurance issuer that offers health insurance coverage in a small group market through a network plan may:

- limit the employers that may apply for such coverage to those eligible individuals who live, work or reside in the network plan's service area; and
- within the service area of the plan, deny coverage to employers if the health insurance issuer has demonstrated, if required, to the satisfaction of the Commission that:
  - it will not have the capacity to deliver services adequately to enrollees of any additional groups because of its obligations

to existing group contract holders and enrollees; and
- it is applying the group health coverage laws uniformly to all employers without regard to the claims experience or any health status-related factors.

VA Code §38.2-3432.2

Eligibility to Enroll

A health insurance issuer offering group health insurance coverage may not establish rules for eligibility of any individual to enroll under the terms of the plan based on any health status-related factors. A health insurance issuer offering group health insurance coverage, may not require an individual to pay a premium or contribution which is greater than a premium or contribution for a similarly situated individual enrolled in the plan on the basis of any health status related factor in relation to the individual or to an individual enrolled under the plan as a dependent of the individual.

A health insurance issuer offering group health insurance coverage may establish premium discounts or rebates or modify applicable copayments or deductibles in return for adherence to programs of health promotion and disease prevention.

VA Code §38.2-3436

Section XI Review

1) The Medicare Supplemental Plan insurer will be putting a radio spot on the air. The radio spot must be reviewed by:
   a. the Executive Officers of the Plan
   b. Commissioner
   c. each state insurance commissioner
   d. the Secretary of Health and Human Services

2) Under Virginia law, a Medicare Supplement buyer's guide, "Guide to Health Insurance for People with Medicare":
   a. must be provided only to persons with Medicare who apply for Medicare Supplement coverage.
   b. must be provided to persons eligible for Medicare by reason of age who are issued hospital or medical expense coverage or to persons eligible for Medicare who are issued group or individual medical expense coverage.
   c. must be provided only to persons with Medicare who are issued Medicare Supplement coverage.
   d. is only required to be provided to persons age 65 or over who request this guide.

3) An applicant for a Medicare Supplement policy had an existing Medicare Supplement policy for the past four years. When this applicant purchased his original Medicare Supplement policy, the applicant had been covered by an employer group health plan for six continuous years prior to application. Because of this creditable coverage, the original Medicare Supplement policy did not apply any preexisting condition exclusions. When this applicant replaces the existing Medicare Supplement policy:
   a. the new Medicare Supplement policy also may not apply preexisting condition exclusions.
   b. may now invoke preexisting conditions as if the applicant had never had any creditable coverage or prior Medicare Supplement coverage.
   c. may invoke preexisting conditions for up to six months under the new Medicare Supplement coverage.
   d. may invoke preexisting conditions for up to twelve months under the new Medicare Supplement coverage.

4) Medicare Supplement policy purchasers have a ___ day free look to review the policy and return it if not satisfied.
   a. 30
   b. 10
   c. 20
   d. 45

5) A long-term care contract is issued in Virginia. It has a premium-paying period of 15 years. The policyholder has had the policy for 10 years and made timely premium payments throughout this period. The insured is age 70, and the insurer has just announced a premium increase of 35%. What option must the insurer give the insured on this fixed premium-paying policy because of the premium rate increase?
   a. to cancel the policy and receive a lump sum benefit
   b. to reduce the policy benefits or convert the policy to a paid up status
   c. to exchange the policy for a different one from the same carrier
   d. the insurer does not have to give any options to this insured because of the premium rate increase

6) An insurer may not deliver or issue a long-term care insurance policy in Virginia unless the option of purchasing a policy including a(n) _____ has been offered to the applicant.
   a. continuation clause
   b. inflation protection feature
   c. accelerated death benefit
   d. waiver of premium

7) Randolph is soliciting a long-term care Partnership policy to the Brown's. What notice is he required to provide them along with the Outline of Coverage at policy issuance?
   a. the Partnership Disclosure Notice
   b. the Personal Worksheet
   c. the Partnership Rate Notice
   d. the Notice Regarding Long-Term Care Insurance Partnership Status

8) Ongoing training for a long-term care insurance producer in Virginia must be completed every ____ months and not be less than ____ hours.
   a. 12, 8
   b. 12, 4
   c. 24, 4
   d. 24, 8

9) An annual statement from an insurer that provides disability income coverage includes a notice of an available rider that will increase the accidental death benefit without requiring insurability for additional premium. Existing insureds can apply for the rider's coverage within 90 days of policy renewal and submit additional premium. The notice concerning the available rider is:
   a. provided on an annual statement, so is not considered advertising under the law.
   b. is information about the existing policy, so is not considered advertising under the law.
   c. is not public since it is only mailed to existing clients, so is not considered advertising under the law.
   d. is advertising.

10) Which of the following is advertising under insurance laws?
   a. a rate sheet provided to appointed agents by an insurer
   b. a commission schedule provided to appointed agents by an insurer
   c. the outline of coverage
   d. an agency contract

11) Each of the following are requirements of the health insurance advertising file according to Virginia Insurance regulations, EXCEPT:
   a. The insurer must maintain a complete advertising file at its home or principal office
   b. The advertising file must be maintained for a period of 10 years
   c. The advertising file must contain every printed, published or prepared advertisement of individual policies
   d. There must be a note attached to each advertisement that states the manner and extent of distribution and any advertised policy's form number, and the file is subject to regular and periodic inspection by the Commission

12) Individual basic medical-surgical expense coverage has a minimum benefit standard in Virginia for in-hospital medical services to a bed patient in a hospital for treatment of sickness or injury that does not need surgical care of an amount not less than 80% of the reasonable charges or:
   a. $5 per day for not less than 31 days during the period of confinement.
   b. $10 per day for not less than 31 days during the period of confinement.
   c. $18 per day for not less than 31 days during the period of confinement.
   d. $25 per day for not less than 31 days during the period of confinement.

13) When an individual accident and sickness policy is being replaced, an insurer or its agent must furnish a replacement notice to the insured:
   a. within ten days of policy delivery
   b. at policy delivery
   c. three days prior to policy delivery
   d. prior to policy issue or delivery

14) Virginia law requires that a health insurance issuer offering group health insurance coverage must provide for certification of the period of creditable coverage:
   a. within one year of the time an individual ceases to be covered under the plan or otherwise becomes covered under a COBRA continuation provision
   b. at the time an individual ceases to be covered under the plan or otherwise becomes covered under a COBRA continuation provision
   c. if an individual requests it at the time when or within 30 days of when the individual ceases to be covered under the plan or otherwise becomes covered under a COBRA continuation provision
   d. if an individual requests it at the time when the individual ceases to be covered under the plan or otherwise becomes covered under a COBRA continuation provision

15) Each group hospital policy, group medical and surgical policy or group major medical policy delivered or issued for delivery in Virginia, or each of these policy types that are renewed, reissued or extended, must provide:
   a. Fitness club membership reimbursement
   b. Coverage for non-allergenic skin products
   c. Treatment for baldness
   d. Continuation of coverage

16) In Virginia, what type of group issues an accident and sickness policy and must include at least 100 persons, been in active existence for at least five years, has not been organized for the purpose of issuing insurance, has a constitution and bylaws that requires meetings to be held regularly, and makes the insurance available to all persons in the group, regardless of health status-related factor?
a. An employer group
b. A creditor group
c. A labor union group
d. An association group

17) An HMO must have a system to provide access to medical care or access by telephone to a physician or licensed health care professional with appropriate medical training who can refer or direct a member for prompt medical care in cases where there is an immediate, urgent need or medical emergency. This access must be available:
a. 24 hours a day
b. 16 hours a day
c. 8 hours a day
d. When necessary

18) When a person enrolls in an HMO in Virginia:
a. The HMO assigns a primary care physician to the enrollee
b. The person has the right to select an HMO primary care health professional from the ones available
c. The HMO assigns a primary care physician and all specialist caregivers to the enrollee
d. The person may never change primary care physicians once one is selected, unless the physician terminates his or her relationship with the HMO.

19) _____ means in connection with a group health plan or health insurance coverage with respect to a calendar year and a plan year, an employer who employed an average of at least one but not more than 50 employees on business days during the preceding calendar year and who employs at least one employee on the first day of the plan year, according to Virginia health insurance law.
a. Large employer
b. Mid-size employer
c. Small employer
d. Self-funded employer

Intentionally Blank

VA PPL LH-2_16298

VIRGINIA LAWS & REGULATIONS COMMON TO ALL LINES OF INSURANCE

Section XII: Virginia Statutes and Regulations Common to Life, Accident and Health, Property, Casualty and Personal Lines Insurance

This section describes Virginia laws and regulations applicable to life, health, property and casualty insurance licensees. Topics include:

- State Corporation Commission
- The Commissioner of Insurance
- Agent licensing
- Fiduciary responsibilities
- Commissions and compensation
- Felony convictions and administrative actions
- Record retention
- Marketing practices
- Virginia Insurance Guaranty Association
- Insurance information and privacy protection

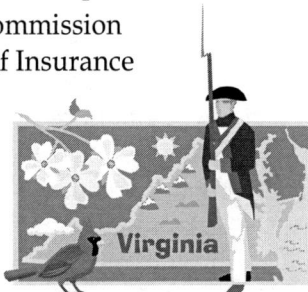

State Corporation Commission and the Commissioner of Insurance

General Powers

The State Corporation Commission (the Commission) regulates the insurance industry through the Bureau of Insurance, which is under the authority of the Commission. The Commissioner of Insurance heads the Bureau of Insurance.

The Commission is charged with the execution of all laws relating to insurance and insurers. All companies, domestic, foreign, and alien, transacting or licensed to transact the business of insurance in Virginia are subject to inspection, supervision and regulation by the Commission. All licenses granting the authority to transact the business of insurance in Virginia are granted and issued by the Commission under its seal.
VA Code §38.2-200

Rules and Regulations, Orders

The Commission, after notice and opportunity for all interested parties to be heard, may issue any rules and regulations necessary or appropriate for the administration and enforcement of Virginia insurance law.
VA Code §38.2-223

Examination

The Commission has power to examine and investigate the affairs of agents and insurers to determine whether they have been or are engaged in any unfair method of competition or in any unfair or deceptive act or practice. It also has the power to gather information from them concerning trade practices and whether their practices adequately and fairly serve the public interest.

Any person who refuses or fails to provide information in a timely manner to the Commission as provided in this section is subject to enforcement and penalty provisions.
VA Code §38.2-515

The Commission may make an examination into the affairs of any person licensed to transact any insurance business in Virginia or any other person subject to the jurisdiction of the Commission when it believes conducting the examination is in the protection of the interests of the people of Virginia.

The Commission may also make an examination into the affairs of:

1. Any person having a contract under which he has the exclusive or dominant right to manage or control any licensed insurer;
2. Any person holding the shares of capital stock or policyholder proxies of any domestic insurer amounting to control either as voting trustee or otherwise;
3. Any person engaged or assisting in, or proposing or claiming to engage or assist in the promotion or formation of a domestic insurer; or
4. Any person seeking a license to transact any insurance business in Virginia.

VA Code §38.2-1317

The Commission examines every insurer licensed in Virginia at least once in every five years. The examination of any foreign or alien insurer or any other foreign or alien person subject to examination is made in cooperation with the insurance departments of other states. In some cases, a report from the state, territory or province where the foreign or alien insurance is domiciled suffices for the examination.

VA Code §38.2-1317

Domestic, Foreign and Alien Insurers

Insurers are classified as *domestic*, *foreign* and *alien*. A domestic insurer is an insurer that is formed, or domiciled, in the state in which it is transacting business. A foreign insurer is one that is domiciled in one state and doing business in other states. When the other states refer to this insurer, they refer to it as a foreign insurer. For example, an insurer is domiciled in Massachusetts. It does business in all states, except New York. In all the states in which it does business outside of Massachusetts, it is a foreign insurer. In Massachusetts, it is a domestic insurer.

Alien insurers are insurers that are formed and domiciled outside of the United States. In any state in which an insurer does business that is domiciled outside of the United States, it is referred to as an alien insurer.

Right to Examine All Persons Engaged in the Business of Insurance

The Commission has the power to examine and investigate the business affairs of any person engaged or alleged to be engaged in the business of insurance in Virginia, including all agents, to determine whether the person has engaged or is engaging in any violation. The Commission has the right to examine all records relating to the writing or alleged writing of insurance by any of these people in Virginia to determine whether they are now or have been violating any applicable provisions.

Any licensee, or any person purporting to be a licensee, or any person whose actions have led any person to believe that he is a licensee, who refuses to permit the Commission or any of its employees or agents, to make an examination or who fails or refuses to comply with the provisions of insurance laws applicable to agents, may, after notice and an opportunity to be heard, be subject to any of the applicable penalties, including the denial, suspension or revocation of his license.

VA Code §38.2-1809

Disciplinary Actions

The Commission may, in addition to or instead of a penalty, place on probation, suspend, revoke or refuse to issue or renew any person's license for any one or more of the following causes:

1. Providing materially incorrect, misleading, incomplete or untrue information in the license application or any other document filed with the Commission
2. Violating any insurance laws, or violating any regulation, subpoena or order of the Commission or of another state's insurance regulatory authority
3. Obtaining or attempting to obtain a license through misrepresentation or fraud
4. Engaging in the practice of rebating
5. Engaging in twisting or any form thereof, where twisting means inducing an insured to terminate an existing policy and purchase a new policy through misrepresentation
6. Improperly withholding, misappropriating or converting any moneys or properties received in the course of doing insurance business
7. Intentionally misrepresenting the terms of an actual or proposed insurance contract or application for insurance
8. Having admitted or been found to have committed any insurance unfair trade practice or fraud
9. Having been convicted of a felony
10. Using fraudulent, coercive, or dishonest practices, or demonstrating incompetence, or untrustworthiness in the conduct of business in Virginia or elsewhere, or demonstrating financial irresponsibility in the handling of applicant, policyholder, agency, or insurance company funds
11. Having an insurance producer license, or its equivalent, denied, suspended or revoked in any other state, province, district or territory
12. Forging another's name to an application for insurance or to any document related to an insurance transaction
13. Improperly using notes or any other reference material to complete an examination for an insurance license
14. Knowingly accepting insurance business from an individual who is not licensed

15. Failing to comply with an administrative or court order imposing a child support obligation
16. Failing to pay state income tax or comply with any administrative or court order directing payment of state income tax.

VA Code §38.2-1831

Cease and Desist Orders

If the Commission has reason to believe that any person has committed a violation of the Insurance Title, or of any rule, regulation, or order issued by the Commission under it, the Commission must issue and serve an order upon that person by certified or registered mail or in any other manner permitted by law.

Contents of Order

The order must include a statement of the charges and a notice of a hearing on the charges to be held at a fixed time and place, which is at least ten days after the date of service of the notice. The order must also require that person to show cause why:

- an order should not be made by the Commission directing the alleged offender to cease and desist from the violation; or
- the Commission should not issue any other appropriate order.

At the hearing, that person has an opportunity to be heard in accordance with the Commission's order.

VA Code §38.2-219

Violation of the Orders

If the Commission finds in the hearing that there is about to be or has been a violation of the insurance laws, it may issue and serve upon any person committing the violation, by certified or registered mail or in any other manner permitted by law:

- an order reciting its findings and directing the person to cease and desist from the violation; or
- another appropriate order as the case and the interests of the policyholders, creditors, shareholders, or the public requires.

Any person who violates a cease and desist order may, upon conviction, be subject to one or both of the following:

1. Punishment as described under **Penalties** (listed below); or
2. The suspension or revocation of any license issued by the Commission.

VA Code §38.2-219

Penalties – Restitution

The Commission may require a person to make restitution in the amount of the direct actual financial loss:

- For charging a rate in excess of that provided by statute or by the rates filed with the Commission by the insurer;
- For charging a premium that is determined by the Commission to be unfairly discriminatory, with the amount of premium restitution being based on a period of one year from the date of determination;
- For failing to pay amounts explicitly required by the terms of the insurance contract where no aspect of the claim is disputed by the insurer;
- For improperly withholding, misappropriating, or converting any money or property received in the course of doing business.

VA Code §38.2-218

Penalties – Submitting Business without an Appointment

Any person submitting business in violation of the appointment requirements, while the person is not a holder of a valid agent's license to transact the class of insurance involved is:

- penalized a sum equal to the first year commission for the placement of that business;
- subject to insurance law penalties; and
- subject to having his or her license placed on probation, suspended, revoked or refused to be issued or renewed.

VA Code §38.2-1823

Penalty for Violations with and without Knowledge or Intent

Any person who knowingly or willfully violates any provision of the Insurance Title (VA Code §38.2) or any rule, regulation, or order issued pursuant to it is punished for each violation by a penalty of not more than $5,000.

Any person who violates without knowledge or intent any provision of the Insurance Title or any rule, regulation, or order issued pursuant to it is punished for each violation by a penalty of not more than $1,000. A series of similar violations resulting from the same act is limited to a penalty in the aggregate of not more than $10,000.

VA Code §38.2-218

Agent Licensing

The purpose of licensing is to ensure that insurance agents are educationally prepared in the line(s) of insurance they will offer, and that they meet certain character standards. The licensing process includes a requirement for pre-licensing education, passing an exam, and having the insurance department evaluate the applicant to make sure he or she meets certain criteria, such as having a good reputation for honesty.

Types of Licenses

Insurance Agent

No person or no insurer or licensed agent may knowingly permit a person to act in Virginia as an agent of an insurer licensed to transact the business of insurance without first obtaining a license as prescribed by the Commission.

Acting as an agent means "selling, soliciting, or negotiating contracts of insurance or annuity on behalf of an insurer licensed in Virginia or receiving or sharing, directly or indirectly, any commission or other valuable consideration arising from the sale, solicitation, or negotiation of any such contract, or both."

VA Code §38.2-1822

Agents offer insurance on behalf of an insurer through an *agency* relationship. In this relationship, the insurer is the *principal*.

The basic qualifications of an applicant are that he or she:

- is at least eighteen years of age, of good character;
- has a good reputation for honesty; and

- meets the other requirements of the Virginia law, including:
  - taking the exam; and
  - paying the application fee.

The application for a license requires information about bankruptcy, a criminal record and other items that can be used to determine the character and reputation of the applicant.

VA Code §38.2-1820

Individual License Residency

There are different licensing requirements for residents and nonresidents of Virginia. For licensing purposes, an individual is considered a **resident** if the individual:

- maintains his principal place of residence within Virginia, or
- maintains a place of residence in a city or town located partly within Virginia and partly within another state, provided the other state has established similar legal or regulatory requirements as to residence of such individuals; and
- declares himself to be a Virginia resident on his federal tax return; and
- declares himself to be a Virginia resident for purposes of paying Virginia income tax and personal property taxes; and
- is able to document this to the satisfaction of the Commission.

The Commission may consider other documentation furnished by the individual, including, but not limited to, a valid current Virginia driver's license or voter registration card, as additional proof of residency.

An individual applying for or holding a license who is unable to document his residency will be deemed not to be a resident of Virginia for purposes of licensing, with the exception that an individual meeting the following conditions may be considered a resident for the purposes of licensing:

- the individual resides outside of Virginia whose principal place of business is in Virginia;
- the individual is able to demonstrate to the satisfaction of the Commission that the laws

of his home state prevent him from obtaining a resident agent license in that state; and

- the individual affirmatively chooses to qualify as and be treated as a resident of Virginia for purposes of licensing and continuing education, both in Virginia and in the state in which the individual resides, if applicable.

VA Code §38.2-1800.1

Nonresident Reciprocity Licensing

Nonresident agents are not required to complete the licensing examination if they are already licensed in the same line of authority as the license for which they are applying, if the insurance supervisory official of the nonresident agent's state of residence grants similar exemptions to Virginia residents seeking licensure in that state.

To be licensed in Virginia, the nonresident agent must:

1. present proof in a form acceptable to the Commission that the applicant is currently licensed as a resident and in good standing in his home state;
2. submit the proper request for licensure and pay the required fees;
3. submit or transmit to the Commission the application for licensure that he or she submitted to his or her home state, or in lieu of that application, a completed Uniform Application.

The nonresident agent's home state must issue nonresident agent licenses to residents of Virginia on the same basis.

VA Code §38.2-1836

Assumed or Fictitious Name

Any individual or business entity conducting the business of insurance in Virginia under an assumed or fictitious name must notify the Bureau of Insurance of the name under which the individual or entity will be doing business. The notification must be made either at the time the application for a license to do business is filed or within thirty calendar days from the date the assumed or fictitious name is adopted.

When the business of insurance is no longer conducted under an assumed or fictitious name, notification to the Bureau of Insurance is required within thirty calendar days from the date the assumed or fictitious name is no longer used.

Foreign business entities comply with nonresident licensing rules.

VA Code §38.2-1822

Insurance Consultant

Persons acting as life and health or property and casualty insurance consultants must be licensed. An *insurance consultant* is defined as "any individual or business entity who acts as an independent contractor in relation to his client and for a fee or compensation, other than from an insurer or agent or surplus lines broker, advises or offers or purports to advise, as to life and health or property and casualty insurance, any person actively or prospectively insured."

Persons not considered an insurance consultant and who do not have to obtain a consultant license include:

- any licensed attorney acting in his professional capacity;
- a trust officer of a bank acting in the normal course of his employment;
- any actuary or certified public accountant who consults during the normal course of his business; and
- any person employed as a risk manager and who consults for his employer only.

VA Code §38.2-1837

A consultant license is generally required when a person:

- represents to members of the public that he provides planning or consulting services beyond those within the normal scope of activities of a licensed insurance agent; or
- charges or receives, directly or indirectly, a fee or other compensation for insurance advice, other than commissions received in the person's capacity as a licensed insurance agent or surplus lines broker resulting from selling, soliciting, or negotiating insurance or health care services as allowed by his license.

Certain administrative fees are allowed to be charged by insurance agents who do not have consultant licenses. The conditions for charging these fees are that:

- the applicant or policyholder consents to the fees in writing before any services are rendered. Written consent must be provided on a form that includes:
  - the applicant's or policyholder's signature;
  - the duration of services and amount of fees to be charged;
  - the services for which the fees are charged;
  - a statement that the agent is entitled to receive a commission from the insurer for selling, soliciting, or negotiating the insurance; and
- a schedule of fees and documentation for services rendered is maintained in the agent's office and is made available to applicants or policyholders upon request.

VA Code §38.2-1812.2

Consultant License Requirements

In order to obtain a consultant license, an individual must submit an application to the Commission and meet the following requirements:

- pass, within 183 calendar days prior to the date of application for such license, the property and casualty or life and health exam, as applicable, unless the applicant already has the license at time of application; and
- through the submission of the application, appoint the clerk of the Commission as the agent for service of process on the applicant in any action or proceeding arising in this Commonwealth out of or in connection with the exercise of the license.

VA Code §38.2-1838

Business Entity Consultant Licensing

Any individual acting as an insurance consultant as an officer, director, principal or employee of a business entity is also required to hold an individual license as an insurance consultant.

A business entity acting as an insurance consultant is required to obtain an insurance consultant license. In order to have the application for this license approved:

- the business entity must pay the required fee; and
- the business entity has designated a licensed producer to be responsible for the business

entity's compliance with the insurance laws, rules and regulations of Virginia.

The Commission may require additional documents reasonably necessary to verify the information in an application.

VA Code §38.2-1838

Application Fee

Each applicant for an insurance consultant's license must submit a $50 nonrefundable application processing fee at the time of initial application for such license.

VA Code §38.2-1838

Written Contracts for Services

A licensed insurance consultant that does not sell, solicit or negotiate insurance as part of his services must enter into a written contract with his client prior to any act as a consultant in Virginia.

A licensed insurance consultant who sells, solicits or negotiates insurance in Virginia as part of his services must enter into a written contract with his client prior to the purchase of any insurance by that client. The contract must include:

- the amount and basis of any consulting fee;
- the duration of employment; and
- additional compensation information if the insurance consultant may also receive commissions, incentives, bonuses, overrides, or any other form of remuneration as a result of his services for selling, soliciting, or negotiating insurance in addition to a consulting fee.

It is prohibited for an insurance consultant to provide or offer to provide insurance products to a public body while at the same time on its behalf evaluate proposals from other insurance agents and recommend the placement of insurance.

VA Code §38.2-1839

Consultant Annual License Renewal

Insurance consultant licenses must be renewed before June 1 of each year. The consultant must submit a renewal application and a non-refundable fee of $50 to the Commission, unless the license has been terminated, suspended or revoked on or before June 30 of that year. The license will be renewed for a one-year period, beginning on July 1 and ending on the following June 30. If the renewal application and fee are not received by the Commission by June 1, the license is terminated, on June 30.

VA Code §38.2-1840

Business Entity Licensing

A business entity acting as an insurance producer is required to obtain an insurance producer license. Application must be made using the Uniform Business Entity Application, or other application acceptable to the Commission. In order to be approved for a license:

- the business entity must pay the required fees; and
- the business entity must designate a licensed producer responsible for the business entity's compliance with the insurance laws, rules and regulations of Virginia.

VA Code §38.2-1820

Business Residency

A business entity is deemed to be a resident of Virginia as long as the business entity:

- if a domestic corporation, has filed its articles of incorporation with the clerk of the Commission, and has been issued a charter by the Commission;
- if a domestic limited liability company, has filed its articles of organization with the clerk of the Commission, and has been issued a certificate of organization by the Commission;
- if a domestic limited partnership, has applied for and received a certificate of limited partnership from the clerk of the Commission;
- if a domestic partnership, has filed its partnership agreement with the clerk of the appropriate court; or
- if a foreign business entity that is not licensed as a resident agent in any other jurisdiction, demonstrates to the satisfaction of the Commission that its principal place of business is within the Commonwealth of Virginia.

VA Code §38.2-1800.1

Resident and Nonresident Business Entity Licensure

Only persons who are licensed and appointed as an agent may act as an agent on behalf of a business entity in the transaction of insurance. Only business entities that are licensed and appointed may act as agents. The Commission may require proof of the business entity's lawful existence before issuing a license to the business entity.

For a nonresident business entity, generally, a **certification by the insurance department** of the business entity's home state is deemed to satisfy the requirement for licensing.

If the nonresident business entity is a corporation it must obtain a **certificate of authority** to transact business in Virginia before the Commission issues a license to such business entity.

If it is a limited liability company or limited partnership it must obtain a **certificate of registration** to transact business in Virginia before the Commission issues a license to such business entity.

VA Code §38.2-1822

Viatical Settlements
Purpose

The Virginia Viatical Settlements Act is implemented by Virginia insurance regulations found in 14 VAC 5-71. The Viatical Settlements Act is found in the Virginia Code §38.2-6000 through 6016.

14VAC5-71-10

A "Viatical settlement contract" means a written agreement establishing the terms under which compensation or anything of value will be paid, which compensation or value is less than the expected death benefit of the insurance policy or certificate, in return for the viator's assignment, transfer, sale, devise or bequest of the death benefit or ownership of any portion of the insurance policy or certificate of insurance. A viatical settlement contract also includes a contract for a loan or other financing transaction with a viator secured primarily by an individual or group life insurance policy, other than a loan by a life insurance company pursuant to the terms of the life insurance contract, or a loan secured by the cash value of the policy. A viatical settlement contract includes an agreement with a viator to transfer ownership or change the beneficiary designation at a later date regardless of the date that compensation is paid to the viator.

14VAC5-71-20

Broker Authority and Licensing

In order to act as a viatical settlement broker in Virginia, the broker must be licensed. Viatical settlement broker is defined as a person licensed in Virginia that on behalf of another and for a fee, commission or other valuable consideration, introduces viators to viatical settlement providers, or offers or attempts to negotiate viatical settlement contracts between a viator and one or more viatical settlement providers. The term does **not** include:

- an attorney;
- a certified public accountant; or
- a financial planner accredited by a nationally recognized accreditation agency,

who is retained to represent the viator and whose compensation is not paid by the viatical settlement provider or viatical settlement purchaser.

VA Code §38.2-6000

The viatical settlement broker's license is a limited license that allows solicitation only of viatical settlements

Life insurance and annuities agents may obtain a viatical settlement broker's license by complying with the licensing requirements in the Viatical Settlement Act and its regulations.

In order to obtain a viatical settlement broker's license, an application and nonrefundable fee of $50 must be submitted to the Commission.

Business Entity License

A business entity may obtain a viatical settlement broker's license. The business must:

- pay a licensing fee; and
- designate a licensed viatical settlement broker as the individual responsible for the business entity's compliance with the laws and related rules and regulations of Virginia.

All applicants for a viatical settlement broker's license must provide satisfactory evidence to the Commission that no disciplinary action has resulted in the suspension or revocation of any federal or state license pertaining to the business of viatical settlements or to the insurance or other financial services business.

Multiple Viators in More than One State

If there is more than one viator on a single policy, and the viators are residents of different states, the viatical settlement broker must hold a license in the state in which the viator having the largest percentage resides or, if the viators hold equal ownership, the viatical settlement broker is required to hold a license in the state of residence of one viator agreed upon in writing by all the viators.

License Renewal

Before June 1 of each year, each viatical settlement broker must pay a nonrefundable renewal fee of $50 and submit a renewal application to the Commission for the renewal of the license effective July 1 of that year.

VA Code 38.2-6001; 14 VAC 5-71-40

Broker vs. Agent

Unless a broker has a written agreement with the viator that makes the broker the agent of the viator, the broker is assumed to be the agent of the viatical settlement provider. A viatical settlement broker may not seek or obtain any compensation from the viator without a written agreement with the viator obtained before performing any services in connection with a viatical settlement.

A viatical settlement broker may perform any activities required of a viatical settlement provider on behalf of the viatical settlement provider.

Definition of Viatical Settlement Provider

Viatical settlement provider means a person, other than a viator, that enters into or effectuates a viatical settlement contract. Viatical settlement provider does not include:

- a bank, savings bank, savings and loan association, credit union, or other licensed lending institution that takes an assignment of a life insurance policy as collateral for a loan;
- the issuer of a life insurance policy providing accelerated benefits;

- an authorized or eligible insurer that provides stop loss coverage to a viatical settlement provider, viatical settlement purchaser, financing entity, special purpose entity or related provider trust;
- a natural person who makes no more than one agreement in a calendar year for the transfer of life insurance policies for any value less than the expected death benefit;
- a financing entity;
- a special purpose entity;
- a related provider trust;
- a viatical settlement purchaser; or
- an accredited investor or qualified institutional buyer as defined respectively in Regulation D, Rule 501 or Rule 144A of the Federal Securities Act of 1933, who purchases a viaticated policy from a viatical settlement provider and does not communicate with the viator or insured who is a resident of this Commonwealth except through a viatical settlement licensee.

If the viatical settlement provider transfers ownership or changes the beneficiary of the insurance policy, the provider must communicate the change in ownership or beneficiary to the insured within 20 days after the change.

Exceptions to Licensing Requirement

Officers, Directors or Employees of Insurers

A license as an insurance producer is not required for an officer, director or employee of an insurer or insurance producer who does not receive commissions on insurance policies and who:

- performs executive, administrative, managerial, or clerical activities which are only indirectly related to the sale, solicitation or negotiation of insurance;
- has functions related to underwriting, loss control, inspection or to claim processing, adjusting, investigating or settling; or
- acts in the capacity of a special agent or agency supervisor assisting insurance producers and whose activities are limited to providing technical advice and assistance to licensed insurance producers and do not include the sale, solicitation or negotiation of insurance.

VA Code §38.2-1821.1

Group Insurance Activities

A license is not required for a person who secures and furnishes information for the purpose of:

- group life insurance;
- group property and casualty insurance;
- group annuities; or
- group or blanket accident and health insurance.

No license is required for a person whose employment responsibilities include enrolling individuals under a group insurance policy, as long as:

- the person receives no commission or other valuable consideration for enrollments; and
- compensation is in no manner contingent upon the number of individuals enrolled or the amount of premium generated by enrollments.

Enrolling individuals for the purposes of exemption from licensure means:

- the process of informing individuals of the availability of coverages;
- calculating the insurance charge;
- assisting with completion of the enrollment application;
- preparing and delivering the certificate of insurance;
- answering questions regarding the coverages; and
- assisting the individual in making an informed decision whether or not enrollment under the group insurance plan is to be elected.

VA Code §38.2-1822

Insurance Plan Administration and Other Administrative Services

A license is not required for a person who:

- secures and furnishes information for the purpose of enrolling individuals under plans, issuing certificates under plans or otherwise assisting in administering plans; or
- performs administrative services related to mass marketed property and casualty insurance. For licensing purposes, administrative services does not include the selling, soliciting, or negotiating of insurance

where no commission is paid to the person for the service.

VA Code §38.2-1821.1

Employee Benefits Plan Administration

A license is not required for an employer or association, officer, director, employee, or the trustee of an employee trust plan who are engaged in the administration or operation of an employee benefits program that includes insurance for the employer's or association's own employees or the employees of its subsidiaries or affiliates, as long as these persons are not in any manner compensated by the insurer.

VA Code §38.2-1821.1

Underwriting Activities

A license is not required of employees of insurers or organizations employed by insurers who are engaged in the inspection, rating or classification of risks, or in the supervision of the training of insurance producers and who are not individually engaged in the sale, solicitation or negotiation of insurance.

VA Code §38.2-1821.1

Advertising without the Intent to Sell Insurance in Virginia

A license is not required for a person whose activities are limited to advertising without the intent to solicit insurance in Virginia through communications in printed publications or other forms of electronic mass media whose distribution is not limited to residents of Virginia as long as the person does not sell, solicit or negotiate insurance that would insure risks residing, located or to be performed in Virginia.

VA Code §38.2-1821.1

Multi-State Property and Casualty Risks

A person who is not a resident of Virginia is not required to be licensed for selling, soliciting or negotiating a contract of insurance for commercial property and casualty covering risks located in more than one state, provided that:

- the person is licensed as an insurance producer to sell, solicit or negotiate insurance in the state where the insured on the contract maintains its principal place of business; and

- the contract of insurance insures risks located in that state.

VA Code §38.2-1821.1

Employee Advice

A salaried, full-time employee is not required to be licensed who counsels or advises his employer about insurance interests of the employer or of the subsidiaries or business affiliates of the employer provided that the employee does not sell, solicit or negotiate insurance or receive direct or indirect commission.

VA Code §38.2-1821.1

Referrals

A non-licensed individual may refer a customer who seeks to purchase any insurance product to a licensed agent and receive compensation for the referral of a customer, as long as:

- the referral does not include a discussion of specific insurance policy terms and conditions;
- the compensation is in the form of a one-time nominal fee of a fixed dollar amount for each referral; and
- the compensation does not depend on whether the referral results in the purchase of insurance by the customer.

VA Code §38.2-1821.1

Agent Appointment

Every licensed agent may sell policies and solicit applications for insurance for any one or more of the classes of insurance for which he is licensed on behalf of an insurer that is also licensed in Virginia for those classes of insurance, even if the licensed agent has not yet been validly appointed by the insurer, as long as the following requirements are met:

- The insurer, within 30 calendar days of the date of execution of the first insurance application or policy submitted by a licensed but not yet appointed agent, either rejects the application or policy or files with the Commission a notice of appointment.
- The insurer must provide to the licensed agent, within the same 30-day period, a verification that the notice of appointment has been filed with the Commission.

         VA PPL LH-2_16298

- Upon receipt of the notice of appointment, the Commission must verify that the agent holds a valid license and that the notice has been properly completed and submitted.

If the Commission determines that the appointment is invalid, it notifies the appointing insurer within five business days of its receipt of the appointment notice. If the appointment is valid, the Commission issues an acknowledgement of appointment to the agent within five business days of its receipt of the appointment notice, and must at the same time, notify the appointing insurer of the issuance of the acknowledgement of appointment.

- An agent whose appointment by an insurer has been terminated by the insurer is prohibited from selling or soliciting applications or policies on behalf of that insurer unless and until reappointed by the insurer. Any selling or solicitation on behalf of that insurer subsequent to the appointment termination and prior to the reappointment constitutes a violation and subjects the agent to penalties.

Each agent's appointment record is public information and is available for public inspection during normal business hours of the Commission. The Commission may charge a reasonable fee to cover the costs incurred in providing this information.

VA Code §38.2-1833

Notices of License Termination, Suspension or Revocation

A valid appointment of an agent authorizes the agent to act for the insurer during the time for which the appointing insurer is licensed to do business in Virginia, unless the appointment is otherwise terminated, suspended, or revoked. No later than 10 calendar days after notice of termination, suspension or revocation of an appointment has been sent to the agent or agency, the agent or agency must immediately cease selling or soliciting on behalf of the insurer.

The insurer must notify the agent of termination within five calendar days, and must notify the Commission within 30 calendar days.

VA Code §38.2-1833; §38.2-1834

Notification of Termination

An insurer or authorized representative of the insurer that terminates the appointment, employment, contract or other insurance business relationship with an agent or other licensee must notify the Commission within thirty calendar days following the effective date of the termination.

A valid reason for any termination for cause must be certified in writing in the notice by an officer or authorized representative of the insurer or agent terminating the relationship. Upon the written request of the Commission, the insurer must provide additional information, documents, records or other data pertaining to the termination or activity of the agent or other licensee whose license was terminated, suspended, revoked, or has lapsed by operation of law.

VA Code §38.2-1834.1

Appointments and Termination

An individual agent's license authorizes him to act as an agent until his license is otherwise terminated, suspended or revoked. A business entity's license that authorizes it to act as an agent is also authorized until the license is terminated, suspended or revoked.

A dissolution or discontinuance of a partnership automatically terminates all licenses issued to the partnership.

All insurance licenses are terminated for the entity within 90 calendar days of receiving notification from the clerk of the Commission of the termination or revocation of:

- a certificate of organization of a domestic LLC;
- a certificate of authority of a domestic corporation;
- a certificate of registration of a foreign LLC; or
- a certificate of authority of a foreign corporation.

VA Code §38.2-1825

 VA PPL LH-2_16298

Maintaining a License

Continuing Education

On a biennial basis every individual resident and nonresident insurance consultant, life and annuities insurance agent, health agent, property and casualty insurance agent and personal lines agent must furnish evidence that required continuing education has been completed.

- Any agent who holds a life and annuities license or a health agent license, or both, must complete 16 hours of continuing education.
- Any agent who holds a personal lines license or a property and casualty license must complete 16 hours of continuing education.
- Generally, any agent who holds licenses from more than one category of licenses must complete 24 hours of continuing education credits with a minimum of eight credit hours in each license category.
- Of the total required credits for each biennium, three credit hours must be in insurance ethics, which may include insurance law and regulations applicable in Virginia.
- Agents may receive no more than 75 percent of their required credits from courses provided by insurance companies or agencies.

VA Code §38.2-1866

Deadline

The continuing education (CE) renewal biennium (two year period) ends December 31 of even numbered years. Each agent holding one or more licenses subject to continuing education requirements must complete all continuing education, exemption, or waiver requirements no later than November 30, or the next working day if November 30 falls on a weekend, of each even-numbered year. The agents must submit to the Board or its administrator proof of compliance, all documents, forms and fees specified, filing proof of completion of approved continuing education course for the appropriate number of hours and the appropriate content, or filing proof of meeting the exemption requirements.

VA Code §38.2-1868.1

Deadline Extension

If an agent failed to submit proof of compliance, or has failed to pay required fees by the November 30 deadline, the agent is given a final opportunity to complete the requirements, provided proof of compliance is received by the Board or its administrator by December 31, or the next working day thereafter if December 31 falls on a weekend.

Failure of an agent to furnish proof of compliance by the applicable date will result in license termination.

VA Code §38.2-1868.1

Failure to Meet CE Requirements

Any agent who fails to submit complete documentation showing proof of compliance with applicable CE requirements, as well as all specified forms and fees, so that they are received by the Board or its administrator by the close of business on the required dates is in noncompliance with the requirements of the CE laws.

Failure of an agent to satisfy the CE requirements within the required time frame, by:

- obtaining the CE credits required and furnishing evidence of them to the Board or its administrator;
- furnishing the Board acceptable evidence of exemption; or
- obtaining a waiver of the requirements for that biennium,

will result, after notification by the Board to the Commission, in the administrative termination of each license held by the agent for which the requirement was not satisfied.

VA Code §38.2-1868.1 and §38.2-1869

CE Status Reports

The CE Board, on or about a date six months prior to the end of each biennium, provides a status report to each agent who has not satisfied the education requirements for that biennium. The report informs the agent of the current compliance status for each license for which the agent needs CE, and the consequences associated with noncompliance. The notice is sent by first-class mail to these agents at their last-known residence addresses as shown in the Commission's records.

Failure of an agent to receive the notification is not grounds for contesting license termination.

VA Code §38.2-1869

Notice of Noncompliance

No administrative termination due to noncompliance with the CE rules becomes effective until the Commission provides at least thirty calendar days' written notice of the impending termination to the agent by first-class mail sent to the agent at the agent's last known residence address as shown in the Commission's records. The notice period begins on the date that the written notice is placed in the United States mail.

Neither the Board, nor its administrator, nor the Commission has the power to grant an agent additional time for completing required continuing education credits, or additional time for submitting proof of compliance, or additional time for seeking waivers or exemption.

VA Code §38.2-1869

Proof of Prior Compliance

Following the notice from the Commission until the compliance deadline is reached, the Board permits agents to demonstrate that the agent had, in fact, submitted, and the CE Board or its administrator had received, proof of compliance on or before the filing deadlines.

VA Code §38.2-1869

Termination of Licenses

No more than fifteen calendar days after the end of the appeal period, the Board or its administrator provides the Commission with a final record of agents who complied with the CE requirements, and the Commission administratively terminates the licenses of those agents who did not submit proper proof of compliance in a timely manner.

Agents who wish to contest the Commission's action in terminating a license must adhere to the Commission's Rules of Practice and Procedure and the Rules of the Supreme Court of Virginia. Failure by the agent to initiate a contest within thirty calendar days following the date of license termination is deemed a waiver by the agent of the right to contest the license termination.

VA Code §38.2-1869

Licensing after Termination

Resident agents who apply for a license after termination of a previous license cannot be issued a license unless the agent has successfully completed, subsequent to the end of the biennium, the licensing examination. In this event, the examination requirements are not subject to waiver under any circumstances.

VA Code §38.2-1869

License Termination and an Agent Who Moves

A resident agent whose license terminates because, within 180 calendar days prior to the end of a biennium, or prior to the expiration of the appeal period for that biennium, the agent moves his residence to another state, and who had not, prior to this relocation, provided proof of compliance for this biennium is not permitted to apply for a new license of the same type until the agent has complied with the requirements of a nonresident license applicant.

VA Code §38.2-1869

Waiver of Continuing Education Requirements

The requirements regarding the number of course credits required may be waived by the Board if good cause is shown. **Good cause** includes long-term illness or incapacity and other emergency situations that prevent the agent from meeting the required continuing education credit hours. Requests for waiver of all course credit requirements must be submitted to the Board or its administrator no later than ninety calendar days prior to the end of the biennium.

In the event that the long-term illness, incapacity, or such other emergency situation manifests itself within 120 calendar days prior to the end of the biennium, requests for waivers of some but not all of the course credit requirements must be submitted to the CE Board or its administrator no later than the normal submission deadline. The CE Board will approve or disapprove the waiver request within thirty calendar days of receipt, and provides written notice of its decision to the applicant for waiver within five calendar days of making its decision.

VA Code §38.2-1870

Licensees Exempt from Continuing Education Requirements

Resident or nonresident agents who were issued a license during the last twelve months of the biennium, and who are not otherwise exempt from the CE requirements for that license, are exempt from fulfilling the CE credit requirements for that license for that biennium.

Licensees may request exemptions from CE requirements, but are not exempt unless the exemption is approved by the CE Board after submission of the exemption request.

VA Code §38.2-1871

Age 65 Licensees Exempt

An agent who has attained or will attain at least the age of sixty-five by the end of a biennium may apply for a **permanent exemption**, subject to submission of proof of the following:

- the agent has had the license for at least 20 years;
- the agent is a resident agent who will have held a Virginia resident license continuously and without interruption for no fewer than the immediately preceding four years by the end of the biennium, and the balance of 20 years in another state of having held equivalent license authority in Virginia for at least twenty of the preceding thirty years; and
- any unlicensed period was not the result of a license revocation or termination by the Commission.

VA Code §38.2-1871

Change of Address

The agent has the responsibility of reporting to the Commission, and to any insurer with which the agent is appointed, any change in residence or name within 30 days. If a licensed resident agent moves from Virginia, his authority to act as a resident agent immediately terminates, whether or not the Commission has been notified.

VA Code §38.2-1826

Appointment Renewal

Prior to August 10 of each year, or the first business day after if August 10 falls on a weekend or holiday, every insurer must remit to the Commission a renewal appointment fee. The insurer must pay a fee in an amount prescribed by the Commission, for each appointment for which notice of appointment termination was not received by the Commission on or before the preceding June 30.

If an insurer fails to pay amounts due by the date due, the Commission:

1. imposes a penalty of $50 per day for each calendar day between the date due and the date full payment is received by the Commission. The renewal appointment fees are not considered paid in full unless and until the penalty has been received by the Commission; and
2. may, in addition to the penalty imposed, administratively terminate the appointment of each agent on whose behalf the appointment renewal fee, including any penalty, was not received by the Commission by the date due and after the insurer has been given due notice and an opportunity to submit the overdue payment.

If the Commission refuses to grant or revokes or suspends a license, any appointment of the license is also revoked or suspended.

VA Code §38.2-1821; §38.2-1834

Hearings

If the Commission believes that any applicant for a license is not of good character or does not have a good reputation for honesty, it may refuse to issue the license, subject to the right of the applicant to demand a hearing on the application.

The Commission generally does not revoke or suspend an existing license until the licensee is given an opportunity to be heard before the Commission. If the Commission refuses to issue a new license or proposes to revoke or suspend an existing license, it will give the applicant or licensee at least ten calendar days' notice in writing of the time and place of the hearing if a hearing is requested. The notice contains a statement of the objections to the issuance of the license, or the reason for its proposed revocation or suspension, as the case may be.

VA Code §38.2-1832

Notice and Revocation

The notice may be given to the applicant or licensee by registered or certified mail, sent to the last known address of record, or the last known business address if the address of record is incorrect, or in any other lawful manner the Commission prescribes. The Commission may summon witnesses to testify with respect to the applicant or licensee, and the applicant or licensee may introduce evidence in his or its behalf.

No applicant to whom a license is refused after a hearing, nor any licensee whose license is revoked, may again apply for a license until after the expiration of a period of five years from the date of the Commission's order, or such other period of time as the Commission prescribes in its order.
VA Code §38.2-1832

Revoking, Suspending or Refusing a Business Entity License

The license of a business entity may be suspended, revoked or refused if the Commission finds, after notice and an opportunity to be heard, that:

- an individual licensee acting at the direction of, on behalf of, or with the permission of the business entity was known to be in violation by one or more of the partners, officers or managers acting on behalf of the business entity; and
- the violation was neither reported to the Commission nor corrective action taken.

In addition to or in lieu of a denial, suspension or revocation of a license, a person may be subject to a penalty.

The Commission has the authority to enforce the provisions of and impose any authorized penalty or remedy against any person who is under investigation for or charged with a violation, even if the person's license or registration has been surrendered, terminated, suspended, revoked, or has lapsed by operation of law.
VA Code §38.2-1832

Fiduciary Responsibilities

All premiums, return premiums, or other funds received in any manner by an agent must be held in a *fiduciary* capacity and must be accounted for by each agent. The agent must, in the ordinary course of business, pay the funds to the insured or his assignee, insurer, insurance premium finance company or agent entitled to the payment.

Generally, all these funds must be maintained in a fiduciary account separate from all other business and personal funds. Funds deposited into the separate fiduciary account may not be commingled or combined with other funds except for the purpose of advancing premiums, establishing reserves for the payment of return premiums, or establishing funds to maintain a minimum balance or to guarantee the adequacy of the account. The agent must maintain an accurate record and itemization of the funds deposited into this account. The commission portion of any premiums deposited to this separate account may be withdrawn at the discretion of the agent.

The separate fiduciary account of a licensed business entity is considered the fiduciary account of an individual agent acting on behalf of the licensed business entity.

Any agent who is a duly appointed agent of an insurer and who has a written contractual relationship with such insurer which includes provisions regarding remittance of funds does not have to maintain a separate fiduciary account for the funds. The funds must be held separately from any personal or nonbusiness funds and be reasonably ascertainable from the books of accounts and records of the agent.
VA Code §38.2-1813

Commissions and Compensation

No insurer may pay any commission or other consideration to anyone for services as an agent within Virginia unless the person is a duly appointed agent of the insurer and, at the time of the transaction, held a valid license as an agent, for the class of insurance involved. No one other than a duly licensed and appointed agent may accept commission or other valuable consideration unless the person, at the time of the transaction, held a valid license as an agent for the class of insurance involved.

This provision does not prevent the payment or receipt of renewal or other deferred commissions or compensation to or by any person if the person was duly licensed and appointed.

Agents may not directly or indirectly share commissions or other compensation paid on account of a transaction under his or her license, with any person not also licensed, for the class of insurance involved in the transaction. If commission is shared, the other agent(s) must also be licensed and qualified for the same class of insurance.
VA Code §38.2-1812

Changing Agents and Commissions

Insurers must accept and honor each request by a policyholder for a change of insurance agent of record. The change is generally effective on the date of the next renewal of the policy. Prior to the effective date of the change, the insurer provides written notice of the change to the current insurance agent of record. The new insurance agent of record is paid all commissions payable on the policy effective prior to the next renewal date of the policy following the policyholder's requested change, excluding any commissions or other compensation payable under an insurer's retirement or deferred compensation plan with the insurance agent. A request for a change of insurance agent of record must be in writing.
VA Code §38.2-1812

Felony Convictions and Administrative Actions

An agent must report to the Commission any felony conviction within 30 days, and include the facts and details regarding the conviction.

Another reporting duty of the agent is to report to the Commission within thirty days of the final disposition of any administration action taken against him in another jurisdiction, or by another government agency in Virginia. The report must include a copy of the order, consent to order or other relevant legal documents.
VA Code §38.2-1826(B)(C)

Record Retention

Insurance licensees must generally retain all records about their insurance transactions for the three previous calendar years. Records of premium quotations that are not accepted by an insured or prospective insured do not have to be retained. Retained records must be made available promptly upon request for examination by the Commission or its employees without notice during normal business hours.
VA Code §38.2-1809(B)

Marketing Practices

Unfair trade practices in the business of insurance are defined in VA Code §38.2-500 through 3-518. Several of these prohibited practices are described in this section.

Rebating

It is illegal to:

1. knowingly permit, offer, or make any insurance contract or agreement which is not plainly expressed in the contract issued.
2. pay, allow or give, or offer to pay, allow or give, directly or indirectly, as inducement to any insurance contract, any rebate of premium payable on the contract, any special favor or advantage in the dividends or other benefits on the contract, any valuable consideration or inducement not specified in the contract, except in accordance with an applicable rating plan authorized for use in Virginia.
3. give, sell, purchase, or offer to give, sell or purchase as inducement to insurance, or in connection with insurance contracts, any stocks, bonds, or other securities of any company, any dividends or profits accrued on any stocks, bonds or other securities of any company, or anything of value not specified in the contract.
4. receive or accept as inducement to insurance, any rebate of premium payable on the contract, any special favor or advantage in the dividends or other benefit to accrue on

the contract, or any valuable consideration or inducement not specified in the contract.

VA Code §38.2-509

Misrepresentation

It is prohibited to make, issue, circulate, cause or knowingly allow to be made, issued or circulated, any estimate, illustration, circular, statement, sales presentation, omission, or comparison that:

1. misrepresents the benefits, advantages, conditions or terms of any insurance policy;
2. misrepresents the dividends or share of the surplus to be received on any insurance policy;
3. makes any false or misleading statements regarding the dividends or share of surplus previously paid on any insurance policy;
4. misrepresents or is misleading as to the financial condition of any person or the legal reserve system upon which any life insurer operates (the legal reserve system is the minimum reserves required under the laws of the jurisdiction in which an insurer operates.);
5. uses any name or title of any insurance policy or class of insurance policies that misrepresents the true nature of the policy or policies;
6. misrepresents any material fact for the purpose of inducing or tending to induce the lapse, forfeiture, exchange, conversion, replacement, or surrender of any insurance policy;
7. misrepresents any material fact for the purpose of effecting a pledge, assignment, or loan on any insurance policy; or
8. misrepresents any insurance policy as being a share of stock.

VA Code §38.2-502

It is illegal to make or cause or allow to be made false or fraudulent statements or representations on or relative to an application or any document or communication relating to the business of insurance in order to obtain a fee, commission, money, or other benefit from any insurer, agent, broker, premium finance company, or individual.

It is illegal to, with respect to any document pertaining to the business of insurance, including payments made to an insurer or by an insurer, affix or cause or allow to be affixed the signature of any other person to the document without the written authorization of the person whose signature appears on the document.

It is illegal to, with respect to any insurance document, obtain or cause or allow to be obtained by false pretense the signature of another person or utilize such signature for the purpose of altering, changing or effecting the benefits, advantages, terms or conditions of any insurance contract or document related to the insurance contract, including payments made to an insurer or by an insurer.

VA Code §38.2-512

Defamation

It is illegal to make false or maliciously critical statements about others in the insurance business. This is known as *defamation*.

Specifically, it is illegal to publish, disseminate, or circulate, directly or indirectly, or aid, abet or encourage the making, publishing, disseminating or circulating of any oral or written statement or any pamphlet, circular, article or literature that is false, and maliciously critical of, or derogatory to, any person with respect to the business of insurance or with respect to any person in the conduct of his insurance business and that is calculated to injure that person.

VA Code §38.2-504

False Advertising

It is illegal to falsely advertise. Specifically, it is illegal to make, publish, disseminate, circulate, or place before the public, or cause or knowingly allow to be made, published, disseminated, circulated, or placed before the public in a newspaper, magazine or other publication, or in the form of a notice, circular, pamphlet, letter or poster, or over any radio or television station, or in any other way, an advertisement, announcement or statement containing any assertion, representation or statement relating to:

- the business of insurance; or
- anyone in the conduct of his insurance business, which is untrue, deceptive or misleading.

VA Code §38.2-503

VA PPL LH-2_16298

Boycott, Coercion and Intimidation

It is illegal to enter into any agreement to commit, or by any concerted action commit, any act of boycott, coercion or intimidation resulting in or tending to result in unreasonable restraint of, or monopoly in, the business of insurance.

VA Code §38.2-505

Unfair Discrimination

No person may:

- Unfairly discriminate or permit any unfair discrimination between individuals of the same class and equal life expectancy:
  - in the rates charged for any life insurance or annuity contract; or
  - in the dividends or other benefits payable on the contract; or
  - in any other of the terms and conditions of the contract;
- Unfairly discriminate or permit any unfair discrimination between individuals of the same class and of essentially the same hazard:
  - in the amount of premium, policy fees, or rates charged for any policy or contract of accident or health insurance;
  - in the benefits payable under such policy or contract;
  - in any of the terms or conditions of such policy or contract; or
  - in any other manner;
- Refuse to insure, refuse to continue to insure, or limit the amount, extent or kind of insurance coverage available to an individual, or charge an individual a different rate for the same coverage solely because of blindness, or partial blindness, or mental or physical impairments, unless the refusal, limitation or rate differential is based on sound actuarial principles;
- Unfairly discriminate or permit any unfair discrimination between individuals or risks of the same class and of essentially the same hazards by refusing to issue, refusing to renew, cancelling or limiting the amount of insurance coverage solely because of the geographic location of the individual or risk, unless:
  - The refusal, cancellation or limitation is for a business purpose that is not a mere pretext for unfair discrimination; or
  - The refusal, cancellation or limitation is required by law or regulatory mandate;
- Make or permit any unfair discrimination between individuals or risks of the same class and of essentially the same hazards by refusing to issue, refusing to renew, cancelling or limiting the amount of insurance coverage on a residential property risk, or the personal property contained in a residential property risk, solely because of the age of the residential property, unless:
  - The refusal, cancellation or limitation is for a business purpose that is not a mere pretext for unfair discrimination; or
  - The refusal, cancellation or limitation is required by law or regulatory mandate;
- (Effective January 1, 2014) Refuse to issue or renew any individual accident and sickness insurance policy or contract for coverage over and above any lifetime benefit of a group accident and sickness policy or contract solely because an individual is insured under a group accident and sickness insurance policy or contract, provided that medical expenses covered by both individual and group coverage must be paid first by the group policy or contract to the extent of the group coverage; or
- Consider the status of a victim of domestic violence as a criterion in any decision with regard to insurance underwriting, pricing, renewal, scope of coverage, or payment of claims on any and all insurance. The term **domestic violence** means the occurrence of one or more of the following acts by a current or former family member, household member, person against whom the victim obtained a protective order or caretaker:
  - Attempting to cause or causing or threatening another person physical harm, severe emotional distress, psychological trauma, rape or sexual assault;
  - Engaging in a course of conduct or repeatedly committing acts toward another person, including following the person without proper authority, under circumstances that place the person in reasonable fear of bodily injury or physical harm;

- Subjecting another person to false imprisonment; or
- Attempting to cause or causing damage to property so as to intimidate or attempt to control the behavior of another person.

VA Code §38.2-508

Twisting

A person may not make, issue, or cause to be made or issued an oral or written statement that misrepresents or makes incomplete comparisons about the terms, conditions, or benefits contained in a policy for the purpose of inducing or attempting or tending to induce the policyholder to forfeit, surrender, retain, exchange, or convert a policy or allow a policy to lapse. Such activity is known as *twisting*.

VA Code §38.2-1831(5)

Virginia Insurance Guaranty Association

A State Guaranty Association is an association governed by individual state regulations, wherein member insurers are responsible for contractual obligations to policyholders if another member is unable to meet them. Insurance companies which are part of these guaranty associations are liable for cash values, death benefits, and other contractual monetary obligations if another of its members is not able to meet them. A typical guaranty association will have a maximum limit of $300,000 per policyholder benefit, and $100,000 per annuity cash value or present value. These limits vary by state, however. The state guaranty association may require all insurance companies doing business in the state to be part of the association, or only those domiciled in that state. Guaranty associations may not be used as a sales tool for the solicitation of insurance business.

In Virginia, member insurers include all insurers who solicit and issue the following types of insurance for Virginia residents:

- Direct, nongroup life, accident and sickness, or annuity policies or contracts and supplemental contracts to any of these;
- Certificates under direct group policies and contracts;
- Unallocated annuity contracts issued by member insurers;

- Annuity contracts and certificates under group annuity contracts including:
  - guaranteed investment contracts;
  - deposit administration contracts;
  - unallocated funding agreements;
  - allocated funding agreements;
  - structured settlement annuities; and
  - any immediate or deferred annuity contracts; and
- Dental benefit contracts entered into with a dental plan organization.

VA Code §38.2-1700

Virginia Life, Accident and Sickness Insurance Guaranty Association Limits on Coverage

The association never pays more than...	
$300,000	in life insurance death benefits
$100,000	in life insurance in net cash surrender and withdrawal values
$250,000	in the present value of annuity benefits, including net cash surrender and net cash withdrawal value
$500,000	for accident and sickness insurance that constitutes basic hospital medical and surgical insurance or major medical insurance
$300,000	for accident and sickness insurance that constitutes disability insurance or long-term care insurance
$100,000	for accident and sickness insurance that DOES NOT constitute disability, basic hospital, medical and surgical insurance, major medical insurance or long-term care insurance including any net cash surrender and net cash withdrawal values

VA Code §38.2-1700

Advertising Prohibition

Virginia's insurance code prohibits using the guaranty association in soliciting sales of insurance. The law states that no person, including an insurer, agent or affiliate of any insurer may make, publish, disseminate, circulate or place before the public, or cause, directly or indirectly, to be made, published, disseminated, circulated or placed before the public, in any newspaper, magazine or other publication, or in the form of a notice, circular, pamphlet, letter or poster, or over any radio station or television station, or in any other way, any advertisement, announcement or

VA PPL LH-2_16298

statement, written or oral, which uses the existence of the association for the purpose of sales, solicitation or inducement to purchase any form of insurance covered by the guaranty association. However, the guaranty association or other entity that does not sell or solicit insurance is not subject to this law.

VA Code §38.2-1715

Insurance Information and Privacy Protection

Much of the information gathered for insurance purposes is protected under privacy rules. These rules apply to insurance purchased primarily for personal, family or household purposes.

VA Code §38.2-601

Pretext Interviews

Insurance institutions, agents, and insurance-support organizations may not use or authorize the use of pretext interview to obtain information in connection with an insurance transaction. In Virginia's laws, a **pretext interview** means an interview whereby a person, in an attempt to obtain information about a natural person, performs one or more of the following acts:

- pretends to be someone he or she is not;
- pretends to represent a person he or she is not in fact representing;
- misrepresents the true purpose of the interview; or
- refuses to identify himself or herself upon request.

A pretext interview may be used when there is, based upon specific information available for review by the Commission, a reasonable basis for suspecting criminal activity, fraud, material misrepresentation, or material nondisclosure in connection with the claim.

VA Code §38.2-603

Notice of Information Collection and Disclosure Practices

An insurance institution or agent must provide a notice of insurance information practices to all applicants or policyholders in connection with insurance transactions:

1. When insurance is being applied for, a notice must be provided no later than:

   a. **At the time of the delivery of the insurance policy** or certificate when personal information is collected only from the applicant or from public records;

   b. **At the time the collection of personal information is initiated** when personal information is collected from a source other than the applicant or public records; or

2. When an application for insurance is made by telephone and personal information is collected from a source other than the applicant or public records, the notice of insurance information practices may be given **orally at the time of application**, as long as, at policy issue, the notice is given in writing or, if the applicant agrees, in electronic format, no later than at the time of the delivery of the insurance policy or certificate.

3. In the case of a policy renewal, a notice must be provided no later than **the policy renewal date**. However, no notice is required in connection with a policy renewal if:

   a. Personal information is collected only from the policyholder or from public records; or

   b. A notice meeting these requirements has been given within the previous 24 months; or

4. In the case of a policy reinstatement or change in insurance benefits, a notice is provided **no later than the time a request for a policy reinstatement** or change in insurance benefits is received by the insurance institution, except that no notice is required if personal information is collected only from the policyholder or from public records.

VA Code §38.2-604

Notice Contents

The notice must be in writing or, if the applicant or policyholder agrees, in electronic format, and include:

- whether personal information may be collected from persons other than an individual proposed for coverage.
- the types of personal information that may be collected and the types of sources and

investigative techniques that may be used to collect such information.

- the types of disclosures made and the circumstances under which the disclosures may be made without prior authorization, if the disclosures occur with such frequency that a general business practice is indicated.
- a description of the rights to access personal information and how the information can be corrected, amended or deleted.
- that information obtained from a report prepared by an insurance-support organization may be retained by the insurance-support organization and disclosed to other persons.

VA Code §38.2-604

Notice of Financial Information Collection and Disclosure Practices

An insurance institution or an agent must provide clear and conspicuous notice of financial information collection and disclosure practices in connection with insurance transactions. An insurance institution or agent may satisfy the notice requirements by providing a **short form notice** at the same time that the insurance institution or agent delivers an opt out notice.

The insurance institution or agent is not required to deliver the complete notice with its short form notice, provided the insurance institution or agent provides the applicant with a reasonable means to obtain such notice.

An insurance agent who is working with a current policyholder and has already provided the policyholder with a notice in the previous 12 months does not have to provide another notice.

VA Code §38.2-604.1

Marketing and Research Surveys

An insurance institution or agent must clearly specify those questions designed to obtain information solely for marketing or research purposes from an individual in connection with an insurance transaction.

VA Code §38.2-605

Consent of Disclosure Authorization Forms

Disclosure authorization forms authorize the disclosure of personal or privileged information about an individual to the insurance institution, agent, or insurance-support organization. These disclosure authorizations must:

- Be written in plain language
- Be dated
- Specify the types of persons authorized to disclose information about the individual;
- Specify the nature of the information that is authorized to be disclosed
- Name the insurance institution or agent and identify the types of representatives of the insurer to whom the individual is authorizing information to be disclosed
- Specify the purposes for which the information is collected
- Advise the individual or a person authorized to act on behalf of the individual that the individual or the individual's authorized representative is entitled to receive a copy of the authorization form

VA Code §38.2-606

Investigative Consumer Reports

An **investigative consumer report** is a consumer report or a portion thereof in which information about a natural person's character, general reputation, personal characteristics, or mode of living is obtained through personal interviews with the person's neighbors, friends, associates, acquaintances, or others who may have knowledge concerning such items of information.

VA Code §38.2-607

There are specific rules insurers and agents must follow if they prepare or request an investigative consumer report. Insurers, agents, or insurance-support organizations may not prepare or request an investigative consumer report about an individual in connection with an insurance transaction involving an application for insurance, a policy renewal, a policy reinstatement or a change in insurance benefits unless the insurance institution or agent informs the individual:

- that he may request to be interviewed in connection with the preparation of the investigative consumer report (this is called a personal interview); and

- that upon request, he is entitled to receive a copy of the investigative consumer report.

VA Code §38.2-607

If an investigative consumer report is to be prepared by an insurance institution or agent, the insurance institution or agent must institute procedures to conduct a personal interview requested by an individual.

If an investigative consumer report is to be prepared by an insurance-support organization, the insurance institution or agent requesting the report must inform the insurance-support organization whether a personal interview has been requested by the individual. The insurance-support organization must also institute reasonable procedures to conduct such interviews, if requested.

VA Code §38.2-607

Access to Recorded Personal Information

If any individual, after proper identification, submits a written request to an insurance institution, agent, or insurance-support organization for access to recorded personal information about himself, the insurance institution, agent, or insurance-support organization must provide this access within 30 business days from the date the request is received.

The personal information provided must identify the source of the information if it is an institutional source. Other than for personal information provided regarding a correction, amendment or deletion, an insurance institution, agent, or insurance-support organization may charge a reasonable fee to cover the costs of providing a copy of recorded personal information to individuals.

VA Code §38.2-608

Correction, Amendment or Deletion of Recorded Personal Information

Within thirty business days from the date of receipt of a written request from an individual to correct, amend, or delete any recorded personal information about the individual within its

possession, an insurance institution, agent, or insurance-support organization may either:

- correct, amend, or delete the portion of the recorded personal information in dispute; or
- notify the individual of:
  - its refusal to make the correction, amendment, or deletion;
  - the reasons for the refusal; and
  - the individual's right to file a statement if the information is not corrected, amended or deleted.

VA Code §38.2-609

If the insurance institution, agent, or insurance-support organization corrects, amends, or deletes recorded personal information, the insurance institution, agent, or insurance-support organization must notify the individual in writing and provide the correction, amendment, or fact of deletion to:

- any person specifically designated by the individual who, within the preceding two years, may have received the recorded personal information;
- any insurance-support organization whose primary source of personal information is insurance institutions if the insurance-support organization has systematically received the recorded personal information from the insurance institution within the preceding seven years; and
- any insurance-support organization that furnished the personal information that has been corrected, amended, or deleted.

When an individual disagrees with an insurance institution's, agent's, or insurance-support organization's refusal to correct, amend, or delete recorded personal information, the individual is permitted to file with the insurance institution, agent, or insurance-support organization:

- a concise statement setting forth what the individual thinks is the correct, relevant, or fair information; and
- a concise statement of the reasons why the individual disagrees with the insurance institution's, agent's, or insurance-support organization's refusal to correct, amend, or delete recorded personal information.

VA Code §38.2-609

If an individual files a statement, the insurance institution, agent, or support organization:

- files the statement with the disputed personal information and provide a means by which anyone reviewing the disputed personal information is made aware of the individual's statement and has access to it;
- must, in any future disclosure by the insurance institution, agent, or support organization of the recorded personal information, clearly identify the matter in dispute and provide the individual's statement along with the recorded personal information being disclosed; and
- furnish the statement to the persons as required.

VA Code §38.2-609

The rights to dispute granted to individuals extend to all natural persons to the extent information about them is collected and maintained by an insurance institution, agent, or insurance-support organization in connection with an insurance transaction. The rights granted do not extend to information about them that relates to and is collected in connection with or in reasonable anticipation of a claim or civil or criminal proceeding involving them.

VA Code §38.2-609

Information Concerning Previous Adverse Underwriting Decisions

No insurance institution, agent, or insurance-support organization may seek information in connection with an insurance transaction concerning:

- previous adverse underwriting decisions experienced by an individual; or
- previous insurance coverages obtained by an individual through a residual market mechanism, other than for requesting the reasons for any previous adverse underwriting decision or the reasons why insurance coverage was previously obtained through a residual market mechanism.

VA Code §38.2-611

Bases for Adverse Underwriting Decisions

Adverse underwriting decisions may not be based:

- on a previous adverse underwriting decision or because an individual previously obtained insurance coverage through a residual market mechanism. However, an insurance institution or agent may base an adverse underwriting decision on further information obtained from an insurance institution or agent responsible for a previous adverse underwriting decision;
- on personal information received from an insurance-support organization whose primary source of information is insurance institutions. However, an insurance institution or agent may base an adverse underwriting decision on further personal information obtained as the result of information received from an insurance-support organization; or
- on the fact that an individual previously obtained insurance coverage from a particular insurance institution or agent.

No insurance institution or agent may base an adverse underwriting decision solely on the loss history of a previous owner of the property to be insured.

VA Code §38.2-612

Information Security Program

Each insurance institution, agent, and insurance-support organization must implement an **information security program** that includes administrative, technical, and physical safeguards for the protection of policyholder information.

Information security programs are designed to:

- ensure the security and confidentiality of policyholder information;
- protect against any anticipated threats or hazards to the security or integrity of the information; and
- protect against unauthorized access to or use of the information that could result in substantial harm or inconvenience to any policyholder.

VA Code §38.2-613.2

Commission Authority and Insurance-Support Organization

The Commission has the power to examine and investigate the affairs of any insurance institution or agent doing business in Virginia to determine whether the insurance institution or agent has been or is engaged in any prohibited conduct.

The Commission has the power to examine and investigate the affairs of any insurance-support organization that acts on behalf of an insurance institution or agent and that either:

- transacts business in Virginia; or
- transacts business outside Virginia and has an effect on a person residing in Virginia, in order to determine whether the insurance-support organization has been or is engaged in any prohibited conduct.

VA Code §38.2-614

Hearings and Procedures

Whenever the Commission has reason to believe that an insurance institution, agent or insurance-support organization has been or is engaged in conduct that is prohibited in Virginia under the insurance laws, or whenever the Commission has reason to believe that an insurance-support organization has been or is engaged in prohibited conduct outside Virginia that has an effect on a person residing in Virginia, the Commission may issue and serve a statement of charges and notice of hearing upon the insurance institution, agent, or insurance-support organization. The date of the hearing must be at least ten days after the date of service.

At the time and place fixed for the hearing, the insurance institution, agent, or insurance-support organization charged has an opportunity to answer the charges against it and present evidence on its behalf. Upon good cause shown, the Commission permits any adversely affected person to intervene, appear, and be heard at the hearing by counsel or in person.

VA Code §38.2-615

Service of Process on Insurance-Support Organizations

For the purpose of the insurance information and privacy protection laws, an **insurance-support organization** transacting business outside Virginia that has an effect on a person residing in Virginia and which is alleged to violate these laws is deemed to have appointed the clerk of the Commission to accept service of process on its behalf.

VA Code §38.2-616

Legal Remedies for the Individual

If any insurance institution, agent, or insurance-support organization fails to comply with the privacy regulations, any person whose rights under them are violated may apply to a court of competent jurisdiction for appropriate equitable relief.

An insurance institution, agent, or insurance-support organization that discloses information in violation of the privacy protection laws is liable for damages sustained by the individual to whom the information relates. No individual, however, is entitled to a monetary award that exceeds the actual damages sustained by the individual as a result of a violation.

In any action brought under these rules, the court may award the cost of the action and reasonable attorney's fees to the prevailing party. An action under the privacy protection laws must be brought within two years from the date the alleged violation is or should have been discovered.

VA Code §38.2-617

Immunity of Persons Disclosing Information

No cause of action in the nature of defamation, invasion of privacy, or negligence can arise against any person for disclosing personal or privileged information according to the privacy protection laws, and a cause of action may not arise against any person for furnishing personal or privileged information to an insurance institution, agent, or insurance-support organization.

However, there is no immunity for disclosing or furnishing false information with malice or willful intent to injure any person.

VA Code §38.2-618

Obtaining Information under False Pretenses

Any person who knowingly and willfully obtains information about an individual from an insurance institution, agent or insurance-support organization under false pretenses will be fined not more than $10,000 or punished by confinement in jail for not more than 12 months, or both.

VA Code §38.2-619

Section XII Review

1) The Commission may make an examination into the affairs of any person licensed to transact any insurance business in Virginia or any other person subject to the jurisdiction of the Commission when:
   a. The Commission considers it the protection of the interest of the people of Virginia
   b. The person being examined gives their consent
   c. The federal government demands it
   d. There is reasonable evidence to support such an examination

2) The Insurance Commissioner has the power to do each of the following, EXCEPT:
   a. License insurance producers
   b. Define licensing requirements based on sex, religion or nationality
   c. Require that fingerprints be submitted to verify the accuracy of information submitted on a license application
   d. Examine and investigate the affairs of every person engaged in the business of insurance in Virginia in order to determine whether the person has engaged in any unfair or deceptive act or practice

3) Each of the following is a prohibited act of an insurance producer, EXCEPT:
   a. Intentionally misrepresenting the terms of an actual or proposed insurance contract or application for insurance.
   b. Having an insurance producer license or other financial services license, or its equivalent, denied, suspended or revoked by a governmental entity.
   c. Failing to pay State income tax or comply with any administrative or court order directing the payment of State income tax.
   d. Replacing a life insurance contract with another life insurance contract

4) When the Commission believes that an insurance agent has violated the insurance laws of Virginia, the Commission must first issue an order to the agent. The order must contain each of the following items, EXCEPT:
   a. A statement of charges
   b. A notice of a hearing giving the time and place
   c. A notice that the agent must show cause why the Commission should not issue a cease and desist order to the agent to stop engaging in the alleged violation
   d. A ruling concerning the penalties, such as license revocation, to which the Commission has determined the agent is subject

5) Any person who knowingly or willfully violates any provision of the Virginia Insurance Title or any regulation issued pursuant to it is punished for each violation by a penalty of not more than:
   a. $1000
   b. $2500
   c. $5000
   d. $7500

6) Any individual or business entity conducting the business of insurance in VA under an assumed or fictitious name must notify the Bureau of Insurance of the name under which the individual or entity will be doing business either at the time the application for a license to do business is filed or within _____ calendar days from the date the assumed or fictitious name is adopted.
   a. 14
   b. 30
   c. 60
   d. 90

7) Insurance Consultant license applicants must pass an appropriate insurance licensing exam within _____ calendar days from the date of application, unless the applicant already has the appropriate license.
   a. 96
   b. 113
   c. 172
   d. 183

 VA PPL LH-2_16298

8) Which of the following must be licensed as insurance agents assuming they only perform the functions listed?
   a. An employee of an insurance rating organization employed by an insurer who analyzes statistics and helps determine premium rates and risk classifications
   b. An employee of an insurer who assists with the enrollment of group insurance applicants
   c. An employee of an insurer who works in underwriting and determines whether applicants meet underwriting standards
   d. An employee of an insurer who contacts people who have asked for rate quotes for insurance through an internet site, determines the best product for them, offers it to them and receives a commission for each sale

9) John is newly licensed in Virginia as a life and health agent. He has not been appointed by an insurance company, but becomes employed at an insurance agency that sells life insurance products through three different insurers authorized to do business in Virginia. John submits a life insurance application to one of these insurance companies, ABX Life Insurance, on June 6, ten days after he is licensed and employed by the insurance agency. When ABX Life Insurance receives the application on June 8 it may do each of the following in order for this sale to be lawful, EXCEPT:
   a. File a notice of appointment of John to the Commission by July 8 if it accepts the application from John
   b. Send a verification notice by July 8 to John that it has filed a notice of appointment to the Commission if it accepts the application from John
   c. Reject John's application
   d. Issue a policy based on the application, pay John for the sale and require the insurance agency to file a notice of John's appointment with the Commission

10) Each agent holding one or more licenses subject to continuing education requirements must complete all CE course, exemption, or waiver requirements no later than _____, or the next working day if this date falls on a weekend, of each _____-numbered year. If the agent does not meet this deadline, the law provides for an additional month extension in which to comply.
   a. November 30; even
   b. November 30; odd
   c. February 28; even
   d. June 30; even

11) In order to renew an insurance license, the licensee must submit each of the following EXCEPT:
   a. specified renewal forms
   b. required fees
   c. verification that the licensee has completed a biennial licensing exam
   d. verification that the licensee has completed the required continuing education

12) An insurance agent acts as a _____ when the licensee handles the funds of others.
   a. professional
   b. attorney
   c. fiduciary
   d. broker

13) A Virginia insurance agent sells an insurance product and then discovers the insurer was not properly licensed in Virginia at the time of the sale. The agent:
   a. may accept commission for the sale from the insurer
   b. may not accept commission for the sale from the insurer
   c. may accept commission for the sale from the insurer if the commission is under $500
   d. may accept a brokerage fee for the sale from the insurer

14) An insurance company that circulates false, malicious or derogatory literature about another insurer's financial position is guilty of:
   a. Rebating
   b. Defamation
   c. Coercion
   d. Discriminatory rate setting

VA PPL LH-2_16298

15) Coercion, boycott or intimidation that results in an unreasonable restraint of trade or a monopoly is generally considered:
   a. lawful
   b. an unfair insurance trade practice
   c. unfair claims settlement
   d. unfair discrimination

16) Misrepresenting a product in order to convince an insured to replace his or her existing policy is:
   a. churning
   b. false advertising
   c. unfair discrimination
   d. twisting

17) The Virginia Life, Accident and Sickness Guaranty Association never pays more than _____ for accident and sickness insurance that constitutes basic hospital medical and surgical insurance or major medical insurance.
   a. $100,000
   b. $250,000
   c. $500,000
   d. $300,000

18) When insurance is being applied for, A Notice of Information Collection and Disclosure Practices must be provided no later than _____ when personal information is collected only from the applicant or from public records.
   a. at the time of the delivery of the insurance policy or certificate
   b. at the time of application
   c. at the time of initial premium submission
   d. one month from policy issue

19) A(n) _____ is a consumer report or a portion thereof in which information about a natural person's character, general reputation, personal characteristics, or mode of living is obtained through personal interviews with the person's neighbors, friends, associates, acquaintances, or others who may have knowledge concerning such items of information.
   a. credit bureau report
   b. investigative consumer report
   c. annotated consumer report
   d. insurance services organization report

20) Any person who knowingly and willfully obtains information about an individual from an insurance institution, agent or insurance-support organization under false pretenses will:
   a. Be fined not more than $10,000
   b. Be fined not more than $20,000
   c. Be jailed for not more than 24 months
   d. Be jailed for not more than 36 months

Life and Health Insurance Glossary of Terms

A

Absolute Assignment: A transfer of all a policy owner's rights irrevocably to another party.

Accelerated Death Benefit: A life insurance rider or provision under which a distribution of the death benefit during the insured's lifetime may be made under conditions specified in the rider. The provisions of the benefit generally require that the insured be terminally ill in order to be eligible for payment.

Accident: An event, unforeseen and unintended.

Accident & Sickness: A form of health insurance that covers loss by bodily injury and sickness.

Accidental Bodily Injury: In health and accidental death and dismemberment policies, a policy definition that requires that the bodily injury be accidental in order for the policy to pay benefits, but does not require that an accident caused the bodily injury in order for the policy to pay benefits.

Accidental Death and Dismemberment (AD&D): Policy or rider that provides lump sum insurance coverage for an accidental death or loss of a certain body part.

Activities of Daily Living (ADL): Normal everyday activities which include eating, bathing, dressing, mobility, transferring, toileting, and continence. Inability to perform these activities is considered a trigger for needing long-term care.

Acute Conditions: Short term illnesses or injuries which develop rapidly and require intense treatment, such as X-rays or surgery.

Additional Purchase Option: *See Guaranteed Insurability*

Adhesion: A legal term referring to the type of contractual agreement found in life insurance policies. Life insurance contracts are not negotiable. The life insurance company draws up the contract and the policy owner must stick to or adhere to its terms.

Adjustable Life Insurance: A form of whole life insurance which allows changes on the policy face amount, premium and period of protection.

Administrative Expense: The portion of premium that goes to pay the insurer for administration of the policy. This may include producing annual statements, processing customer service changes on the contract, providing ongoing customer service through the insurer's home office, and so on. Some administrative expenses may be charged directly to policyholders rather than being paid through the premium. For example, in a variable product, if a policyholder transfers money among the subaccounts more often than a specified number of times annually, the transfers may be subject to an administrative charge.

Agent: The person who is given authority by the insurer to solicit insurance, obtain applications, delivery policies, collect premium and provide service. The agent represents the insurance company, not the policy owner, although the agent has certain responsibilities to act in the best interests of both the insurance company and the policy owner.

Agent Solicitation: In contrast to direct response solicitation, a solicitation of insurance that occurs when an insurance agent or producer offers to sell a policy to a potential customer.

Agency: The relationship between the insurance company and the agent. The agent represents the principal, who is the insurer, in insurance transactions

Aleatory Contract: A contract that is conditioned upon an uncertain event. In a life insurance policy, the insurer's promise to pay the policy proceeds is conditioned upon the uncertain event of death.

Alien Insurer: An insurer that is formed and domiciled outside of the United States and transact insurance business in a state.

Annual Reset Method: A return calculation method used in equity-indexed products where the index value at the beginning of the year is compared to the value at the end of the year. Declines are ignored when the calculation results in a negative number; 0% is the least amount credited, not a negative number.

Annuitant: Party on an annuity contract. If an annuity contract is annuitized, the annuitant's life is generally used to determine the amount of the annuity payments.

Annuitization: Conversion of annuity contract values to an irrevocable stream of income payments.

Any Gainful Occupation: A definition in a disability income insurance policy that pays benefits when an insured is unable to work in any occupation that pays compensation. This definition is distinguished from the "own occupation" definition in disability income insurance policies.

Application: A document used by the insurance company to evaluate the risk of a proposed insured and policy owner. It includes information concerning the medical condition, occupation and avocation of the insured. Once a policy is issued, the application becomes part of the policy contract.

Attained Age: The age an insured has reached on a given date. When a group policy is converted to an individual policy or a term policy is converted to permanent coverage, the insurer may require the conversion premium to be based on attained age, which is the age at the time of conversion.

Automatic Premium Loan: A provision in the policy or a rider added authorizing the insurance company to use the loan value to pay any premium not paid by the end of the grace period.

Averaging: As pertains to equity-indexed contracts, averaging may be used in the return calculation and the index return is averaged over the contract's return calculation period.

B

Base Rate: As distinguished from a bonus rate, the normal crediting rate on cash values.

Beneficiary: The party receiving proceeds at the death of an insured on a life insurance or health insurance policy. This term may also mean the person to be the recipient of a participant's retirement benefits at the participant's death.

Banded Method of Investing: A method of interest rate determination. Under this method, the insurer tracks the return of investments purchased with premiums from contracts opened within the same period of time. Also known as the bucket method of investing.

Bonus Rate: A rate paid on cash values that is greater than the normal crediting rate, or base rate.

Bucket Method of Investing: *See Banded Method of Investing*

Business Overhead Expense Insurance (BOE): A form of disability income insurance that is specifically designed to pay benefits based on business overhead expenses The idea behind the policies is that the disability of certain members of the business, such as the owner or key employees, will cause the business to have difficulty paying overhead expenses. Business overhead policies are the oldest form of business disability income policies

Buy-Sell Agreement: An agreement that arranges the selling of a business interest in case of an owner or shareholder's death, disability, retirement, divorce, or voluntary or involuntary withdrawal from the business. There are four types of buy-sell agreements: 1) Stock Redemption, 2) Cross Purchase, 3) Wait and See, 4) Third Party Buy Out

C

Cancellation: Termination of a contract of insurance in force by voluntary act of the insurance company or insured.

Cap: A term used with equity-indexed life and annuity products. It is the limit on a percentage increase from one return calculation period to the next return calculation period.

Capital Sum: The payment amount under an Accidental Death and Dismemberment policy for losses other than accidental death.

Capitation: To number by the head. Capitation refers to the practice of paying for patient care based on the number of patients under the care of a physician.

Cash Refund Annuity or Payout: An annuity or life settlement option that includes a lump-sum payment upon the death of the annuitant or beneficiary. A life with cash refund annuity pays income over the life of the annuitant and pays a lump-sum payment to the named beneficiary if the annuitant dies before the amount paid by the purchaser has been distributed. A life with cash refund settlement pays income over the life of the beneficiary who received the life insurance proceeds and pays a lump-sum payment to the beneficiary named at time of settlement if the original beneficiary dies before the amount of the settlement is distributed.

Cash Surrender Value: The amount of money that the insurance company must pay to the owner of an insurance policy should the policy be canceled or surrendered.

Cash Value: Permanent life insurance policy and deferred annuity accumulations that belong by law to the life insurance policy owner while living. The life insurance company that issues the policy can include certain restrictions to their access. If the contract is surrendered, the policy owner has a right to receive the cash values, less outstanding loans, surrender charges and other miscellaneous charges from the insurer.

Catch-Up Contributions: Additional contribution amounts that may be made to IRA and qualified retirement plans by persons age 50 and older and to HSAs by persons age 55 and older.

Centers for Medicare and Medicaid (CMS): The federal agency that runs the Medicare program. In addition, CMS works with the States to run the Medicaid program.

Change of Insured Provision: A feature in some key employee insurance policies that allows the insured to be changed on the policy, with evidence of insurability.

Change of Beneficiary: As pertains to individual health insurance, a policy provision that states that the owner of a policy that includes a death benefit has the right to change the beneficiary without the consent of the beneficiary, unless an irrevocable beneficiary has been named.

Chronic Condition: A long-term or permanent illness or condition for which skilled, custodial, or personal care is needed.

Claim: The demand for benefits as provided by the policy.

Claims Form: A provision in health insurance policies that requires that the insurer must furnish claim forms to the claimant within fifteen days of notice of the claim. If the insurer does not furnish the claim forms within this time frame, the claimant fulfills the requirement to provide proof of loss by providing written proof covering the occurrence, the character and event of the loss for which the claim is made.

COBRA: stands for the Consolidated Omnibus Budget Reconciliation Act of 1985, and includes requirements for group health plans regarding health care continuation.

Cognitive Impairment: As pertains to long-term care insurance, a deficiency in a person's short or long-term memory, orientation as to person, place and time, deductive or abstract reasoning, or judgment as it relates to safety awareness.

Coinsurance: a certain portion of the net amount of the claim after the health insurance deductible is paid that is also payable by the insured, while the insurance company pays their share of the remaining claim. The amount the patient must pay is the coinsurance. For example, the insurer may pay 80% and the insured pay 20% of the cost of covered care.

Collateral Assignment: Under a collateral assignment, a portion of the death benefit is assigned as long as necessary to secure the lender's rights. No more of the proceeds can go to the lender than the amount of the debt owed however, because the extent of a lender's insurable interest in a life insurance policy does not exceed the amount of the debt.

Commission: Fee paid to an insurance producer by the insurance company for the sale of the insurer's policy.

Commission Load: Premium cost of a policy allocated to the payment of commissions.

Common Disaster Provision: A death benefit provision in life insurance policies that pays benefits to the class II or secondary beneficiary only if the primary beneficiary does not survive the insured for a specified number of days.

Community-Based Services: As pertains to long-term care, locally based services that are aimed at helping older individuals remain independent while utilizing custodial and personal care. They may include chores and meal preparation or ADL assistance. These services can be performed in the home or at a daytime care facility.

Concealment: The intentional nondisclosure of a material fact. Concealment in the application of insurance may cause the policy to be void if the concealment was done knowingly.

Conditional Contract: A contract that contains responsibilities that must be fulfilled by one party in the contract in order for the other party to be responsible to fulfill its obligations in the contract. An insurance contract is conditional because it gives the insured responsibilities or conditions in order for the insurer's ongoing obligations to be fulfilled.

Conditional Receipt: Provided to an insurance applicant when premium is paid prior to the completion of insurance underwriting and policy issue. The receipt states that if the premium is paid as required, the coverage will be in effect from the date of the conditional receipt assuming the passing of normal underwriting requirements.

Conditionally Renewable: Provision in an insurance contract that provides that the insured may renew the contract to a stated date or a certain age, subject to the right of the insurance company to decline to renew the policy under conditions defined in the contract.

Consideration: One of the required elements of a valid contract. Consideration is something of value that induces the parties involved into making a contractual agreement. Consideration may be monetary, or may be in the form of a promise or an act. Under an insurance contract, premium is the consideration.

Consumer Report: A report ordered by the underwriters requesting information about the person's credit, character, reputation, etc.

Contingent Beneficiary: The beneficiary who will receive death proceeds if all primary beneficiaries are deceased at the time insurance death proceeds are payable

Contract: An agreement between two or more parties by which rights are exchanged for lawful consideration.

VA PPL LH-2_16298

Contributory Plan: Employer-sponsored insurance plan in which the employees contribute some or all of the premiums for the insurance.

Convalescent Care Rider: An accelerated death benefit rider that is payable when the insured enters a convalescent care facility, such as a skilled nursing facility, and normally payable only if the insured enters the facility due to chronic or terminal illness.

Convertibility: A feature of term insurance policies and riders that provides the option to convert to a permanent policy without requiring evidence of insurability. It is also a feature of group life and health insurance and allows group coverage to be converted to individual coverage.

Copayment: A form of medical cost sharing in a health insurance plan that requires an insured person to pay a fixed dollar amount when a medical service is received. The insurer is responsible for the rest of the reimbursement.

Cost of Living Benefit: (Also known as inflation protection) A benefit or rider in insurance that increases policy benefits on a scheduled basis.

Credit Life Insurance: Decreasing term insurance based on the balance of the loan.

Creditable Coverage: Coverage applied to a new health insurance plan based on length of coverage in a prior plan. Creditable coverage requirements are found in HIPAA and state laws governing termination of a health plan or of health coverage. Creditable coverage laws remove or reduce preexisting condition periods and waiting periods in new plans for the insureds with creditable coverage.

Creditable Coverage Certificate: A certificate required to be given by health insurance plan sponsors subject to HIPAA to insureds whose insurance coverage is terminated that provides their creditable coverage amount.

Custodial Care: As pertains to long-term care, non-medical care which requires no special training or professional skills, however, it may be provided by a trained aide. It is usually aimed at assisting elderly or disabled people with ADLs, but can also include assistance with household chores, such as cleaning, cooking, and laundry.

D

Death Benefit: The amount specified in the life insurance contract that is to be paid out at the death of the insured.

Decreasing Term: A form of term insurance that provides a death benefit which declines throughout the term of the contract. This type of insurance is sometimes referred to as mortgage insurance or credit life insurance. The death benefit is based on the decreasing loan balance.

Deductible: For health insurance purposes, a fixed dollar amount during the benefit period – usually a year that an insured person pays before the insurer starts to make payments for covered medical services. Plans may have both per individual and family deductibles.

Deductible: For tax purposes, the ability to reduce taxable income by subtracting an amount paid for certain expenses. For example, certain retirement plan contributions are deductible for tax purposes, as are certain insurance premium payments.

Defamation: False or malicious statements against another insurance company.

Deferred Annuity: Annuity contract that does not begin annuitization payments within the first year from inception of the contract.

Defined Benefit Plan: A type of qualified retirement plan that promises to pay a specified benefit upon a plan participant's retirement. The benefit is generally calculated by a formula that includes factors such as salary and length of service.

Defined Contribution Plan: A type of qualified retirement plan where contributions are defined and the plan does not promise to pay a specific benefit upon retirement. The employer and/or the employee contribute to the plan. The contributions are invested based on the specifications of the plan and the choices of the employee, and the amount available at retirement is based on the employee's accumulated assets within the plan.

Direct Rollover (also known as Direct Transfer): A nontaxable transaction that occurs when an eligible distribution is moved directly from one eligible qualified retirement plan to another.

Disability Buy-Out Policy: Disability insurance used to fund buy-sell agreements and that pays benefits based only on total disability. Under these policies, total disability generally means that the insured is unable to perform the substantial and material duties of the insured's regular occupation, the insured is under the care of the physician, and the insured is not working in any position for the firm.

VA PPL LH-2_16298

Disability Income Insurance: A form of health insurance that compensates the insured for loss of income due to a disability.

Dividend: The payment of surplus to policy holders due to favorable experience related to return, mortality rates, and/or expense charges.

Direct Response Solicitation: This solicitation occurs when a person sees or hears public advertisements for an insurance company and requests an application based on those advertisements.

Domestic Insurer: An insurer that is formed, or domiciled, in the state in which it is transacting business.

Dread Disease Coverage: A form of limited health insurance coverage that pays based on being diagnosed with a dread disease, such as cancer. It may pay a lump sum upon diagnosis along with paying for benefits based on care received.

E

Effective Date: The date on which an insurance policy goes into effect and provides protection.

Elimination Period: The waiting period after a health insurance policy goes into effect and before benefits begin. The elimination period may vary based on the type of benefit to be paid.

Emergency Care: Type of health care that is generally defined in insurance coverage as necessary care that a person reasonably believes to be immediately necessary to preserve life, prevent serious impairment to bodily functions, organs or part, or prevent placing the physical or mental health of the individual in serious jeopardy.

Employer Group Health Plan: Under federal regulations, a plan maintained by an employer or employee organization to provide health care to individuals who have an employment-related connection to the employer or employee organization or to their families

Endodontic Services: Dental care services such as root canals that treat conditions on the inside of the tooth – the tooth's pulp.

Endowment: A life insurance policy that pays the face amount at the end of a specified period or at a specified age of the insured. An endowment pays a death benefit if the insured dies prior to the end of the specified period or specified age.

Entire Contract: An insurance provision that specifies that the policy along with the attached application copy, addendums and riders constitutes the insurance contract.

Estate Taxes: Taxes due on transfers of property or wealth at the death of the property owner.

Essential Health Benefits: A category of benefits in health insurance plans subject to the ACA's provisions that may not have annual or maximum benefit limits. States and insurers ensure that ACA qualified health plans include these benefits.

Excess Premium: A condition that exists in level premium insurance policies where premium in the earlier years of a policy includes amounts that are in excess of the cost of insurance. These excess amounts are used to offset the higher cost of insurance as the insured ages and the likelihood of death or sickness increases.

Exclusion Ratio: As pertains to taxation of annuity income payments and life settlement option payments, the ratio applied to each payment which results in the portion of each payment that is not taxable. Under most circumstances, earnings only are taxable in these payments. Generally, the taxable earnings are spread over the payment stream and reported to the payee annually for tax purposes.

Exclusions: Conditions listed in the insurance contract which are not covered and for which no benefits are payable. These conditions must be specifically listed in the policy, addendum or rider. Some exclusions are temporary, and are removed after the policy has been in effect after a specified period, which also must be stated in the policy, addendum or rider, as applicable.

Extended Term: A nonforfeiture option provided in life insurance where the policyholder is given a term insurance policy. The term of the insurance is equal to the length of time the cash values will purchase.

F

Face Amount: The amount of the death benefit of a life insurance policy on the date of policy inception. It is listed on the front page, or face page, of an insurance policy. Depending on the life insurance policy type, the face amount may differ from the actual death benefit payable over the life of the policy.

Fair Credit Reporting Act: A federal Act that requires that an applicant be advised that a consumer report may be requested by the underwriters and which includes provisions for disputing information within a consumer report.

Family Coverage: An individual life insurance plan where the spouse and each child in a family is covered

VA PPL LH-2_16298

by term insurance attached to a permanent policy on the life of the other spouse. The children are generally covered for an amount that would pay for their death expenses. There is generally a provision that allows the children's coverage to be converted to their own individual coverage once they reach adulthood.

Fee-For-Service Care: Under this type of care, every time a physician provides a service, the physician is paid a fee.

Fiduciary: A person in a position of authority whom the law obligates to act solely on behalf of the person he or she represents and in good faith. A fiduciary is required to act in the best interests of the person represented, insofar as his or her fiduciary relationship extends. Handling funds of others is a fiduciary responsibility of an insurance agent. The agent must act in the best interest of the person paying premiums, for example, by properly remitting the premium as the person intends and as contractually required.

Fixed Account: A type of account in a variable life or annuity product that pays a guaranteed rate and is backed by the insurer's general account. The other accounts in a variable product are subaccounts that are part of the insurer's separate account.

Fixed Annuity: An annuity type that includes a fixed interest rate guaranteed for a specified period, and which has a minimum guaranteed interest rate.

Flexible Premium Policies: A deferred annuity or life insurance contact that accepts differing premium amounts, subject to contract and state requirements. Life insurance premiums may vary under these policies, but the policy may have the danger of lapse if premiums are not sufficient to keep the policy in force.

Flexible Spending Accounts or Arrangements (FSA): Accounts offered and administered by employers that provide a way for employees to set aside, out of their paycheck, pretax dollars to pay for the employee's share of insurance premiums or medical expenses not covered by the employer's health plan. The employer may also make contributions to a FSA. Typically, benefits or cash must be used within the given benefit year or the employee loses the money. Flexible spending accounts can also be provided to cover childcare expenses, but those accounts must be established separately from medical FSAs.

Floor: The lowest rate credited to an annuity or to life insurance cash values. The floor may be 0% in contracts that use an earnings calculation that could result in a negative crediting rate, such as in equity index contracts.

Foreign Insurer: An insurer that is domiciled in one state and doing business in other states.

Formulary: A formulary is a list of medications that are used to treat various conditions and is used by physicians within a plan as a guide for prescribing medication appropriate to a patient's condition.

Free Look Period: The period of time, generally ten to fifteen days, from the date the issued contract is received by the policy owner in which the owner is able to cancel the policy and have the premiums contributed refunded without surrender charges. In some cases, the free look period is as long as 30 days or more.

Free Withdrawal: An informal term applied to withdrawals of annuity or life insurance cash values that are without surrender charges during the period of time surrender charges would normally apply. For example, a contract may allow 10% of deferred annuity accumulations to be withdrawn on an annual basis without surrender charges, and any withdrawal amounts in excess of this during that year to be assessed a surrender charge. Taxes may still apply to the withdrawal.

G

General Account: The investment portfolio of a life insurance company that holds assets of the insurance company.

Grace Period: A specified period from the premium due date, generally thirty or thirty-one days depending on the state, in which to make a premium payment. In some states, insurers are required to extend the grace period under certain circumstances. During the grace period, the insurance continues in force.

Graded Premium Policy: A modified whole life policy in which the initial premium is low and then increases over a period of time, usually 5 years, after which it becomes a level premium.

Grandfathered: A term applied to the status of existing plans and products that are subject to prior law and not required to adhere to current law.

Grantor: the person who establishes a trust.

Group Insurance: As distinguished from individual insurance, insurance that is issued to groups that are approved through state law to offer insurance to group members. Employer sponsored group insurance is the most common form of group insurance. Each insured member receives a certificate of coverage rather than a policy.

VA PPL LH-2_16298

Guaranteed Insurability: The ability to add to or continue insurance coverage without proving insurability.

Guaranteed Renewable: A life and health insurance policy provision that guarantees that the contract may be renewed as long as premium is paid.

H

Hazard: A hazard is a condition that creates or increases a chance of loss. There are three types of hazards that are of concern in insurance. These are physical hazards, moral hazards and morale hazards.

Health Insurance: Insurance which protects against financial loss due to sickness or bodily injury. Also known as "Accident and Health," or "Accident and Sickness" insurance.

Health Savings Account: An account used to pay for qualified medical services, used in conjunction with a high deductible individual health plan

High-Water Mark Index Benefit Calculation Method: A return calculation method used in equity-indexed products where the index value at specified periods during the contract's term, such as on the policy anniversary. If the index is higher, then the benefit calculation is performed based on the average return over that year and earnings are calculated. If the index is lower, no calculation is performed and the cash value remains the same in that year (adjusted for premiums paid in).

HIPAA: the federal Health Insurance Portability and Accountability Act of 1996. It includes employer group health insurance portability requirements and privacy protections for certain health information.

Home Care: As pertains to long-term care, personal, non-medical care which may include help with household chores, running errands, meal preparations, and ADL assistance.

Home Health Care: As pertains to long-term care, medical services rendered to an individual, such as giving injections, IV's, or any prescribed medical treatment. Home health care may also include therapy.

Human Life Value Approach: An economic estimate of human life value to determine the appropriate amount of life insurance to purchase that involves calculating a dollar value that represents the financial loss an income earner's death will cause, based on anticipated earnings over a lifetime, to the income earner's family.

I

Immediate Annuity: An annuity in which annuitization occurs within the first 12 months from contract inception.

Incontestability Clause: A clause in a policy providing that after the policy has been in effect for a specified number of years, the insurance company is not able to contest it (i.e., deny coverage) based on statements made in the application.

Indemnity: A legal principle where an insured is to be brought back to the financial position the insured was in prior to the loss or damage the insurance covers. The insured is not to make a profit from the insurance benefits. Indemnity bars the insured from collecting payment from both Workers Compensation and an employer's group health plan, for example, when Workers Compensation is the insurer responsible for a work injury and is responsible for paying medical expenses for work injuries.

Individual Insurance: As distinguished from group insurance, insurance issued directly to an individual policyowner by the insurer. Individual insurance may cover more than just one individual. An individual policy may cover a family or several partners in a business.

Individual Retirement Account (IRA): A federally created plan that allows for contributions to a savings plan structured to provide retirement accumulations and income. Individual retirement accounts have associated tax benefits and are owned by individuals. IRA types include traditional IRA, Roth IRA, SIMPLE IRA and SEP IRA.

Inflation Protection: *See Cost of Living Benefit.*

Insurability: The overall acceptability of an individual as an insurance risk. Factors used to determine insurability include health, financial situation, occupation, life expectancy, exposure to risks and other factors determined by the insurance company.

Insurable Interest: A legal concept underlying insurance contracts. It means that the insured or policy owner has to suffer financially or be harmed in another way if a loss occurs in order for insurance to be issued.

Insurance: An agreement between an insurance policyholder and the insurer where the payment of premium by the insured requires the insurance company through an insurance contract to provide payment, based on the principal of indemnity, for certain losses.

Insurance Consultant: An individual or business entity who acts as an independent contractor and for a fee or compensation provides insurance advice.

Insured: The measuring life of a life insurance policy. At the insured's death, the insurance policy pays a death benefit.

Investigative Consumer Report: An in-depth form of consumer report that may be obtained by the insurer for underwriting purposes. It may include information on a consumer's character, general reputation, personal characteristics, or mode of living based on personal interviews with neighbors, friends, or associates of the consumer reported on or with others with whom he is acquainted or who may have knowledge concerning any such items of information.

Irrevocable Beneficiary: A beneficiary named by an insurance policyowner which cannot be changed without the written permission of the irrevocable beneficiary.

J

Joint and Survivor Annuity or Life Settlement: A life annuity and life settlement option that makes payments over the life of two or more payees and continues to make payments until the last of the payees dies. A joint and survivor annuity or life settlement can be structured to make the same payment amount over the lives of all the payees, or can be structured to reduce the payment upon the death of the first payee.

Joint Life Annuity or Life Settlement: A life annuity and life settlement option that is payable until the death of one of two payees.

Joint Life Insurance: A form of life insurance whose premium is based on the life expectancies of two or more insureds, and pays a death benefit upon the death of the first insured to die.

K

Key Employee: For purposes of qualified retirement plan rules, a key employee is defined as an officer earning over $170,000. A 5% owner of the employer; or A 1% owner of the employer earning over $150,000.

Key Employee Insurance: An insurance policy on the life of a key employee whose death or disability would cause the employer financial loss. The company is always the beneficiary. Also known as key person insurance.

L

Lapse: Condition that occurs when the payments on a policy are not paid on time or during the grace period, or are stopped altogether. It is a cessation of coverage due to the failure to pay premiums as required. A lapsed policy, can be reinstated if the insured meets certain tests and the policy holder pays sufficient premium to put the insurer back in the financial position it would have been in had the policy never been allowed to lapse.

Legal Reserve: The minimum reserves required of an insurer under the laws of the jurisdiction in which an insurer operates. Reserve requirements vary based on the type of insurance being offered.

Legal Actions: An individual health insurance provision that sets boundaries upon the time period during which legal action may be sought. This provision states that legal action to collect from a claim must not begin for at least sixty days from the time a proof of loss form is filed with the insurer, and must be taken in a period no longer than three years from that time.

Level Premium: A premium amount on an insurance policy that normally does not change over the life of the policy or within a renewal period and that cannot be arbitrarily changed while the policy is in place.

Life and Period Certain Annuity: An annuity payment option that makes payments for the life of the annuitant or a specified period of time, whichever is greater.

Life and Period Certain Settlement: A life settlement option that makes payments for the life of the beneficiary or a specified period of time, whichever is greater.

Life Expectancy: For insurance purpose, the average number of years remaining for a person of a given age to live as shown in approved mortality tables.

Life Income Annuity or Life Income Settlement Option: Also called a straight life annuity or straight life settlement. This is a payout option that makes payments for the life of the annuitant or life settlement beneficiary. Payments cease upon the death of the annuitant or beneficiary.

Life Insurance: Insurance that pays benefits to compensate for the financial loss due to the insured's death. Some health insurance policies may include a life insurance benefit, such as accidental death and dismemberment insurance.

Lifetime Maximum Benefit: The total amount of benefits which could be paid by an insurance company for the term of existence of a health insurance policy. The ACA prohibits health plans subject to its requirements from having annual and maximum lifetime benefits on essential health benefits. Limited health insurance policies and other health policies not

VA PPL LH-2_16298

subject to the ACA may still use lifetime maximum benefits.

Limited Pay Policy: A whole life policy with premium payments paid for a period shorter than the insured's whole life. These policies provide protection until the earlier of death or the insured's 100 year birth-date. Examples include single premium, 10-pay (10 years of premium payments), 20-pay (20 years of premium payments) and paid-up at age 65 (premiums paid until age 65).

Living Benefit: *See Accelerated Death Benefit*

Long-Term Care: A variety of services that help people with health or personal needs and activities of daily living over a period of time. Long-term care can be provided at home, in the community, or in various types of facilities, including nursing homes and assisted living facilities. Most long-term care is custodial care.

Long-Term Care Rider: An accelerated death benefit rider that is payable when the insured enters a long term care facility, such as a skilled nursing facility, and normally payable only if the insured enters the facility due to chronic or terminal illness.

Long-Term Care Insurance: Private insurance designed to aid individuals in paying for long-term care. Care may be received in the home, in a community facility, or in a residential facility, depending on the policy.

Long-Term Disability: In group insurance, a disability having a duration for two years or more.

Long-Term Care Partnership: State programs designed to eliminate the need for moderate-income persons to use Medicaid by encouraging the purchase of long-term care insurance policies. Expansion of state Partnership programs was authorized under the Deficit Reduction Act of 2005 (the DRA).

Low Cost Loan: A life insurance policy loan where the interest rate charged on the amount of the loan is a few percentage points higher than the amount credited to the cash value equal to the loan amount.

M

Major Medical Insurance: A type of health insurance that provides benefits for most types of medical expenses with high limits and subject to a deductible and co-insurance.

Managed Care: Any health delivery system that includes the utilization of a network of providers and a process of overseeing the types of care and services provided by the physicians and other parties supplying health care inside of the network.

Master Policy: In group insurance, the master policy is a contract between the employer, or other sponsoring group, and the insurance company.

Material Change: A term used in conjunction with modified endowment contracts (MECs). A material change to a life insurance contract that is exempt from tax treatment as a MEC solely due to issue date will be considered a MEC if a material change to the contract is made. Material changes include certain increases in the death benefit; a term policy's conversion to a permanent insurance policy; and an exchange of one policy for another.

Material Fact: As pertains to the issue and enforceability of an insurance contract, a fact that, if known to the insurer at time of application, would have caused the insurer to deny coverage or issue coverage under substantially different conditions.

Maximum Out-of-Pocket Expense: The maximum dollar amount a group member is required to pay out of pocket during a year. Until this maximum is met, the plan and group member shares in the cost of covered expenses. After the maximum is reached, the insurance carrier pays remaining covered expenses for the year.

Medicaid: A joint Federal and State program that helps with medical costs for some people with low incomes and limited resources. Medicaid programs vary from state to state, but most health care costs are covered if an individual qualifies for both Medicare and Medicaid.

Medical Information Bureau (MIB): An association of most life and health insurers in the United States. The MIB contains information about the medical condition of applicants and insureds and is used in underwriting life and health insurance.

Medical Waiver: *see Nursing Home Waiver*

Medicare: Federally regulated program that provides health care benefits to those who are eligible for Social Security. Benefits include hospital insurance and supplementary medical insurance.

Medicare Advantage Plan: A Medicare program that gives more choices among health plans. Anyone who has Medicare Parts A and B is eligible, except those who have End-Stage Renal Disease (unless certain exceptions apply).

Medicare Cost Plan: A Medicare Cost Plan is a type of HMO. In a Medicare Cost Plan, if services outside of the plan's network are received without a referral, Medicare-covered services will be paid for under the Original Medicare Plan, except that the plan pays for emergency services, or urgently needed services outside the service area.

Medicare HMO: A type of Medicare managed care plan where a group of doctors, hospitals, and other health care providers agree to give health care to Medicare beneficiaries for a set amount of money from Medicare every month. The beneficiary usually must get care from the providers in the plan.

Medicare Supplement Plans: Also known as Medigap Plans. Health insurance policies that have been authorized through Medicare legislation to supplement Medicare coverage that fill the "gaps" in Medicare coverage and do not provide the same benefits as Medicare.

Medigap Plans: *See Medicare Supplement Plans*

Mini-Med Plans: Health insurance plans with a limited menu of benefits that are paid on a per visit or per day basis providing the types of benefits of a medical expense plan, but with much lower limits.

Minimum Guaranteed Rate or Return: The minimum interest rate contractually guaranteed to be paid on life insurance and annuity cash values.

Misrepresentation: Written or oral statements made by the insured, the insurer, or a representative of the insurer, which misstates information regarding the risk, terms, coverages, benefits, returns, or other material fact related to the contract.

Modified Endowment Contract (MEC): A life insurance product that is subject to taxation rules that include taxation of loans as distributions and which treat withdrawals as though they are comprised of earnings before principal or cost basis. In order to avoid being treated as a MEC, a life insurance contract must meet the "seven-pay test" described in the IRS Code Section 7702.

Money Laundering: The process of engaging in acts with the purpose of concealing the origin of the criminally derived proceeds so that they appear to have been obtained legitimately.

Moral Hazard: A hazard considered in underwriting insurance and issuing policies that any individual may be dishonest or have another negative character trait that increases the frequency or severity of a loss.

Morale Hazard: A hazard considered in underwriting insurance and issuing policies that any individual may possess an attitude that causes him or her to take less care of property or other insured risk because it is insured.

Mortality Expense: The insurer bases and collects premium based on statistical data that indicates that a certain percentage of insureds will suffer losses at a certain frequency percentage. In life insurance the loss the insured suffers is death. The frequency that death occurs within a population is called the mortality risk. The portion of premium charged based on mortality risk is known as mortality expense.

Multiple Indemnity: A multiple indemnity provision states that a benefit under a policy will be increased by a stated multiple, such as double or triple the normal benefit amount.

N

National Association of Insurance Commissioners (NAIC): Organization comprised of state insurance commissioners which drafts model insurance regulation and collects and reports statistics and other information on the insurance industry.

Needs Approach: A method of determining the appropriate life insurance coverage amount where the producer assists the customer in defining expenditures that will occur throughout life, and then subtracts from that amount the amount of assets available to meet these expenses.

Network: The physicians, hospitals, clinics, group practices and other health care providers participating in the managed care plan.

Noncancellable: Noncancellable contracts guarantee that the premium on a contract will never go up at renewal, up through a specified period or age. As long as premium is paid by the insured, the contract will renew and continue through its specified length.

Non-Contributory Plan: An employer sponsored group insurance plan in which the employees do not contribute to the plan and the employer pays the full premium.

Nonduplication of Benefits: This is a contract provision in many health insurance policies and required by law in some instances. For example, an insurance policy is not allowed to cover the same benefits as any State or Federal program except Medicaid.

Nonforfeiture Values: Nonforfeiture values are those values that belong to the policy owner by law if the policy owner surrenders the policy. Generally, there are three nonforfeiture options offered to a life insurance policy owner: the cash value, the extended term, and the reduced paid-up insurance options.

Non-Occupational Coverage: A policy or provision in health insurance which excludes coverage for care due to accidents occurring on the job and disease arising from a job that are covered by Workers Compensation.

Nonparticipating Insurance: Life insurance that does not include the payment of dividends because the policy owner does not participate in the surplus of the policy.

Non-Qualified Long-Term Care Insurance: A long-term care insurance policy which does not qualify its owner for Federal tax benefits. Partnership policies must be qualified long-term care insurance policies.

Nursing Home: For long-term care insurance, accelerated death benefit and premium waiver provision purposes, generally defined as a state licensed residential facility which provides 24-hr skilled nursing care to elderly or disabled persons. Other services consist of room and board, personal and custodial care, medication, therapy, rehabilitation, and communal dining. Rooms may be private or semi-private.

Nursing Home Waiver: a feature of deferred annuities that allows a partial or full surrender of the contract if a party on the contract as specified in the policy provisions is confined to a nursing home, a long-term care facility, a hospital or other qualified facility as defined in the policy. Also known as a medical waiver.

O

Open Enrollment Period: A period of time in which a new group health member or eligible dependents may enroll in a health plan.

Optionally Renewable: An insurance contract in which the insurer reserves the unrestricted right to terminate the coverage at any anniversary or premium due date.

Ordinary life insurance: Also known as whole life and straight life. Life insurance that requires a level premium payment, has a guaranteed death benefit and a guaranteed minimum rate applicable to cash values.

Original Age: The age of an insured at original issue of an insurance policy. When a group policy is converted to an individual policy or a term policy is converted to permanent coverage, the insurer may allow the conversion premium to be based on original age, which is the age at the time the original group or term policy was effective.

Orthodontic Services: Dental care involving treatment for putting teeth in proper alignment. Orthodontists are specialists who use braces, retainers and other appliances to straighten or otherwise put teeth and jaw in their proper positions.

Own Occupation: A definition in disability income insurance policies that pay benefits when an insured is disabled and unable to work in his or her regular occupation. This definition is often used for insurance designed for highly paid professionals.

P

Paid-Up Additions: An option found on dividend paying life insurance policies. The policy owner has the option to use dividends to purchase additional insurance on a single premium basis at the insured's attained age.

Paid-Up Policy: A life insurance policy that continues in force and requires no further premium payments.

Participating Insurance: Life insurance policies that may include the payment of dividends because the policy owner participates in the earned surplus of the insurance company

Participation Rate: In equity index products, the percentage of change in the index that is used in the return calculation. For example, if the participation rate in a contract is 85% and the index increases by 5%, the rate of return that will be applied to the cash values is 4.25%.

Patient Protection and Affordable Care Act (ACA): A federal act signed into law on March 23, 2010 with the primary purpose of ensuring that no one has to be uninsured. It combines reforms to both public and private health care systems with the aim to provide an affordable, accessible health care system for all. The ACA expands Medicaid so that previously uncovered, lower income segments of the population who are unable to obtain or cannot afford private coverage are provided with health care coverage. It includes mandated benefits in individual and employer sponsored health insurance coverage.

Payee: The person who receives annuitization payments, immediate annuity payments and life settlement payments. In some cases a person other than the insured or named beneficiary may be a payee. Most commonly, however, the insured or named beneficiary is also the payee.

Payment of Claims: An individual health care provision that requires that any death benefits payable will be paid to a named beneficiary on the policy, or to the estate of the insured if a beneficiary is not named. Any other payment will be made to the insured.

Payor Policy: A policy insuring a minor's life where premiums are waived if the premium payor dies or becomes totally disabled. This feature is found on juvenile life insurance.

VA PPL LH-2_16298

Period Certain Annuity or Life Settlement: An annuity or life settlement payout option that lasts for a specified period of time. Payments end at the end of the period.

Periodontic Services: Dental services that include care for the gums and bone structure supporting the teeth and include more aggressive cleaning and scaling services for gum disease.

Permanent Life Insurance: Life insurance policies that include the accumulation of cash values.

Persistency Rate: The ratio of policies that renew as a percent of total like policies issued by the insurer. A high persistency rate means a high number of policies stay in effect and a low persistency rate means that many policies are lapsing and nonrenewing.

Personal Care: *See Custodial Care*

Physical Examination and Autopsy Provision: An individual health insurance policy that allows, in the event of death, the insurer to examine the person of the insured and to make an autopsy where allowed by law.

Physical Hazard: A hazard considered in insurance underwriting that a physical condition of property is present that increases the chance of loss.

Point-to-Point Index Benefit Calculation Method: A return calculation used in equity-indexed contracts where the index value at the end of the term is compared to the index at the beginning of the policy and where no earnings are credited during the term.

Policy Loan: A loan against cash values accumulated in a life insurance policy.

Policyowner: Party on a life insurance contract who is normally the premium payer and has the right to change the beneficiary, to withdraw funds, take loans, make premium payments, and in some cases add or change beneficiaries.

Point of Service Plans (POS): Health plans that allow for the use of both HMO and non-network providers.

Portfolio Method of Investing: An interest rate determination method. Under this method, all premiums received for the same insurance product are included as one portfolio for the purpose of establishing interest rates.

Preexisting Condition: A preexisting condition is a health condition or problem that existed before a health care policy or contract was effective and for which medical advice, diagnosis, care, or treatment was recommended. Each health insurance policy or contract will define preexisting condition in its' policy terms and state the applicable time periods coverage is excluded for preexisting conditions, as allowed under the law.

Preferred Issue: Decision to issue a policy to an applicant who falls within the lowest risk boundaries of the insurer's underwriting standards for the policy. Preferred rates represent the lowest rates offered by an insurer for its coverage.

Preferred Provider: A health care provider chosen by the managed care network or organization or a managed care sponsor (such as an employer) to provide the health care services outlined in the managed care plan.

Preferred Provider Organization (PPO): An organization that contracts with health care professionals and hospitals to provide health care according to the organization's health plan. Unlike HMOs which compensate physicians on a capitation basis, PPOs compensate health care providers by compensating through a fee schedule.

Premature Withdrawals (also known as Premature Distributions): Withdrawals from products and plans with federal tax benefits that apply only to withdrawals that occur after a certain age. Premature withdrawals are withdrawals taken before this specified age (for example, age 59 ½) and are subject to additional taxation. The additional taxation is referred to as a tax penalty. Annuities, IRAs, qualified retirement plans, and MECs all have premature withdrawal penalties.

Premium: Money paid to the insurer to pay for the risk the insurer assumes for paying claims and for meeting the insurance contract's provisions. Premiums must be paid to keep the policy in force.

Presumptive Disability: Defined conditions that automatically meet a disability insurance policy's definition of total disability, such as the loss of a limb.

Primary Beneficiary: Also known as Class I beneficiary. The beneficiary who has the first right to the death proceeds of an insurance contract.

Primary-Care Physician: the physician that gives most of the care to a patient. A primary care physician is typically a family doctor, pediatrician and may be a gynecologist/obstetrician. Managed care plans allow members to select a primary-care physician.

Principal: In the insurer-agent agency relationship, the insurer is the principal. The agent acts on behalf of the insurer as principal in insurance transactions. For tax purposes, the term principal is used to mean cost-basis

VA PPL LH-2_16298

or the contributions made to an insurance contract through premium payments.

Principal Sum: The payment for accidental death under an accidental death and dismemberment policy.

Probate: The legal process of ensuring clear title to property in an estate prior to transferring this property to heirs upon the death of the property owner.

Probationary Period: The period of time from policy inception before a sickness will be covered under a health insurance policy.

Proof of Loss: An individual health insurance policy provision that places a time limit upon the period in which a proof of loss form is given to the insurer. It requires that the proof of loss be filed within ninety days of loss, or if the loss is a continuing loss within ninety days after the period for which the insurer is liable.

Prosthodontic Services: A type of dental care dealing with constructing and fitting implants and dentures, and providing therapy and care for TMJ.

Q

Qualified Distributions: Distributions from a qualified plan, HSA or IRA that meet certain conditions and qualify for special tax treatment.

Qualified Long-Term Care Insurance: Long-term care insurance that receives special tax treatment under federal tax laws. Partnership policies must be qualified long-term care contracts.

Qualified Long-Term Care Services: Necessary diagnostic, preventive, therapeutic, curing, treating, mitigating, and rehabilitative services, and maintenance or personal care services, which are required by a chronically ill individual, and are provided pursuant to a plan of care prescribed by a licensed health care practitioner.

Qualified Retirement Plan: A retirement plan that receives special tax treatment under federal tax laws.

R

Rated: A term used to denote that a policy risk that has been classified as substandard and a premium rate higher than the standard rate is charged for the policy's coverage.

Recurring Disability: Definition found in a disability income policy provision that specifies the duration of time during which the recurrence of a condition will be considered a continuation of a prior disability for the

purposes of applying the elimination period and/or benefit period.

Reduced Paid-Up Insurance: A nonforfeiture option under which a policy owner uses the nonforfeiture values of a policy to purchase a reduced amount of insurance for which no further premium is due.

Reduction of Coverage: A provision which allows the policy owner to reduce the benefits received from his or her policy without needing to show proof of insurability. This offer may be required by law to be made to a policyowner if his or her policy is going to lapse.

Referral: The method used by a primary-care physician to give permission to a patient within the managed care network to receive medical care not provided by the primary-care physician.

Reinstatement: Reinstatement is a restoration and, according to most courts, a continuation of the original contract. The policy may be reinstated up to three years after the due date of defaulted premium payments. Reinstatement of the policy generally requires evidence of insurability, payment of premium in arrears, plus interest. In addition, any outstanding loans must be repaid to the company with interest. In long-term care policies, special reinstatement provisions allow an extended period to reinstate if the reason for lapse is tied to cognitive impairment.

Renewability: Feature of insurance policies that gives the policyowner the ability to continue the policy at specified periods of time. Renewability may be allowed annually or at the end of a longer specified number of years.

Renewal Rate: The rate paid on cash values in life insurance after the policy is renewed.

Required Beginning Date: As pertains to traditional, SEP and SIMPLE IRA plans and to qualified retirement defined contribution plans, the date on which distributions must be taken from the plan, which is generally no later than age 70 ½.

Residual Disability: A partial disability where the insured is able to work following a total disability. Some disability policies pay a residual disability benefit to prevent insureds from being discouraged from returning work as soon as reasonably possible after a total disability.

Retained Interest: Generally, as pertains to a trust, any interest or right the grantor of the trust continues to have in the property within the trust. If such an interest is retained by the grantor, the trust cannot be considered an irrevocable trust for tax purposes.

Return of Premium: An insurance contract provision which causes premiums paid to be refunded to the insured or beneficiary under certain conditions. Benefits paid under the policy are subtracted from the return of premium amount.

Revocable Beneficiary: A beneficiary on an insurance contract who can be changed by the policy owner at any time.

Rider: An additional, optional life insurance policy benefit that requires the payment of additional premium.

Rollover: A nontaxable transaction that occurs when an eligible distribution is moved from one eligible retirement plan to another eligible retirement plan and the distribution is first made to the plan participant, who then places it into an eligible retirement plan within sixty days.

S

Separate Account: An investment account used by life insurance companies to hold assets in variable product sub-accounts. It is considered a separate legal entity from the life insurance company.

Settlement Options: Options for the payment of death benefits to life insurance policy beneficiaries. Options include life income, income for a fixed period, income for a fixed amount, income for a fixed period and life, and joint and survivor income.

Seven-Pay Test: Applied to life insurance policies to determine if they are modified endowment contracts. Under this test, if the calculated net level premium during the first seven years of the contract, which is calculated based on assumptions in the IRS code, is less than the amount paid in the first seven years of the contract, the contract is considered a MEC. The seven-pay pest applies to life insurance policies issued after June 20, 1988, a life insurance policy exchanged for another policy after June 20, 1988, and to policies that undergo a material change, as defined under the Internal Revenue Code.

Short-Term Disability: Under group insurance, a disability condition that triggers policy benefit payments for two years (104 months) or less.

Sickness: as defined in accident and sickness insurance, illness or disease.

Single Premium Annuity: An annuity that accepts only one premium only.

Single Premium Life: A life insurance contract that accepts only one premium only.

Skilled Care: A form of health care that is performed by a professionally trained individual, such as a licensed nurse, physician, or therapist.

Skilled Nursing Facility: A facility which provides room and board, 24-hour nursing care and rehabilitation, along with other medical services, and has been certified by Medicare.

Spending Down: A term used in relation to Medicaid eligibility, where persons transfer assets and spend income in a manner that makes them eligible to receive Medicaid. Federal and state law governs this activity and impose penalties related to some spending down activities.

Split-Dollar Insurance: Insurance arrangement where two parties, generally employer and employee, split the cost of premiums. Split-dollar arrangements may also include the splitting of cash values, dividends and the death benefit.

Standard Issue: The decision to issue a policy to an applicant falling within the normal boundaries of underwriting standards for that type of policy.

State Guaranty Association: Associations made up of insurance companies doing business in a particular state and/or domiciled within a particular state. Insurance companies that are part of a state guaranty association are liable for a specified amount of contractual obligations if another of its members is not able to meet them.

Statement of Good Health: A statement where an insurance applicant signs and affirms that his or her health condition has not changed since the time of life or health insurance application or medical exam and that his or her life insurance and/or health insurance risks have not changed since that time. It is generally required at the time of policy delivery in order to complete the issue of the policy.

Stop Loss: Provides that after the insured pays out a certain amount of out of pocket expenses, the company will pay 100% of all eligible expenses after that amount during a calendar or plan year.

Subaccounts: Separate accounts used for variable life insurance and variable annuities containing pools of securities with specified investment objectives.

Subaccount Unit: A share in a variable subaccount.

Subrogation: A legal term for the process through which an insurer is able to recover damages from the party liable for damages once the insurer has paid an insured or other claimant. To subrogate means "to substitute." The insurer's right to recover damages are substituted for the insured's right to the damages since the insurer paid damages on behalf of the insured.

Substandard Issue: The decision to issue a policy when a risk is not deemed to be outside underwriting standards, but is considered to be of high risk within those standards. The insurer generally has three basic options when it offers a substandard policy issue to an applicant. It may:
- issue the policy with a higher premium than would be required for a standard policy
- issue the policy with limited benefits
- issue the policy with certain exclusions

Surrender Charge: A percentage charged against certain withdrawals and surrenders taken from life insurance and annuity contract cash values.

Surrender Charge Period: The period of time in which surrender charges apply.

Survivorship Life: Life insurance that pays a death benefit upon the death of the last to die of two or more insureds.

T

Term: This word refers to a variety of periods of time in insurance products. It may refer to the entire length of time a policy is in force, which for a whole life policy is up to age 100. It may refer to the length of time from one renewal period to the next, as in a 5-year term CD annuity or a 5-year term equity-indexed annuity which may be renewed after 5-years. It may refer to the length of time before premiums will change, as in term life insurance.

Term Life Insurance: Life insurance policy that does not accumulate cash values, but pays a death benefit only. The policy is in force for a certain period of time, or term, and generally may be renewed for additional terms.

Time of Payment of Claims: A provision in individual health insurance contracts that requires the insurer must generally pay claims immediately upon receipt of written proof of loss. An insurer may have up to thirty days after receipt of proof of loss to pay certain claims, such as periodic payment claims.

Total Disability: A condition defined in a disability income policy that triggers the payment of benefits for total disability, which are normally the highest benefit amounts paid under the policy. Generally, total disability is defined to mean that the insured is either unable to perform the duties of his or her regular occupation or unable to perform the duties of any gainful occupation, is under a doctor's care, and is not working.

Trigger Events: Events in a business' buy-sell agreement that cause the buy-sell transaction to take place. Trigger events may include death, disability, divorce, bankruptcy and retirement.

Triggering Conditions: A condition defined in an insurance contract that, if met, makes the insured eligible for benefit payments. For example, an accident is a triggering condition under an accident and sickness policy, a partial disability is a triggering condition under a disability income policy and the inability to perform two activities of daily living is a triggering condition under a long-term care policy.

Twisting: Sales practice which involves selling a policy to replace another policy issued by a different insurer for the purpose.

U

Unbundled: A term used to describe a life insurance policy where elements of premium expenses are separated for the purposes of keeping the policy in force and for accumulating cash values. In such a contract, the amount of premium that is used to pay for the cost of insurance and administrative expenses is separated from the remaining amount, which is used for cash values and to pay for future premiums if premium payments are skipped. Universal life and current-assumption life use an unbundled premium structure.

Underwriting: The process of evaluating an insurance risk to determine whether an insurance policy should be issued, and if so, at what rate and with what conditions or exclusions, if any besides those within the policy's normal terms.

Unilateral Contract: A contractual agreement in which one party is responsible to fulfill the terms of the contract. Insurance contracts are unilateral because the insurer is the party responsible to fulfill the insurance contract's terms. An insured or policyowner may have duties under the contract that will remove the insurer's responsibility to fulfill certain of the contract's terms, but an insured may not be found in breach of contract by a court of law, where the insurer can be found to be in breach of contract.

Unit of Insurance: (Also known as exposure unit.) A unit of measurement used to determine pricing in insurance policies. It varies based on the type of risk being insured. A unit may be referred to as an amount of the death benefit in life insurance, e.g., one unit = $1000 of

VA PPL LH-2_16298

death benefit. A unit of health insurance may equal $1000 in policy benefits.

Universal Life: Permanent life insurance that includes the unbundling of policy components. Universal life policies do not require level premium payments and include adjustable death benefit amounts.

Usual, customary, and reasonable (UCR) charges: Conventional health insurance indemnity plans operate based on usual, customary, and reasonable (UCR) charges. UCR charges mean that the charge is the provider's usual fee for a service that does not exceed the customary fee in that geographic area, and is reasonable based on the circumstances.

V

Variable Annuity: Type of annuity contract that includes variable sub-account investing. The return on the annuity is not guaranteed.

Variable Life: Type of whole life insurance policy that includes variable sub-account investment of cash values. Level premium payments are required under this type of policy.

Variable Universal Life: Type of life insurance policy that combines the features of variable life and universal life. Level premium payments are not required under this type of policy.

Viatical Settlement: A contract which allows a policy owner to sell his or her life insurance policy to a viatical settlements company or an individual. The owner receives a lump sum equal to the face value of the policy. The buyer then assumes responsibility to pay all premiums, and will receive the death benefit upon the original owner's death.

Vested: A person with nonforfeitable rights to benefits funded by an employer's contributions in a qualified retirement plan.

Vesting: Increasing ownership in contract or plan values over time. In qualified retirement plans, an employee may have rights to employer contributions to the plan that increase over a three to five year period. In some equity-indexed contracts that do not apply surrender charges, the percentage of cash value available to the owner increases over time through a vesting schedule.

W

Waiting Period: See probationary period.

Warranty: A statement made on the insurance application that is warranted to be true in all respects. However, in the absence of fraud, all statements made on life and health insurance applications are representations, not warranties.

Whole Life: See ordinary life insurance.

Withdrawal Charge: see Surrender Charge

Workers Compensation Categories of Disability: Four types of disability that are covered by Workers Compensation insurance which are: temporary partial disability; temporary total disability; permanent partial disability; and permanent total disability.

Workers Compensation Insurance: A form of insurance that covers employer risks such as injury, disability or death that occurs to employees while on the job.

Z

Zero Cost Loan: A life insurance policy loan where the interest charged on the amount of the loan is equal to the amount credited to the cash value equal to the loan amount.

VA PPL LH-2_16298

Section Review Answers

Section I

1. C Straight or Ordinary Life insurance includes the following characteristics: Level Premium Payments; Coverage to Age 100; Cash Values; Level Face Amount

2. A Limited pay whole life insurance requires payments for a certain, or limited, period. Limited pay life insurance policies can have premium periods of any length, such as twenty years, or up to age 65.

3. C Universal life insurance was developed to be a flexible form of insurance that can be used to meet almost any need. Premium amounts can be changed, premium payments may be skipped or suspended for a time, and the death benefit can be changed, all during the life of the policy.

4. C Variable life and annuity contracts provide that contract amounts are to be allocated to a separate account and invested in shares of a specified investment company. The separate account which must be registered under the Investment Company Act of 1940. The agents who sell variable insurance products must be licensed by the securities regulators and must comply with the variable licensing requirements of the state in which they do business.

5. D Variable universal life is a life insurance product that combines the features of variable life and universal life insurance.

6. B Death benefit provisions vary among current-assumption whole life insurance policies. Some policies provide a guaranteed death benefit, like other whole life insurance policies. Others offer death benefits similar to universal life insurance policies, including both a level death benefit option and a death benefit option that correlates the death benefit to cash values so that it increases or decreases based on the cash value level.

7. C A decreasing term policy is used in both business and personal situations to protect against the financial risk assumed when a loan is taken.

8. C Variable annuities are annuity contracts which allow the accumulation of earnings based on subaccounts that are similar to mutual funds. The insurer does not guarantee the return on subaccounts, although the insurer may offer some guarantees by pegging the value of the annuity every several years or by guaranteeing the death benefit amount.

9. A The annuitant is generally the measuring life on the contract. If the contract is an income annuity, the annuitant's life expectancy is used to determine the payout amount over a life income annuity option.

10 A One annuity payment option allows the purchaser to specify a fixed period of time that the payments will continue. This option is known as a "period certain" payout. Generally, the minimum period is five years, but some annuity companies allow for a period as short as three years. The maximum term may be limited.

11. A Fixed annuities may either be "flexible premium" annuities or "single premium" annuities. A single premium annuity is one that accepts only one premium contribution.

12. A Fixed annuity contracts generally have back-end charges levied when a contract is surrendered or when withdrawals are made, called a surrender charge.

13. A A surrender provision in some annuities includes a waiver of surrender charges if the rate ever falls below a specified percentage or falls more than a specified percentage lower than the initial rate. This percentage is referred to as a bail out rate or as the rate floor.

14. C Survivorship life pays a death benefit upon the death of the last to die of two or more insureds. The most common use of survivorship life is to supply insurance coverage to pay for estate taxes at the death of a surviving spouse.

15. A Some policies allow the insured to purchase increased amounts of insurance without providing proof of insurance through a guaranteed insurability option.

Section II

1. C A waiver of premium for disability rider for juvenile life policies waives the premium when the payor, which is the person paying the premiums, becomes disabled.

2. B A waiver of premium rider provides that the insurer will waive the premium on a life insurance policy should the insured or policy holder become disabled. Waiver of premium riders do not generally continue to age 100 or

VA PPL LH-2_16298

policy maturity. Most of these riders provide coverage through age 60 or 65.

3. A The policy owner (or policy holder) is typically the purchaser and payer of the premium. It is up to the owner to name the insured and beneficiaries of the policy. The owner also has several other rights, including the right to make withdrawals from the policy.

4. A The policyowner (or policyholder) is typically the purchaser and payer of the premium. It is up to the owner to name the insured and beneficiaries of the policy. The owner also has several other rights, including being able to increase or decrease coverage within contract specifications.

5. D The parties to a contract must each provide valuable consideration in a contractual relationship. The premium is the consideration by the insured and the promise to fulfill policy obligations is the consideration given by the insurer.

6. A Beneficiaries receive the life insurance policy proceeds upon the death of the insured. Any person, natural or non-natural, may be named as a beneficiary.

7. C Beneficiaries may be designated as revocable or irrevocable. If an owner designates a beneficiary as irrevocable, the beneficiary cannot be changed without the permission of that beneficiary.

8. C An insurer may include a deferment or common disaster period in beneficiary designations. These clauses will pay benefits to the class II or secondary beneficiary only if the primary beneficiary does not survive the insured for a specified number of days.

9. A Life insurance policies must allow for reinstatement after the policy lapses due to nonpayment of premium. The policy holder must make written application within three years from the date of default in premium payments and submit evidence of insurability that is satisfactory to the insurance company. Overdue premium must be paid, including accrued interest at a rate stated in the policy, and not to exceed 8% along with any policy loan amounts and loan interest owed to the insurer.

10. A Participating Life Insurance is life insurance that may include the payment of dividends from the insurer because the policy owner participates in the earned surplus of the insurance company.

11. D Life insurance policies include an incontestability clause that gives the maximum amount of time the insurer has to contest the validity of the policy. The reason for this is that the policy holder should be able to rely on the coverage for which he or she is paying premium. The allowable contestability period gives the insurer time in which to verify the application representations and supporting information supplied by the insured and policy holder.

12. D These are all provisions in individual life insurance contracts.

13. C A life income with refund settlement option pays out income for the life of the payee. If the payee passes away before an amount equal to the original death benefit is paid out, the named beneficiary will continue to receive payments until this amount is paid, or will receive a lump sum.

14. B No individual life insurance policy may be delivered or issued for delivery in Virginia unless it has printed on it a notice that states that during a ten-day period from the date the policy is delivered to the policyowner, the policy is surrendered to the insurer or its agent with a written request for cancellation, the policy is void from the beginning and the insurer will refund any premium paid for the policy. An insurer may extend this right to examine period to more than ten days if the period is specified in the policy.

15. B Each individual life insurance policy must contain a provision that the insured is entitled to a grace period of not less than 31 days within which the payment of any premium after the first premium may be made.

16. D In Virginia, under the mandatory "grace period" provision, the policyholder has seven additional days to pay premium if the policy has a weekly premium payment schedule, ten additional days to pay premium if the policy has a monthly premium payment schedule, and thirty-one additional days to pay premium for policies with any other premium payment schedule.

17. D A life insurance policy where premium payments are in default is subject to reinstatement. The policy may be reinstated within three years from default, if certain conditions are met.

18. C A life insurance policy must provide that it is incontestable after it has been if force, during the lifetime of the insured, two years from its

VA PPL LH-2_16298

date of issue, except for nonpayment of premiums.

Section III

1. C The agent has the important role of not submitting improper risk to the insurer through the application and supporting documents, if the agent knows the risk will not meet the insurer's standards.

2. D Material misrepresentation and concealment may cause a contract to be void. When a court determines that concealment, misrepresentation or breach of warranty meets the legal standards of fraud, the insurance coverage is void.

3. A Gramm-Leach-Bliley includes provisions that deal with disclosure of nonpublic personal information to nonaffiliated third parties, and how and why this may or may not be done, as well as the requirement of the financial institution to provide a disclosure of the institution's disclosure process.

4. D Licensees must provide an opt-out notice to consumers when given notice by a financial institution of its policies concerning disclosing nonpublic personal information.

5. C The three major credit reporting bureaus are Equifax, Experian and TransUnion

6. D Consumer reports can be generated for the following reasons: Because of a court order; and because the consumer has given written authorization to do so for employment purposes, for underwriting insurance, or to determine the eligibility for a government issued license, or other government benefit where financial responsibility or status must be reviewed.

7. A Consumer reports include the consumer's credit information, employment information, their current and past addresses, and the source of the information.

8. A If an adverse action, such as denying credit or insurance, occurs due to the information on the consumer report, the user of the report may disclose the contents of the report to the consumer.

9. C The FACT Act expands some of the consumer protections found in the Fair Credit Reporting Act. It was passed with the intent to help decrease errors in credit reports and other reporting problems associated with identity theft.

10. B Insurers have raised the concern that the presence of STOLI and IOLI transactions in the market cause life insurance premiums to rise. STOLI and IOLI funders generally have a greater capacity to pay insurance premiums and keep large policies in force than does the general marketplace; the general marketplace allows life insurance policies to lapse by nonpayment of premium at a greater rate than will large investors. The persistency rate in the life insurance market therefore increases and the insurer's requirement to pay a death benefit on a policy climbs closer to a 100% certainty. Insurance companies argue that when institutional investors buy a policy on which a death claim would not otherwise be paid, this affects their ability to provide lower premiums for all customers.

11. B Life insurance policies may not have an issue or effective date that is earlier than six months before the original application for the insurance is made. Since John's birthdate is less than six months prior to August 9, John's policy may be backdated to his birthdate, June 2.

12. D Under the Final Rules for the USA Patriot Act, a transaction must be reported if it is conducted or attempted by, at, or through an insurance company and involves or aggregates at least $5,000 in funds or other assets.

13. B Insurance companies must provide training for their producers concerning their responsibilities under the company's anti-money laundering program. An insurance company should provide for independent testing of their anti-money laundering program on a periodic basis to ensure that it complies with the requirements of the final rule and that it functions as designed.

14. B The negative impacts of failing to maintain an effective anti-money laundering program are as follows: Financial penalties (some cases in the banking and brokerage industry have resulted in fines as high as $100 million); Injurious impact on share-holder value of a financial institution; Damage to a company's reputation and integrity (which are fundamental to a company's continuance).

15. B The Bank Secrecy Act includes the regulatory requirement applicable to insurance companies to report the receipt of cash or certain non-cash instruments totaling more than $10,000 in one transaction or two or more related transactions.

16. C Virginia law provides that all statements, declarations and descriptions in any application for an insurance policy or for the reinstatement of an insurance policy are deemed representations and not warranties. No statement in an application or in any affidavit made before or after loss under the policy may bar a recovery upon a policy of insurance unless it is clearly proven that the answer or statement was material to the risk when assumed and was untrue. *VA Code §38.2-309*

17. C An adverse underwriting decision is permissible if, during the underwriting process, it is revealed that the applicant has had positive HIV-related test results following testing protocol, or has been diagnosed as having AIDS or HIV infection. An adverse underwriting decision is not permissible if it is based solely on the presence of symptoms, as disclosed in an application for life or accident and sickness insurance coverage. An adverse underwriting decision is permissible, however, if the symptoms disclosed in the application for coverage are confirmed as being HIV-related through the use of medical records or HIV-related tests.

18. B The Virginia Code in Section 38.2-301 defines insurable interest for life, accident and sickness policies. This code section states that any individual of lawful age may take out an insurance contract upon himself for the benefit of any person and that no person is allowed to knowingly procure or cause to be procured any insurance contract upon another individual unless the benefits under the contract are payable to: the insured or his personal representative; or a person having an insurable interest in the insured at the time when the contract was made.

19. B Virginia insurance law provides that: a wife or husband may effect an insurance contract upon each other.

20. B Under Virginia law, a policy is deemed to have been received by the owner of the policy as of the date of its issuance if six months have passed since its issue and the owner of the policy has paid the premiums for those six months. *VA Code §38.2-3301.1*

Section IV

1. D The insured is the measuring life of the contract. A non-natural person, such as a trust or a corporation, may own life insurance policies. The insured, however, must be a natural person.

2. B Group insurance is issued through a master policy. Each insured in the group is issued a certificate of coverage.

3. B Distributions from Roth IRAs that are considered "qualified distributions" are not taxable upon receipt. In addition, under the special tax rules that apply to Roth IRAs, earnings accumulate without taxation as long as qualified distributions are made when they are withdrawn.

4. C Ed must be 59 ½ and the withdrawal must be taken 5 tax years after the contribution was made.

5. B This withdrawal meets the definition of "qualified distribution" from a Roth, and so is not tax because the IRA holder has reached age 59½.

6. C Defined contribution plans include 401(k) plans, 403(b) plans, employee stock ownership plans (ESOPs), money purchase plans and profit-sharing plans.

7. B The "human life value" approach results in a dollar value that represents the financial loss an income earner's death will cause, based on anticipated earnings over a lifetime, to the income earner's family. The human life value calculated for this purpose is the present value of the family's share of the deceased income earner's future earnings.

8. A Under a "cross-purchase" buy-sell agreement, the owners of the business each purchase a policy on the life of the other owners.

9. B Businesses may have more than one key employee. In such a case, "first-to-die" or "joint life" insurance may be used. Under this type of policy, two or more insureds are named. In the family market, joint life is usually utilized in order to save the expense associated with writing two separate individual policies.

10. C Loans from non-MEC policies are not taxable, but if taken from a MEC, they are taxable.

Section V

1. D When an advertisement uses the terms "nonmedical," "no medical examination required," or similar terms when issue of the insurance policy is not guaranteed, these terms must be accompanied by further disclosure that explains that issuance of the policy may depend upon the answers to health questions contained in the application.

VA PPL LH-2_16298

2. B An advertisement may not represent that premium payments will not be required for every year of the policy in order to maintain the illustrated death benefits, unless that is the fact. An advertisement may not use certain terms to describe a plan using nonguaranteed elements to pay a portion of future premiums. Prohibited terms are: vanish; vanishing premium; and similar terms that imply the policy becomes paid-up.

3. C An advertisement must not contain statements indicating that because a prospect has agreed to furnish names of potential purchasers, he is entitled to any specific benefits not available to all policyholders generally.

4. B If an individual receives any financial benefit directly or indirectly, greater than required union scale wages, that fact must be clearly and prominently disclosed in the advertisement by language identical or substantially similar to the following: THIS IS A PAID ENDORSEMENT.

5. A When advertising group health plans, the agent and insurer must follow state law in the state in which they are advertising. Virginia law states that an advertisement that is intended to be seen or heard beyond the limits of the jurisdiction in which the insurer or agent is licensed may not imply licensing beyond those limits.

6. A The Virginia insurance laws defines an annuity "recommendation" as "advice provided by an insurance agent, or an insurer where no agent is involved, to an individual consumer that results in a purchase or exchange of an annuity in accordance with that advice."

7. A Exceptions to the replacement rules include when there is an application to the existing insurer that issued the existing life insurance because a contractual change or a conversion privilege is being exercised; or when the existing policy or contract is being replaced by the same insurer pursuant to a plan filed and approved by the commission; or when a term conversion privilege is exercised among corporate affiliates.

8. B The notice states that "A replacement occurs when a new policy or contract is purchased and, in connection with the sale, you discontinue making premium payments on the existing policy or contract, or an existing policy or contract is surrendered, forfeited, assigned to the replacing insurer, or otherwise terminated or used in a financed purchase."

9. B Virginia insurance law and regulation allow life insurance policies to include an accelerated payment of benefits provision. One of the conditions for payment of the benefit during the lifetime of the insured is: If a qualified health care provider or court of competent jurisdiction has determined that the insured is no longer able to perform two of the following activities of daily living: bathing; dressing; continence; eating; toileting; or transferring.

10. A The accelerated benefit must allow the insured to authorize a lump sum payment. The payment may not be made as an annuity contingent upon the insured's life.

11. D In Virginia, defined groups able to offer life insurance are employer groups, creditor groups, labor unions, associations, credit unions and associations that provide funeral plans and insurance. Groups cannot be formed just for the purpose of being able to obtain group insurance.

12. B To exercise a conversion privilege on a group life policy, one condition is: Application for the individual policy must be made within 31 days after the termination.

13. D Except when policy loans are made to pay premiums, the insurer may defer issuing a policy loan for up to six months after the date on which the loan is applied.

14. C It is a violation of the Viatical Settlements Act for any person to enter into a viatical settlement contract within a two-year period commencing with the date of issuance of the insurance policy or certificate however, an exception to this law occurs when the viator submits independent evidence to the viatical settlement provider that one or more of the following conditions have been met within the two-year period: The insured is terminally or chronically ill.

15. C It is prohibited for an insurer or insurance agent to make any representation, or use any device, title, descriptive name or identifier that has the tendency or capacity to confuse or mislead a service member into believing that the insurer, insurance agent or product offered is affiliated, connected or associated with, endorsed, sponsored, sanctioned or recommended by the U.S. Government, the United States Armed Forces, or any state or federal agency or government entity.

Section VI

1. A An accidental injury is generally defined as "injury to the body as a result of an accident."

2. C For partial disabilities, a loss-of-income calculation may apply in policies that use a stated percentage for total disabilities. 25% of $4000 = $1000.

3. C BOE insurance pays benefits based on covered overhead expenses. The policy defines what items are covered and what items are excluded.

4. D Care provided by medical expense plans includes care by physicians, such as physical exams, but does not include long-term skilled nursing care, adult day care or orthodontic care.

5. D A hospital indemnity policy pays a specified benefit on a daily or monthly basis when an insured is confined to a hospital.

6. B In a managed care network, physicians who provide primary care are encouraged to try to provide all the care they reasonably and appropriately can prior to referring a patient to a specialist.

7. A Managed care plans generally divide emergency care into two classifications: urgent and life-threatening. Life-threatening refers to conditions that could result in death, serious disability, disfigurement, or a long-term medical problem. Many managed care plans require that they be notified within 24 to 48 hours of the member's treatment for a life-threatening condition.

8. A Medically necessary dental, hearing and vision care includes care such as that required after an accident, or care required due to an infection.

9. A In order to be eligible for an HSA, neither the employee or the employee's spouse can have health coverage that is not an HDHP, if the non-HDHP plan covers the employee.

10. B Under HSA rules, qualified medical expenses include fees paid to physicians, for prescription medicines, and for necessary hospital services not paid for by insurance.

11. D Distributions from HRAs may be made to reimburse any of the following: current and former employees; spouses and dependents of those employees; most people that could be claimed as a dependent on the employee's return.

12. D Medigap Plan M includes the same benefits as Plan A and pays 50% of the Medicare Plan A deductible and includes coverage for the skilled nursing facility care coinsurance amount

13. A METs and MEWAs are only available for single employer groups. Together, these single employers form a multiple employer trust. The insurer told the business it did not meet this standard, since the one business was not a single employer, but several businesses under common control.

14. C This question provides an example of a health insurance plans including a deductible carryover into the first three months of the next plan year of the deductible if it has not yet been met by the insured.

15. B The reason creditable coverage certificates are not necessary to prove coverage for preexisting condition purposes is that the ACA disallows preexisting conditions in qualified health plans. However, health plans will still issue certificates and documents with proof of health plan coverage length and termination because of continuation requirements in COBRA.

16. C Custodial care can include some health related care, but no skilled medical care. This type of care is assistance with ADLs – eating, toileting, transferring, bathing, dressing and continence.

17. D Long-term care policies may calculate benefits as indemnity or actual cost of care contracts. Indemnity contracts pay a fixed amount per day, or the actual cost of care, whichever is lower. Actual cost of care contracts pay for the actual cost of care, up to specified limits.

18. B Oral surgery services include extracting teeth and pre-operative and post-operative care. Oral surgery services include anesthesia.

19. C A nonscheduled plan will pay for services based on the amount the dentist or specialist charges, subject to limits of insurance and generally include coinsurance and deductibles.

20. A The Patient Protection and Affordable Care Act (ACA) was signed into law on March 23, 2010. This Act is implemented over several years, beginning in 2010, with most provisions being implemented by 2015.

Section VII

1. A The "entire contract and changes clause" states that the policy is the entire contract of insurance and that no changes may be made unless it is approved by the insurer and an endorsement of the change is attached to the policy. An agent may not change the policy or waive any of its provisions.

2. B The NAIC's Uniform Policy Provisions Model Law, which specifies provisions found in individual accident and sickness insurance policies, has been adopted by all fifty states. It includes mandatory provisions for these policies, as well as optional provisions.

3. B These are mandatory provisions in individual health insurance contracts, and are standard provisions applicable in all states.

4. B A reinstated policy will cover loss resulting from accidental injury immediately upon reinstatement, but will not cover loss due to sickness that begins ten days or less after reinstatement.

5. A A reinstated policy will cover loss resulting from accidental injury immediately upon reinstatement, but will not cover loss due to sickness that begins ten days or less after reinstatement.

6. A January 13 is 90 days after the period for which the insurer is liable for the injury. The "proof of loss" mandatory individual health insurance policy provision places a time limit upon the period in which a proof of loss form is given to the insurer. Under the provision, the proof of loss must be filed within ninety days of loss, or if the loss is a continuing loss, the proof of loss must be given within ninety days after the period for which the insurer is liable. If it is not reasonably possible for the claimant to furnish the proof of loss within that time period, it must be submitted no later than within one year, except due to legal incapacity.

7. B Under the "payment of claims" provision, any death benefits payable will be paid to a named beneficiary on the policy, or to the estate of the insured if a beneficiary is not named.

8. B July 31, 2016 is three years and 90 days after the date of the loss. Under the "legal actions" provision, boundaries are set upon the time period during which legal action may be sought. This provision states that legal action to collect from a claim must not begin for at least sixty days from the time a proof of loss form is filed with the insurer, and must be taken in a period no longer than three years from the time in which the proof of loss form is required to be filed.

9. A Grace period is a required provision for individual health insurance policies. The other provisions are optional.

10. A The Insurance with Other Insurers – Other Than Expense Incurred Basis is an optional provision in individual health policies. It is used when the benefits are not paid on an expense-incurred basis. The insurer's liability is limited to its proportionate share of the expenses incurred if other coverage is in force and the insurer is not notified of it until after the commencement of the policy. The total expense is $120. The total coverage is $400. Insurer A's share of the total is ¼, Insurer B's share of the total is ¾.

11. A The conformity with state statutes optional provision removes conflict in the policy's language with state laws. It amends any provision in the policy on the issue date that is in conflict with a state statute so that it conforms with state law.

12. C The optional provision concerning loss involving intoxicants or narcotics specifies that the insurer will not be liable for any loss sustained or contracted in consequence of the insured's being intoxicated or under the influence of any narcotic unless administered on the advice of a physician.

13. B Noncancellable contracts guarantee that the premium on a contract will never go up at renewal, up through a specified period or age.

14. D A nonrenewable health plan is a short-term coverage plan, and is also known as cancelable or term coverage. This type of health plan provides coverage for 6 to 12 months.

15. D The accidental death rider pays double or triple a stated amount of the AD&D benefit if death occurs as a result of an accident. The definition of accident under these riders does not include disease and death must be the direct result of accidental injury. The rider also specifies that death must occur within a specified number of days from the accident, generally from 90 to 120 days. The coverage from this type of rider generally ends at a specified age, such as age 70.

16. B Under the time limit on certain defenses clause, once an individual health insurance policy has been issued, the insurer may not void the policy or deny a claim for loss or disability due to misstatements in the application unless fraudulent, after three years.

17. B The ACA includes provisions that disallow lifetime maximum limits on essential health benefits in policies subject to the ACA. The Virginia Code §38.2-3440 addresses lifetime and annual limits on essential health benefits in

VA PPL LH-2_16298

group and individual health plans and is effective as of January 1, 2014, as follows: "Notwithstanding any provision of § 38.2-3406.1; 38.2-3406.2; or 38.2-3418.5; or any other section of this title to the contrary, a health carrier offering group or individual health insurance coverage shall not establish a lifetime limit on the dollar amount of essential health benefits for any covered person. A health carrier shall not establish any annual limit on the dollar amount of essential health benefits for any covered person."

18. A The Virginia Bureau of Insurance provided the following explanation of what are considered essential health benefits under the ACA in its Essential Health Benefits Guidance published in April 2013 for insurance companies. This Guidance is subject to change as the ACA is more fully implemented in the Commonwealth.

Section VIII

1. D Medicare Part A is hospital insurance and Part B is medical expense insurance.

2. B Generally, Medicare Part A covers the following: Inpatient care in hospitals; inpatient stays in a skilled nursing facility (not long-term care); hospice care services; home health care services; inpatient care in a Religious Nonmedical Health Care Institution.

3. D To qualify for Social Security Disability payments, the individual must have earned a specified number of work credits. Generally, the individual must have earned 40 credits, of which 20 must have been earned in the last ten years. Four credits are the maximum number of credits that may be earned each year.

4. D If an individual qualifies for Social Security Disability payments, the first benefit is paid the sixth full month after the date Social Security finds that the disability began.

5. D Generally, Social Security Disability payments continue as long as the individual remains disabled. If the person's health improves, and/or they are able to go back to work, benefits will cease.

6. D Medicare is a federal health insurance program, primarily for seniors. Medicare is provided to people age 65 and over, people under 65 that have certain disabilities and anyone, regardless of age, with permanent kidney failure that requires dialysis or a kidney transplant.

7. A The enrollment period for Medicare Part D is from October 15-December 7 of each year.

8. D Medicare supplement policies, or "Medigap" insurance policies, are designed to fill the gaps Medicare coverage leaves. These policies are structured to pay items such as Medicare coinsurance amounts and Medicare deductibles and to provide coverage for services not paid for by Medicare.

9. B Medicare includes health coverage through Part A and Part B. Part A is hospitalization insurance and Part B is medical expense insurance.

10. A Medicare Part A home health care coverage generally applies if the individual is homebound, and therefore unable to get care services outside the home. The individual must need skilled nurse or skilled physical, speech or occupational therapist care. Home health care for assistance with bathing, toileting, feeding and personal care are covered, if considered home health care, and not simply custodial care.

11. B Individuals who did not enroll in Medicare during the initial enrollment period may sign up between January 1-March 31 each year. Coverage for these enrollees begins July 1. Late enrollees may be subject to higher premium rates.

12. B Low income individuals who are aged (aged means age 65 and older), or blind and disabled are eligible for Medicaid coverage.

Section IX

1. B Partial disability is generally defined to mean the inability to perform some, but not all, of the important duties of the insured's regular occupation. A specified percentage of time the insured is able to work in the occupation may also be included in the partial disability definition, such as "the insured's inability to engage in his or her regular occupation for longer than 50% of the time normally spent in performing the usual duties of the regular occupation."

2. A If people are covered by more than one health coverage plans, the payment of benefits must be coordinated between the plans when more than one plan covers a sickness or injury. Circumstances that may result in being covered by more than one health plan include being involved in an auto accident and the applicable auto insurance providing medical expense coverage. Health plan language varies regarding how its coverage is applied when

VA PPL LH-2_16298

there is duplicate coverage. Many insurers however, use the coordination of benefits provision developed by the National Association of Insurance Commissioners.

3. B If individual health coverage is in place along with an employer health plan, the individual health plan does not generally include a coordination of benefits provision. Generally, this means that the individual health coverage will be the primary payor and the employer plan will be the secondary payor when both plans apply to the same sickness, injury or accident.

4. C Premiums for medical expense insurance may be included in the medical expense deduction for federal income tax purposes.

5. A Amounts received under a qualified long-term care contract are treated like amounts received under Accident and Health Insurance contracts. If a taxpayer itemizes deductions and owns a qualified long-term care contract, the taxpayer can take advantage of deductions and exclusions relate to long-term care premiums and benefits.

6. A Long-term care insurance premiums and benefits are generally treated the same as premiums and benefits from accident and health insurance policies, for tax purposes. Employer paid premiums are deductible to the employer, benefits are not taxable to the employee, and if the employee pays any of the premiums, they may be deductible as part of medical insurance expenses on the employee's individual federal tax return.

7. B All states have enacted laws requiring certain employers to provide financial protection against disability and death due to work-related occurrences. These laws are called "Workers Compensation" laws. Workers Compensation is another form of social insurance.

8. C If a group plan calls for the employer and employee to split the premiums paid for the disability insurance, and the employee will be receiving the benefits from the policy, then the amount of premium paid by the employer is deductible to the employer for tax purposes, and the amount of benefits received by the employee that is attributable to the employer-paid premium is considered taxable income. The benefits received by the employee that are attributable to the premium paid by the employee are exempt from income taxation.

9. A Group health plans are subject to Federal taxation rules applicable to accident or health plans. The health benefits provided to employees are not included in the wages of employees. Contributions and payments made by the employer in accordance with governing law are tax deductible to the employer.

10. B Business overhead expense disability insurance premiums are deductible to the business. When benefits are received, they are taxable. However, the benefits will be used to pay for business expenses, e.g., electricity and rent, which are deductible to the business.

11. C Under a situation when a disability income policy is used for a buy-sell agreement, and a corporation owns the policy and will receive benefits, and the employee or shareholder is named as insured, premiums are not tax deductible to the corporation. Benefits received by the corporation are also not taxable. If the benefits received by the corporation are used to make payments to an employee, the payments are taxable as income to the employee, and deductible as compensation by the corporation.

12. D Key person disability income insurance premiums are not deductible to the business, and the benefits from the policy paid to the business are not includable in business income. The employee pays no taxes on the benefits; benefits are paid to the business.

13. D Workers Compensation statutes include four categories of disability, and payments made vary based on the category of disability under which the injury falls. Generally, the four categories of disability are: temporary partial disability; temporary total disability; permanent partial disability; permanent total disability.

14. D All states have laws that require the payment of benefits to workers injured on the job or who have an occupational disease or work-related illness. Payments are made for medical expenses, rehabilitation, disability and death. Benefits are payable regardless of who is at fault.

15. C Generally, the owner has the following rights under a health insurance contract, as applicable to the coverage: selecting the deductible; selecting the elimination period; selecting the benefit period; selecting the benefits included in the insurance, subject to legal requirements; selecting the preferred provider or other providers paid for under the policy; appealing denials of coverage; adding riders or additional

VA PPL LH-2_16298

coverages available for additional premium; and adding additional insureds under the coverage, such as a spouse and dependent children.

16. C All group or individual accident and sickness insurance policy contracts delivered or issued for delivery in Virginia that provide that coverage of a dependent child terminates upon the child's attainment of a specified age, must also provide that attainment of the specified age will not terminate the child's coverage while the dependent child is and continues to be both: incapable of self-sustaining employment by reason of intellectual disability or physical handicap; and chiefly dependent upon the policyowner for support and maintenance.

Section X

1. D The agent is crucial in the underwriting process. This is because they gather underwriting information through the application, evaluate risk, often do a preliminary assignment of premium, may authorize preliminary coverage, and may reject applicants on behalf of the insurer.

2. A Once the agent has completed the fact-finding process with the customer, the agent will be ready to discuss specific products and plans that may meet the customer's needs. Whenever the agent discusses product and plan options with the customer, the agent has a responsibility to provide clear and accurate information about the programs discussed.

3. C The agent may be called upon to screen out unacceptable risks for the insurer. The agent may determine that an applicant does not meet minimum underwriting standards. In some cases, the agent must inform the applicant that the insurer will not be able to write a policy for that applicant. Or, the agent may try to work with the applicant to determine if there is another method of covering the risk that will meet minimum underwriting requirement.

4. B Documentation may be asked for by the underwriters after the application is submitted, such as an APS and other medical care documentation. An APS must be completed by a physician who treated the medical condition under question.

5. B In the health insurance underwriting process, if additional documentation is required from the applicant, the underwriting department will request the documentation directly from the applicant or will notify the agent or agency that these items are needed. The request for information and documentation generally include a specified period of time in which the request must be fulfilled. If the information is not received within the specified time, the application file is generally closed, and any premium received is returned.

6. A An Attending Physician Statement generally includes: Patient's (insured's) name; Patient's address; If related to an insured's employment, a statement for the physician to designate whether the patient is able to return to work, and if unable, when it is anticipated the patient will be able to return to work; An area for the physician to indicate the physician's diagnosis and prognosis; An area for additional remarks for the physician; The physician's name, license number, address, phone number and signature.

7. C It is generally prohibited for an agent to commingle funds that belong to the insurer with other funds, such as those of an insurance agency. Generally, it is prohibited to treat the funds in a trust account as a personal asset, as collateral for either a personal or business loan, or as a personal asset on a financial statement. The Insurance Commissioner may have a trust account examined and audited at any time.

8. D When premium for a health insurance policy is not collected at time of application, it must be collected at policy delivery. The policy generally becomes effective when the premium is collected and a statement of good health is signed, unless there is a written agreement with the insurer to make the policy effective under some other condition.

9. A When evaluating applicants, underwriters determine whether insurance on the applicant will be rejected; issued on a substandard basis; issued on a standard basis; or issued on a preferred basis. Insurers reject applications for insurance when they find that the applicant represents a risk that falls outside of the underwriting standards established by the insurance company.

10. D Important factors when considering replacement include waiting period, preexisting conditions, benefits and limits, exclusions and the financial strength of the insurer. Since all insurers must be authorized by the state and meet the state's financial, legal and policy form

VA PPL LH-2_16298

requirements, it doesn't matter very much whether the insurer is domestic or foreign.

11. C Emergency care is generally defined as necessary care that a person reasonably believes to be immediately necessary to preserve life, prevent serious impairment to bodily functions, organs or part, or prevent placing the physical or mental health of the individual in serious jeopardy.

12. C Parties to contracts must be recognized as having the legal ability to enter into them. Insurance policyholders must be of legal age and must also be considered legally competent to enter into the agreements.

13. B Insurance contracts are aleatory. This means that the outcome is affected by chance, and that the values exchanged may not be equal. Only if a peril or other insured cause of loss occurs will payment be made by the insurance company. Under insurance contracts, if a loss occurs, the premium is much less than the benefit received. The value received is not generally equal to the value paid.

14. A Insurance contracts are written by the insurer, and the policyholder may only negotiate terms according to the options the insurer gives. This makes them contracts of adhesion. If there is a contractual dispute involving the wording or terms of an insurance contract, a court generally rules in favor of the insured because the insured had nothing to do with the construction of the contract's terms. Ruling in favor of the insured is a legal principal followed by courts when interpreting an insurance contract when there is ambiguity because the insurance policy is a contract of adhesion.

15. C An aleatory contract is one whose outcome is affected by chance and which has values exchanged that are not equal.

Section XI

1. B According to Virginia insurance regulations, an issuer of Medigap policies must provide a copy of any Medicare Supplement advertisement intended for use in Virginia to the Commission. This filing requirement applies to all Medigap policy advertising, whether through written, radio or television medium.

2. B Insurers issuing accident and health policies delivered or issued for delivery in Virginia which provide hospital or medical expense coverage to a person eligible for Medicare by reason of age, must provide a Medicare Supplement buyer's guide, "Guide to Health Insurance for People with Medicare." Delivery of the buyer's guide must be made whether or not the group policy qualifies as a Medicare Supplement policy.

3. A If a Medicare Supplement policy or certificate replaces another Medicare Supplement policy or certificate, the replacing issuer must waive time periods applicable to preexisting conditions, waiting periods, elimination periods and probationary periods in the new Medicare Supplement policy or certificate for similar benefits to the extent the time was spent under the original policy.

4. A Under Virginia law, Medigap policies must have a prominent notice when delivered that states that he or she has the right to return the certificate within thirty days of its delivery and to have the premium refunded if the insured person is not satisfied for any reason.

5. B At age 70, if a long-term care insurer imposes a rate increase of 30%, it must offer the reduced policy benefits nonforfeiture option and the reduced paid-up option to the insured.

6. B All long-term care insurance applicants must be offered inflation protection in Virginia.

7. D Partnership policy insurers must provide the Notice Regarding Long-Term Care Insurance Partnership Status to the insured at the issuance of a policy intended to be a Partnership policy. It must be provided with the Outline of Coverage.

8. C Agents must undergo an initial training of not less than 8 hours and ongoing training every 24 months thereafter of not less than 4 hours.

9. D This notice is considered direct mail and is issued to members of the insurance buying public, so is advertising.

10. C Disclosure materials provided to applicants and purchases, such as the outline of coverage, are considered advertisements.

11. B Under Virginia's insurance regulations, it is required that each insurer maintain at its home or principal office a complete file containing: every printed, published, or prepared advertisement of individual policies; and typical printed, published, or prepared advertisements of blanket, franchise, and group policies. There must be a note attached to each advertisement that states the manner and extent of distribution and any advertised policy's form number. These documents must be maintained

VA PPL LH-2_16298

for a period of the longer of 4 years or until the filing of the next regular report on examination of the insurer.

12. B In-hospital medical services, consisting of physician services rendered to a person who is a bed patient in a hospital for treatment of sickness or injury other than that for which surgical care is required, in an amount not less than: 80% of the reasonable charges; or $10 per day for not less than 31 days during the period of confinement.

13. D Upon determining that a sale involves replacement an insurer or its agent must furnish the applicant, prior to policy issue or delivery, a replacement notice. One copy of the notice must be retained by the applicant and an additional copy signed by the applicant must be retained by the insurer. A direct response insurer must also deliver a replacement to the applicant upon issuance of the policy. These notices are not required in the solicitation of accident only and single premium nonrenewable policies.

14. B A health insurance issuer offering group health insurance coverage must provide for certification of the period of creditable coverage: at the time an individual ceases to be covered under the plan or otherwise becomes covered under a COBRA continuation provision; in the case of an individual becoming covered under a COBRA continuation provision, at the time the individual ceases to be covered under such provision; and at the request, or on behalf of, an individual made not later than 24 months after the date of cessation of the coverage.

15. D Continuation of coverage must be provided in each group hospital policy, group medical and surgical policy or group major medical policy plans issued in Virginia even when federal COBRA laws do not apply to a plan.

16. D Association groups may be authorized to issue accident and sickness insurance. The association or associations must: 1) Have at the outset a minimum of 100 persons; 2) Have been organized and maintained in good faith for purposes other than that of obtaining insurance; 3) Have been in active existence for at least five years; 4) Have a constitution and bylaws; 5) Does not condition membership in the association on any health status-related factor relating to an individual; 6) Makes health insurance coverage offered through the association available to all members and those eligible through the member, regardless of any health status-related factor; 7) Does not make health insurance coverage offered through the association available other than in connection with a member of the association; and 8) Meets any additional requirements imposed under the laws of Virginia.

17. A A health maintenance organization must have a system to provide to its members, on a 24-hour basis: access to medical care; or access by telephone to a physician or licensed health care professional with appropriate medical training who can refer or direct a member for prompt medical care in cases where there is an immediate, urgent need or medical emergency.

18. B At the time of enrollment an HMO enrollee must have the right to select a primary care health care professional from among the HMO's affiliated primary care health care professionals. An enrollee who is dissatisfied with his primary care health care professional has the right to select another primary care health care professional from among the health maintenance organization's affiliated primary care health care professionals, subject to availability.

19. C Small employer groups are subject to the provisions found in Virginia Code §38.2-3431 to 3437 and in 14VAC 5-234-10 to 100. Small employer means in connection with a group health plan or health insurance coverage with respect to a calendar year and a plan year, an employer who employed an average of at least one but not more than 50 employees on business days during the preceding calendar year and who employs at least one employee on the first day of the plan year.

Section XII

1. A The Commission may make an examination into the affairs of any person licensed to transact any insurance business in Virginia or any other person subject to the jurisdiction of the Commission when it believes conducting the examination is in the protection of the interests of the people of Virginia.

2. B The Commissioner's powers include licensing insurance producers, requiring that fingerprints be submitted to verify the accuracy of information submitted on a license application, examine and investigating the affairs of every person engaged in the business of insurance in Virginia in order to determine whether the

VA PPL LH-2_16298

person has engaged in any unfair or deceptive act or practice.

3. D Prohibited acts of insurance producers include: intentionally misrepresenting the terms of an actual or proposed insurance contract or application for insurance; having an insurance producer license or other financial services license, or its equivalent, denied, suspended or revoked by a governmental entity; failing to pay State income tax or comply with any administrative or court order directing the payment of State income tax.

4. D If the Commission has reason to believe that any person has committed a violation of the Insurance Title, or of any rule, regulation, or order issued by the Commission under it, the Commission must issue and serve an order upon that person by certified or registered mail or in any other manner permitted by law. The order must include a statement of the charges and a notice of a hearing on the charges to be held at a fixed time and place, which is at least ten days after the date of service of the notice. The order must also require that person to show cause why an order should not be made by the Commission directing the alleged offender to cease and desist from the violation or why the Commission should not issue any other appropriate order. This order does not include any ruling or judgment. At the hearing, that person has an opportunity to be heard in accordance with the Commission's order.

5. C Any person who knowingly or willfully violates any provision of the Insurance Title or any regulation issued pursuant to it is punished for each violation by a penalty of not more than $5,000.

6. B Any individual or business entity conducting the business of insurance in Virginia under an assumed or fictitious name must notify the Bureau of Insurance of the name under which the individual or entity will be doing business. The notification must be made either at the time the application for a license to do business is filed or within thirty calendar days from the date the assumed or fictitious name is adopted.

7. D In order to obtain a consultant license, an individual must submit an application to the Commission and meet the following requirements: pass, within 183 calendar days prior to the date of application for such license, the property and casualty or life and health exam, as applicable, unless the applicant

already has the license at time of application and through the submission of the application, appoint the clerk of the Commission as the agent for service of process on the applicant in any action or proceeding arising in this Commonwealth out of or in connection with the exercise of the license.

8. D An employee of an insurer who contacts persons looking for insurance rate quotes, determines appropriate product, offers product and receives commissions for sales is required to be licensed as a producer. The other employees described in the answer options are excepted from licensing.

9. D Every licensed agent may sell policies and solicit applications for insurance for any one or more of the classes of insurance for which he is licensed on behalf of an insurer that is also licensed in Virginia for those classes of insurance, even if the licensed agent has not yet been validly appointed by the insurer, as long as the following requirements are met: 1) The insurer, within 30 calendar days of the date of execution of the first insurance application or policy submitted by a licensed but not yet appointed agent, either rejects the application or policy or files with the Commission a notice of appointment. 2) The insurer must provide to the licensed agent, within the same 30-day period, a verification that the notice of appointment has been filed with the Commission. 3) Upon receipt of the notice of appointment, the Commission must verify that the agent holds a valid license and that the notice has been properly completed and submitted.

10. A Each agent holding one or more licenses subject to continuing education requirements must complete all continuing education, exemption, or waiver requirements no later than November 30, or the next working day if November 30 falls on a weekend, of each even-numbered year.

11. C Any agent who fails to submit complete documentation showing proof of compliance with applicable CE requirements, as well as all specified forms and fees, so that they are received by the Board or its administrator by the close of business on the required dates is in noncompliance with the requirements of the CE laws.

12. C All premiums, return premiums, or other funds received in any manner by an agent must be

held in a fiduciary capacity and must be accounted for by each agent.

No one other than a duly licensed and appointed agent may accept commission or other valuable consideration unless the person, at the time of the transaction, held a valid license as an agent for the class of insurance involved.

14. B   It is illegal to make false or maliciously critical statements about others in the insurance business. This is known as defamation.

15. B   It is an unfair insurance trade practice to enter into any agreement to commit, or by any concerted action committing, any act or boycott, coercion or intimidation resulting in or tending to result in unreasonable restraint of, or monopoly in, the business of insurance.

16. D   Inducing a person to lapse, forfeit, surrender or replace a contract by misrepresenting or providing incomplete information is known as "twisting." Twisting is illegal in all states.

17. D   The maximum amount of coverage available through the guaranty association for accident and sickness insurance that constitutes basic hospital medical and surgical insurance or major medical insurance is $500,000.

18. A   When insurance is being applied for, a notice must be provided no later than at the time of the delivery of the insurance policy or certificate when personal information is collected only from the applicant or from public records.

19. B   This is the definition of an investigative consumer report.

20. A   Any person who knowingly and willfully obtains information about an individual from an insurance institution, agent or insurance-support organization under false pretenses will be fined not more than $10,000 or punished by confinement in jail for not more than 12 months, or both.

VA PPL LH-2_16298